The Colors of Poverty

The Colors of Poverty

Why Racial and Ethnic Disparities Persist

Ann Chih Lin and David R. Harris, Editors

The National Poverty Center Series on Poverty and Public Policy

Russell Sage Foundation ◇ New York

The Russell Sage Foundation

The Russell Sage Foundation, one of the oldest of America's general purpose foundations, was established in 1907 by Mrs. Margaret Olivia Sage for "the improvement of social and living conditions in the United States." The Foundation seeks to fulfill this mandate by fostering the development and dissemination of knowledge about the country's political, social, and economic problems. While the Foundation endeavors to assure the accuracy and objectivity of each book it publishes, the conclusions and interpretations in Russell Sage Foundation publications are those of the authors and not of the Foundation, its Trustees, or its staff. Publication by Russell Sage, therefore, does not imply Foundation endorsement.

Library of Congress Cataloging-in-Publication Data

The colors of poverty: why racial and ethnic disparities persist / Ann Chih Lin and David R. Harris, editors.
    p. cm.
  Includes bibliographical references and index.
  ISBN 978-0-87154-539-8
  1. Poor—United States—Cross-cultural studies.   2. Poverty—United States—Cross-cultural studies.   3. Minorities—United States—Economic conditions.   4. Minorities—United States—Social conditions.   I. Lin, Ann Chih.   II. Harris, David R., 1969–
  HV4045.C65 2008
  362.5'20973—dc22   2008010269

The paper used in this publication meets the minimum requirements of American National Standard for Information Sciences—Permanence of Paper for Printed Library Materials. ANSI Z39.48-1992.

Text design by Suzanne Nichols.

RUSSELL SAGE FOUNDATION
112 East 64th Street, New York, New York 10021
10 9 8 7 6 5 4 3 2 1

Contents

Contributors

Ann Chih Lin is associate professor of public policy in the Gerald R. Ford School of Public Policy and associate professor of political science at the University of Michigan.

David R. Harris is deputy provost, vice provost for social sciences, and professor of sociology at Cornell University.

Scott W. Allard is associate professor in the School of Social Service Administration at the University of Chicago.

Heather E. Bullock is associate professor of psychology and director of the Center for Justice, Tolerance, and Community at the University of California, Santa Cruz.

George Farkas is professor of sociology, demography, and education at Pennsylvania State University.

Michèle Lamont is Robert I. Goldman Professor of European Studies and professor of sociology and African and African American studies at Harvard University.

Selina A. Mohammed is assistant professor of nursing at the University of Washington, Bothell.

Devah Pager is associate professor of sociology and faculty associate at the Office of Population Research at Princeton University.

Lincoln Quillian is associate professor of sociology and faculty fellow in the Institute for Policy Research at Northwestern University.

Rozlyn Redd is a graduate student in sociology at Columbia University.

SANFORD F. SCHRAM is professor in the Graduate School of Social Work and Social Research at Bryn Mawr College.

MARIO LUIS SMALL is associate professor of sociology and the College and research associate at the Population Research Center of the National Opinion Research Center at the University of Chicago.

JOE SOSS is professor and Cowles Chair for the Study of Public Service in the Hubert H. Humphrey Institute of Public Affairs at the University of Minnesota.

MICHAEL A. STOLL is professor and chair of the Department of Public Policy and associate director of the Center for the Study of Urban Poverty at the University of California, Los Angeles.

CHRISTOPHER UGGEN is Distinguished McKnight Professor and chair of the Department of Sociology at the University of Minnesota.

DARREN WHEELOCK is assistant professor of social and cultural sciences at Marquette University.

DAVID R. WILLIAMS is the Florence Sprague Norman and Laura Smart Norman Professor of Health in the Department of Society, Human Development, and Health at the School of Public Health, and professor in the Departments of African and African American Studies and Sociology, Harvard University.

Acknowledgments

This book had its genesis as part of a proposal to the U.S. Department of Health and Human Services (HHS) that the University of Michigan put together for a new National Poverty Center (NPC). As junior faculty at Michigan, we had socialized with each other's families and chatted at various campus events. But we had never worked together until Rebecca Blank and Sheldon Danziger brought us into the NPC. We are grateful to them for the opportunity to put this project together under the NPC's auspices, and for the funding and advice that they provided along the way. Sheldon actually first introduced us to each other, and he has continued to be an exceptional mentor and perennial friend to us both.

Support from the NPC allowed us to invite potential authors and discussants to a planning conference, and later to a two-day event at which we previewed the book chapters. For extremely helpful comments and encouragement we are indebted to Richard Alba and Scott Page, who were our interlocutors at the first conference, and Charles Hirschman, Vincent Hutchings, Jeffrey Morenoff, Steven Morgan, Ted Mouw, Alice O'Connor, and Alford Young, who discussed chapter drafts at the second. We could not have organized either conference without the input and assistance of Kristin Seefeldt, Laura Lee, and Sarah Marsh at the NPC. For expert logistical help we also thank Susan Carpenter and Patricia Rayl.

The Russell Sage Foundation has sponsored some of the best social science on American poverty and race, and it is an honor to receive its support. Eric Wanner awarded us a Presidential Grant to complete the volume. Aixa Cintron has been its champion from the beginning. We benefited greatly from their suggestions on the right topics to include. Suzanne Nichols, with infinite patience and a little prodding, hauled us back on track whenever we attempted to run off the rails. We are also grateful for the comments of the two anonymous reviewers, who helped the authors and us to improve the book.

When we first took on this project, neither of us realized that most of our work would travel through phone and Internet. The miracles of modern technology made the transition to long-distance collaboration easy enough, though we might have traded less sports commentary and academic gossip had we remained on the same campus. One person, however, has every reason to point out the downside of this mode of collaboration: Anne, who patiently put up with phone calls that cut into evenings, weekends, holidays, and at least three Harris summer vacations, and who made one especially important part of the book possible. We owe you a lot more than this thank you.

Somewhere in the fifth, or fifteenth, draft of the introduction, one of us said to the other: "This is the book I went to graduate school to study." We are fortunate to have been instructed by such wonderful authors: Chris, Darren, David, Devah, George, Heather, Joe, Lincoln, Mario, Michael, Michèle, Rozlyn, Sandy, Scott, and Selina. For both of us this project is a tangible sign of the passion for a more just society that brought us to academia, and a shout-out to those we grew up with who did not have or could not have taken advantage of the opportunities we had. To them, to Jamal, and for all like them, we dedicate this book.

Chapter 1

Why Is American Poverty Still Colored in the Twenty-First Century?

Ann Chih Lin and David R. Harris

In the United States, one of every three African American children and one of every four Latino children lives in poverty. For white children, the number is one in seven (U.S. Census Bureau 2007). Substantial progress for racial minorities has occurred over the last forty years, and yet the life chances of the average black or Latino child are still very different from those of his average white or Asian classmate. Will more and better education close these gaps? Is a renewed commitment to personal responsibility necessary? Can government fix this problem—or will government make it worse?

These questions are familiar to anyone—citizen, journalist, scholar, or politician—who has worried about poverty in the United States. But that these questions have persisted so long should give us pause. Despite excellent research into the causes and consequences of poverty, despite extensive evaluation of policies liberal and conservative, the same answers—education reform, individual effort, government attention—continually vie for precedence. Better answers are needed: answers that build on the knowledge gained from nearly half a century of fighting poverty, but that also suggest different approaches and models for progress.

The authors in this volume draw on all the social sciences—economics, history, anthropology, political science, psychology, and sociology—to offer these answers. They consider what disciplines have learned about specific aspects of poverty, and how these connect to race. They propose new questions that need to be studied, and in some cases solutions that could be tried. But all of their essays lead to a common insight: that debates about the causes of racial and ethnic disparities, and about the best solution to them, are fundamentally misconceived. Fifty years of research into the various aspects of poverty and race point not to one most important cause of poverty, but to a process: any type of disadvantage makes one vulnerable to more disadvantages, and the increased vulnerability reduces the probability that any single solution, however effective, will make an overall difference in a disadvantaged person's life. Like a hospital stay prolonged when a weakened patient keeps getting new infections, poverty has no root cause. The solution is not any particular cure. It is to figure out how to reduce vulnerability, to prevent disadvantages from cumulating.

Consider Jamal, now seven years old, a boy that one of us has known for the last two years. He is a black child in a school that is more than 75 percent white, and a poor child in a school where less than 15 percent of students receive free or reduced lunch. His teachers report that he has at least five siblings under the age of twelve, not all with the same father, that his home is not well maintained, that he frequently tries to get extra food during snack time, and that he sometimes comes to school dirty. Although his mother rarely attends school activities, and never comes to PTA meetings, everyone seems to know that she dresses, speaks, and interacts differently than the white and nonwhite middle class moms in the school.

At five, Jamal entered kindergarten. On class trips and activities organized by volunteer parents and college students, he quickly gained a reputation as disruptive, but also as artistic and engaged in the classroom. He was interested in learning and often tried to do the right thing. It seemed that despite his circumstances, Jamal might do well in school and avoid a future of economic instability. After all, he was in a school where teachers regularly volunteered to organize enrichment activities, where middle class parents and affluent children were accessible role models, and where college student volunteers provided frequent opportunities for one-on-one help.

By second grade, however, Jamal was increasingly having academic and social problems. His second-grade class had an unusually large number of boys, many of whom were extremely disruptive and encouraged Jamal's outbursts. He rarely completed homework assignments and could not depend on anyone at home to help with lessons he did not master in class. During the last two months of the school year, on a classroom visit and two field trips, we were struck by how different this Jamal was from the kindergartener of two years before. It was harder to see the good child inside Jamal—the boy who sometimes managed to do the right thing and who tried to be a learner. Instead, we saw a child who, though only seven years old, seemed angry, frustrated, and hardened. He was less engaged in his schoolwork and less interested in following classroom rules. He was physically and verbally aggressive toward other children. He did not listen to adults and challenged authority when reprimanded. Several times the teacher or one of the classroom aides physically restrained Jamal to prevent him from attacking a classmate or to keep him from running out of the classroom. Jamal was no longer a disruption. He was now a serious threat to the classroom community.

It is impossible to argue that Jamal's rapidly dwindling opportunities are the result of a school system that pays too little attention to the academic talents and needs of minority children. Jamal has had extraordinary teachers—the teachers that affluent parents vie to have assigned to their own children. Additionally, during most weeks Jamal received individual attention from a speech therapist, a reading specialist, the school psychologist, a special education teacher, and in-class volunteers. The principal, who frequently stopped by to see Jamal, even reserved a spot in her office for him to regroup when he started to lose control in the classroom.

It is also not possible for us to argue that Jamal, at seven, made too many bad choices and is wholly responsible for the situation he is in today. We have seen Jamal work hard. Some of his classmates, equally disruptive but from more advantaged backgrounds, seemed to maintain promising trajectories despite their behavior and apparent disinterest in school.

No one knows what will become of Jamal, but it is clear that he is on a disturbing path. Between kindergarten and second grade, adults and children at school solidified their assessment of Jamal as a "bad kid." Over the same period, Jamal seemed to have accepted that he would always get in trouble, and he slowly stopped trying quite so hard to do the right thing. Also over this period, Jamal was exposed to yet another two years of poverty. His less affluent home environment did not adequately prepare him for kindergarten, and did not enforce accountability or provide academic support. Nor did his parents use medical diagnoses to shield Jamal from the consequences of his impulses, as the parents of some of his more affluent classmates did. If left unchecked, this cascade of disadvantage will likely make it difficult for Jamal to graduate from high school, to avoid prison, to earn a living wage, to sustain a long-term romantic relationship, to guide his own children toward economic self-sufficiency, and to live a long and healthy life.

CASCADES

We offer Jamal's story to illustrate the core message of this book: disadvantages cascade. Difficult but solvable problems—the lack of dependable food, clothing, or shelter; the inability to control oneself; the presence of a disruptive peer group; a home environment that does not or cannot support learning—exacerbate and are exacerbated by other disadvantages. When multiple disadvantages exist, even solutions exacerbate problems: Jamal may receive extra help at school, but that extra attention also reinforces the teachers', the other parents', and his own belief that he is bad.

By contrast, advantages insulate. Being affluent does not guarantee parental attention, good behavior, academic support, or friends of good character. Doing well in school does not prevent job loss or guarantee a successful marriage. The presence of enough advantages, however, makes it easier to cushion the negative impact of single disadvantages. When problems come one at a time, or at least slowly enough to allow for solutions to create stability, bad choices or bad luck are less likely to result in a bad life.

Much previous writing about poverty was motivated by debates over the relative significance of different root causes: economic structure, mainstream and underclass cultures, or government capabilities and responsibilities. We start from a different position: that poverty may be rooted in many causes, but what matters is how it spreads and flourishes. Poverty reflects not single causes but cumulative disadvantages. Everyone is vulnerable to some of these, but some people are vulnerable to many, and each new disadvantage is made harder to overcome given the lingering effect of past ills. Thus fixing blame and attempting a remedy are doomed to fail if the solution does not also protect against new vulnerabilities—whether these be created by the economy, enabled by culture, or institutionalized by government.

Disadvantages do not cascade by accident. Within any society, resources, status, and opportunities are distributed through many different mechanisms. In the American context, one of the most important and consistent mechanisms is race. In the course of American history, the meaning of race—whether Irish are white, whether Asians are colored, and how many black ancestors make one black—has changed. What has not is the use of race to create categories that guide the distribution of opportunities. Over time, this means that it is not necessary to trace Jamal's actions to biological difference, or the actions of those around him to prejudice or hatred, to conclude that race has influenced Jamal's life. It is only necessary to see that Jamal's race creates a vulnerability to negative treatment, and thus a higher probability of experiencing and exacerbating the disadvantages he has already suffered.

Why focus on race, when nonracial vulnerabilities to poverty also exist? We put race at the center of any attempt to assess vulnerability to poverty because in the United States, our economy, our cultural frameworks and repertoires, and our government policies have been shaped by a history of racial relations and racially inflected decision making. As a result, our institutions, practices, and beliefs can foster racial disadvantage without any deliberate effort to discriminate. This remains true even as the changing racial and ethnic environment of the United States challenges historical precedents about who the targets of racial disadvantage are now, and who they may be in the future. The growing diversity of the American racial landscape spurs us to review the mechanisms by which race and ethnicity—white, black, Latino, Asian—are linked to advantage and disadvantage.

Together, the cumulative operation of disadvantage and the close connection between race and vulnerability demonstrate the need for a new framework for understanding the racial and ethnic disparities that characterize poverty in the United States. Our book provides this framework. Each chapter in this volume examines one area of social life in which disadvantage or vulnerabilities to poverty are embedded: discrimination, beliefs about inequality, culture, education, health, social networks, residential location, incarceration, and welfare policy. The chapters explain these vulnerabilities and show their links to race and ethnicity—not only because some groups do worse, but also because the connection of race to bad outcomes results in more vulnerability down the line. These vulnerabilities result in a system of advantages and disadvantages that explains why poverty is substantially less common for whites and Asians than for blacks and Latinos. The authors also point out what still needs to be studied, and examine policy strategies to sever some of the connections between race and vulnerability, or to prevent disadvantages from cascading until they cannot be reversed. The result is a comprehensive assessment of racial disparities in poverty for the student, the scholar, the journalist, and the policy maker.

We group our examination of these systems of vulnerability into three categories. The first section includes those in which race influences perceptions, cognitive structures, and expectations: interpersonal and institutional discrimination, beliefs about economic inequality, and culture. The second focuses on social mechanisms in which race is a contributing, but implicit factor: education, health, and social networks. The third examines four policy areas in particular detail—residential segregation, incarceration, income support, and social services—to show how racial disparities have been embedded, consciously or unconsciously, in policy design and implementation.

In the rest of this introduction, we discuss each of these sections. In doing so, we illustrate why an approach that takes the cumulative impact of disadvantage seriously is different from thinking about each of these mechanisms as an independent cause of racial disparities in poverty. We start, however, by explaining what race has become in twenty-first century America, and why it still matters.

ASSIGNING DISADVANTAGE BY RACE

In 1965, the coattails of the civil rights movement made possible a little-known piece of legislation with far-reaching effects. Until then, immigration quotas were explicitly fixed to replicate the racial and ethnic distribution in the America of the 1890 census. Thus, in 1960, 75 percent of the foreign-born came from Europe, and less than 15 percent came from Latin America and Asia combined (Gibson and Lennon 1999). But the 1965 Hart-Celler Act abolished these quotas, instead allowing families and employers to sponsor new immigrants. Hart-Celler was not intended to change the racial makeup of the United States: if all citizens had immediate family who wanted to leave other countries for America, and if employable migrants were equally distributed across countries, the racial and ethnic balance of the United States would have remained constant. But because Asian, Latin American, and African workers were more likely to desire migration, and newer citizens were much more likely to sponsor family members than long-settled ones, Hart-Celler set the stage for a racial and ethnic restructuring of American society.

The most obvious aspect of this restructuring is the change in racial composition. In 1960, whites were 88.6 percent of the American population, and blacks 10.5 percent; other racial groups made up less than 1 percent, and Hispanics were not systematically counted (Gibson and Jung 2002). By 2000, the white population had dropped nearly 18 percent; the black and Hispanic populations were virtually equal to one another, at 12.4 and 12.5 percent respectively; and Asians had reached 3.6 percent. This change was almost entirely fueled by immigrants, more than 50 percent of whom were from Latin America, and more than 25 percent from Asia (U.S. Census Bureau 2003).

The change in numbers has been accompanied by a change in the way Americans think about race. In the 1960s, a belief in racial inferiority was still acceptable, even as the civil rights movement questioned the legality of embedding these beliefs in state practice. Nearly fifty years later, it has become common to point to the many successful African Americans, Asians, and Latinos in American life as proof that no reasonable person could any longer believe in the inherent inferiority of a particular racial group. These examples of successful individuals, however, have their own consequences. They delegitimize conversations about group success and failure, which seem to mock Americans' ideas about individual merit (see Bullock, chapter 3, this volume). They divert attention to attitude and perseverance as solutions for economic difficulty or social prejudice, and in doing so obscure the operation of any other mechanisms. They impede the creation of multiethnic alliances between America's new immigrants and its settled residents, by providing the accusation that group-based organization is an effort to obtain illegitimate group rights.

The increasingly diverse racial landscape also complicates the analytical meaning of race and draws attention to the historically specific ways it has been used in the United States. Race is often a synonym for disadvantage, yet today's new immigrants are concentrated at the top as well as the bottom of the educational distribution, and Asian Americans have a higher median household income than any other racial group (DeNavas-Walt, Proctor, and Mills 2004). Race implies a shared history and culture, yet Asian immigrants—even from the same country—may not share the same language, and Latino immigrants from South America have a very different history than those from Central America or Mexico. Race implies a sense of solidarity, yet black immigrants from Africa or the Caribbean may feel quite different from African Americans who have been in the United States for generations. Indeed, even the definition of race is more a government artifact than an empirical recognition of groupings that people might have chosen, or that they might recognize. Indians, Koreans, and Filipinos are all considered Asian despite the fact that the Asian countries they came from had very little historical relationship. Arabs are recoded as white even when they check Other and name themselves as Arab or Middle Eastern, or when they give a Middle Eastern country of origin on the U.S. Census (Grieco and Cassidy 2001). Hispanic is considered an ethnic rather than a racial category, even though in practice scholars, policy makers, and the media implicitly reject this distinction by distinguishing between non-Hispanic whites, non-Hispanic blacks, and Hispanics (Hirschman, Alba, and Farley 2000).

Thus the first task facing a volume on racial and ethnic disparity is to examine how connections between race, privilege, disadvantage, and achievement are constructed. The chapters on discrimination, attitudes, and culture do just that. In chapter 2, Devah Pager assesses the major social scientific approaches to the measurement of discrimination: surveys asking for self-reported experiences of unequal treatment, or of self-reported attitudes of distrust or dislike; statistical analyses of large-scale socioeconomic datasets; and experimental approaches testing differences in treatment related to race, gender, or ethnicity. Though each has advantages and disadvantages, all suggest that "overt forms of prejudice and discrimination have declined, but . . . subtle and unconscious forms of bias persist. Unfortunately, these unconscious sources of discrimination remain among the most difficult to identify, legislate, and change" (chapter 2, this volume). Structural forms of discrimination, including the social patterning of opportunity and the spatial distribution of resources, can aggregate over time and across different social spheres, so that even small inequalities can have substantial effects over time and space. Chapter 2 also illustrates the power of social categories to affect social outcomes, even when those categories are inconsistent with how individuals see themselves.

Heather Bullock follows in chapter 3 with an examination of American attitudes about wealth, poverty, and achievement. Reviewing literature from social psychology, sociology, and political science, she shows that beliefs in individualism and upward mobility intersect with beliefs about the relative worth of different races. This intersection gives legitimacy to existing hierarchies of wealth and social status, and justifies stereotypes about blacks and Latinos. Rather than try to separate so-called true beliefs in merit from ostensibly disguised racism, sexism, or classism, Bullock concludes that it is more important to see how the combination of these beliefs affects important public policy domains, especially those related to education and income support. Central to her discussion is the evidence that poor and nonpoor, white and nonwhite, all share these beliefs. Thus change in racial and ethnic disparities is not simply a matter of increasing understanding, awareness, or appreciation across different groups. Instead, it requires deliberate efforts to recognize stereotypes that usually go unquestioned, and context-specific attempts to challenge them.

Finally, in chapter 4, Michèle Lamont and Mario Small explain how early discussions of the relationship between poverty and culture essentialized specific beliefs and behaviors by attributing them to the history or the circumstances of specific racial groups. Instead, they propose six alternative approaches to the concept of culture: frames, repertoires, narratives, cultural capital, symbolic boundaries, and institutions. All of these turn the analyst's focus away from a particular race or ethnicity, and instead toward smaller venues: families, neighborhoods, peer groups, policies, or political movements. Each also shows that numerous choices exist within cultures, so that cultural processes never produce outcomes in a deterministic way. Poverty can reproduce itself through culture, but the way to break this cycle is not by changing a culture of poverty. Instead, cycles are broken when the link between culture and a specific set of circumstances produces its own set of possibilities for change.

One of the most important implications of Lamont and Small's analysis is that by turning away from approaches that equate culture to an entire race, scholars and policy makers often find that the same values are shared across racial groups, by both the poor and the nonpoor. In acting on these values, however, people in

advantaged and disadvantaged circumstances, under conditions of racial privilege or racial vulnerability, will have different options. This suggests that assessing the options available under different conditions is more likely to explain individual behavior and group outcomes than simply assuming that because
particular options are chosen, they must have been preferred. A black single
mother in a closely knit community, and a white middle class mother who moves
into a less affluent neighborhood after divorce, will have different options. The
white mother may not be able to get her ex-husband to take responsibility for
their child without a court order; the black mother, with fewer resources to navi-
gate the court system, may rely instead on ongoing relationships with the father
and his family. These differences in behavior would not be the result of different
preferences, but rather of the availability of different pathways to achieving a
common goal.

These chapters provide an important foundation for the rest of the volume, and
for future explorations of the connections between race and poverty. They draw
attention to the importance of looking for the mechanisms that connect group
identity to group outcomes, rather than looking only at disproportionate representation. They also show that the intersection of race and poverty has a reciprocal effect on practices, attitudes, and habits. Current disparities in neighborhood
quality, employment rates, school achievement, access to resources, single parent-
hood, and imprisonment create expectations and coping mechanisms that may
guide future behavior, even if the original gaps are closed. Disadvantages cascade
because disparity is enabled through discrimination, attitudes, or culture, and the
resulting disparity then serves to justify future discrimination, new attitudes, or
cultural adaptations.

Each of these authors makes clear that discrimination, attitudes, and culture do
not exist only in the mind. Rather, they are best understood within specific venues
and in conjunction with specific policies. The next set of chapters in this volume
thus explores three areas—education, social networks, and health—where initial,
tiny disparities between groups can develop into large and seemingly insur-
mountable differences. These differences in human capital, social capital, and
physical and psychological well being have been exhaustively studied, and they
often serve as the target of simple, group-specific interventions: more education,
better peer support, or more access to medical care. Our chapters show, however,
that the mechanisms in each of these areas are complex, interactive, and stubborn;
they suggest that the first goal of policy should not be to remedy inequality, but to
avoid concentrating it.

ANALYZING DIFFERENCES BY RACE

The chapters on discrimination, attitudes about achievement, and culture make
clear that the close association of race and disadvantage is deeply rooted in the assumptions and experiences of both the poor and nonpoor. But these associations
are not the only explanation for their connection. Indeed, race is often considered

only incidental to other causes of poverty: inadequate education, poor social connections, health problems and the lack of health care. Even if one believes that racial discrimination is primarily responsible for consigning racial minority groups to bad schools, bad neighborhoods, or inferior medical care, it might not be necessary to address discrimination before creating better schools, better neighborhoods, or accessible health insurance. In other words, the best way to overcome racial disparities could be to look past race, focusing instead on the correlates of poverty.

Certainly an approach like this has much to recommend it. College graduation rates, for instance, vary greatly by race: 31 percent of whites have at least a bachelor's degree, compared to 18 percent of blacks and 12 percent of Hispanics. By contrast, nearly 50 percent of Asians hold a bachelor's or advanced degree (U.S. Census Bureau 2006). This suggests that if preparation for and access to college were made more available to everyone, all groups would benefit and racial gaps in both education and income would decrease. To take another example, in 2001 black infants were more than twice as likely as Asian, Hispanic, or non-Hispanic white babies to die before their first birthday. Indeed, black infant mortality was higher than infant mortality in most developed countries, and higher than in many less developed countries—Cuba, the Russian Federation, Bulgaria, and Chile, to name just a few. But given that infant mortality has dropped between 40 and 70 percent for all racial groups over the past twenty years (National Center for Health Statistics 2005), the solution is presumably obvious; better prenatal and well-baby care simply need to be more widely implemented.

Another argument for non-race-specific approaches is that the coincidence of race and disadvantage can be misleading. The last section laid out the tremendous change that immigration has created in the racial makeup of the United States: about 40 percent of Hispanics and 70 percent of Asians are foreign-born, compared to fewer than 7 percent of non-Hispanic whites and blacks (U.S. Census Bureau 2003). This suggests that racial disparities in income, education, or opportunity may be caused not by factors related to race or ethnicity, but simply by being new members of society. If so, any gaps might disappear as immigrants, and their children and grandchildren, blend into American society; and policies might be directed, not at decreasing discrimination or ensuring equal treatment, but at aiding integration and Americanization.

Racial and ethnic disparities might even be a source of advantage for some groups. Some scholars of immigration have argued, for instance, that though poor blacks in highly segregated neighborhoods have limited chances for upward mobility, the segregation (voluntary or involuntary) of immigrants into ethnic enclaves and social networks can buffer them from the effects of concentrated poverty and societal prejudice. Their customs and cultures, though sometimes an obstacle to integration in America, can serve to cement social ties among coethnics and lead to mutual aid. Their expectations for success are nurtured by comparisons with their home country, which makes hardship easier to bear. And though some immigrants come with very little, others migrate with resources, or may be able to draw on transnational resources to ease their transition and invest in future success (Zhou 1997).

Any discussion of racial and ethnic disparities in poverty must therefore confront two important arguments: that racial disparities will disappear as the causes of poverty are addressed, and that some racial disparities result from the strengths of a group and cannot, or should not, be redressed. Our chapters on education, health, and social capital consider these issues. In chapter 5, George Farkas looks at the results of No Child Left Behind (NCLB), a policy that chose to address racial gaps in academic achievement by implementing school reform focused on universal standards. In chapter 6, David Williams and Selina Mohammed use the California Health Interview Study (CHIS) to examine the relative contribution of socioeconomic status, race, ethnicity, country of origin, and immigrant status to health status. Finally, in chapter 7, Lincoln Quillian and Rozlyn Redd assess the voluminous literature on social capital to consider the extent to which social networks, especially those linked to race and ethnicity, might explain both poverty and economic success.

If education alone could help to reduce racial and ethnic disparities in poverty, one would expect to find that differences in poverty rates could explain why black and Latino children fare less well in school, with corresponding difficulties in later life. George Farkas's chapter, however, begins with a startling fact: both race and socioeconomic status affect vocabulary skills well before children turn three years old. Thus black and Latino children enter pre-school at a substantial disadvantage to their white playmates, and do not catch up. Through an examination of studies on early childhood achievement, Farkas finds that parental income, marital status, education, and interaction with children not only influence what children know before they start school, but also create strategies that will determine the ability tracking that children will experience. Put another way, racial and ethnic disparities that affect adults are passed down to their children, and at present formal education does comparatively little to redress these. Farkas concludes that without consistent attention and support throughout their schooling, directed at helping children who are most at risk, racial disparities in academic achievement will remain intact even if the overall level of education improves.

The multifaceted picture of education that Farkas draws is in many ways similar to the story that David Williams and Selina Mohammed tell about health in chapter 6. Their analysis shows that while poverty has severely detrimental effects on health—one study suggesting, for example, that the effect size is comparable to that of cigarette smoking (Hahn et al 1995)—race does as well, over and above the effect of socioeconomic status (SES). Compounding both is that illness and its correlates (obesity, stress, disability) also cause socioeconomic disadvantage such that "the relationship between SES and health status is dynamic and reciprocal" (Williams and Mohammed, chapter 6, this volume). Williams's and Mohammed's discussion of the CHIS data also shows, however, that the relationship between race and health is by no means straightforward. Looking within race at the experiences of national origin groups shows considerable variation, especially among Latinos and Asians. For instance, Puerto Rican, Filipino, Chinese, and

Vietnamese health does not improve as economic status improves, a result that has also been observed for some measures of black health. Immigrants can have better health than whites, presumably because those who anticipate arduous migration circumstances are likely to start with fewer chronic conditions and better than average health. On the other hand, stress linked to migration, adaptation, and SES can produce lower levels of emotional health for some but not all national-origin groups of Latinos and Asians. The upshot is that race proxies, often imperfectly, for a wide variety of vulnerabilities that improvements in SES alone cannot overcome.

In recent years, one of the most popular explanations for vulnerabilities of this sort has been social capital, that is, contacts, knowledge, and support gained from peers. Because the advantaged are likely to know people who are also advantaged, the contacts, knowledge, or support they gain from their acquaintances are likely to be useful in raising their income, finding good jobs, or increasing their health, education, and other resources. By contrast, the poor may also have close ties and relationships, but their peers are also likely to be poor and thus unable to provide information or contacts that could improve their friends' economic and social well being. This type of sorting, known as homophily, "contributes to the advantage of the advantaged and the disadvantage of the disadvantaged" (Quillian and Redd, chapter 7, this volume). The tendency of people of the same race to associate, or their forced association through racial segregation or bias, exacerbates the effects of class homophily: if the poor primarily associate with others who are poor and of their own race, the range of social capital that they can access is even narrower.

Quillian and Redd explain this process in chapter 7 and then examine the evidence for four social capital explanations most commonly applied to persistent racial gaps in poverty: that limited job search networks cause differential rates of employment, that neighborhoods are more likely to be plagued with crime when residents distrust each other and the police, that immigrants are able to draw on coethnic sources of socioeconomic support to assist their economic mobility, and that school friendship networks play an important role in academic achievement. They find evidence that high levels of social capital can result in safer neighborhoods, more prosperous immigrant communities, and slightly higher school achievement, but not that social capital influences the probability of getting a better job. These conclusions are further evidence that racial disparities in poverty are not only a by-product of the human tendency to prefer people similar to oneself. Although higher levels of social capital can provide some protection from the disadvantages of poverty, they do not address many of the other vulnerabilities that this volume describes. Increasing access to contacts of a higher social class, or to resources and information that those contacts provide, is not a solution to racial disparities. The pathways through which race allocates opportunity and concentrates disadvantage need closer attention.

The final section of the book brings together the arguments of the previous two sections—that race and poverty are deeply intertwined in the beliefs and expectations of Americans, and that increasing the human or social capital of the poor is not enough to overcome racial disparities—by showing that public policy is, in and of itself, a primary contributor to racial vulnerability in the United States. Housing, crime, and antipoverty policies continue to concentrate advantage and disadvantage, exacerbating the legacy of policies that fostered racial discrimination, and undercutting their own stated goals to improve the well being of all Americans, including the poor. These chapters show that it is simply shortsighted to argue that Americans have gotten beyond race, or to assume that policies are race-neutral because they do not mention race. Creating a race-blind society requires that we pay attention to the effects of race, and not that we seek to forget it.

ENSHRINING DISADVANTAGE THROUGH POLICY

After the Civil War and through the first half of the twentieth century, poverty in the United States had many faces and many colors. Black and white sharecroppers in the American South, Midwestern farmers chased off their farms by bank failures and drought, American Indians on reservations, and immigrants in city tenements—"the wretched refuse" of Europe's "teeming shores"—all bore the face of poverty, and public sentiment alternately condoled with their precarious economic conditions or vilified their shiftlessness, ignorance, or cultural failings. Racial prejudice was ubiquitous. Indian children were removed from their parents to be civilized; Chinese and Japanese immigrants were the target of riots, deportation, and internment; Southern and Eastern Europeans were spoken of as biologically inferior to their Northern European counterparts; and rights that blacks had supposedly been guaranteed after the Civil War were systematically stripped away by Jim Crow laws in the South and de facto segregation in the North.

Yet, as these examples suggest, the institutions that created vulnerability to poverty and reinforced inferior status were different for each group. And, over time, through political action and coalition building, through political necessities wrought by the Great Depression, two world wars, and America's changing role in the world, many of these institutions changed as well. As a result, by the second half of the twentieth century, the face of poverty was more and more often a black face (see chapters 3 and 11, this volume). Despite occasional attention to other groups, such as whites in Appalachia, race and poverty became intertwined in public perception and policy.

President Lyndon Johnson made this connection clear. In a commencement speech at Howard University, he famously said that the next stage of the battle for civil rights was to seek "not just equality as a right and a theory, but equality as a fact and equality as a result." Inequality, he said, had two aspects: "inherited, gateless poverty" exacerbated by living without "training and skills. . . in slums, without decent medical care," and "the devastating heritage of long years of slavery; and a century of oppression, hatred, and injustice." Thus freedom, "the right to share, share fully and equally, in American society—to vote, to hold a job, to enter a public place, to go to school" was a start, but not enough. "You do not take a person who, for years, has been hobbled by chains and liberate him, bring him up to the starting line of a race and then say, "You are free to compete with all the others," and still justly believe that you have been completely fair" (Johnson 1965, 635–40).

The civil rights policies enacted in this period attempted to address these fundamental inequalities between whites and blacks by dramatically changing the conditions of political participation, the social mores of public places, private choices about friendship and marriage, and the composition of American schools, workplaces, and leisure activities. But necessary as they were, these changes only began to remove the chains that had hobbled blacks. They did not address the ways in which race was embedded in American law and society through institutions and outcomes: through the neighborhoods that blacks lived in, the laws that defined criminal behavior, or the poverty that far too many blacks experienced. Equally important, the civil rights victories of the 1960s failed to address a policy-making process and a set of policy preferences that, though not race-specific, had racial impacts. Without intent to discriminate, and with every intent to honor American principles such as majority opinion, federalism, and personal responsibility, American social policy after the 1960s has continued to disadvantage blacks, and in some cases Latinos, relative to whites.

In chapter 8, Michael Stoll illustrates the racial impact of the policies shaping the American landscape. There is perhaps no more common belief about poverty than that it is a problem of the urban ghetto. Stoll's discussion of place, however, shows that this easy generalization can be misleading: although central cities contain heavily black and poor neighborhoods, rural poverty rates are higher than metropolitan poverty rates, and poverty within suburbs is growing, especially for Latinos and Asians. The role that discriminatory mortgage lending, public housing practices, and racial steering played in the creation of poor black neighborhoods is well known (Allard, chapter 9, this volume), and Stoll summarizes the evidence that overt racial housing discrimination still exists, helping cause racial segregation in suburbs as well as in cities. But he also points to other factors—suburban sprawl, development and zoning regulations, and immigration to nontraditional destinations—that do not originate in the desire for racial segregation, but often create or exacerbate it. Moreover, the resulting segregated neighborhoods also impose significant economic disadvantages, in particular distance from job opportunities and mass transportation alternatives. In other words, the suburban and rural poor also suffer from the spatial mismatch between residence and jobs that scholars have identified as a problem for the urban poor. If policy makers fail to notice either that racial segregation and economic disadvantage coexist in places other than the central city, or the disproportionate racial impact of policy decisions about sprawl, local development, or immigrant settlement, the United States could unintentionally recreate the kinds of racial disadvantage previously caused by deliberate racial segregation.

The racial consequences of the tight connection between place and poverty are made even clearer in chapter 9, where Scott Allard discusses the availability of social services. Such services—providing help with employment-related needs such as job training, child care, or transportation; meeting basic needs through food and clothing pantries or emergency cash assistance; or addressing problems such as substance abuse and domestic violence—are commonly thought of as services for the poor. Indeed, the welfare reforms of 1996 shifted funding away from income support toward services, in the expectation that services could help recipients permanently leave the welfare rolls. Allard finds, however, that in both rural and urban areas, services are more likely to be accessible to those living in low-poverty census tracts, and especially likely to be inaccessible in census tracts with high concentrations of blacks. Put another way, those in high poverty, highly black neighborhoods are least likely to find accessible services even though they might need them the most. Hispanics, who are less segregated than blacks, experience more uneven accessibility: generally, the more mixed-race the area, the more accessibility Hispanics have. However, even Hispanic neighborhoods located near one another can have very different access to services, and the increasing presence of Hispanics in poor rural areas bodes ill for their future access.

Racial disparities in policy are not only caused by the lack of access to benefits; they also include a greater vulnerability to sanctions. The most obvious case, of course, is that of criminal sanctions, and—in particular—imprisonment. Due in large part to changes in penalties for drug offenses, the reduced use of parole, and the spread of mandatory minimum sentencing, the number of people in American prisons today is more than ten times greater than in 1974. The consequences are especially stark when examined by race: the rate of incarceration for black men is more than seven times greater, and for Hispanic men nearly two times greater, than that for whites. In chapter 10, Darren Wheelock and Christopher Uggen trace this disparity to different types and rates of offending as well as to different treatment by the criminal justice system. Both can result from policy choices that correspond with other correlates of racial disparity: poverty, the drug economy, and greater emphasis on policing and enforcement, for instance, are all more common in black and Hispanic neighborhoods.

Wheelock and Uggen, however, are most interested in the results of this disparity for the future life chances of ex-prisoners and their families and communities. They document a wide variety of collateral consequences that affect ex-prisoners after release, such as restrictions on employment, jury duty, financial aid for college, public housing, and income assistance. All of these are likely to limit income, civic participation, and social mobility, not only for prisoners but also for their families and communities. Moreover, they raise the probability of continued disparities in incarceration: with less income, fewer opportunities for education, less influence on convictions, laws, and penalties, and a greater probability of living in neighborhoods with many ex-offenders, blacks and Hispanics are more likely to commit crimes, more likely to be arrested when they do, and more likely to be imprisoned as a result.

In chapter 11, Joe Soss and Sandy Schram place the potential for policy to perpetuate racial disparities in its broader historical and political context. Like Allard, they explore welfare—the paradigmatic case of poverty policy. But instead of focusing on the distribution of benefits, they examine the impact of welfare reform on civic disparities—"how recent policy changes position different groups vis-à-vis major institutions of the state, market, and civil society" and "organize governance and establish terms of membership in distinctive ways for different racial and ethnic groups." Welfare policy, for instance, has depended heavily on state and local regulation since its inception, and states with the highest concentrations of African Americans have also had the least expansive and most punitive programs. In effect, blacks are thus disproportionately denied not just benefits, but also the guarantee of equality that characterizes federal programs with uniform eligibility standards. Similarly, a major change in welfare eligibility in the 1996 reforms reduced the membership rights of immigrants. Despite their legal status, all new permanent residents were denied eligibility for both family and old-age assistance, and states were allowed to choose whether pre-1996 immigrants who had not become citizens would be kept on the rolls.

Soss and Schram argue, however, that the best evidence for racial disparities in welfare reform lies in its implementation. They show that states with higher proportions of African Americans and Hispanics are more likely to impose sanctions and to choose more restrictive policies. States with more African Americans are also likely to devolve authority to counties and other local jurisdictions, increasing the probability that implementation will vary by geography. The result is that local differences cumulate, nationwide, to a welfare regime in which the majority of white recipients experience the most generous welfare programs and the majority of black recipients experience the most restrictive. They also find that Hispanics and Asians, who are more likely to have language difficulties, are especially vulnerable to the effects of "work-first" policies. Soss and Schram then situate these findings in the larger question of government regulation of the lives of its citizens, arguing that both welfare reform and the rise in incarceration leave blacks and Hispanics under significantly more supervision and intervention in their choices. Moreover, these differences also create potential divisions between poor and middle class minorities, which could end in the middle class refusal to acknowledge racial vulnerability.

THE PERSISTENCE OF RACIAL DISPARITY

Soss and Schram's analysis brings the volume full circle, to the question we posed at the beginning. Why focus on race, when nonracial disparities in poverty also exist? Will racial disparities in poverty persist as the definition of race in America expands beyond black and white? The chapters clearly show that racial disparity characterizes American beliefs about poverty and achievement, the indicators and mechanisms of social mobility and well being, and the policies that disproportionately affect the poor. Read together, they also show that disadvantages in one area create disadvantages and vulnerabilities in others, cascading to stymie attempts to find the independent effects of individual factors. Finally, a clear pattern emerges across these chapters, with disadvantages more likely to be experienced by Latinos, and especially blacks, than Asians or whites.

We believe that cumulative disadvantage provides the most compelling explanation for why racial disparities in poverty are difficult to understand and influence. The increased racial diversity of American society, the economic and social stability that people of all races have achieved, and the growing rejection of overt racism remove many of the historic barriers to racial equality in the United States. But the implication of cumulative disadvantage is that racial disparities yield only slowly to overall improvement in equality, because any remaining disadvantages increase one's vulnerability to other disadvantages. Meanwhile, segregation in schools, social networks, and neighborhoods means that the advantaged are unlikely to see the consequences of inaction, or to understand how a complex web of forces and choices act to keep them comfortable while the poor are desperate.

For too long, the policy debate has been dominated by the search for magic bullets, policies that address one determinant of economic success. Welfare reform was seen as the solution for the economic, cultural, and social deficiencies of the poor: make expectations for employment clear, and recipients will respond by adopting a work ethic, earning enough money to educate their children, and abandoning their social isolation to enter a society of workers. No Child Left Behind was seen as a solution for intergenerational poverty: hold schools accountable for teaching students basic skills early, and they will be able to find work, go to college, and improve their lives. Certainly welfare reform and NCLB have been the cause of necessary improvements in welfare and education. But, as the chapters by Allard, Soss and Schram, and Farkas show, these programs also created new forms of racial disparity and failed to address others. Rather than adopt a holistic approach to the causes of poverty, welfare reform did not address the effects of limited education, inaccessible services, and other impediments to work, and NCLB fails to address the role that families play in the development of their children's skills.

Affirmative action and other equal opportunity policies represent yet another type of magic bullet: if blacks and Latinos are able to go to the good schools that Asians and whites attend, to get the good jobs that their networks make available, or to live in their neighborhoods with access to services and employers, racial disparities will dissipate. We disagree. Although equal opportunity removes some disparities, it does not address those that are embedded in race-neutral policies, or correct for differences in locational, economic, intergenerational, and racial privilege that affect one's ability to take advantage of opportunities.

This book does not promote a set of policy proposals to replace the magic bullets we have criticized. Many of the chapters highlight innovative programs focusing directly on racial disparities, and we applaud these. They should be understood, however, as building blocks of the comprehensive solutions necessary to deal with cascades of disadvantage. The most important message to take from this book is that, to succeed, our policies need to be explicit in confronting race and holistic in their scope.

Jamal's story, which opened this chapter, illustrates the human cost of abandoning the problems of racial inequality to luck, pluck, or political posturing. To wait is to implicitly conclude that providing our own children with every possible opportunity, showering ourselves with ever more luxuries, financing yet another military action, and keeping taxes on the wealthy a little lower are more important than helping a new cohort of Jamals live up to their true potential. The problem of poverty in the United States is also a problem of color. Admitting, understanding, and working with this fact are necessary steps in changing it.

REFERENCES

DeNavas-Walt, Carmen, Bernadette D. Proctor, and Robert J. Mills. 2004. *Income, Poverty, and Health Insurance Coverage in the United States, 2003.* Current Population Reports, P60-226. Washington: U.S. Census Bureau.

Gibson, Campbell, and Kay Jung. 2002. *Historical Census Statistics on Population Totals By Race, 1790 to 1990, and By Hispanic Origin, 1970 to 1990, For The United States, Regions, Divisions, and States.* Working Paper No. 56. Washington: U.S. Census Bureau.

Gibson, Campbell, and Emily Lennon. 1999. *Historical Census Statistics on the Foreign Born Population of the United States, 1850–1990.* Working Paper No. 29. Washington: U.S. Census Bureau.

Grieco, Elizabeth M., and Rachel C. Cassidy. 2001. *Overview of Race and Hispanic Origin.* Census 2000 Brief. March. Washington: U.S. Bureau of the Census. Accessed at http://www.census.gov/prod/2001pubs/cenbr01-1.pdf.

Hahn, Robert A., Elaine Eaker, Nancy D. Barker, Steven M. Teutsch, Waldemar Sosniak, and Nancy Krieger. 1995. "Poverty and Death in the United States: 1973 and 1991." *Epidemiology* 6(5): 490–97.

Hirschman, Charles, Richard Alba, and Reynolds Farley. 2000. "The Meaning and Measurement of Race in the U.S. Census: Glimpses in the Future." *Demography* 37(3): 381–93.

Johnson, Lyndon B. 1965. "To Fulfill These Rights: Commencement Address at Howard University, June 4, 1965." *Public Papers of the Presidents of the United States: Lyndon B. Johnson, 1965.* Volume II. Washington: Government Printing Office.

National Center for Health Statistics. 2005. *Health, United States, 2005, with Chartbook on Trends in the Health of Americans.* Washington: Government Printing Office.

U.S. Census Bureau. 2003. The Foreign-Born Population: 2000. Census 2000 Brief. December. Washington: Government Printing Office. Accessed at http://www.census.gov/prod/2003pubs/c2kbr-34.pdf.

———. 2006. "Table 10. Educational Attainment of the Population 25 Years and Over , by Citizenship, Nativity, and Period of Entry, Age, Sex, Race, and Hispanic Origin." 2006 Annual Social and Economic Supplement, Current Population Survey. Washington: Government Printing Office. Accessed at http://www.census.gov/population/www/socdemo/education/cps2006.html.

———. 2007. "Table POV03. People in Families with Related Children under 18 by Family Structure, Age, and Sex, Iterated by Income-to-Poverty Ratio and Race." 2007 Annual Social and Economic Supplement, Current Population Survey. Washington: Government Printing Office. Accessed at http://pubdb3.census.gov/macro/032007/pov/toc.htm.

Zhou, Min. 1997. "Segmented Assimilation: Issues, Controversies, and Recent Research on the New Second Generation." *International Migration Review* 31(4): 975–1008.

Part I

Group Identity and Group Outcomes

Chapter 2

The Dynamics of Discrimination

Devah Pager

In 1927, a New York clothing manufacturer advertised for help with a notice typical of that time period: "White Workers $24: Colored Workers $20" (Schiller 2004, 190; see also Darity and Mason 1998, table 1). At the time, ads like these were common, with the explicit understanding that whites were more highly valued and should be paid accordingly. Today, of course, such overt forms of discrimination have all but vanished. The Civil Rights Act of 1964 bars discrimination on the basis of race, color, religion, sex, or national origin, rendering previously common forms of unequal treatment illegal. With the shifting legal context, the social context of discrimination has transformed dramatically as well. Today the vast majority of Americans endorse the principle of racial equality and repudiates acts of racial discrimination. Yet, despite these progressive developments, a range of social science evidence indicates that significant discrimination persists in contemporary society. Whether conscious or unconscious, explicit or covert, individual or institutional, systematic differences in the treatment of whites and minorities contribute to the economic marginalization of minority groups. This chapter examines the ways in which discrimination continues to operate by asking five basic questions: What is discrimination? What is the relationship between discrimination and poverty? How can we identify discrimination when it takes place? What causes discrimination? How can we reduce the incidence of discrimination? In answering these questions, we will examine the range of evidence available from social science research, as well as considering the factors that are not adequately captured by existing measures of discrimination.

WHAT IS DISCRIMINATION?

Racial discrimination, according to its most simple definition, refers to unequal treatment of persons or groups on the basis of their race or ethnicity. In defining racial discrimination, the National Research Council differentiates between differential treatment and differential effects, creating a two-part definition: "(1) *differential treatment on the basis of race* that disadvantages a racial group and (2) *treatment on the basis of inadequately justified factors other than race* that disadvantages a racial group (differential effect)" (Blank, Dabady, and Citro 2004, 39-40). The second component of this definition broadens its scope to include decisions and processes that may not themselves be racially motivated, but have the ultimate consequence of systematically disadvantaging minority groups. Beyond more conventional forms of intentional discrimination, institutional processes such as these are important to consider in assessing how valued opportunities are conditioned by race.

WHAT IS THE RELATIONSHIP BETWEEN DISCRIMINATION AND POVERTY?

Not all those who have experienced racial discrimination are poor, and not all those who are poor experience racial discrimination, but there is reason to believe that a significant relationship exists between the two. Racial bias and discrimination can contribute to blocked opportunities and economic marginality in several ways. First, discrimination by gatekeepers across a range of social institutions inhibits members of minority groups from key social, economic, and residential opportunities that form the basis of economic self-sufficiency. To the extent that employment discrimination contributes to elevated rates of unemployment, underemployment, lower wages, or less stable employment conditions, members of racial minority groups will experience greater economic insecurity and elevated risks of poverty. To the extent that discrimination in mortgage or lending markets contributes to higher rates of loan default or financial instability, members of minority groups will experience greater economic hardship. Discrimination across a wide range of social and economic domains adds to the psychic and financial burdens of everyday life in ways that contribute to pervasive disadvantage among minority individuals and communities. Second, discrimination (both past and present) underlies systematic differences in the structural conditions facing minority and white households. For example, persistent residential segregation—caused in part by past and ongoing discrimination—has led to poor African American children growing up in environments that often differ radically from those of their white counterparts. Nearly 30 percent of poor black children, for example, grow up in high poverty neighborhoods yet fewer than 3 percent of poor white children do (Jargowsky 1997, table 3.7). This concentration of poverty compounds initial disadvantages by increasing the frequency and intensity of harmful environmental exposure, including joblessness, failing schools, poor housing stock, and crime (Massey and Denton 1993). Poor white children, by contrast, more often experience conditions in which their exposure to poverty is in part offset by exposure to the networks and resources of their nonpoor neighbors (Brooks-Gunn, Duncan, and Aber 1997). Individual disadvantage is thus compounded by the structural by-products of systemic discrimination.

In light of these dynamics, it becomes important to consider the significance of discrimination in the context of persistent poverty among members of racial or ethnic minority groups. Although racial discrimination can affect minorities of any status, its consequences are particularly acute for those with few alternative resources. For each of these reasons, it is critical that we understand how to identify discrimination, its causes, and how we might reduce its effects. The remainder of this chapter takes each of these questions in turn.

IDENTIFYING DISCRIMINATION WHEN IT TAKES PLACE

Discrimination has long been both a fascinating and a frustrating subject for social science—fascinating because it is a powerful mechanism underlying many historical and contemporary patterns of inequality; frustrating because it is elusive and difficult to measure. More than a century of interest has resulted in numerous techniques aimed to isolate and identify its presence and to document its effects. I consider some of the dominant methods used to study discrimination, examining their primary contributions as well as their possible limitations (for a fuller discussion, see Blank, Dabady, and Citro 2004). In thinking about each of these methods, the primary question we seek to answer is, How do we really know when or where discrimination is at work?

Perceptions in Everyday Settings: "I Know It When I See It"

To some, discrimination is as easy to spot as a train wreck in daylight. We notice subtle cues in the ways we or others are treated—a curt exchange with the shop clerk, the security guard who keeps a watchful eye, the cab driver who doesn't stop. Most of us can think of at least one instance—whether related to age, gender, race, disability, sexual orientation, or any other stigmatized identity—in which we, or someone close to us, was treated unfairly on the basis of a single status distinction. In these instances, it doesn't take a social scientist to certify the case as discrimination.

Social scientists have capitalized on the insights and interpretations individuals have of their experiences. Numerous surveys have asked African Americans and other minorities about their experiences with discrimination in the workplace, in their search for housing, and in other everyday social settings (Smith 2001; Schuman et al. 2001). One startling conclusion from this line of research is the frequency with which discrimination is reported. A recent Gallup poll, for example, found that nearly half of all black respondents reported having experienced discrimination at least once in one of five common situations in the past month (shopping, at work, dining out, using public transportation, with police). Further, the frequency with which discrimination is reported does not decline among blacks higher in the social hierarchy; in fact, middle class blacks are as likely to perceive discrimination as are their working class counterparts, if not more (Hochschild 1995; Feagin and Sikes 1994; Kessler, Mickelson, and Williams 1990). Likewise, a 2001 survey found that more than 30 percent of blacks, and nearly 20 percent of Hispanics and Asians, reported that they had been passed over for a job or promotion because of their race or ethnicity (Schiller 2004).

What can we make of these findings? One important conclusion is that African Americans and other minority groups perceive discrimination to be pervasive in their lives. This is an important finding in its own right. Research shows that those who perceive high levels of discrimination are more likely to experience depression, anxiety, and other negative health outcomes (Kessler, Mickelson, and Williams 1990). But what we don't know from this line of research is the extent to which these trends represent perceptions rather than fact. Although some instances of discrimination leave little room for doubt, many others are subject to misinterpretation or distortion. A curt shop clerk might have been having a bad day; the security guard may be vigilant with all passersby; the cab driver may simply not have seen the pedestrian waving him down. What may be blatant evidence of discrimination from one vantage point could be a simple misunderstanding from another.

The problem with relying on perceptions for our measure of discrimination is not only that some cases may be blown out of proportion. The opposite can be just as much of an issue—acts of discrimination are often imperceptible to the victim. Thanks to social norms and legal sanctions, contemporary forms of discrimination are rarely overt, leaving countless instances of discriminatory action entirely invisible to the very individuals who have been targeted.[1] Although highly relevant to the concrete lived experiences of individuals, the use of perceptions can only provide one incomplete account of the prevalence of discrimination. In order to get closer to the source of discriminatory action, researchers have turned their attention to the potential discriminators themselves.

Self-Reports and Research: "I'm Not Racist, But. . . ."

Rather than relying on the perceptions of victims, other social science research focuses on the general attitudes of dominant groups for insights into when and how racial considerations come into play. The most well-developed line of work in this area is the long tradition of survey research on racial attitudes. Similar questions have been asked for several decades on national polls such as Gallup, the General Social Survey, among others, gauging white Americans' views on issues of race relations and racial inequality. Because the same questions have been asked over many years, we are able to chart changes in the expressed racial attitudes of Americans over time. And indeed, according to these items, much has changed in race relations since Jim Crow. In the 1940s and 1950s, for example, fewer than half of whites on surveys believed that white students should go to school with black students or that black and white job applicants should have an equal chance at getting a job. By the 1990s, by contrast, more than 90 percent of white survey respondents would endorse the principle that white and black students and job applicants should be treated equally by schools and employers (Schuman et al. 2001). These changes in attitudes over time indeed suggest a substantial decline in prejudice, and imply that overt forms of racial hostility and discrimination are no longer acceptable among the majority of the American public.

One of the main criticisms of attitude research is of its vulnerability to social desirability bias, or the pressure for respondents to give politically correct responses to questions even if this means distorting or lying about their beliefs. In charting trends in racial attitudes over time, it is hard to separate the changing beliefs of respondents from the increasing pressures to provide socially appropriate (nondiscriminatory) responses. Indeed, some critics question the interpretation of trends in survey measures as indicative of meaningful change in underlying racial attitudes. Pointing to the lack of support for policies aimed to achieve the widely supported principles of equality—such as busing programs to achieve racial integration in schools or affirmative action programs to support diversity in higher education and the workplace—these researchers question the endorsement of principles of equality as superficial (Kinder and Sears 1981; Bobo, Kluegel, and Smith 1997; McConahay 1986). If not linked to support for meaningful social change, what exactly do these attitudes tell us about the state of race relations today? Of course, policy attitudes are the product of multiple influences, including but not limited to attitudes about race (Sniderman et al. 1991). Nevertheless, the discrepancy between attitudes of principles versus policy raises important questions about the meaning of survey responses.

Further pointing to the persistence of racialized attitudes, white Americans continue to express strong negative stereotypes about racial and ethnic minorities. Though we are less likely to attribute group differences to biological sources than we were in earlier eras, the persistence of cultural stereotypes remains an important feature of contemporary race relations. Tom Smith (1991), for example, reports on a series of 7-point scales assessing a range of characteristics associated with whites, Jews, blacks, Asian Americans, Hispanic Americans, and southern whites.[2] Racial and ethnic minorities are consistently rated more negatively relative to whites. Blacks were rated most negatively, with particularly strong stereotypes as lazy, violence prone, and welfare dependent. Hispanics were a close second in negative ratings, falling behind even blacks on associations with characteristics such as poverty, intelligence, and patriotism. Asians are seen in a moderately negative light, roughly comparable to views of southern whites. The dimension on which Asians score most negatively was patriotism. Overall, these measures indicate that perceptions of difference across racial-ethnic groups remain pervasive in American society, with racial and ethnic minorities viewed in a consistently negative light relative to whites.[3] To the extent that these attitudes translate into differential treatment, persistent racial stereotypes and prejudice may be one source of contemporary discrimination (for a discussion of the relationship between attitudes and behavior, particularly those related to prejudice and discrimination, see Merton 1949; LaPiere 1934; Pager and Quillian 2005).

Though little research has focused on views of nonwhites, some evidence suggests that dynamics among minority groups show similar signs of racial bias. Black respondents demonstrate rankings very similar to those of whites, with whites rated most favorably, followed by Asians, blacks, and then Hispanics (Yoon 1995).[4] It is not the case, then, that whites are the only group influenced by negative racial stereotypes. Likewise, Lawrence Bobo and Vincent Hutchings (1996) find that a substantial proportion of blacks, Asians, Hispanics, and whites perceive members of other groups as zero-sum competitive threats for social resources. In explaining these perceptions, the authors point to varying levels of racial alienation, prejudice, beliefs about the sources of inequality, as well as simple self-interest. Together, these analyses suggest that discrimination, whether by whites or others, may be motivated by competition among groups, in addition to any influence of prejudice or racial stereotypes.

Statistical Analyses: "Everything But the Kitchen Sink"

Perhaps the most common approach to studying discrimination is by investigating inequality in outcomes between groups. Rather than focusing on the attitudes or perceptions of actors that may be correlated with acts of discrimination, this approach looks to the possible consequences of discrimination in the unequal distribution of employment, housing, or other social and economic resources. Using large-scale datasets from the census or other large samples of the population, researchers can identify systematic disparities between groups and chart their direction over time. Persistent inequalities in employment, home ownership, or mortgage rates, for example, or high levels of residential or occupational segregation, indicate trouble in the social system. These disparities cannot be automatically attributed to discrimination, but they do provide clues for further investigation. Particularly in cases where discrimination cannot be reduced to the specific actions of any one individual, such as more complex, institutional sources of discrimination, it is only by observing aggregate outcomes that these more subtle and expansive sources of discrimination can be identified.

But statistical analyses can provide more than descriptive estimates of inequality, moving further toward isolating the effects of discrimination. Many researchers use statistical models to estimate the causal effect of race on a wide range of social and economic outcomes among individuals with otherwise equivalent characteristics. For example, a widely cited study by economists at the Boston Federal Reserve Bank analyzed 3,000 mortgage applications from individuals in the Boston area in 1990. Controlling for differences in the consumer's credit history, current financial status, loan type, and a wide range of other relevant variables, the study found that black and Hispanic clients were 82 percent more likely to be turned down for a loan than their white counterparts (Munnell et al. 1996). By taking into account the complex array of factors that contribute to mortgage decisions—including all those factors that lenders themselves claim to be determinative—this study reveals the systematic ways in which race continues to shape access to opportunity.

In response to the Boston Fed study, some critics have questioned whether omitted variables or statistical misspecifications may have inflated the estimates (for reviews, see Ladd 1998, 48–53; Ross and Yinger 2002, chapter 6). Although the results have held up under extensive scrutiny, these debates point to the primary limitation of statistical studies of discrimination. It is difficult to effectively account for the many factors relevant to inequality outcomes, leaving open the possibility that the disparities we attribute to discrimination may in fact be explained by some other unmeasured cause or causes.[5] Although sophisticated techniques exist that minimize these concerns, some degree of uncertainty remains. Thus, though the strength of this line of research is the strong statistical power to detect differences between groups, its limitation is in the ability to conclusively explain them.

EXPERIMENTAL APPROACHES TO MEASURING DISCRIMINATION

Experimental approaches to measuring discrimination excel in exactly those areas where statistical analyses flounder. Experiments allow researchers to more directly measure causal effects by presenting carefully constructed and controlled comparisons. For example, Joshua Correll and his colleagues (2002) had subjects play a videogame in which they had to identify and shoot armed targets but not shoot unarmed figures. Whether the figures that appeared were white or black was assigned randomly. The results revealed that subjects were quicker to pull the trigger when targets were black, regardless of whether they were armed. This illustrates the ways in which deeply embedded stereotypes about black criminality guide behavior consistent with stereotyped expectations. Though this study was conducted using undergraduate research subjects, the implications may extend to the potential for mistreatment in real-world contexts, such as the recent shooting of Amadou Diallo, an unarmed black man, by New York City police. Whether conscious or not, stereotypes of black criminality color snap-decisions about whether a target is armed and dangerous, and whether extreme action is warranted.

Laboratory experiments offer some of the strongest evidence of causal relationships, but we have little way of knowing the extent to which their findings relate to the kinds of actual decisions made in their social contexts—to hire, to rent, to move, for example—that are most relevant to understanding the forms of discrimination that produce meaningful social disparities. Seeking to bring more realism to the investigation, some researchers have moved experiments out of the laboratory and into the field. Field experiments offer a direct measure of discrimination. Typically referred to as audit studies, these experiments involve the careful selection, matching, and training of individuals (called testers) to play the part of a job or apartment-seeker or consumer. By presenting equally qualified individuals who differ only by race or ethnicity, researchers can assess the degree to which racial considerations affect access to opportunities. Audit studies have documented strong evidence of discrimination in the context of housing searches (Yinger 1995), car sales (Ayres and Siegelman 1995), applications for insurance (Wissoker, Zimmerman, and Galster 1998), home mortgages (Turner and Skidmore 1999), in the provision of medical care (Schulman et al. 1999), and even in hailing taxis (Ridley, Bayton, and Outtz 1989).

For example, between 2000 and 2002, the U.S. Department of Housing and Urban Development conducted an extensive series of audits measuring housing discrimination against blacks, Latinos, Asians, and Native Americans, including nearly 5,500 paired-tests in nearly thirty metropolitan areas. Evidence of bias across multiple dimensions of housing searches is clear, with minorities substantially disadvantaged relative to similar whites. Among renters, blacks and Latinos experienced adverse treatment in roughly one out of five cases. Minority renters were told about fewer units and were shown fewer units relative to similarly positioned whites. Similar overall patterns were found for Asian and Native American renters, though the results were less consistent.[6] Among homebuyers, blacks, Hispanics, and Asians each experienced adverse treatment in roughly 20 percent of cases. Adverse treatment included differences in reports of housing availability, inspections, assistance with financing, and encouragement from the real estate agent (see Turner et al. 2002, 2003). And whereas overall levels of discrimination have declined on many dimensions since 1989, the level of geographic steering away from white neighborhoods that black and Hispanic homebuyers experienced has increased over time.[7] Far from being a thing of the past, active discrimination among realtors and rental agents remains an important source of residential segregation and inequality between groups. As we will see, these dynamics have important implications that extend well beyond the specific context of housing, forming one link in a much larger system of discrimination.

One limitation of experimental methods in general, and of audit studies in particular, is that only a narrow range of characteristics can be included in any one study.[8] Because experiments rely on carefully controlled research designs, researchers must limit their focus to a small number of experimental characteristics (race), holding other characteristics constant (gender, age, educational attainment). A few recent audit studies, however, have incorporated more complex designs, allowing race to vary according to other dimensions of interest. For example, Marianne Bertrand and Sendhil Mullainathan (2004) examined the effects of race on employment and the ways in which increasing skill can condition the effects of race. In this study, the researchers mailed résumés to employers in Boston and Chicago using racially identifiable names to signal race (for example, Jamal and Lakisha for African Americans, and Brad and Emily for whites).[9] White names triggered a callback rate 50 percent higher than that of equally qualified black applicants.[10] Further, the findings indicated that improving the qualifications of applicants benefited white applicants but not blacks, leading to a wider racial gap in response rates for those with higher skills. These results suggest that employers are more likely to overlook or dismiss evidence of objective skills among black applicants, but respond favorably to the same information among whites.

Another recent series of audit studies compared the effects of race to the stigma of being an ex-offender. In these studies, young men posing as job applicants filled out applications for entry-level jobs in Milwaukee and New York City, presenting fictitious résumés reflecting equal qualifications. In some cases, the applicants also indicated they had recently been released from prison for a felony drug charge.[11] The results demonstrated that employers were roughly twice as likely to hire a white applicant as an equally qualified black applicant and, further, were just as likely to hire a white applicant just released from prison as an equally qualified black or Hispanic applicant with no history of criminal involvement (Pager 2003; Pager and Western 2005). By calibrating the effect of race against the stigma of a felony conviction, these studies provide a concrete estimate of the magnitude of discrimination in low-wage labor markets. Not only do blacks have to work twice as hard to receive equal treatment to whites, they have no better prospects than a white individual just returned from prison.

Each of these methods provides a window into the dynamics of race in contemporary society, and offers compelling evidence for the persistence of discrimination across a wide range of domains. Though each method has limitations, the consistency of findings across studies is strong evidence of the persistence of discrimination. Employers, lenders, real estate agents, and other key gatekeepers continue to use race as a factor in their decisions, shaping opportunities in ways that systematically disadvantage minorities. Understanding the sources of discrimination in contemporary society remains an important goal for academics and policy makers who wish to address this important social problem.

WHAT CAUSES DISCRIMINATION?

Given the compelling evidence that discrimination remains an important factor in shaping access to contemporary opportunities, how can we explain the underlying basis for the differential treatment we observe? At the aggregate, all forms of discrimination have the same consequences—excluding potentially qualified individuals from opportunities solely on the basis of their group membership. In each case, however, discriminatory decisions can be the product of a complex set of considerations, and it is helpful to consider the multiple influences underlying these decisions.

Dating back to the early writings of Gordon Allport and Theodore Adorno, the historical literature on discrimination largely emphasized the role of prejudice, or a deep distaste or hatred for members of an out-group. Personal feelings or attitudes about members of minority groups, for example, were seen as the predominant source of racial discrimination (Pettigrew 1975; Adorno et al. 1950; Allport 1954; Becker 1971). Indeed, as described, contemporary research indicates that negative racial stereotypes remain, and many whites show signs of resentment when asked about federal efforts to improve the status of racial minorities (Kinder and Sanders 1996). It would be a mistake, though, to assume that all discrimination, or even the most common forms, represents deeply felt prejudice or animosity toward African Americans or other minorities. In fact, as mentioned, most researchers studying racial attitudes would agree that the level of explicit or conscious racial prejudice in this country has declined precipitously since the 1950s.

If by discrimination we do not mean racial animus, what do we mean? The economics literature on discrimination has increasingly emphasized a process referred to as statistical discrimination, by which individuals are judged according to the real or perceived characteristics of the group to which they belong (Phelps 1972; Arrow 1972; Aigner and Cain 1977). For example, a police officer may use race as a proxy for criminality, a doctor for treatment compliance, and a mortgage lender for risk of loan default. Because criminality, treatment compliance, and default risks are difficult to observe directly, evaluators rely on indirect information inferred from group membership. Even rational, nonprejudiced decision makers, then, may wind up systematically favoring whites over nonwhites if their estimate of overall reliability among whites is higher.

What remains contested is the degree to which these group-level attributions reflect accurate assessments. According to standard economic arguments, statistical discrimination is a rational and efficient mechanism for dealing with the problems of information shortages. Relying on group averages may lead certain individuals to be unfairly dismissed, but overall the strategy should yield an efficient distribution of decisions. Competing arguments, on the other hand, argue that statistical discrimination is largely based on exaggerated and distorted differences between groups (Tomaskovic-Devey and Skaggs 1999; Bielby and Baron 1986). Although mean differences may exist between groups on some valued characteristics, these differences are often inflated, leading to much larger differences in individual evaluations than would be warranted by actual group-level characteristics (Rothschild and Stiglitz 1982). Indeed, when asked to rate the characteristics of stereotyped groups (according to dimensions for which objective information is available), individuals tend to exaggerate group differences and to underestimate the level of within-group dispersion (Ryan 1995; McCauley 1995). To take one example, a 1991 survey asked, "of all the people arrested for violent crimes in the United States last year, what percent do you think were black?" The modal response was "60 percent," an exaggeration of roughly 35 percent.[12] Likewise, Americans on average estimate that blacks make up roughly 50 percent of the nation's poor, nearly double the actual proportion (Gilens 1999). The degree of overestimation for these characteristics differs little for residents of urban and rural communities, or areas with either high or low concentrations of blacks. Pervasive racial stereotypes, amplified through selective media portrayals, can thus substantially distort the evidence according to which group attributions are formed. Rational-actor models emphasizing the utility of statistical discrimination may thus be missing a substantial degree of bias built in to the otherwise-rational inference process.

Further, researchers disagree over the degree to which inaccurate group assessments can persist over time. Perfect-market models assume that inefficiencies will be automatically eliminated over time, as relevant actors discover their practices to be suboptimal and correct for necessary modifications (Oettinger 1996). Factors such as segregation, imperfect information flows, and negative feedback effects, however, impede awareness of changes and work to preserve existing outcomes (Tomaskovic-Devey and Skaggs 1999; Whatley and Wright 1994). As labor economist Kenneth Arrow argued, "Each employer has a very limited range of experience, and so prior beliefs can remain relatively undisturbed. Indeed, to the extent that discrimination takes the form of segregation, then there will in fact be little experimentation to find out abilities. . . . The very fact of segregation will reinforce beliefs in racial differences" (1998, 97). Segregation limits whites' exposure to non-whites, thus reducing opportunities to recalibrate group assessments and preserving outdated attributions. Without direct contact, media representations may be the most common source of information available to employers (or the general public) about the characteristics of blacks today. Unfortunately, media coverage of successful black professionals has not kept pace with coverage of blacks in poor neighborhoods or behind bars (Entman and Rojecki 2000).

Perhaps more disturbingly, even with exposure to accurate information about group members, stereotypes demonstrate a stubborn resistance to change. Creative social psychological experiments have demonstrated the numerous ways in which individuals unconsciously resist the integration of counterstereotypic information through biases in the gathering, processing, and recall of information (Fiske 1998; Bodenhausen 1988; Trope and Thomson 1997). The heuristic value of stereotypes shapes perception in ways that privilege evidence confirming of stereotypes while discounting that which is contradictory. Although sometimes efficient when dealing with accurate expectations, these processes can lead individuals to retain false beliefs far longer than optimal.

Understanding the processes that shape discrimination remains an important goal for social scientists. Overall, the evidence suggests that overt forms of prejudice and discrimination have declined, but that subtle and unconscious forms of bias persist. Unfortunately, these unconscious sources of discrimination remain among the most difficult to identify, legislate, and change.

Structural Discrimination

Most of the research on discrimination, and indeed each of the mechanisms discussed, thus far focuses on dynamics between individuals. It is easiest to conceptualize discrimination in terms of the actions of specific individuals, with the attitudes, prejudices, and biases of majority group members shaping actions toward minority group members. Yet it is important to recognize that each of these decisions takes place within a broader social context. Recognizing the ways in which these contexts shape individual and group outcomes is a critical component of understanding the underlying dynamics of discrimination. In some cases, the distinction is blurry. When an employer discriminates against a minority job seeker, is this an individual act of discrimination, motivated by the prejudices and assumptions of that particular employer, or does the employer's decision reflect a larger system of discrimination within that corporate environment? When a doctor prescribes a course of treatment to a minority patient that is less effective than what he or she would prescribe to a white patient, is this individual bias, or does the decision represent the influence of a larger medical establishment that uses race as a predictor of treatment compliance or insurance status? Although each case has its own unique circumstances, the consistency of discrimination within and across domains encourages us to direct our attention beyond individual actors to consider the larger institutional context in which discrimination takes place.

A focus on structural and institutional sources of discrimination allows us to further recognize the ways in which opportunities can be allocated on the basis of race in the absence of direct prejudice or bias. Numerous processes take place at the organizational, institutional, and societal level that systematically disadvantage minorities without any necessary conscious intent. These structural forms of discrimination are often ostensibly race-neutral, but can nevertheless exclude or subordinate blacks or other minorities.

For example, a common practice used by firms to recruit new workers is through employee referrals. In doing so, employers can avoid extensive advertising for and screening of prospective applicants. Indeed, some evidence suggests that referrals often do produce better-quality applicants, and that referred employees often make a better fit than those recruited other ways (Fernandez, Castilla, and Moore 2000). Whatever the advantages, however, the use of referrals has the added consequence of reproducing the existing racial composition of the company. Because of high levels of social segregation, in firms where a majority of employees are white, new referrals are also likely to be white (Braddock and McPartland 1987). Ted Mouw, for example, found that employee referrals in predominantly white firms reduce the probability of a black hire by nearly 75 percent relative to newspaper ads (2002).[13] Focusing more directly on the context of working class jobs that represent critical pathways out of poverty, Diedre Royster (2003) found that access to and support from informal social networks was a critical factor differentiating the employment trajectories of otherwise similar black and white graduates of a vocational high school in Baltimore. The wide-ranging economic consequences that follow from segregated social networks corresponds to what Glenn Loury referred to as the move from "discrimination in contract" to "discrimination in contact" (2001, 452). According to Loury, whereas earlier forms of discrimination primarily reflected explicit differences in the treatment of racial groups, contemporary forms are more likely to be perpetuated through informal networks of opportunity that, though ostensibly race-neutral, systematically disadvantage members of historically excluded groups.

Although the majority of this literature has focused on the white-minority divide, the use of employee referrals also has implications for competition between minority groups. In fact, research on ethnic niches suggests that Hispanics and Asians have likewise been able to capitalize on the use of networks to benefit members of their own group at the expense of other minorities (for example, Portes and Landolt 1996; Light and Gold 2000). Roger Waldinger and Michael

Lichter (2003), for example, found a substantial number of firms and industries in Los Angeles in which Latino workers have been able to internally regulate the recruitment process through extensive kinship and community networks. These low-skill jobs provide critical economic footholds for those whose employment options are otherwise limited; to the extent that ethnically homogenous recruitment networks regulate the hiring process, members of out-groups become excluded from potentially valuable employment opportunities. "Where incumbents' networks essentially seize hold of the recruitment process, employers rarely, if ever, have the opportunity to consider applicants who differ from the workers whom they already employ. Under these circumstances, out-group workers find themselves excluded, but not as the result of actions motivated by prejudices of employers" (Waldinger and Lichter 2003, 150). In this context, then, employers are rarely confronted with the opportunity to discriminate against members of excluded groups, given that such individuals never make it into the applicant pool. Forms of structural discrimination, through which existing inequalities are reproduced through informal social processes, instead preclude opportunities in ways that contribute to systematic disadvantage.

The spatial distribution of resources also contributes to structural forms of discrimination. The majority of job growth over the past two decades—including low-skill and low-wage work—has been concentrated in suburban areas, far from the reach of central city (and largely minority) residents. The cost of transportation to these jobs is often prohibitive, particularly for entry-level jobs for which compensation is minimal. Even among those willing to make the journey, information about job opportunities in the distant suburbs is less likely to make its way to central-city residents. These barriers of access—including both transportation and information—reduce the pool of black applicants for suburban jobs, with a corresponding reduction in black employment overall (Kain 1968; Wilson 1987; Fernandez and Su 2004).[14] Again, suburban employers may not actively seek to avoid minority workers (but see Ellwood 1986), but the spatial disconnect between jobs and minority workers can effectively lead to the same outcome.

Similarly, the allocation of resources for public schools is associated with systematic disadvantage to minority communities. According to Gary Orfield and Chungmei Lee, more than 60 percent of black and Latino students attend high poverty schools, compared to 30 percent of Asians and 18 percent of whites (2005, 18). Public schools receive a large fraction of their funding from local property taxes, with schools in affluent neighborhoods benefiting from the wealthier tax base. Some efforts are made to redistribute resources from rich to poor school districts, but sizable disparities remain (Augenblick, Myers, and Anderson 1997). Further, beyond simple funding levels, the broader resources of schools in poor neighborhoods are substantially limited: teachers in poor and minority schools tend to have less experience, shorter tenure, and are more likely to have emergency credentials rather than official teaching certifications (Orfield and Lee 2005). At the same time, schools in high poverty neighborhoods are faced with a greater incidence of social problems, including teen pregnancy, gang involvement, and unstable households (Massey and Denton 1993). Despite fewer resources, these schools are expected to manage a wider array of student needs. The resulting lower quality of education common in poor and minority school districts implies that students in these schools will be less prepared for future opportunities, including employment and higher education, which represent critical pathways out of poverty (Orfield and Lee 2005; see Farkas, chapter 5, this volume).

Each of these cases is an example of structural forms of discrimination, not necessarily motivated by any racial considerations, but with the ultimate consequence of systematically disadvantaging racial minorities. Recalling our two-part definition of discrimination proposed earlier, these cases of disparate impact (as opposed to disparate treatment) represent an equally powerful form of racial discrimination in contemporary society. Unfortunately, unlike individual acts of discrimination, structural sources are far more difficult to identify, evaluate, and change. Because these patterns are not produced by any single decision maker, but rather through a complex web of decisions that evolve over time, they are far more resistant to intervention and thus far more likely to persist.[15]

Systems of Discrimination

The significance of discrimination is reinforced still further when we look beyond the impact of any given individual or institution to the complex and interwoven systems through which the effects of discrimination become magnified. To take one vivid example, consider the implications of pervasive discrimination in housing markets described earlier. Minority home-seekers are routinely directed toward minority neighborhoods in their search for housing. At the same time, white residents quickly move out of neighborhoods when more than a small percentage of blacks move in (Schelling 1971; Conley 1999). The combination of racial channeling and white flight perpetuates high levels of residential segregation, which is in turn associated with a growing concentration of poverty (Massey and Denton 1993). Residence in a segregated, high poverty neighborhood is itself associated with a wide range of negative social outcomes, including poorer schools, fewer nearby jobs, more limited social networks, and greater exposure to crime and violence (Yinger 2001; Williams 2004). Discrimination in housing markets also serves to channel minority residents toward poorer housing stock, which in turn contributes to negative health outcomes. Poor blacks and Hispanics are roughly twice as likely as poor whites to live in homes with rodents or cockroaches, or in housing with chipped plaster or peeling paint—conditions linked to asthma, lead poisoning, and other serious health risks (Yinger 2001, 377). These health problems in turn place greater financial burden on minority families, including emergency room visits and other health care costs and the costs of missed work or schooling (Mullahy and Wolfe 2001).

Previous research has documented strong evidence of discrimination in the context of housing searches (Yinger 1995), car sales (Ayres and Siegelman 1995), applications for insurance (Wissoker, Zimmerman, and Galster 1997), home mortgages (Turner and Skidmore 1999), medical care (Schulman et al. 1999), and even in hailing taxis (Ridley, Bayton, and Outtz 1989). Although the existing body of research investigates what are only a few of the nearly infinite domains of social life, it demonstrates the wide range of contexts in which race profoundly limits opportunity. Consider how each of these everyday interactions cumulate across the life course in the form of sequential and additive disadvantage. For racial minorities, everyday life achievements take longer, require more effort, and impose greater financial and psychic costs.

Table 2.1 presents a schematic of some of the primary domains in which discrimination may be associated with significant racial disparities. As illustrated, discrimination is not isolated to one social sphere or to any one set of actions or actors. In this way, even relatively small incidents of discrimination—when experienced at multiple intervals or across multiple contexts—can have substantial effects on aggregate outcomes. Discrimination in educational settings or labor markets increases pressures for youth to opt out, turning instead to opportunities in the informal or illegal economy; discrimination in credit markets contributes to higher rates of loan default, with negative implications for minority entrepreneurship and home ownership; discrimination in housing markets leads to residential segregation, which in turn limits access to employment opportunities. It is difficult to capture the cumulative consequences of discrimination using traditional research designs. Nevertheless, to accurately account for the impact of discrimination, it is critical to recognize the ways in which discrimination in one domain (or at one stage) can impose negative spillover effects into other arenas.

Cumulative Effects

Just as the effects of discrimination can accrue across multiple domains, they can cumulate across the life course. Indeed, blocked opportunities early on can have long-term consequences for an individual's future social and economic well being. For example, standard economic models inform us that investments in skill are a function of the expectations of future returns. As job-seekers make attempts to secure employment, they receive explicit and implicit feedback from employers about their suitability for various kinds of jobs and their desirability to various kinds of employers. The information gathered during these initial searches is likely to guide subsequent search behavior and to influence expectations of the returns to investments in work-related capital. If blacks perceive high levels of discrimination in the labor market, their incentives to invest in the development of cognitive skills or labor market credentials will be weakened early on (Darity and Mason 1998; Loury 2002).

An abundance of social-psychological literature documents the powerful negative feedback effects created by the internalization or imposition of early acts of discrimination. As victims of discrimination come to expect disapproval or rejection, their internal defenses become activated. The tension caused by such interactions can be resolved through either an active disidentification with the initial goal, thereby preserving the congruence between one's aspirations and one's

TABLE 2.1 / Mapping Discrimination: Actions and Actors

Source Points	Housing and Lending	↔	Education	↔	Labor Markets	↔	Criminal Justice	↔	Health Care
Access	Steering; redlining		Acceptance; financial aid		Interviewing; hiring		Racial profiling; arrests		Access to care; insurance
Progress	Mortgage approval; loan pricing; resale value		Tracking; grades; special education retention		Wages; promotion; layoffs; firing		Plea bargaining; sentencing; parole violations		Quality of care; price of care; referrals
Key actors	Landlords; sellers; lenders; neighbors		Teachers; administrators; fellow students		Employers; customers; coworkers		Police; prosecutors; judges; juries; parole boards		Health care workers; administrators; insurance companies

Source: Adapted from Blank, Dabady, and Citro (2004, 67).

achievements, or through an internalization of negative attributions, with an associated lowering of expectations for success (Crocker, Major, and Steele 1998; Fanon 1967).

Loury described the complex consequences of stigma in what he terms "the logic of self-confirming stereotypes" (2002, 26–33). In this discussion, he articulated three key components of this cycle by which initial evaluations—no matter how innocent—can have serious consequences for the distribution of outcomes among groups. The first stage involves an initial evaluation, say, by employers of job applicants, for which employers must draw inferences on the basis of limited and difficult-to-observe information. Following what could be a rational cognitive process, employers are likely to make statistical inferences, based on perceived associations between observed characteristics (such as race, gender, age, criminal history) and job-relevant concerns. Whether or not an employer seeks to intentionally exclude members of certain social categories, internalized expectations about these categories can, as we have seen, play a significant role in the evaluation process.

In the second stage of this cycle, the employer's initial evaluation provides the applicant with feedback regarding the degree to which his or her job-relevant characteristics are noticed and appreciated, and, likewise, the probability that future investments in job-relevant skills will be rewarded. To the extent that racial-ethnic minorities feel that their job-relevant characteristics are devalued by employers, the incentive to invest in such skills will decline (see also Arrow 1998). Whether or not the individuals themselves internalize negative attributions, a rational cost-benefit analysis of job search behavior indicates that the returns are lower for members of stigmatized groups. Although some may intensify their efforts to overcome these barriers, many will likely resign themselves to failure (Crocker and Major 1989).

Finally, through the interaction of initial (category-based) evaluations and feedback effects, an equilibrium can be reached. As initial rejections create disincentives for stigmatized individuals to persevere, a congruence between employer expectations and applicant characteristics is achieved. The result of this negative feedback loop is that, over time, it becomes entirely "rational" for employers to make decisions on the basis of "functionally irrelevant attributes" (Loury 2002, 27): as negative expectations lead to real differences in job-relevant attributes, the perceived link between racial identity and productivity becomes real (see also Merton 1948).

Perhaps even more damaging, the mechanisms producing this outcome can remain entirely hidden. Employers mistakenly believe that the disadvantage racial minorities suffer is attributable to some intrinsic property of the group, whereas in fact this association is at least in part produced by faulty expectations. Poverty and joblessness are thus seen as the confirmation of expectations rather than the consequence thereof, perpetuating an unchallenged system of misattributions and faulty judgments.

More broadly, Larry Bobo and his colleagues argued that the largely invisible structural forces that perpetuate racial disadvantage reinforce whites' beliefs in black inferiority, and legitimate existing inequalities as the assumed result of fair competition. "A large number of white Americans have become comfortable with as much racial inequality and segregation as a putatively nondiscriminatory polity and free market economy can produce: hence the reproduction and, on some dimensions, the worsening of racial inequalities. These circumstances are rendered culturally palatable by the new ideology of laissez-faire racism" (Bobo, Kluegel, and Smith 1997, 41). Cass Sunstein (1991) discussed similar themes in his article, "Why Markets Don't Stop Discrimination." According to him, "the beneficiaries of the status quo tend to [conclude] that the fate of victims is deserved, or is something for which victims are responsible, or is part of an intractable, given, or natural order. . . . The reduction of cognitive dissonance thus operates as a significant obstacle to the recognition that discrimination is a problem, or even that it exists" (32). The perpetuation of racial inequality through structural and institutional channels can thus be conducive to legitimating ideologies of race-blindness, exonerating the majority group from responsibility and shifting blame toward minorities for their own disadvantage.

WHAT ARE EFFECTIVE STRATEGIES FOR REDUCING DISCRIMINATION?

The pervasiveness of racial stereotypes and the persistence of discrimination can seem like grounds for despair. Racial bias appears so deeply embedded in American society and its institutions that there sometimes seems little possibility for its eradication. And yet, there are grounds for hope. Despite the pervasiveness of racial stereotypes—the content of which has changed very little over time—the expression of racial bias has been shown to vary substantially over time and across social contexts. Examining the contexts in which discrimination becomes more or less prevalent can help us to identify strategies for reducing discrimination more broadly. I consider four factors that matter for the expression (or reduction) of racial discrimination.

LAW MATTERS   There is substantial evidence to suggest that the legal context can and does matter for the expression of discrimination. The adoption of broad antidiscrimination statutes in the mid-1960s significantly changed the ways in which employers, landlords, and other key gatekeepers conducted business. And there is convincing evidence to suggest that these legal changes, far from resulting in merely superficial change (making discrimination more covert), did in fact expand opportunity significantly for blacks in the 1960s and 1970s,. For example, James Heckman and Brook Payner (1989) examined changes in the level of black employment and wages in the manufacturing industry in South Carolina between 1960 and 1980. After taking into account a wide range of competing factors—including changes in educational attainment by race, labor supply, and local economic conditions—the authors concluded that federal antidiscrimination programs directly contributed to the increase in black economic attainment (see also

Donahue and Heckman 1991). Reductions in the poverty rates of black families during this time period provides further (indirect) evidence for the wide-ranging effects of equal opportunity laws and enforcement (Harrison and Bennett 1995, 195).

The more proactive approach represented by affirmative action policy has also demonstrated substantial positive effects. Affirmative action requirements for federal contractors, for example, have been associated with a 25 percent increase in the share of minority workers and a significant increase in the occupational status of Latinos and African Americans (Edelman and Petterson 1999; Reskin 1998). Harry Holzer and David Neumark (2000) reported that firms that have affirmative action policies in place have higher rates of minority employment and smaller racial wage gaps. Further, though minorities hired under affirmative action had on average lower levels of education than whites, their performance ratings on the job were virtually identical to those of whites (Holzer and Neumark 2000, 533; for a parallel case in higher education, see Bowen and Bok 1998).[16] Together, antidiscrimination law and affirmative action have provided twin vehicles for the enforcement and promotion of equal opportunity for America's racial minorities, contributing to reductions in poverty and spurring an unprecedented growth of black upward mobility (Wilson 1987, chapter 5).

Finally, it is important to emphasize that the effectiveness of antidiscrimination law is only as great as the corresponding commitment to enforcement (Leonard 1990). The Department of Housing and Urban Development, for example, has partnered with the Department of Justice to investigate and enforce fair housing laws, resulting in a number of large settlements against major insurance and real estate companies. Perhaps in part as a result of this effort, the rate of discrimination against blacks and Latinos in home purchasing declined between 1990 and 2000, and the number of mortgage loans to blacks and Hispanics nationwide increased 60 percent, compared to 16 percent for whites (Turner et al. 2002; Squires 1999). The same has not been true in the case of employment, where the Equal Employment Opportunity Commission (EEOC) has shown great reluctance to proactively identify and prosecute discriminatory employers.[17] In fact, the number of EEOC claims focusing on racial discrimination declined through the 1990s, relative to increasing numbers of claims on the basis of gender and disability (Donahue and Siegelman 2003). The low rates of detection and enforcement in cases of hiring discrimination leave employers largely immune to antidiscrimination law, potentially undermining the substantial gains of earlier decades. The legal environment can have important effects on the expression of discrimination, but only with the appropriate monitoring and enforcement.

INSTITUTIONS MATTER   A second contextual factor related to the expression of discrimination is the institutional environment. Institutions can adopt specific procedures and develop well-defined norms to encourage or reduce the incidence of discrimination. The U.S. military, for example, is one institution in which we have seen a remarkable advancement of African Americans over time. African Americans are well represented among high-ranking officers, and the level of integration on military barracks is far beyond that in the society at large. Further, the children of military personnel who attend Department of Defense schools demonstrate higher test scores and a smaller racial test score gap than their civilian peers (Brown 2006). In their study of the U.S. Army, Charles Moskos and John Butler (1996, 13) attributed the significant progress toward racial equality to three primary factors: an absolute organizational commitment to nondiscrimination, with serious consequences for those who violate these norms; high standards of performance for all recruits; and opportunities to reach and maintain standards, through education, training, and mentoring. Although the army is quite distinct from mainstream American institutions, Moskos and Butler argued that many of these lessons can be generalized to nonmilitary settings in which diversity and racial equality are made priorities.

Indeed, beyond the specific case of the army, the public sector more generally has achieved a strong track record in reducing racial disparities. The public sector is characterized by a highly rationalized system of hiring, promotion, and remuneration, thought to shield against forms of discrimination that may prevail in some private sector firms (DiPrete and Soule 1986; Moulton 1990). Empirical evidence suggests that the wage gaps by race and gender are substantially lower in the public sector than they are in corresponding private sector occupations, and that a disproportionate number of blacks and women are employed in public sector positions (Grodsky and Pager 2001; Ehrenberg and Schwarz 1986). Stable career jobs in the public sector represented a critical stepping stone for poor and working class families and the emergence of a significant black middle class.

Finally, these lessons have been shown to apply in some private sector contexts as well. Firms that have in place formal and systematic protocols for personnel management decisions are more effective in reducing the impact of racial bias, as evidenced by higher rates of minority employment (Reskin 1998; Holzer 1998). Strong institutional commitments to reducing discrimination can have large effects. By putting into place procedures to counteract the effects of individual bias or pervasive racial stereotypes, organizations can work to effectively overcome individual and systemic forms of discrimination.

TECHNOLOGY MATTERS As suggested, decisions made in informal settings or with wide personal discretion are often those most vulnerable to the influence of conscious or unconscious racial bias. Conversely, the formalization of decision making can help reduce the impact of subjective bias. Recent technological developments offer some promising strategies toward this end. Mortgage lenders, for example, increasingly use automated credit scoring systems, based on a formula that takes into account an individual's assets and credit risks. Based on these formal criteria, there is little room for the biases of individual lenders to influence ratings of creditworthiness. Further, increasing numbers of mortgage lenders now offer this service online, with no in-person contact. In these cases, the race of the applicant can often remain unknown by the lender until well into the process (Harris 2002). According to a study by Susan Gates, Vanessa Perry, and Peter Zorn

(2002), the use of automated underwriting systems is associated with a nearly 30 percent increase in the approval rate for minority and low-income clients, and more accurate predictions of default than traditional methods. Technologies such as these, which demonstrate the capacity to increase performance and decrease discrimination, offer promising directions for future efforts to reduce discrimination, and to increase access to opportunities for valued social goods.

Similarly, the internet offers promising possibilities for reducing discrimination in employment, housing, and consumer markets. For example, previous research has found that African Americans and Hispanics pay on average 2 percent more for new cars relative to whites. Among online consumers, by contrast, minority buyers pay roughly the same prices as whites even after controlling for consumers' income, education, and neighborhood characteristics (Morton, Zettelmeyer, and Silva-Risso 2003). Research on the impact of the internet remains limited, but similarly promising scenarios may be possible for employment and housing searchers. Although in these cases in-person contact is typically required at some point in the process, initial screening and information gathering—in some cases even rapport-building—can be achieved before the race of the job- or home-seeker becomes known (Harris 2002). Of course, for these technologies to reduce rather than exacerbate racial disparities, the issue of access must be addressed. Currently the digital divide remains large, with black and Latino households less likely to own a computer and less likely to have access to the internet than their white counterparts (Hoffman and Novak 1998). Increasing access to internet technology and capacity in schools, public libraries, and community centers will help to reduce these disparities, and promote the full potential of new technologies for reducing racial discrimination.

THE ECONOMY MATTERS   A final contextual factor affecting the expression of discrimination is the economy. When the labor market is slack—that is, when the number of job openings relative to the number of job seekers is small—employers can be extremely selective in their hiring practices. For those who prefer some racial-ethnic groups to others, the abundance of applicants allows them to have their pick, even if their preferences are irrelevant to the actual quality of workers (Myers 1989). In tight labor markets, by contrast, when the demand for labor is acute, employers are less able to exert nonessential preferences. In this context, even employers with preferences for white workers will often be forced to give minority workers a chance. Indeed, during the economic expansion of the 1990s, we saw significant gains in employment and earnings for young low-skill minority men (Freeman and Rodgers 1999; but see Western and Pettit 2005). Likewise, earlier periods of economic expansion, such as that following World War II, have been associated with the increasing economic status of African Americans (Smith and Welch 1989). Macroeconomic conditions are of course difficult to control, but this research suggests that investments in job creation and economic growth can have important effects for reducing racial discrimination.

Although none of these factors are a cure-all for the problems of discrimination, they are compelling evidence that certain environments can and do reduce the incidence of discrimination. It may be the case, then, that rather than focusing on the attitudes or biases of individuals, we should focus more on the contexts in which individual preferences are expressed.

CONCLUSION

This review suggests that discrimination remains an important source of disadvantage for minority groups, contributing to limited opportunities in employment, housing, consumer markets, health care, and numerous other domains. Although it is difficult to quantify the degree to which poverty among minorities can be explained by discrimination, the pervasiveness of these effects suggests that the impact is substantial.

But there is still much to be learned. Very little research on discrimination, for example, goes beyond the perspective of white Americans. Although no group has a level of power or institutional control comparable to whites, ethnic niches can command substantial influence over the allocation of resources and opportunities at the local level. Particularly in urban contexts where divisions of space, class, race and culture intersect, racial dynamics between minority groups can produce complex patterns of discrimination that extend well beyond the divisions of black and white. Future research would benefit from investigations of discrimination that include multiple minority groups, examining forms of discrimination that originate from white-minority relations as well as between distinct minority groups.

Likewise, additional research is needed to better specify the complex nature of discrimination, among individuals, within institutions, across domains of social life, and over the life course. Single point estimates of discrimination within particular domains substantially underestimate the cumulative effects of discrimination over time, and the ways in which discrimination in one domain can trigger disadvantage in many others. Developing models to better capture systems of discrimination will move us toward a fuller understanding of discrimination in contemporary society.

Discrimination is not the only cause of racial disparities in poverty. Indeed, as the other chapters in this volume suggest, persistent inequality between racial and ethnic groups is the product of complex and multifaceted influences. Nevertheless, the weight of existing evidence suggests that discrimination does continue to affect the allocation of contemporary opportunities; and, further, given the often covert, indirect, and cumulative nature of these effects, our current estimates may in fact underestimate the degree to which discrimination contributes to the poor social and economic outcomes of minority groups. Great progress has been made since the early 1960s, but the problems of racial discrimination remain an important factor in shaping contemporary patterns of social and economic inequality.

NOTES

1. Likewise, research suggests that individuals may underestimate or suppress the incidence of discrimination in their own lives, even when conscious of high levels of discrimination against their group (Crosby 1984; Taylor et al. 1990).

2. Respondents were asked to rate members of a designated group on a continuum between two polar statements (for example, rich-poor). Respondents were asked about ratings for each group sequentially, without direct comparisons between groups.

3. Likewise, despite the progressive changes in racial attitudes generally, Patricia Devine and Scott Elliot (1995) found that the content of racial stereotypes has changed little over time. What has changed, rather, is the conscious effort on the part of nonprejudiced individuals to inhibit the activation of these stereotypes (Devine 1989). Although these conscious strategies have successfully resulted in a substantial reduction in the expression of racial bias, actions taken under pressure remain vulnerable to the influence of implicit racial attitudes (Macrae, Hewstone, and Griffiths 1993).

4. Korean merchants have demonstrated strong preferences for hiring Hispanic workers, but not blacks, resulting in part from perceptions of work ethic and dependability across these groups (Kim 1999; Min 1996; Yoon 1997; Weitzer 1997; for an overview of research on black racial attitudes, see Farley, Hatchett, and Schuman 1979; Jaynes and Williams 1989, chapter 3).

5. These concerns are even more evident in statistical analyses of racial differences in labor market outcomes where, even after controlling for education, work experience, region, and a wide range of factors associated with labor market success, a whole host of employment-related characteristics typically remain unaccounted for. Characteristics such as reliability, motivation, interpersonal skills, and punctuality, for example, are each important to finding and keeping a job, but these are characteristics that are virtually impossible to measure using survey data.

6. Asian renters experienced a similar overall mean level of discrimination, but because of high levels of variation across tests the difference was not statistically significant. Native American renters did not experience adverse treatment on most dimensions, but were significantly more likely to be denied information about the availability of housing units relative to whites (Turner and Ross 2003a, 2003b).

7. Unlike trends for homebuyers and for African American renters, the results of the recent HUD study indicate that discrimination against Hispanic renters has not declined. In fact, Hispanics are now more likely to experience discrimination in seeking rental units than African Americans are (Turner et al. 2002). Native American homebuyers also experienced significant steering away from white neighborhoods, though no measure from an earlier time point is available for comparison (Turner and Ross 2003b).

8. Other critiques of the audit methodology have focused on the problems of effective tester matching, the use of overqualified testers, the limited sampling frame for the selection of firms and jobs to be audited; experimenter effects, and the ethics of audit research (for a more extensive discussion of these issues, see Heckman 1998; Pager 2007). In addition, audit studies are often costly and difficult to implement, and can

only be used for selective decision points (such as hiring decisions but not promotions).

9. For a similar study testing a wider range of ethnic-gender groups, see the Discrimination Research Center (2004). Also, see David Figlio (2005) for a nonexperimental, but clever study of the effects of racially identifiable names on teachers' expectations of students (comparing sibling pairs in which one sibling has a racially identifiable name but the other does not).

10. Whites received callbacks in 10.06 percent of cases compared to 6.70 percent for blacks. Callback rates were slightly higher for women than men, but overall levels of discrimination differed little by gender.

11. In most cases, application forms ask applicants to report, "Have you ever been convicted of a felony? If yes, please explain" (for more information on how testers reported criminal background information, see Pager 2003).

12. This survey item comes from the 1991 National Race and Politics Survey (accessed at http://sda.berkeley.edu:7502/archive.htm). The proportion of violent arrests involving blacks was 45 percent in 1990 (FBI 1990).

13. This estimate comes from a model with controls for spatial segregation, occupational segregation, city, and firm size. Analyses apply to noncollege jobs only.

14. Hispanics and Asians are less affected by the dynamics of spatial mismatch, presumably due to their lower levels of residential segregation and greater access to suburban jobs (Holzer 1996).

15. The legal basis for challenging certain structural forms of discrimination falls under the disparate impact doctrine, first established by the 1991 Supreme Court decision in Griggs v. Duke Power Co., and codified into law in the 1991 Civil Rights Act (Blank, Dabady, and Citro 2004). In these cases, organizational practices can be deemed illegal if they produce unequal outcomes by race and are not justified by business necessity. Disparate impact claims have been critical in removing barriers to minority groups not motivated by explicit racial intent (and therefore not covered by traditional definitions of discriminatory treatment). Over time, however, changes in the judicial interpretation of this doctrine have increased the burden of proof for plaintiffs; correspondingly, the proportion of cases that have prevailed under this doctrine has declined since 1991 (Songer 2005).

16. Hispanic males were the only group that showed lower average performance ratings under affirmative action.

17. Unlike the HUD studies, there are no time series for audit studies of employment. Recent employment audits do, however, reveal similar levels of discrimination to those from the previous decade (Pager 2003; Bendick, Jackson, and Reinoso 1994).

REFERENCES

Adorno, Theodor, E. Frankel-Brunswik, D. Levinson, and R. Sanford. 1950. *The Authoritarian Personality*. New York: Harper.

Aigner, Dennis J., and Glen G. Cain. 1977. "Statistical Theories of Discrimination in Labor Markets." *Industrial and Labor Relations Review* 30(2): 749–76.

Allport, Gordon. 1954. *Nature of Prejudice*. Cambridge, Mass.: Addison-Wesley.

Arrow, Kenneth J. 1972. "Models of Job Discrimination." In *Racial Discrimination in Economic Life*, edited by A.H. Pascal. Lexington, Mass.: D.C. Heath.

———. 1998. "What Has Economics to Say about Racial Discrimination?" *Journal of Economic Perspectives* 12(2): 91–100.

Augenblick, John, John Myers, Amy Berk Anderson. 1997. "Equity and Adequacy in School Funding." *Future of Children* 7(3): 63–78.

Ayres, Ian, and Peter Siegelman. 1995. "Race and Gender Discrimination in Bargaining for a New Car." *The American Economic Review* 85(3): 304–21.

Becker, Gary S. 1971. *The Economics of Discrimination*, 2nd ed. Chicago, Ill.: University of Chicago Press.

Bendick, Marc, Jr., Charles Jackson, and Victor Reinoso. 1994. "Measuring Employment Discrimination Through Controlled Experiments." *Review of Black Political Economy* 23(1): 25–48.

Bertrand, Marianne, and Sendhil Mullainathan. 2004. "Are Emily and Brendan More Employable than Lakisha and Jamal? A Field Experiment on Labor Market Discrimination." *American Economic Review* 94(4): 991–1013.

Bielby, William T., and James N. Baron. 1986. "Men and Women at Work: Sex Segregation and Statistical Discrimination." *American Journal of Sociology* 91(4): 759–99.

Blank, Rebecca, Marilyn Dabady, and Constance Citro, editors. 2004. *Measuring Racial Discrimination: Panel on Methods for Assessing Discrimination*. Committee on National Statistics, Division of Behavior and Social Sciences and Education. Washington, D.C.: The National Academies Press.

Bobo, Lawrence, and Vincent L. Hutchings. 1996. "Perceptions of Racial Competition in a Multiracial Setting." *American Sociological Review* 61(6): 951–73.

Bobo, Lawrence, James Kluegel, and Ryan Smith. 1997. "Laissez-Faire Racism: The Crystallization of a 'Kinder, Gentler' Anti-black Ideology." In *Racial Attitudes in the 1990s: Continuity and Change*, edited by Steven A. Tuch and Jack K. Martin. Westport, Conn.: Praeger.

Bodenhausen, Galen. 1988. "Stereotypic Biases in Social Decision Making and Memory: Testing Process Models of Stereotype Use." *Journal of Personality and Social Psychology* 55(5): 726–37.

Bowen, William and Derek Bok. 1998. *The Shape of the River*. Princeton, N.J.: Princeton University Press.

Braddock, J.H. and J.M. McPartland. 1987. "How Minorities Continue to be Excluded from Equal Employment Opportunities." *Journal of Social Issues* 43(1): 5–39.

Brooks-Gunn, Jeanne, Greg J. Duncan, and J. Lawrence Aber, editors. 1997. *Neighborhood Poverty, Volume 1: Context and Consequences for Children*. New York: Russell Sage Foundation.

Brown, Charles. 2006. "Relatively Equal Opportunity in the Armed Forces: Impacts on Children of Military Families." Unpublished manuscript.

Conley, Dalton. 1999. *Being Black, Living in the Red: Race, Wealth, and Social Policy in America*. Berkeley, Calif.: University of California Press.

Correll, Joshua, Bernd Wittenbrink, and Charles M. Judd. 2002. "The Police Officer's Dilemma: Using Ethnicity to Disambiguate Potentially Threatening Individuals." *Journal of Personality and Social Psychology* 83(6): 1314–29.

Crocker, Jennifer, and Brenda Major. 1989. "Social Stigma and Self-Esteem: The Self-Protective Properties of Stigma." *Psychological Review* 96(4): 608–30.

Crocker, Jennifer, Brenda Major, and Claude Steele. 1998. "Social Stigma." In *Handbook of Social Psychology*, vol. 4., edited by Daniel Gilbert, Susan Fiske, and Gardner Lindzey. New York: Oxford University Press.

Crosby, Faye. 1984. "The Denial of Personal Discrimination." *American Behavioral Scientist* 27(3): 371–86.

Darity, William A. and Patrick L. Mason. 1998. "Evidence on Discrimination in Employment: Codes of Color, Codes of Gender." *The Journal of Economic Perspectives* 12(2): 63–90.

Devine, Patricia. 1989. "Stereotypes and Prejudice: Their Automatic and Controlled Components." *Journal of Personality and Social Psychology* 56(1): 5–18.

Devine, Patricia, and Scott Elliot. 1995. "Are Stereotypes Really Fading? The Princeton Trilogy Revisited." *Personality and Social Psychology Bulletin* 21(11): 5–18.

DiPrete, Thomas, and Whitman Soule. 1986. "The Organization of Career Lines: Equal Employment Opportunity and Status Advancement in a Federal Bureaucracy." *American Sociological Review* 51(3): 295–309.

Discrimination Research Center. 2004. "Names Make a Difference: The Screening of Resumes by Temporary Employment Agencies in California." Berkeley, Calif.: Discrimination Research Center. Accessed at http://drcenter.org/staticdata/pdfs/name_resume_study.pdf.

Donahue, John J. III., and James Heckman. 1991. "Continuous versus Episodic Change: The Effect of Federal Civil Rights Policy on the Economic Status of Blacks." *Journal of Economic Literature* 29(4): 1603–43.

Donahue, John J. III, and Peter Siegelman. 2003. "The Evolution of Employment Discrimination Law in the 1990s: A Preliminary Empirical Investigation." In *Handbook of Employment Discrimination Research*, edited by L.B. Nielsen and R.L. Nelson. Dordrecht, Netherlands: Springer.

Edelman, Lauren B. and Stephen Petterson. 1999. "Symbols and Substance in Organizational Response to Civil Rights Law." *Research in Social Stratification and Mobility* 17: 107–36.

Ehrenberg, Ronald, and Joshua Schwarz. 1986. "Public-Sector Labor Markets." In *Handbook of Labor Economics*, edited by O. Ashenfelter and R. Layard. New York: North-Holland.

Ellwood, David. 1986. "The Spatial Mismatch Hypothesis: Are There Teenage Jobs Missing in the Ghetto?" In *The Black Youth Employment Crisis*, edited by Richard B. Freeman and Harry J. Holzer. Chicago, Ill.: University of Chicago Press.

Entman, Robert M., and Andrew Rojecki. 2000. *The Black Image in the White Mind: Media and Race in America*. Chicago, Ill.: University of Chicago Press.

Fanon, F. 1967. *Black Skins, White Masks*. New York: Grove.

Farley, Reynolds, Shirley Hatchett, and Howard Schuman. 1979. "A Note on Changes in Black Racial Attitudes in Detroit: 1968–1976." *Social Indicators Research* 6(4): 439–43.

Feagin, Joe R., and Melvin P. Sikes. 1994. *Living with Racism: The Black Middle-Class Experience*. Boston, Mass.: Beacon Press.

Federal Bureau of Investigation (FBI). 1990. "Crime in the United States." Uniform Crime Reports, 1990.

Fernandez, Roberto, Emilio Castilla, and Paul Moore. 2000. "Social Capital at Work: Networks and Employment at a Phone Center." *American Journal of Sociology* 105(5): 1288–356.

Fernandez, Roberto, and Celina Su. 2004. "Space and the Study of Labor Markets." *Annual Review of Sociology* 30(2004): 545–69.

Figlio, David N. 2005. "Names, Expectations and the Black-White Test Score Gap." NBER Working Paper 11195. Cambridge, Mass.: National Bureau of Economic Research.

Fiske, Susan. 1998. "Stereotyping, Prejudice, and Discrimination." In *Handbook of Social Psychology*, vol.4, edited by Daniel Gilbert, Susan Fiske, and Gardner Lindzey. New York: Oxford University Press.

Freeman, Richard B., and William M. Rodgers III. 1999. "Area Economic Conditions and the Labor Market Outcomes of Young Men in the 1990s Expansion." NBER Working Paper 7073. Cambridge, Mass.: National Bureau of Economic Research.

Gates, Susan Wharton, Vanessa Gail Perry, and Peter Zorn. 2002. "Automated Underwriting in Mortgage Lending: Good News for the Underserved?" *Housing Policy Debate* 13(2): 369–91.

Gilens, Martin. 1999. *Why Americans Hate Welfare: Race, Media and the Politics of Antipoverty Policy*. Chicago, Ill.: University of Chicago Press.

Grodsky, Eric, and Devah Pager. 2001. "The Structure of Disadvantage: Individual and Occupational Determinants of the Black-White Wage Gap." *American Sociological Review* 66(August): 542–67.

Harris, David R. 2002. "Poverty Research and Antipoverty Policy After the Technological Revolution." In *Understanding Poverty*, edited by Sheldon H. Danziger and Robert H. Haveman. Cambridge, Mass.: Harvard University Press.

Harrison, Roderick J., and Claudette E. Bennett. 1995. "Racial and Ethnic Diversity." In *State of the Union: America in the 1990s*, vol. 2, *Social Trends*, edited by R. Farley. New York: Russell Sage Foundation.

Heckman, James J. 1998. "Detecting Discrimination." *The Journal of Economic Perspectives* 12(2): 101–16.

Heckman, James, and Brook Payner. 1989. "Determining the Impact of Federal Antidiscrimination Policy on the Economic Status of Blacks: A Study of South Carolina." *The American Economic Review* 79(1): 138–77.

Hochschild, Jennifer L. 1995. *Facing Up to the American Dream: Race, Class, and the Soul of the Nation*. Princeton, N.J.: Princeton University Press.

Hoffman, D. L., and T. P. Novak. 1998. "Bridging the Racial Divide on the Internet." *Science* 280(17): 390–91.

Holzer, Harry. 1996. *What Employers Want: Job Prospects for Less-Educated Workers*. New York: Russell Sage Foundation.

———. 1998. "Why Do Small Establishments Hire Fewer Blacks than Larger Ones?" *Journal of Human Resources* 33(4): 896–914.

Holzer, Harry, and David Neumark. 2000. "Assessing Affirmative Action." *Journal of Economic Literature* 38(September): 483–568.

Jargowsky, Paul. 1997. *Poverty and Place: Ghettos, Barrios, and the American City*. New York: Russell Sage Foundation.

Jaynes, Gerald Davis, and Robin M. Williams, Jr., editors. 1989. *A Common Destiny: Blacks and American Society*. Washington, D.C.: National Academy Press.

Kain, J. F. 1968. "Housing Segregation, Negro Employment, and Metropolitan Decentralization." *The Quarterly Journal of Economics* 82(2): 165–97.

Kessler, Ronald C., Kristin D. Mickelson, and David R. Williams. 1990. "The Prevalence, Distribution, and Mental Health Correlates of Perceived Discrimination in the United States." *Journal of Health and Social Behavior* 40(3): 208–30.

Kim, Dae Young. 1999. "Beyond Co-Ethnic Solidarity: Mexican and Ecuadorean Employment in Korean-Owned Businesses in New York City." *Ethnic and Racial Studies* 22(3): 581–605.

Kinder, Donald R., and Lynn M. Sanders. 1996. *Divided by Color: Racial Politics and Democratic Ideals*. Chicago, Ill.: Chicago University Press.

Kinder, Donald R., and David O. Sears. 1981. "Prejudice and Politics: Symbolic Racism Versus Racial Threats to the Good Life." *Journal of Personality and Social Psychology* 40(3): 414–31.

Ladd, Helen F. 1998. "Evidence on Discrimination in Mortgage Lending." *The Journal of Economic Perspectives* 12(2): 41–62.

LaPiere, Richard T. 1934. "Attitudes vs. Actions." *Social Forces* 13(2): 230–37.

Leonard, Jonathan. 1990. "The Impact of Affirmative Action Regulation and Equal Employment Law on Black Employment." *The Journal of Economic Perspectives* 4(4): 47–63.

Light, Ivan, and Stephen J. Gold. 2000. *Ethnic Economies*. San Diego, Calif.: Academic Press.

Loury, Glenn C. 2001. "Politics, Race, and Poverty Research." In *Understanding Poverty*, edited by Sheldon H. Danziger and Robert H. Haveman. Cambridge, Mass.: Harvard University Press.

———. 2002. *The Anatomy of Racial Inequality*. Cambridge, Mass.: Harvard University Press.

Macrae, C. N., M. Hewstone, and R. G. Griffiths. 1993. "Processing Load and Memory for Stereotype-Based Information." *European Journal of Social Psychology* 23(1): 77–87.

Massey, Douglas S., and Nancy A. Denton. 1993. *American Apartheid: Segregation and the Making of the Underclass*. Cambridge, Mass.: Harvard University Press.

McCauley, Clark R. 1995. "Are Stereotypes Exaggerated? A Sampling of Racial, Gender, Academic, Occupational, and Political Stereotypes." In *Stereotype Accuracy: Toward Appreciating Group Differences*, edited by Yueh-Ting Lee, Lee J. Jussim, and Clark R. McCauley. Washington, D.C.: American Psychological Association.

McConahay, J. B. 1986. "Modern Racism, Ambivalence, and the Modern Racism Scale." In *Prejudice, Discrimination, and Racism*, edited by J. F. Dovidio and S. L. Gaertner. San Diego, Calif.: Academic Press.

Merton, Robert. 1948. "The Self-Fulfilling Prophesy." *Antioch Review* 8(2): 193–210.

———. 1949. "Discrimination and the American Creed." In *Discrimination and National Welfare: A Series of Addresses and Discussions*, edited by R. M. MacIver. New York: Harper and Brothers.

Min, Pyong Gap. 1996. *Caught in the Middle: Korean Communities in New York and Los Angeles*. Berkeley, Calif.: University of California Press.

Morton, Fiona Scott, Florian Zettelmeyer, and Jorge Silva-Risso. 2003. "Consumer Information and Price Discrimination: Does the Internet Affect the Pricing of New Cars to

Women and Minorities?" NBER Working Paper 8668. Cambridge, Mass.: National Bureau of Economic Research.

Moskos, Charles, and John Sibley Butler. 1996. *All That We Can Be: Black Leadership and Racial Integration the Army Way*. New York: Basic Books.

Moulton, Brent. 1990. "A Reexamination of the Federal-Private Wage Differential in the United States." *Journal of Labor Economics* 8(2): 270–93.

Mouw, Ted. 2002. "Are Black Workers Missing the Connection? The Effect of Spatial Distance and Employee Referrals on Interfirm Racial Segregation." *Demography* 39(3): 507–28.

Mullahy, John, and Barbara L. Wolfe. 2001. "Health Policies for the Non-Elderly Poor." In *Understanding Poverty*, edited by Sheldon Danziger and Robert Haveman. New York: Russell Sage Foundation and Harvard University Press.

Munnell, A. H., G.M.B. Tootell, L. E. Browne, and J. McEneaney. 1996. "Mortgage Lending in Boston: Interpreting HMDA Data." *American Economic Review* 86(1): 25–53.

Myers, Samuel. 1989. "How Voluntary is Black Unemployment and Black Labor Force Withdrawal?" In *The Question of Discrimination: Racial Inequality in the U.S. Labor Market*, edited by Steven Shulman and William Darity, Jr. Middletown, Conn.: Wesleyan University Press.

Oettinger, Gerald S. 1996. "Statistical Discrimination and the Early Career Evolution of the Black-White Wage Gap." *Journal of Labor Economics* 14(1): 52–78.

Orfield, Gary, and Chungmei Lee. 2005. "Why Segregation Matters: Poverty and Educational Inequality." Civil Rights Project Working Paper. Cambridge, Mass.: Harvard University.

Pager, Devah. 2003. "The Mark of a Criminal Record." *American Journal of Sociology* 108(5): 937–75.

———. 2007. "The Use of Field Experiments for Studies of Employment Discrimination: Contributions, Critiques, and Directions for the Future." *Annals of the American Academy of Political and Social Science* 609: 104–33.

Pager, Devah, and Lincoln Quillian. 2005. "Walking the Talk: What Employers Say Versus What They Do." *American Sociological Review* 70(3): 355–80.

Pager, Devah, and Bruce Western. 2005. "Discrimination in Low Trust Labor Markets." Paper presented at the Annual Meetings of the American Sociological Association. Philadelphia, Pa., August 9, 2005.

Pettigrew, T. F. 1975. *Racial Discrimination in the United States*. New York: Harper and Row.

Phelps, Edmund. 1972. "The Statistical Theory of Racism and Sexism." *American Economic Review* 62(4): 659–61.

Portes, Alejandro, and Patricia Landolt. 1996. "Unsolved Mysteries: The Downside of Social Capital." *American Prospect* 7(26): 28–31.

Reskin, Barbara. 1998. *The Realities of Affirmative Action in Employment*. Washington, D.C.: American Sociological Association.

Ridley, Stanley, James A. Bayton, and Janice Hamilton Outtz. 1989. "Taxi Service in the District of Columbia: Is It Influenced by Patrons' Race and Destination?" Mimeograph. Washington, D.C.: The Washington Lawyers' Committee for Civil Rights Under the Law.

Ross, Stephen, and John Yinger. 2002. *The Color of Credit: Mortgage Discrimination, Research Methodology, and Fair-Lending Enforcement*. Cambridge, Mass.: MIT Press.

Rothschild, Micahel, and Joseph E. Stiglitz. 1982. "A Model of Employment Outcomes Illustrating the Effect of the Structure of Information on the Level and Distribution of Income." *Economic Letters* 10(3/4): 231–36.

Royster, Diedre. 2003. *Race and the Invisible Hand: How White Networks Exclude Black Men from Blue Collar Jobs.* Berkeley, Calif.: University of California Press.

Ryan, Carey S. 1995. "Motivations and the Perceiver's Group Membership: Consequences for Stereotype Accuracy." In *Stereotype Accuracy: Toward Appreciating Group Differences,* edited by Yueh-Ting Lee, Lee J. Jussim, and Clark R. McCauley. Washington, D.C.: American Psychological Association.

Schelling, Thomas C. 1971. "Dynamic Models of Segregation." *Journal of Mathematical Sociology* 1(2): 143–86.

Schiller, Bradley. 2004. *The Economics of Poverty and Discrimination,* 9th ed. Upper Saddle River, N.J.: Pearson Education.

Schulman, Devin, Jesse Berlin, William Harless, Joh Kerner, Shyrl Sistrunk, Bernard Gersh, Ross Dube, Christopher Taleghani, Jennifer Berke, Sankey Williams, John Eisenberg, and Jose Escarce. 1999. "The Effect of Race and Sex on Physicians' Recommendations for Cardiac Catheterization." *New England Journal of Medicine* 340(8): 618–26.

Schuman, Howard, Charlotte Steeh, Lawrence Bobo, and Maria Krysan. 2001. *Racial Attitudes in America: Trends and Interpretations,* rev. ed. Cambridge, Mass.: Harvard University Press.

Smith, James P., and Finis R. Welch. 1989. "Black Economic Progress After Myrdal." *Journal of Economic Literature* 27(2): 519–64.

Smith, Tom W. 1991. "Ethnic Images." General Social Survey Technical Report 19. Chicago, Ill.: University of Chicago, National Opinion Research Center.

———. 2001. *Intergroup Relations in a Diverse America: Data from the 2000 General Social Survey.* New York: American Jewish Committee.

Sniderman, Paul, Thomas Piazza, Philip Tetlock, and Ann Kendrick. 1991. "The New Racism." *American Journal of Political Science* 35(2): 423–47.

Songer, Michael. 2005. "Going Back to Class? The Reemergence of Class in Critical Race Theory Symposium: Note: Decline of Title VII Disparate Impact: The Role of the 1991 Civil Rights Act and the Ideologies of Federal Judges." *Michigan Journal of Race and Law* 11(Fall): 247.

Squires, Gregory. 1999. "The Indelible Color Line: 9 *The American Prospect* 42(January/February): 67–70.

Sunstein, Cass R. 1991. "Why Don't Markets Stop Discrimination." *Social Philosophy and Policy* 8(2): 22–37.

Taylor, Donald M., Stephen C. Wright, Fathali M. Moghaddam, and Richard N. Lalonde. 1990. "The Personal/Group Discrimination Discrepancy: Perceiving My Group, But Not Myself, to be a Target of Discrimination." *Personality and Social Psychology Bulletin* 16(2): 254–62.

Tomaskovic-Devey, Donald, and Sheryl Skaggs. 1999. "Sex Segregation, Labor Process Organization, and Gender Earnings Inequality." *American Journal of Sociology* 108(1): 102–28.

Trope, Yaacov, and Erik P. Thomson. 1997. "Looking for Truth in All the Wrong Places? Asymmetric Search of Individuating Information about Stereotyped Group Members." *Journal of Personality and Social Psychology* 73(2): 229–41.

Turner, Margery Austin, and Stephen L. Ross. 2003a. Discrimination in Metropolitan Housing Markets: National Results from Phase 2—Asians and Pacific Islanders. Washington: Department of Housing and Urban Development. Accessed at http://www.huduser .org/publications/pdf/phase2_final.pdf.

———. 2003b. Discrimination in Metropolitan Housing Markets: National Results from Phase 3—Native Americans. Washington: Department of Housing and Urban Development. Accessed at http://www.huduser.org/publications/hsgfin/hds_phase3.html.

Turner, Margery Austin, Stephen L. Ross, George Gaister, and John Yinger. 2002. "Discrimination in Metropolitan Housing Markets: National Results from Phase 1 of HDS 2000." Washington, D.C.: Urban Institute and Metropolitan Housing and Communities Policy Center. Accessed at http://www.huduser.org/intercept.asp?loc=/Publications/pdf/ Phase1_Report.pdf.

———. 2003. "Discrimination in Metropolitan Housing Markets: National Results from Phase 2 – Asians and Pacific Islanders." Washington, D.C.: Urban Institute and Metropolitan Housing and Communities Policy Center. Accessed at http://wwww .huduser.org/publications/pdf/phase2_final.pdf.

Turner, Margery Austin, and Felicity Skidmore, editors. 1999. *Mortgage Lending Discrimination: A Review of Existing Evidence*. Washington, D.C.: Urban Institute Press.

Waldinger, Roger, and Michael Lichter. 2003. *How the Other Half Works: Immigration and the Social Organization of Labor*. Berkeley, Calif.: The University of California Press.

Weitzer, Ronald. 1997. "Racial Prejudice Among Korean Merchants in African American Neighborhoods." *The Sociological Quarterly* 38(4): 587–606.

Western, Bruce, and Becky Pettit. 2005. "Black-White Wage Inequality, Employment Rates, and Incarceration." *American Journal of Sociology* 111(2): 553–78.

Whatley, Warren, and Gavin Wright. 1994. "Race, Human Capital, and Labour Markets in American History." In *Labour Market Evolution*, edited by George Grantham and Mary MacKinnon. London and New York: Routledge.

Williams, Donald R. 2004. "Racism and Health." In *Closing the Gap: Improving the Health of Minority Elders in the New Millennium*, edited by Keith Whitfield. Washington, D.C.: Gerontological Society of America.

Wilson, William Julius. 1987. *The Truly Disadvantaged: The Inner City, the Underclass, and Public Policy*. Chicago, Ill.: University of Chicago Press.

Wissoker, Douglas A., Wendy Zimmerman, and George Galster. 1997. *Testing for Discrimination in Home Insurance*. Washington, D.C.: Urban Institute.

Yinger, John. 1995. *Closed Doors, Opportunities Lost*. New York: Russell Sage Foundation.

———. 2001. Housing Discrimination and Residential Segregation as Causes of Poverty." In *Understanding Poverty*, edited by Sheldon H. Danziger and Robert H. Haveman. Cambridge, Mass.: Harvard University Press.

Yoon, In-Jin. 1995. "Attitudes, Social Distance, and Perceptions of Influence and Discrimination Among Minorities." *Journal of Group Tension* 25(1): 35–56.

———. 1997. *On My Own: Korean Businesses and Race Relations in America*. Chicago, Ill.: University of Chicago Press.

Chapter 3

Justifying Inequality: A Social Psychological Analysis of Beliefs About Poverty and the Poor

Heather E. Bullock

A news story reports that 12.6 percent of the United States population was poor in 2004. No demographic information is provided. Who do you think the poor are?

You watch a television program about low-income mothers trying to make ends meet. One of the mothers featured says that employers don't want to hire her because of her Spanish accent. Who is responsible for her situation?

While visiting the city, you give a homeless man a dollar. Your friend tells you that handouts only encourage laziness. Do you regret giving him money?

When you were growing up you believed that with hard work anyone could move up the socioeconomic ladder. At your child's high school graduation, though, you notice that a lot of the graduates who aren't going on to college are black and from poorer families. Is there a level playing field for everyone?

Each of these scenarios raises everyday questions about inequality. Our answers, and the beliefs that inform them, play an important role in justifying or challenging economic disparity. This chapter examines the ideological foundations of inequality in the United States, particularly how beliefs about individualism, meritocracy, and opportunity influence understandings of poverty. It also explores how *classism* (attitudes and stereotypes that derogate poor and working class people), *sexism* (attitudes and stereotypes that devalue women), and *racism* (attitudes and stereotypes that devalue people of color) constrain upward mobility and have a cumulative impact on disadvantage.

THE IDEOLOGICAL ROOTS OF INEQUALITY

In the United States, ideological support for economic inequality rests on two deeply cherished beliefs: individualism and the possibility of upward mobility. Individualism refers to a cluster of beliefs emphasizing independence, the pursuit of self-fulfillment, and individual responsibility for achievement. The prominence of individualism over collectivism in the national identity and political thought of the United States and other Western nations is amply documented by cross-cultural research (Oyserman, Coon, and Kemmelmeier 2002). As Juri Allik and Anu Realo (2004) observed, "it was in the United States where individualism obtained the status of a system that secures, guards, and encourages free competition and capitalism and any attempt to subordinate individuals to the primacy of society as a whole is perceived as an inevitable route to totalitarianism" (30–31). Individualism is evident in many aspects of public life in the United States, including popular culture (advertisements proclaiming "just do it") and cultural narratives (the character Rocky and his triumph over adversity).

Individualism is also evident in the tendency to view poverty and wealth as reflecting merit and personal effort. Dominant attributions for wealth and poverty illustrate how social class, unlike race and gender, is regarded as an achieved or earned status rather than an ascribed characteristic (Weber 1998). In one of the first large U.S. studies of attributions for poverty, Joseph Feagin (1975) found that the role of characterological flaws in causing poverty (laziness, substance abuse, lack of thrift) were supported more strongly than structural causes (discrimination, inferior schools, low wages) or fatalistic attributions (bad luck, unfortunate circumstances). This finding is indicative of a national inclination toward viewing poverty as a sign of personal and moral failure (Katz 1989; Cozzarelli, Wilkinson, and Tagler 2001; Shirazi and Biel 2005). As the poor deserve their economic status, so do the rich: individualistic explanations for wealth—drive, ability-talent, willingness to take risks, hard work—enjoy greater support than structural attributions—economic bias, political influence, inheritance (Hunt 2004; Kluegel and Smith 1986; Smith 1985; Smith and Stone 1989).

The high value placed on personal accomplishment is tied to the belief that individuals can shape their destiny and that with hard work and perseverance upward mobility is possible. Indeed, the belief that anyone can advance, regardless of their family of origin, economic status, or ethnicity, is so central to our national identity that it is the heart of the so-called American dream, "the promise that all Americans have a reasonable chance to achieve success as they define it—material or otherwise—through their own efforts, and to attain virtue and fulfillment through success" (Hochschild 1995, xi). From this vantage point, economic disparity is acceptable as long as mobility is possible. Alexis de Tocqueville aptly described this fundamental tenet when he asserted that "what is most important for *Démocratie*, is not that there are no great fortunes, but that great fortunes do not remain in the same hands" (cited in Schleifer 1980, 268).

Rising inequality has not detracted from the belief that upward mobility is possible. Although such mobility has not increased over the past thirty years, and economic disparity has reached historic levels (David C. Johnston, "Richest are Leaving Even the Rich Far Behind." *The New York Times*, June 5, 2005, 1.1.), findings from national opinion polls underscore the extent to which inequality is accepted and normalized. More Americans today than twenty years ago believe it possible to move from poverty to affluence through hard work (Janny Scott and David Leonhardt, "Shadowy Lines that Still Divide," *The New Times*, May 15, 2005, 1.1). Some public opinion data suggests that tolerance for inequality has grown as disparity itself has risen: between 1974 and 1984, the number of Americans believing that money and wealth in this country should be more evenly distributed dropped by 20 percent, and has held steady at 63 percent (McCall 2003). Even among adolescents, belief in the possibility of financial success is firmly entrenched. A Charles Schwab (2007) poll of 1,000 teenagers found that nearly 73 percent of respondents believed they would earn "plenty of money" and 53 percent expected to surpass their parents financially. Boys expected to earn $174,000 annually and girls $114,200, far exceeding national median incomes for full-time male and female workers.

The broader context of these beliefs is demographic inequality that reinforces race, gender, and class-based stereotypes. The hardship of poverty falls disproportionately on ethnic minorities and female-headed households. In 2005, 24.9 percent of blacks and 21.8 percent of Hispanics lived below official poverty thresholds compared to 11.1 percent of Asians and 8.3 percent of for non-Hispanic whites (U.S. Census Bureau 2006). Households headed by single mothers are also especially vulnerable, with the highest rates of poverty found among black (45.3 percent) and Hispanic (44 percent) female-headed households. These concentrations of disadvantage are transformed into causes: into characterizations of poverty as a minority problem (Gilens 1999; Quadagno 1994) or a reflection of weak sexual mores and the decline of the nuclear family (Lind 2004; Orloff 2002). Characterizations including laziness, sexual promiscuity, irresponsible parenting, disinterest in education, and disregard for the law intersect in stereotypes about the poor, people of color, and women. This fusion is especially pronounced for certain subgroups of the poor, such as welfare recipients and the urban poor (Gans 1995; Henry, Reyna, and Weiner 2004). Shorthand terms such as *underclass*, *Cadillac queen*, and *trailer trash* call to mind specific ethnic groups, further illustrating the association of class, race, and gender in popular discourse and public consciousness.

Such biases are likely to develop early in life. Children make judgments about class at an early age, and as they grow older their conceptualizations become more consistent with dominant stereotypes (Chafel 1997). In research with youth ranging in age from six to seventeen, Robert Leahy (2003) found that as children grew older, their descriptions of the rich and poor shift from emphasizing physical characteristics (appearance, possessions) to personal characteristics (abilities, traits). Similarly, the perceived legitimacy of inequality and individualistic attributions for poverty and wealth become more common with age. By age eleven, the belief that the poor could not work harder had increased substantially, and thereafter inequality was less likely to be seen as a problem that could be solved by having the rich give to the poor (Leahy 2003).

In adolescence, class-based stereotyping is common, particularly among white middle class teens. After showing photographs of poor, neutral, or wealthy strangers to a predominantly white sample of middle class adolescents, Dianne Skafte (1989) asked them to rate the target on a series of characteristics. Although poor strangers were rated as working harder and as more generous, they were also judged to steal more often, feel worse about themselves, and make friends less easily than neutral or wealthy strangers. Wealthy strangers were perceived as being more intelligent, more likely to be successful, and happier than poor or neutral strangers. Although poor strangers of both sexes were evaluated less favorably than their wealthy counterparts, poor girls received the lowest ratings, suggesting that some subgroups of the poor are judged more harshly than others.

The media plays a key role in the transmission of stereotypes about the poor. News stories exaggerate the relationship between minority status and poverty by overrepresenting African Americans in features about poverty (Gilens 1999). In Rosalee Clawson and Rakuya Trice's (2000) content analysis of photographs published in five major news magazines between 1993 and 1998, African Americans were pictured in 49 percent of stories about poverty but made up only 27 percent of the poor. Conversely, whites were significantly underrepresented, appearing in only 33 percent of stories but making up 45 percent of those in poverty. Hispanics were underrepresented by 5 percent and Asian Americans were invisible. The absence of images depicting Asian Americans in poverty may reflect their stereotypical association with industriousness and intelligence, just as stereotypes about the weak work ethic of African Americans may contribute to their overrepresentation (Clawson and Trice 2000). These findings speak to the importance of examining the prevalence and content of media representations of diverse low-income groups, and looking carefully at potential real world consequences. For instance, visual representations may intersect with and reinforce racial biases. After viewing a videotaped vignette, Franklin Gilliam (1999) found that white respondents were less likely to recall seeing a white than a black welfare recipient.

Theories of the ideological underpinnings of stratification and symbolic racism ground these findings (Bobo and Kluegel 1993; Bobo and Hutchings 1996; Kinder and Winter 2001; Schuman and Krysan 1999). Ideology-based theories draw their evidence from the relationship of anti-welfare attitudes to individualistic attributions, belief that equality of opportunity is preferable to equality of outcomes, and the notion that inequality is an inevitable consequence of meritocratic democracies. Theories of symbolic or modern racism explain white opposition to welfare policies as "racial hostility that is vented indirectly, for example, agreeing with statements such as 'the government pays too much attention to blacks,' or 'blacks who receive welfare could get along without it if they tried'" (Bobo and Kluegel 1993, 446).

Researchers have tried to tease apart the relative predictive power of beliefs about poverty and opportunity and symbolic racism by pitting them against each other in regression analyses. However, if beliefs about gender (promiscuity), race (laziness), and poverty (lack of work ethic) collectively fuel antiwelfare sentiment, models assessing relative importance may be less useful than those examining the intersection of beliefs. Although feminist conceptions of intersectionality focus primarily on the navigation of multiple identities, the underlying message of this scholarship, that complex social constructs cannot be easily isolated, is applicable here as well (McCall 2005). As such, references to welfare recipients and welfare policy must be analyzed in terms of their potential to activate intersecting, not solo, biases. The following section delves deeper into these intersections, and their interaction with social location.

INTERSECTIONS OF IDEOLOGY WITH RACE, CLASS, AND GENDER

Stereotypes do not exist in isolation from other belief systems, nor are they universally endorsed across groups. Just as rates of poverty are distributed across race, class, and gender groupings, belief in dominant ideology also varies. Research examining support for dominant ideology indicates that people of color are more likely to see systemic inequities and express skepticism about equality of opportunity than whites (Hochschild 1995). This trend is reflected in demographic variability in beliefs about poverty and wealth. Joseph Feagin (1975) found that White Protestants and Catholics, people with middle-income earnings, and those with moderate levels of education have been found to favor individualistic explanations for poverty. African Americans, low-income earners, and those with less education were found to favor structural explanations (Feagin 1975). Greater support for structural causes of poverty has been found among women than among men, liberals than conservatives, and welfare recipients than those who have not received public assistance (Kluegel and Smith 1986; Cozzarelli, Wilkinson, and Tagler 2001; Hunt 1996; Bullock 1999). Even among children, low-income and African American children express greater concern for the poor and willingness to challenge the economic structure than their white middle class peers (Leahy 2003). Similarly, Judith Chafel and Carin Neitzel (2005) found that children with low socioeconomic status (SES) and black or biracial children were more likely to talk about the need for more humane treatment of the poor than financially secure white children.

Other researchers have conducted more fine-tuned, predictive analyses to examine how demographic variables influence the causal beliefs of diverse ethnic groups. For instance, Matthew Hunt (1996) found that income was a stronger negative predictor of individualistic explanations for poverty among African Americans than European Americans or Latinos, education was a stronger predictor of individualistic attributions among Latinos and whites than African Americans; and being a woman was a stronger predictor of structural attributions for whites than Latinos. Different life histories and experiences can also shape attributional patterns. Among first-generation Mexican American farmworkers, support for structural attributions may be rooted in the recognition of widespread poverty and discrimination, whereas individualistic beliefs may be a way of acknowledging the personal resolve needed to survive immigration (Bullock and Waugh 2005).

Beliefs about wealth have received less attention in the research literature than beliefs about poverty, a bias that may indicate the tendency to see poverty, not wealth, at the core of inequality. In one of the few intergroup comparisons of Latino, African American, and European American beliefs, all three groups preferred individualistic to structural attributions for wealth (Hunt 2004). This "remarkable consensus" (Hunt 2004, 841) did not extend to structural attributions for wealth which received greater support from African Americans and Latinos than whites. Among all three groups, structural attributions for poverty were favored over individualistic causes, but again African Americans and Latinos expressed stronger support for structural explanations than whites.

One set of explanations for these group differences focuses on attributional bias. The most notable is the actor-observer effect, where individuals attribute their own (negative) outcomes to situational factors but the (negative) outcomes of others to personal causes (Jones and Besbitt 1972). Overall, difference in support for individualistic and structural attributions among the poor (actors) and nonpoor (observers) reflect this discrepancy. This type of explanation, however, overlooks the contextual and power-based dimensions of these patterns. That those who hold more social power are more likely to attribute poverty to laziness than to discrimination has significant implications for the maintenance of inequality. As Emily Kane and Elise Kyyrö (2001) observed, "by masking the existence of inequalities, defining them as good, or construing them as inevitable, ideologies and the beliefs derived from them can legitimate and perpetuate unequal relationships between social groups" (710).

Critical race theory (CRT), critical race feminism (CRF) (Delgado and Stefancic 2001; Wing 2003), and theories of social control (Piven and Cloward 1993) offer theoretical frameworks for analyzing the relationship between power, ideology, and group-level differences in beliefs about how resources should be distributed. Both CRT and CRF treat race as a social construct that is (re)created to maintain and regulate white economic and political power. Theorists from this tradition call into question whether stereotypical characterizations are best understood as benign misperceptions or as hierarchy-enhancing beliefs (Augoustinos, Tuffin, and Every 2005; Limbert and Bullock 2005). Similarly, social control theories highlight how stigma inhibits identification with devalued groups. The stigma associated with welfare receipt may keep eligible poor and working class people from applying for benefits, particularly publicly visible forms of aid such as food stamps. It also makes low-paying jobs appear more desirable than public assistance, a function that benefits businesses and corporations, not service and other low-wage workers (Piven and Cloward 1993).

Viewed through these theoretical lenses, attributions for poverty are part of a larger, interrelated network of hierarchy enhancing or attenuating beliefs. Correlational research in social psychology supports this perspective. Individualistic attributions are correlated with belief in a just world (Cozzarelli, Wilkinson, and Tagler 2001), the Protestant work ethic (Wagstaff 1983), social dominance (Lemieux and Pratto 2003), political conservatism (Zucker and Weiner 1993), and stereotypes about welfare recipients (Bullock 1999). Conversely, structural explanations are correlated with political liberalism and the rejection of beliefs that situate responsibility on the individual.

The following section delves more deeply into these relationships and their differential impact on the poor and the nonpoor. In each case, I show how ideology contributes to disadvantage and cumulates differently across race, gender, and class.

HIERARCHY-LEGITIMIZING BELIEFS AND THE NONPOOR

Among groups that hold significant social and economic power, individualistic beliefs and stereotypes about race, class, and gender are likely to influence perceptions of the access and treatment the poor should receive in major institutions. Ideological biases may be used to justify policies and structures that further restrict prospects for mobility and deepen disadvantage, particularly for low-income minorities. The effects of dominant ideology and stereotyping on classroom bias and welfare policy are offered as two illustrations.

Dominant Ideology, Stereotyping, and the Construction of Educational Disadvantage

Stereotypes about race-ethnicity, class, and intelligence as well as discriminatory treatment from teachers, other relevant authorities, and peers can influence educational goals, school involvement, and, ultimately, the persistence of inequality (Hauser-Cram, Selcuk, and Stipek 2003; Lott 2001). According to what is known as the Pygmalion effect, teachers act on classist and racist expectations about student competence; in response, student performance confirms these lowered expectations, creating a self-fulfilling prophecy (Ferguson 2003; Rosenthal and Jacobson 1968; Rosenthal 2003). Stronger effects have been observed among African American students and low SES students (Smith, Jussim, and Eccles 1999).

Despite widespread popular belief in this phenomenon, numerous scientific critiques of self-fulfilling prophecies have been raised. The magnitude of expectancy effects tends to be small (Jussim and Harber 2005), calling into question the robustness of this phenomenon. Other researchers assert that the alleged power of self-fulfilling prophecies is grounded in the accuracy of teachers' perceptions, not their bias. Methodological debates about the costs and benefits associated with naturalistic versus experimental studies of teacher expectancy also plague the literature. In spite of these caveats, concern about teacher expectancies remains high.

Rather than trying to document the self-fulfilling or cyclical nature of stereotyping, other research suggests that even if teachers do not act on biased attitudes, deep-rooted prejudice may compromise fairness in the classroom (McCombs and Gay 1988). An experiment by La Vonne Neal and her colleagues (2003) vividly illustrates this point. One hundred and thirty-six teachers watched videotapes in which student ethnicity (African American versus European American) and walking style ("standard" erect posture versus a stylized "stroll" associated with African Americans) was manipulated. Male students of both races with an "African American stroll" were rated as lower in achievement, higher in aggression, and more likely to need special education than students of either ethnicity with a "standard" walk. These findings reflect dominant beliefs that associate "acting black" with intellectual inferiority and laziness, and are indicative of the biases low-income youth and students of color may confront. Interviews with poor minority students of color indicate that young people themselves regard teachers as having lower academic expectations for "bad kids" or kids "who start trouble" (Rosenbloom and Way 2004).

Despite being largely discredited by the scientific community, genetic arguments about the intellectual inferiority of minorities and the poor still make their way into public discourse (Herrnstein and Murray 1994; Rushton and Jensen 2005). In Herrnstein and Murray's controversial but widely read book, *The Bell Curve* (1994), arguments about the racial and class heritability of intelligence are used to justify eliminating Head Start programs. Attacks on affirmative action in education have a similar structure (Augoustinos, Tuffin, and Every 2005). Cultural deficit models also locate responsibility for the achievement gap within individuals, but the focus shifts from nature to nurture. Deficit models (culture of poverty, cultural underclass) contend that poor whites and ethnic minorities do not endorse values, such as respect for education, common in mainstream culture. The transmission of these values from parent to child is seen as perpetuating low educational and occupational achievement (for a comprehensive review of cultural models, see Lamont and Small, chapter 4, this volume). From this vantage point, the devaluation of education by poor people of color is the source of low achievement, a perspective grounded in individualism.

These stereotypes, independently and through their interactions with structural disparities in the public schools (overcrowding, high student to teacher ratios, and teacher turnover), deepen the disadvantage that low-income and minority students of color face (Hochschild 2003; Kozol 2005). The highest numbers of deficiencies are reported in schools that serve more than 50 percent minorities or 70 percent poor students (National Center for Education Statistics 2000a). It is unlikely that high rates of basic shortcomings (non-functioning toilets, broken windows) would be tolerated in more affluent schools. Such inequities convey the same message as racist and classist stereotypes: white, middle class students are more deserving of resources than poor and minority students.

Dominant Ideology, Stereotypes, and the Social Construction of Welfare Policy

The influence of dominant ideology and stereotypes on the nonpoor, particularly the white middle class, has been most closely examined in relation to attitudes toward welfare policy. The most recent large-scale illustration of antiwelfare mobilization occurred in the 1990s among voters who resonated with then presidential candidate Bill Clinton's pledge "to end welfare as we know it" (1995, 80). Before passage of the Personal Responsibility and Work Opportunity Reconciliation Act of 1996 (PRWORA), welfare was among the most unpopular social programs (Jacoby 1994; Weaver, Shapiro, and Jacobs 1995). A study by Susan Fiske and her colleagues (1999) examining the perceived warmth and competence of seventeen commonly stereotyped groups illustrates this unpopularity. Of the groups that were examined, including migrant workers, feminists, and blacks, only welfare recipients were both disliked and disrespected. This low regard is further illustrated by polling data showing greater support for assisting the poor than for welfare, leading Tom Smith to conclude "that which we call welfare by any other name would smell sweeter" (1987, 75).

What accounts for welfare's unpopularity? Part of the answer lies in the long tradition of categorizing the poor in terms of their deservingness (Katz 1989; Piven and Cloward 1993). Historically and today, these distinctions are grounded in dominant beliefs about individualism and personal responsibility for poverty (Weiner 1995). Widows, children, people with disabilities, and veterans are considered among the deserving poor, while single mothers, welfare recipients, people with substance abuse issues, able-bodied men, and high-school drop-outs constitute the so-called undeserving poor. Experimental studies document how policy preferences are affected by this differentiation. For example, Lauren Appelbaum (2001) found that participants were more likely to recommend no benefits when targets were from undeserving groups and when their poverty was attributed to personal causes. Survey research similarly finds that individualistic attributions for poverty are correlated with opposition to welfare spending and progressive welfare policies (Kluegel and Smith 1986).

Individualistic judgments about poverty are consistent with the stereotype that welfare recipients, unlike the poor, prefer welfare to work (Henry, Reyna, and Weiner 2004). This perception situates welfare recipients as violating dominant ideology that equates work with morality and individual initiative and poverty with personal shortcomings, a view that undoubtedly shapes policy attitudes. For instance, unlike proposals to expand welfare benefits, initiatives to increase the minimum wage enjoy strong support among the general population (Pew Research Center 2005), a difference that may be partially attributed to their perceived associations with work.

Among European Americans, the "outsider" or "other" status of welfare recipients is furthered by both racism and sexism (Neubeck and Cazenave 2001; Smith 1987). Indirect and direct effects of racism on white opposition to welfare underscore this point. For instance, one analysis found that the impact of antiblack attitudes on opposition to welfare was mediated by the stereotype that welfare recipients are personally responsible for their poverty (Henry, Reyna, and Weiner 2004). Other studies find direct effects. Various measures of racism, mostly focusing on European American attitudes toward African Americans, are positively correlated with antiwelfare attitudes (Kinder and Sanders 1996). In Martin Gilens's (1999) analysis of national survey data, stereotyping blacks as lazy and the poor as undeserving emerged as the strongest predictors of white opposition to welfare, followed by conservativism and individualism. Stereotypes about black welfare mothers were nearly twice as strong in predicting antiwelfare attitudes than stereotypes of white welfare mothers (Gilens 1999). These biases are manifested in the real world adoption of restrictive welfare policies, such as family cap regulations, in states with higher percentages of minority recipients (Soss et al. 2001).

Poverty and racism are not solely white versus black phenomena: research paradigms must be expanded to examine attitudes among and beliefs toward majorities and minorities at national, state, and local levels. In states such as California, ethnic attitudes toward Latinos may have a stronger influence on whites' policy preferences than attitudes toward other ethnic minority groups. Cybelle Fox's (2004) contextualized analysis of stereotyping, ethnic context, and antiwelfare attitudes underscores this point. In areas of the United States with fewer Latinos, whites stereotyped Latinos as having a poor work ethic, and opposed welfare spending on these grounds. In states with a higher percentage of Latinos, whites perceived Latinos more positively; however, these favorable attitudes did not translate into greater support for welfare programs. Instead, the more hardworking Latinos were perceived to be, the less whites wanted to spend on welfare. Similar findings did not emerge for African Americans, who were viewed as lazier than Latinos, regardless of ethnic context. To explain the counterintuitive relationship between perceived industriousness and opposition to welfare spending, Fox drew on comparative processes, speculating that Latinos may be the model minority against which African Americans are judged. She asserted, "since Latinos can make it without welfare, so the logic goes, so can blacks, and therefore spending on welfare should be decreased. Alternatively, whites may fear that Latinos will follow what they see as the path of blacks and become lazy if the welfare system is allowed to grow too large" (616).

These findings illustrate what could be characterized as stereotype spillover: how stereotypes about diverse racial-ethnic groups reinforce, negate, or interact with each other. As Fox's findings make clear, marginalized groups do not exist in isolation, nor do social judgments about them. Thus, it is not only how antiblack stereotypes affect the treatment of African Americans but also how these stereotypes influence the treatment of other ethnic groups. Examining these interactions will not only yield a more multifaceted understanding of intergroup relations, it will also yield a more sophisticated understanding of how stereotypes contribute to disadvantage across diverse groups, eventually shaping policy preferences across different racial-ethnic contexts.

In its most simple form, economic practicality would suggest that those who are less likely to draw on social programs organize against them (Bobo and Kluegel 1993; Kinder and Winter 2001). Indeed, across racial groups, support for welfare programs decreases as earnings increase. But the greater support found for welfare spending among middle-income voters of color, relative to their white counterparts, speaks to the necessity of more complex constructions of self-interest, particularly those that take group belonging into account. Legitimizing ideologies have different social and political implications across diverse groups: in some instances, group loyalty or identification, regardless of direct personal benefits, has proven a stronger explanatory variable than simple group membership (Luttmer 2001). This point is further illustrated by research examining the impact of dominant ideology on the poor.

HIERARCHY-LEGITIMIZING BELIEFS AND THE POOR

Although low-income groups have considerably less social power and authority over policy decisions and the distribution of resources, the endorsement of dominant ideology among the poor still has important consequences. Two areas, welfare stigma and stereotype threat, illustrate the potential social and economic repercussions of these beliefs among low-income groups.

Concentrating Disadvantage Through Welfare Stigma

Disidentification from stigmatized social groups, such as welfare recipients, may lead even those who would benefit from more generous assistance programs to oppose them. In William Epstein's (2004) review of national polling data, even the poorest respondents share the upper quintiles' preference for personal responsibility, limited welfare payments, restrictive reform initiatives, and hostility toward welfare recipients. In twenty-one years of polling between 1973 and 1998, only 23.2 percentage points separated the poorest and wealthiest quintiles on approval for the statement, "We're spending too much money on welfare." This difference, which is relatively small in light of the sizable resource gap between these groups, illustrates that simple self-interest alone is not a sufficient explanatory variable.

The humiliation and degradation associated with welfare receipt or welfare stigma may lead recipients to disidentify from others receiving aid (Seccombe 1999) and even facilitate disidentification from the poor among those who are not aid recipients. The psychological underpinnings of social distancing are illustrated in Michelle Fine and Lois Weis's (1998) analysis of poor and working class white men experiencing the consequences of deindustrialization. Explaining that he "never had to" apply for public assistance, Ron revealed a personal history of food stamp use while distinguishing himself from other recipients:

> You know, we look at welfare as being something less than admirable. . . . I think it
> [falling back on the government] is more common for black people. . . . I mean social

services, in general, I think, is certainly necessary, and Sheila [wife] and I have taken advantage of them. We've got food stamps several times. . . . But you know, as soon as I was able to get off it, I did. (Fine and Weis 1998, 26)

Other qualitative studies with low-income participants find similar distancing, typically by disparaging the work ethic or integrity of welfare recipients (Seccombe 1999). Grounded in individualism and racism, such interpretations of economic hardship are apt to weaken the formation of strong interracial alliances among the poor, to deepen community and neighborhood tensions, and to legitimize scapegoating of low-income people of color.

Strongly held convictions about personal responsibility and belief in upward mobility through hard work among low-income groups, most notably African Americans, may also temper structural critiques of inequality (Hochschild 1995; Fine and Weis 1998). Seemingly incongruent individualistic and structural beliefs often coexist (Hunt 1996, 2004). In Heather Bullock and Wendy Limbert's (2003) study of welfare recipients enrolled in an educational program for low-income individual and families, poverty and wealth were attributed to structural sources and income inequality was regarded as unjust, but American dream ideology was also supported, and respondents expressed confidence in their own prospects for upward mobility.

The perceived permeability of class boundaries and the belief that poverty is transitory may also contribute to social distancing and the blunting of structural critiques of inequality. Belief in personal mobility can be self-protective, allowing individuals to find hope in the midst of economic hardship and to negotiate institutional discrimination. The denial of personal discrimination (Crosby 1984), or the tendency for disadvantaged individuals to perceive less discrimination against themselves personally than against the groups to which they belong, helps explain why marginalized groups believe in personal advancement even when formidable barriers are present.

The concept of dual consciousness is also used to explain the simultaneous belief in personal agency and structural inequality, particularly among ethnic minorities (Hunt 1996, 2004). Although research finds stronger support for structural than individualistic attributions among people of color, support for individualistic causes is often relatively strong as well. This pattern may allow disadvantaged groups to maintain a sense of control over their economic situation while acknowledging the role of larger structural forces in the maintenance of inequality.

Collectively, these studies underscore the importance of studying perceptions in all their complexity and contradiction. Social judgments are rarely binary and should not be treated as such. Beliefs serve multiple functions: they can legitimate or disrupt class and race hierarchies, allow someone to retain a sense of personal control over hardship, or create distance between oneself and economically similar others. These responses cannot be stripped of the context in which they exist; they must be examined with an eye toward the interests served by the acceptance of widespread belief in upward mobility, individual responsibility for poverty, and the permeability of class boundaries. Doing so will provide a more sophisticated understanding of welfare stigma as well as the conditions that facilitate it.

CONCENTRATING DISADVANTAGE THROUGH STEREOTYPE THREAT

Some of the most compelling evidence regarding the impact of stereotypes on people of color and the poor comes from research on stereotype threat. As a phenomenon driven by racist, classist, and sexist stereotypes about intellectual inferiority and poor work ethic, stereotype threat is situation-specific. Claude Steele (1997) described stereotype threat as

> the social-psychological threat that arises when one is in a situation or doing something for which a negative stereotype about one's group applies. This predicament threatens one with being negatively stereotyped, with being judged or treated stereotypically, or with the prospect of conforming to the stereotype. . . . And for those who identify with the domain to which the stereotype is relevant, this predicament can be self-threatening. (614)

The possibility of confirming negative stereotypes may impair performance or lead to disidentification with the area in which the stereotype is relevant, such as school. In part, stereotype threat is believed to be such a powerful and problematic phenomenon because individual endorsement of negative beliefs is not necessary; simple awareness of their presence in society causes the effect.

Support for stereotype threat comes from experimental studies documenting diminished math scores for women and reduced standardized test scores for African Americans and students from low socioeconomic backgrounds (Spencer, Steele, and Quinn 1999; Croizet et al. 2001; Régner, Huguet, and Monteil 2002). In a series of related studies, Claude Steele and Joshua Aronson (1995) asked black and white college students to complete a test of difficult GRE items. When the test was described as ability-diagnostic, black participants did less well than white participants; however, when the test was described as nondiagnostic, blacks and whites performed equally well. In another experiment, the same pattern of results emerged when participants reported their race on a demographic questionnaire immediately before taking the test: identifying their race was sufficient to depress the performance of black students. Parallel findings have emerged for socioeconomic status: when low SES students were led to believe that the test could measure their intellectual ability, they answered fewer items correctly, but they performed just as well as high SES students when they thought the test was nondiagnostic (Croizet and Claire 1998).

These performance effects interact with and magnify long-standing educational inequities. Significant differences on standardized tests and classroom performance continue to divide across race-ethnicity and class lines (McLoyd 1998; Suzuki and Aronson 2005). High school completion rates also differ, with students who live in low-income families leaving high school at four times the rate of their peers in high-income families (National Center for Education Statistics 2006). Ethnicity is also associated with rates of secondary school completion. In

2006, 63.2 percent of all Hispanics between the ages of twenty-five and twenty-nine had completed secondary education, compared with 93.4 percent of whites and 86.3 percent of blacks (National Center for Education Statistics 2007a). For those who complete high school, significant barriers to higher education remain. Of all undergraduate students, only 26 percent are from low-income families (National Center for Education Statistics 2000b) and only 32 percent are racial-ethnic minorities (National Center for Education Statistics 2007b). For marginalized groups, the activation of stereotype threat may well contribute to the widening of these gaps.

Just as negative stereotypes clearly harm the performance of some groups, "positive" stereotypes may confer benefits. As so-called "model minorities," Asian Americans are stereotyped as "being untroubled and compliant, excelling in math and science and succeeding in spite of racial barriers and discrimination" (Asher 2002, 268). It can be argued that even when valued qualities are posited, stereotyping is not a positive phenomenon. Nevertheless, cultural assumptions touting the skills of ethnic groups such as Asian Americans and Indian Americans may confer a stereotype "boost". In a study documenting both stereotype boost and threat, Margaret Shih, Todd Pittinsky, and Naliny Ambady (1999) found that Asian American women performed better on a math test when their ethnic identity was made salient, but worse when their gender identity was activated, compared with a control group for whom neither identity was activated.

At best, however, stereotype boost is a highly conditional and relatively limited phenomenon. Unlike Shih and her colleagues (1999), Sapria Cheryan and Galen Bodenhausen (2000) found that focusing Asian American participants' attention on their ethnicity created difficulties with concentration, not improved test performance. Procedural differences used to make ethnicity salient in these two studies appear to underlie these disparate outcomes. In the Shih, Pittinsky, and Ambady analysis (1999), subtle, indirect prompts, such as asking about language use, were used to promote private reflection about one's ethnicity, whereas Cheryan and Bodenhausen (2000) encouraged participants to focus on public perceptions of their ethnic group. Discussing their findings, they explained:

> This focus presumably led them to contemplate the possibility of failing to exhibit the positive quantitative skills commonly expected of Asians. Just as fear of confirming a negative stereotype can undermine performance, so can fear of failing to confirm a positive stereotype. However, the latter effect appears to be limited to conditions in which public expectations of success are salient. (401)

Fear of not living up to widespread public assumptions about "model minorities" appears well founded. Colin Ho, Denise Driscoll, and Danielle Loosbrock (1998) found that a hypothetical Asian American student who performed poorly on math assignments was awarded fewer points by "unmotivated" graders (those who worked quickly or were not instructed on accuracy) than a European American target with identical scores.

These findings not only highlight the potential of stereotypes to enhance or deflate test performance, but also the importance of examining stereotype boost and threat in terms of multiple rather than single identities. Most empirical studies of stereotype threat and boost examine a single identity, such as race, gender, or class, but people possess multiple intersecting identities. Research examining stereotype boost inadvertently risks reifying monolithic constructions of so-called model minorities if diverse experiences of ethnicity, socioeconomic status, and immigration histories are ignored (Asher 2002).

Many questions remain about the pathways through which stereotypes inhibit or enhance performance. Beyond stereotype threat, subjective understandings of and responses to dominant ideology by marginalized groups need more study. A growing body of ethnographic and qualitative research examines the intersections of race, gender, and class is filling this gap in with literature (Bettie 2000; Fine et al. 2004; Jones 2003; Weis 2003). Socially embedded analytical strategies like these are advantageous because low-income informants-participants are active agents in the construction of identities and beliefs, not passive receptacles of dominant conceptions. As such, beliefs about poverty may emerge as a potential source of shame and humiliation, or a site of critical resistance.

This point is illustrated by two conceptually and methodologically different studies, both of which raise provocative questions about the meanings low-income youth attach to dominant beliefs about poverty. In the first study (Weinger 1998), low-income youth between five and twelve years of age were shown photographs of a rundown house and a suburban style ranch house. They were then asked a series of questions about what they imagined the children and adults who lived in each house were like. Low-income children were acutely aware of class, describing poverty in terms of crisis and hardship: meeting basic survival needs like food and confronting social rejection. Middle class status, by contrast, was described as relatively worry-free. The majority of low-income children spoke about family closeness, strong coping skills, and other positive characteristics when speaking about the poor, yet a small but potentially meaningful percentage of participants talked instead about stereotypical characteristics such as lacking intelligence. These findings highlight the stigmatizing aspects of poverty and, albeit inconclusively, suggest that negative beliefs may be internalized among a minority of the poor.

Constance Flanagan and her colleagues' (1997) study of students attending inner-city (poor), urban ring (blue collar), and suburban schools (affluent) offers an alternative perspective, illustrating the importance of critically examining the context and function of beliefs. They found that inner-city adolescents were more likely than their urban and suburban peers to make dispositional attributions for poverty and wealth. Urban ring and suburban youth were more likely to make structural attributions or to give explanations that included both structural and dispositional causes. Compared to their peers, inner-city youth also perceived the school system as more alienating and reported receiving stronger message from their families about the importance of self-reliance and academic success.

Flanagan and her colleagues conclude that systemic blame poses little threat to suburban adolescents because institutions tend to work for them, whereas adopting structural explanations could imply limited prospects for those living in economically depressed communities. Emphasis on self-reliance and dispositional explanations can be interpreted as belief that it is "incumbent on the individual to create his or her own success and that those who rely on the system may be disappointed" (Flanagan et al. 1997, 62). As with adults, the adoption of individual-centered explanations may serve an important self-protective function allowing poor adolescents to hold long-range career and education plans in the face of adversity. As these authors observe, "although minority youth from poor neighborhoods may be aware of the system's failures, it may be necessary for them to disregard those failures in order to remain committed to education and the American Dream" (1997, 61).

In sum, the research reviewed here points to the significant impact that dominant ideology and stereotypes have on the poor. It is important to keep in mind, however, that differences in social position or power cannot be rectified through attitudinal change alone. For this reason, researchers must remain focused on the interface of structural inequities and beliefs, attending to the social landscape as closely as they attend to cognitive interpretations of these structures.

REDUCING PREJUDICE AND STEREOTYPING: POSSIBILITIES AND CHALLENGES

Many attempts have been made to reduce racial prejudice and improve intergroup relations through cognitive restructuring (breaking down "us" versus "them" distinctions or fostering inclusive multiple social identities; see Dovidio, Glick, and Rudman 2005; Oskamp 2000) and enhancing empathy for disadvantaged groups (Batson et al. 1997). Theories of intergroup contact, however, have received the most attention by researchers. At the heart of this body of work is the notion that intergroup contact, if carefully constructed, can reduce negative affect and stereotypes. A number of optimal conditions for successful intergroup contact have been identified, including equal status between the groups, a common intergroup goal, and a context that promotes cooperation (Pettigrew 1998).

The very nature of these conditions belies the difficulty of creating successful intergroup contact situations outside of carefully controlled experiments. Unequal status, for instance, is the very core of race and class inequity: not easily manipulated or controlled in real world situations. For this reason, contact-based interventions are usually tested in readily controllable settings such as the classroom, with improved interpersonal relations as the desired outcome. Thus, the development of interracial friendships is more likely to be the goal of contact-based interventions, and it is a more probable outcome than deep-rooted structural or institutional change. Yet as chapters 2, 8, 10, and 11 of this volume document, persistent inequality is best redressed through structural change. Concern regarding the generalizability of positive attitudes across situations and from individuals to groups raises further questions about the promise of intergroup contact, as do critics' claims that ethnic hatred or animosity is not the root problem.

Despite these limitations, positive effects of contact on the reduction of prejudice are well documented by psychological and sociological research (Dovidio, Glick, and Rudman 2005; Pettigrew 1998). Intergroup contact is used as a strategy for attitudinal change in a wide range of everyday settings: desegregated classrooms, university service learning programs that provide opportunities for interracial and interclass interactions, and "walk a mile in my shoes" programs that partner welfare recipients with nonpoor community members. Such strategies include learning about the outgroup (Pettigrew 1998) or generating affective ties (McClelland and Linnander 2006). In a large meta-analysis of 515 studies investigating the effects of intergroup contact, Thomas Pettigrew and Linda Tropp (2006) found that greater intergroup contact was associated with lower levels of prejudice. Although the effect sizes of these effects are only small to medium, the large number of samples included in the study make these findings robust.

The positive outcomes associated with intergroup contact are compellingly illustrated through specific examples. For example, in Stephen Wright and Linda Tropp's (2005) study of intergroup contact in classrooms, white children in racially integrated, bilingual classrooms were found to hold more positive attitudes toward Latino children and to select Latino children as best friends. English-only classrooms, whether integrated or segregated, do not show this effect. Clearly, contact alone is not enough for reducing prejudice across all contexts. Tropp (2003) found that even a single experience of prejudice negatively influenced how members of devalued groups felt in intergroup settings and their expectations for future interactions. Perceiving oneself as a target of discrimination reinforced these negative outcomes, and having close relationships with outgroup members facilitated more positive attitudes toward cross-group interactions. These findings are a powerful reminder that contact must be studied from multiple vantage points; though the focus of prejudice reduction efforts necessarily remains on dominant groups, individual and social consequences of contact on marginalized groups should not be overlooked (Tropp and Pettigrew 2005).

Beyond contact-based approaches, targeted, context-specific interventions also show promise, particularly in terms of reducing the negative consequences of stereotyping on marginalized groups. For instance, in two randomized field experiments, Geoffrey Cohen and his colleagues (2006) tested whether completing brief in-class writing assignments reaffirming personal adequacy and self-integrity could lessen the effects of stereotype threat on the academic performance of African American students. This brief exercise was associated with a significant increase in black students' grades, resulting in a 40 percent reduction in the racial achievement gap among study participants. These impressive findings should not be interpreted as either a quick fix or a solution to persistent educational inequities, however. As the researchers note, their findings rest "on an obvious precondition: the existence in the school of adequate material, social, and psychological resources and support to permit and sustain positive academic outcomes" (Cohen et al. 2006, 1309). This interpretation again affirms that attitudes, beliefs, and cognitive interventions must always be considered in conjunction with broader social structures.

In the face of growing inequality, changing racial and ethnic demographics, and persistently high poverty rates, particularly among people of color, understanding legitimizing ideologies and intervening to reduce their negative impact on marginalized groups takes on heightened urgency. Clearly, much remains to be learned about the prevalence, dynamics, and consequences of legitimizing ideologies, and how dominant beliefs and stereotypes intersect with and magnify structural disadvantage across diverse groups. Equally crucial is investigation of the processes that contribute to critical resistance among both privileged and marginalized groups. As we study the beliefs that maintain inequality, we must also direct our energies toward understanding how individual, social, and situational variables contribute to the rejection of pejorative stereotypes and the development of counterhegemonic frameworks for understanding inequality. In doing so, we can gain crucial insight into the persistence and reduction of race, gender, and class disparities.

REFERENCES

Allik, Jüri, and Anu Realo. 2004. "Individualism-Collectivism and Social Capital." *Journal of Cross-Cultural Psychology* 35(1): 29–49.

Appelbaum, Lauren D. 2001. "The Influence of Perceived Deservingness on Policy Decisions Regarding Aid to the Poor." *Political Psychology* 22(3): 419–42.

Asher, Nina. 2002. "Class Acts: Indian American High School Students Negotiate Professional and Ethnic Identities." *Urban Education* 37(2): 267–95.

Augoustinos, Martha, Keith Tuffin, and Danielle Every. 2005. "New Racism, Meritocracy, and Individualism: Constraining Affirmative Action in Education." *Discourse and Society* 16(3): 315–40.

Batson, Daniel C., Marina P. Polycarpou, Eddie Harmon-Jones, Heidi J. Imhoff, Erin C. Mitchener, Lori L. Bednar, Tricia R. Klein, and Lori Highberger. 1997. "Empathy and Attitudes: Can Feeling for a Member of a Stigmatized Group Improve Feelings Toward the Group?" *Journal of Personality and Social Psychology* 72(1): 105–18.

Bettie, Julie. 2000. "Women Without Class: Chicas, Cholas, Trash and the Presence/Absence of Class Identity." *Signs: Journal of Women in Culture and Society* 26(1): 1–35.

Bobo, Lawrence, and Vincent L. Hutchings. 1996. "Perceptions of Racial Group Competition: Extending Blumer's Theory of Group Position to a Multiracial Social Context." *American Sociological Review* 61(6): 951–72.

Bobo, Lawrence, and James R. Kluegel. 1993. "Opposition to Race-Targeting: Self-Interest, Stratification Ideology, or Racial Attitudes?" *American Sociological Review* 58(4): 443–64.

Bullock, Heather E. 1999. "Attributions for Poverty: A Comparison of Middle-Class and Welfare Recipient Attitudes." *Journal of Applied Social Psychology* 29(10): 2059–82.

Bullock, Heather E., and Wendy M. Limbert. 2003. "Scaling the Socioeconomic Ladder: Women's Perceptions of Class Status and Opportunity." *Journal of Social Issues* 59(4): 693–709.

Bullock, Heather E., and Irma M. Waugh. 2005. "Beliefs about Poverty and Opportunity among Mexican Immigrant Farmworkers." *Journal of Applied Social Psychology* 35(6): 1132–49.

Chafel, Judith A. 1997. "Societal Images of Poverty: Child and Adult Beliefs." *Youth & Society* 28(4): 432–63.

Chafel, Judith A., and Carin Neitzel. 2005. "Young Children's Ideas About the Nature, Causes, Justification, and Alleviation of Poverty." *Early Childhood Research Quarterly* 20(4): 433–50.

Cheryan, Sapna, and Galen V. Bodenhausen. 2000. "When Positive Stereotypes Threaten Intellectual Performance: The Psychological Hazards of 'Model Minority' Status." *Psychological Science* 11(5): 399–402.

Clawson, Rosalee A., and Rakuya Trice. 2000. "Poverty as We Know It: Media Portrayals of the Poor." *Public Opinion Quarterly* 64(1): 53–64.

Clinton, William J. 1995. "Address Before a Joint Session of the Congress on the State of the Union: January 24, 1995." In *Public Papers of the Presidents of the United States*. Washington: U.S. Government Printing Office.

Cohen, Geoffrey, L., Julio Garcia, Nancy Apfel, and Allison Master. 2006. "Reducing the Racial Achievement Gap: A Social-Psychological Intervention." *Science* 313(5791): 1307–9.

Cozzarelli, Catherine, Anna V. Wilkinson, and Michael J. Tagler. 2001. "Attitudes Toward the Poor and Attributions for Poverty." *Journal of Social Issues* 57(2): 207–27.

Croizet, Jean-Claude, and Theresa Claire. 1998. "Extending the Concept of Stereotype Threat to Social Class: The Intellectual Underperformance of Students from Low Socioeconomic Backgrounds." *Personality and Social Psychology Bulletin* 24(6): 588–94.

Croizet, Jean-Claude, Michel Desert, Marion Dutrevis, and Jacques-Phillippe Leyens. 2001. "Stereotype Threat, Social Class, Gender, and Academic Under-Achievement: When Our Reputation Catches Up To Us and Takes Over." *Social Psychology of Education* 4(3–4): 295–310.

Crosby, Faye J. 1984. "The Denial of Personal Discrimination." *American Behavioral Scientist* 27(3): 371–86.

Delgado, Richard, and Jean Stefancic. 2001. *Critical Race Theory: An Introduction*. New York: New York University Press.

Dovidio, John F., Peter Glick, and Laurie A. Rudman, editors. 2005. *On the Nature of Prejudice: Fifty Years after Allport*. Malden, Mass.: Blackwell Publishing.

Epstein, William M. 2004. "Cleavage in American Attitudes toward Social Welfare." *Journal of Sociology and Social Welfare* 31(4): 177–202.

Feagin, Joseph R. 1975. *Subordinating the Poor: Welfare and American Beliefs*. Englewood Cliffs, N.J.: Prentice-Hall.

Ferguson, Ronald F. 2003. "Teachers' Perceptions and Expectations and the Black-White Test Score Gap." *Urban Education* 38(4): 460–507.

Fine, Michelle, April Burns, Yasser A. Payne, and Maria E. Torre. 2004. "Civics Lessons: The Color and Class of Betrayal." *Teachers College Record* 106(11): 2193–223.

Fine, Michelle, and Lois Weis. 1998. *The Unknown City: Lives of Poor and Working-Class Young Adults*. Boston, Mass.: Beacon Press.

Fiske, Susan T., Jun Xu, Amy C. Cuddy, and Peter Glick. 1999. "(Dis)respecting Versus

(Dis)liking: Status and Interdependence Predict Ambivalent Stereotypes of Competence and Warmth." *Journal of Social Issues* 55(3): 473–89.

Flanagan, Constance A., Patreese Ingram, Erika M. Gallay, and Erin E. Galley. 1997. "Why are People Poor? Social Conditions and Adolescents' Interpretations of the Social Contract." In *Social and Emotional Adjustment and Family Relations in Ethnic Minority Families*, edited by Ronald D. Taylor and Margaret C. Wang. Mahwah, N.J.: Lawrence Erlbaum Associates.

Fox, Cybelle. 2004. "The Changing Color of Welfare? How Whites' Attitudes Toward Latinos Influence Support for Welfare." *American Journal of Sociology* 110(3): 580–625.

Gans, Herbert. J. 1995. *The War Against the Poor: The Underclass and Antipoverty Policy*. New York: Basic Books.

Gilens, Martin. 1999. *Why Americans Hate Welfare: Race, Media, and the Politics of Antipoverty Policy*. Chicago, Ill.: University of Chicago Press.

Gilliam, Franklin D. 1999. "The 'Welfare Queen' Experiment: How Viewers React to Images of African-American Women on Welfare." *Nieman Reports* 53(2): 49–52.

Hauser-Cram, Penny, Sirin R. Selcuk, and Deborah Stipek. 2003. "When Teachers' and Parents' Values Differ: Teachers' Ratings of Academic Competence in Children from Low-Income Families." *Journal of Educational Psychology* 95(4): 813–20.

Henry, P. J., Christine Reyna, and Bernard Weiner. 2004. "Hate Welfare But Help the Poor: How the Attributional Content of Stereotypes Explains the Paradox of Reactions to the Destitute In America." *Journal of Applied Social Psychology* 34(1): 34-58.

Herrnstein, Richard J., and Charles Murray. 1994. *The Bell Curve: Intelligence and Class Structure in American Life*. New York: Free Press.

Ho, Colin P., Denise M. Driscoll, and Danielle Loosbrock. 1998. "Great Expectations: The Negative Consequences of Falling Short." *Journal of Applied Social Psychology* 28(19): 1743–59.

Hochschild, Jennifer L. 1995. *Facing Up to the American Dream: Race, Class and the Soul Of The Nation*. Princeton, N.J.: Princeton University Press.

———. 2003. "Social Class in the Public Schools." *Journal of Social Issues* 59(4): 821–40.

Hunt, Matthew O. 1996. "The Individual, Society, or Both? A Comparison of Black, Latino, and White Beliefs about the Causes of Poverty." *Social Forces* 75(1): 293–322.

———. 2004. "Race/Ethnicity and Beliefs About Wealth and Poverty." *Social Science Quarterly* 85(3): 827–53.

Jacoby, William G. 1994. "Public Attitudes toward Government Spending." *American Journal of Political Science* 38(2): 336–61.

Jones, Edward E., and Richard E. Nisbett. 1972. "The Actor and the Observer: Divergent Perceptions of the Causes of Behavior. In *Attribution: Perceiving the Causes of Behavior*, edited by Edward E. Jones, David.E. Kanouse, Harold H. Kelley, Richard E. Nisbett, Stuart Valins, and Bernard Weiner. Morristown, N.J.: General Learning Press.

Jones, Sandra J. 2003. "Complex Subjectivities: Class, Ethnicity, and Race in Women's Narratives of Upward Mobility." *Journal of Social Issues* 59(4): 803–20.

Jussim, Lee, and Kent D. Harber. 2005. "Teacher Expectations and Self-Fulfilling Prophecies: Knowns and Unknowns, Resolved and Unresolved Controversies." *Personality and Social Psychology Review* 9(2): 131–55.

Kane, Emily W., and Elise K. Kyyrö. 2001. "For Whom Does Education Enlighten? Race,

Gender, Education, and Beliefs about Social Inequality." *Gender & Society* 15(5): 710–33.

Katz, Michael B. 1989. *The Undeserving Poor: From the War on Poverty to the War on Welfare.* New York: Pantheon Books.

Kinder, Donald R., and Lynn M. Sanders. 1996. *Divided By Color: Racial Politics and Democratic Ideals.* Chicago, Ill.: University of Chicago Press.

Kinder, Donald R., and Nicholas Winter. 2001. "Exploring the Racial Divide: Blacks, Whites, and Opinions on National Policy." *American Journal of Political Science* 45(2): 439–56.

Kluegel, James R., and Eliot R. Smith.1986. *Beliefs About Inequality: Americans' Views of What Is and What Ought to Be.* Hawthorne, N.Y.: Aldine de Gruyter.

Kozol, Jonathon. 2005. *The Shame of the Nation: The Restoration of Apartheid Schooling in America.* New York: Crown Publishers.

Leahy, Robert L. 2003. *Psychology and the Economic Mind: Cognitive Processes and Conceptualization.* New York: Springer Publishing.

Lemieux, Anthony F., and Felicia Pratto. 2003. "Poverty and Prejudice." In *Poverty and Psychology: From Global Perspective to Local,* edited by Stuart. C. Carr and Tod S. Sloan. New York: Kluwer Academic/Plenum.

Limbert, Wendy M., and Heather E. Bullock. 2005. "'Playing the Fool:' U.S. Welfare Policy from a Critical Race Perspective." *Feminism and Psychology* 15(3): 253–74.

Lind, Amy. 2004. "Legislating the Family: Heterosexist Bias in Social Welfare Policy Frameworks." *Journal of Sociology and Social Welfare* 31(4): 21–35.

Lott, Bernice. 2001. "Low-Income Parents and the Public Schools." *Journal of Social Issues* 57(2): 247–59.

Luttmer, Erzo F. P. 2001. "Group Loyalty and the Taste for Redistribution." *Journal of Political Economy* 109(3): 500–528.

McCall, Leslie. 2003. "Do They Know and Do They Care? American's Awareness of Rising Inequality." Unpublished paper. Accessed at http://www.rci.rutgers.edu/~/lmccall.

———. 2005. "The Complexity of Intersectionality." *Signs: Journal of Women in Culture and Society* 30(3): 1771–800.

McClelland, Katherine, and Erika Linnander. 2006. "The Role of Contact and Information in Racial Attitude Change Among White College Students." *Sociological Inquiry* 76(1): 81–115.

McCombs, Regina C., and Judith Gay. 1988. "Effects Of Race, Class, And IQ Information on Judgments of Parochial Grade School Teachers." *Journal of Social Psychology* 128(5): 647–52.

McLoyd, Vonnie, C. 1998. "Socioeconomic Disadvantage and Child Development." *American Psychologist* 53(2): 185–204.

National Center for Education Statistics. 2000a. *Condition of America's Public School Facilities: 1999.* NCES 2000-032. Washington, D.C.: NCES (June).

———. 2000b. *Low-Income Students: Who Are They and How Do They Pay for Their Education?* NCES 2000-169. Washington, D.C.: NCES (March).

———. 2006. *Dropout Rates in the United States: 2004.* NCES 2007-024. Washington, D.C.: National Center for Education Statistics (November).

———. 2007a. *The Condition of Education 2007*. NCES 2007-064. Washington, D.C.: National Center for Education Statistics (June).

———. 2007b. *Status and Trends in the Education of Racial and Ethnic Minorities*. NCES 2007-039. National Center for Education Statistics (September).

Neal, La Vonne, I., Audrey D. McCray, Gwendolyn Webb-Johnson, and Scott T. Bridgest. 2003. "The Effects of African American Movement Styles on Teachers' Perceptions and Reactions." *Journal of Special Education* 37(1): 49–57.

Neubeck, Kenneth J., and Noel A. Cazenave. 2001. *Welfare Racism: Playing the Race Card Against America's Poor*. New York: Routledge.

Orloff, Ann, S. 2002. "Explaining US Welfare Reform: Power, Gender, Race, and the US Policy Legacy." *Critical Social Policy* 22(1): 96–118.

Oskamp, Stuart, editor. 2000. *Reducing Prejudice and Discrimination*. Mahwah, N.J.: Lawrence Erlbaum.

Oyserman, Daphna, Heather M. Coon, and Markus Kemmelmeier. 2002. "Rethinking Individualism and Collectivism: Evaluation of Theoretical Assumptions and Meta-Analyses." *Psychological Bulletin* 128(1): 3–72

Pettigrew, Thomas F. 1998. "Intergroup Contact Theory." *Annual Review of Psychology* 49: 65–85.

Pettigrew, Thomas F., and Linda Tropp. 2006. "A Meta-Analytic Test of Intergroup Contact Theory." *Journal of Personality and Social Psychology* 90(5): 751–83.

Pew Research Center. 2005. *The 2005 Political Typology*. Washington, D.C.: Pew Research Center.

Piven, Frances F., and Richard A. Cloward. 1993. *Regulating the Poor: The Functions of Public Welfare*, 2nd ed. New York: Vintage Books.

Quadagno, Jill. 1994. *The Color of Welfare: How Racism Undermined the War on Poverty*. New York: Oxford University Press.

Régner, Isabelle, Pascal Huguet, and Jean-Marc Monteil. 2002. "Effects of Socioeconomic Status (SES) Information on Cognitive Ability Inferences: When Low-SES Students Make Use of a Self-Threatening Stereotype." *Social Psychology of Education* 5(3): 253–69.

Rosenbloom, Susan R., and Niobe Way. 2004. "Experiences of Discrimination among African American, Asian American, and Latino Adolescents in an Urban High School." *Youth & Society* 35(4): 420–51.

Rosenthal, Robert J. 2003. "Covert Communication in Laboratories, Classrooms, and the Truly Real World." *Current Directions in Psychological Science* 12(5): 151–54.

Rosenthal, Robert J., and Lenore Jacobson. 1968. *Pygmalion in the Classroom: Teacher Expectations and Pupils' Intellectual Development*. New York: Holt, Rinehart & Winston.

Rushton, J. Phillipe, and Arthur R. Jensen. 2005. "Wanted: More Race Realism, Less Moralistic Fallacy." *Psychology, Public Policy, and Law* 11(2): 328–36.

Schleifer, James T. 1980. *The Making of Tocqueville's Democracy in America*. Chapel Hill, N.C.: University of North Carolina Press.

Schuman, Howard, and Maria Krysan. 1999. "A Historical Note on Whites' Beliefs about Racial Inequality." *American Sociological Review* 64(6): 847–55.

Schwab, Charles. 2007. "Teens & Money Survey Findings: Insights into Money Attitudes, Behaviors and Concerns of Teens." No. 0307-5638. San Francisco, Calif.: Charles Schwab and Boys and Girls Clubs of America. Accessed at http://www.aboutschwab.com/teen-survey2007.pdf.

Seccombe, Karen. 1999. "So You Think I Drive A Cadillac?" *Welfare Recipients' Perspectives on the System and its Reform*. New York: Allyn & Bacon.

Shih, Margaret, Todd L. Pittinsky, and Nalini Ambady. 1999. "Stereotype Susceptibility: Identity Salience and Shifts in Quantitative Performance." *Psychological Science* 10(1): 80–83.

Shirazi, Rez, and Anders Biel. 2005. "Internal-External Causal Attributions and Perceived Government Responsibility for Need Provision: A 14-Culture Study." *Journal of Cross-Cultural Psychology* 36(1): 96–116.

Skafte, Dianne. 1989. "The Effect of Perceived Wealth and Poverty on Adolescents' Character Judgments." *The Journal of Social Psychology* 129(1): 93–99.

Smith, Alison E., Lee Jussim, and Jacquelynne Eccles. 1999. "Do Self-Fulfilling Prophecies Accumulate, Dissipate, or Remain Stable Over Time?" *Journal of Personality and Social Psychology* 77(3): 548–65.

Smith, Kevin B. 1985. "I Made it Because of Me: Beliefs about the Causes of Wealth and Poverty. *Sociological Spectrum* 5(3): 255–67.

Smith, Kevin B., and Lorene H. Stone. 1989. "Rags, Riches, and Bootstraps: Beliefs About the Causes of Wealth and Poverty." *The Sociological Quarterly* 30(1): 93–107.

Smith, Tom W. 1987. "That Which We Call Welfare By Any Other Name Would Smell Sweeter: An Analysis of The Impact of Question Wording on Pattern Response." *Public Opinion Quarterly* 51(1): 75–83.

Soss, Joe, Sanford F. Schram, Thomas P. Vartanian, and Erin O'Brien. 2001. "The Hard Line and the Color Line: Race, Welfare, and Get-Tough Reform." In *Race and the Politics of Welfare Reform*, edited by Sanford F. Schram, Joe Soss, and Richard C. Fording. Ann Arbor, Mich.: University of Michigan Press.

Spencer, Steven J., Claude M. Steele, and Diane M. Quinn. 1999. "Stereotype Threat and Women's Math Performance." *Journal of Experimental Social Psychology* 35(1): 4–28.

Steele, Claude M. 1997. "A threat is in the air: How Stereotypes Shape Intellectual Identity and Performance." *American Psychologist* 52(6): 613–29.

Steele, Claude M, and Joshua Aronson. 1995. "Stereotype Threat and the Intellectual Test Performance of African Americans." *Journal of Personality and Social Psychology* 69(5): 797–811.

Suzuki, Lisa, and Joshua Aronson. 2005. "The Cultural Malleability of Intelligence and its Impact on the Racial/Ethnic Hierarchy." *Psychology, Public Policy, and Law* 11(2): 320–27.

Tropp, Linda R. 2003. "The Psychological Impact of Prejudice: Implications for Intergroup Contact." *Group Processes & Intergroup Relations* 6(2): 131–49.

Tropp, Linda R., and Thomas F. Pettigrew. 2005. "Relationships between Intergroup Contact and Prejudice Among Minority and Majority Status Groups." *Psychological Science* 16(12): 951–57.

U.S. Census Bureau. 2006. *Income, Poverty, and Health Insurance Coverage in the United States: 2005*. Publication P60-231. Washington: U.S. Government Printing Office.

Wagstaff, Graham F. 1983. "Attitudes to Poverty, the Protestant Work Ethic, and Political Affiliation: A Preliminary Investigation." *Social Behavior and Personality* 11(1): 45–47.

Weaver, Kent R., Robert Y. Shapiro, and Lawrence R. Jacobs. 1995. "Trends: Welfare." *Public Opinion Quarterly* 59(4): 606–27.

Weber, Lynn. 1998. "A Conceptual Framework for Understanding Race, Class, Gender, and Sexuality." *Psychology of Women Quarterly* 22(1): 13–32.

Weiner, Bernard. 1995. *Judgments of Responsibility: A Foundation for a Theory of Social Conduct.* New York: Guilford Press.

Weinger, Susan. 1998. "Poor Children 'Know Their Place': Perceptions of Poverty, Class, and Public Messages" *Journal of Sociology & Social Welfare* 25(2): 100–118.

Weis, Lois. 2003. "Acquiring White Working-Class Identities: Legitimate and Silenced Discourse Within the School." In *Silenced Voices and Extraordinary Conversations: Re-imagining Schools*, edited by Michelle Fine and Lois Weis. New York: Teachers College Press.

Wing, Adrien K. 2003. *Critical Race Feminism: A Reader.* 2nd ed. New York: New York University Press.

Wright, Stephen C., and Linda R. Tropp. 2005. "Language and Intergroup Contact: Investigating the Impact of Bilingual Instruction on Children's Intergroup Attitudes." *Group Processes & Intergroup Relations* 8(3): 309–28.

Zucker, Gail S., and Bernard Weiner. 1993. "Conservatism and Perceptions of Poverty: An Attributional Analysis." *Journal of Applied Social Psychology* 23(4): 925–44.

Chapter 4

How Culture Matters: Enriching Our Understanding of Poverty

Michèle Lamont and Mario Luis Small

The term *culture* figures prominently in the literature on poverty, race, and ethnicity, though rarely with much theoretical or empirical sophistication. Conceived rather vaguely as a group's norms and values, as its attitudes toward work and family, or as its observed patterns of behavior,[1] culture has been discussed by many poverty experts without the depth or the precision that characterize their analyses of such matters as demographic trends, selection bias, or the impact of public policies on work and family structure. This lack of sophistication is reflected in many practices, such as the use of *culture* and *race* interchangeably, as if all members of a racial group shared a unified set of beliefs or pattern of behavior, or the use of culture as a residual category to explain unaccounted-for variance in statistical model, or the use of culture exclusively as an intermediary mechanism—an intervening variable that helps explain why structural conditions such as neighborhood poverty lead to unwanted outcomes, but not an independently causal force.[2] By contrast, other scholars reject cultural explanations altogether, arguing that culture cannot be studied scientifically or that cultural explanations inevitably blame the victims for their problems.

Poverty scholarship tends to reveal a rather thin understanding of culture. Over the last two decades, however, cultural sociologists have produced theoretical and empirical research yielding a subtle, heterogeneous, and sophisticated picture of how cultural factors shape and are shaped by poverty and inequality. They have used concepts such as *frames, cultural repertoires, narratives, symbolic boundaries, cultural capital,* and *institutions* to study how poor individuals interpret and respond to their circumstances, yielding insights that may be used to understand racial disparities in poverty. This literature has not coalesced into a coherent perspective on culture, but all of these approaches allow social scientists to move beyond the assumption that racial groups have inherent cultural traits, such as an Asian work ethic. These new concepts allow us to understand racial disparities in a way that avoids the cultural stereotypes that have too often characterized poverty policies and produced research of minimal explanatory power.

This new scholarship is often ignored by scholars of poverty and race, for at least two reasons. First, much of it has been conducted by social scientists who are not part of the community of economists, demographers, sociologists, and political scientists working on poverty and policy.[3] Second, much of it is based on data-gathering techniques—participant observation, in-depth interviewing, comparative historical research, and content analysis—that are unfamiliar to quantitative social scientists. Lacking the training to distinguish between good and bad practitioners of these techniques, many quantitative researchers are tempted to dismiss qualitative work as anecdotal or worse, nonempirical (which too often seems to mean nonquantitative). Even quantitative research in the sociology of culture, such as research on cultural consumption and on networks, too often remains ignored by the interdisciplinary core of inequality scholars, much to the detriment of scholarship (for an attempt to rectify the situation, see Furstenburg 2007).[4]

The consequences of ignoring this scholarship are not limited to the ivory tower. Culture is the subject or subtext of the recurrent public debates about poverty. It remains the subtext of the distinction between the deserving and undeserving poor, and it underlies claims that the welfare system has been too permissive (see Bullock and Soss and Schram, chapters 3 and 11, this volume). It is referenced, often crudely, in the discussions of American individualism, responsibility, hard work, and fairness that characterize debates on poverty and immigration. The writings of influential policy researchers such as George Borjas (2001), David Ellwood (1988), and Lawrence Mead (1986) rely on assumptions about culture among the poor—assumptions often stemming from the culture of poverty theory—that have been criticized by sociologists of culture repeatedly since their emergence in the early 1960s (for example, Valentine 1968; Young 2004). Policy discourse often relies on unsubstantiated assumptions about American culture (for example, about what its core values are), assumptions that, in addition to lacking empirical foundation, have become part of a powerful narrative that equates liberalism with moral decadence and laissez-faire economics with fairness (Guetzkow 2006; O'Connor 2001; Somers and Block 2005).[5]

These issues cannot be resolved without taking seriously the scholarship on poverty among sociologists of culture. In what follows we do not summarize or review all of this literature; in fact, we ignore many important works, to retain argumentative coherence. Rather, we identify those works we believe exemplify significant improvements on thin and dated conceptions of culture, discuss the pitfalls any new work on culture should avoid, and chart a research agenda for the study of poverty in the context of race that takes into account the difficulties in research on culture. Our review does not state where the field is headed—it states where we believe it should head. Although the scholarship we review has much to offer poverty research, it still varies widely in the extent to which its empirical claims can be evaluated quantitatively. In addition, its attempts at depicting subtlety have often come at the cost of lost parsimony. We take pains, therefore, to identify the limitations of the work we review and to suggest issues that culture scholars should address.

Many of the concepts we discuss (such as repertoires, frames, and narratives) may be turned into variables through content analysis or survey data analysis, and studied with statistical models (for an illustration concerning the use of content analysis, see Benson and Saguy 2005; for an illustration of the use of surveys to study boundary work, see Bail 2008). However, several of the analytical tools we describe are more suited to process-tracing (on process tracing, see Bennett and George 2005; on how qualitative methods can identify causal mechanisms, see Lin 1998). It is necessary to examine not only whether two phenomena are associated, but also how one leads to the other, or under what circumstances it does so—questions often best addressed with the help of qualitative data. Tackling such questions has been needed in the study of poverty for some time. In a review of the evidence on the spread of single-parent families, David Ellwood and Christopher Jencks, noting that "quantitative social science does best with sharp turning points and tight links between dependent and independent variables," skeptically concluded that "quantitative models have done about as well as could be expected given the limits of our methods for investigating a complex system" (2004, 60). Getting beyond these limitations is essential to understanding the social and cultural mechanisms that affect racial and ethnic differences in poverty.

BACKGROUND AND CONCEPTS

For years, the most prominent, if controversial, theory of culture and poverty was Oscar Lewis's culture of poverty (1969). Lewis argued that this culture emerged when populations that were socially and economically marginalized from a capitalist society developed patterns of behavior to deal with their low status. This behavior was characterized by low aspirations, political apathy, helplessness, disorganization, provincialism, and the disparagement of so-called middle class values (190–2). Once such a culture was in place, Lewis argued, it developed mechanisms that tended to perpetuate it even if structural conditions changed.[6]

Lewis's work was in part an attempt to bridge the structure-culture divide that had long been a feature of opposing explanations for poverty. Cultural explanations emphasized values and norms that directed behavior; structural explanations emphasized economic and structural constraints on behavior. However, the idea that the culture of poverty was self-perpetuating placed Lewis, in the eyes of many, on the cultural side. The debates that followed devolved into caricatures of the complex social processes involved: some blamed poverty on the inadequate values of the poor; others blamed "the system." The cultural conservatism of the 1980s polarized research even further, such that politically moderate social scientists were wary of associating themselves with cultural explanations for fear of being considered reactionary (Patterson 1997; Wilson 1987).[7]

Beginning in the 1980s, sociological research on these questions began to follow multiple trajectories. Some scholars have examined the interaction between culture and structure with respect to issues such as agency, free will, and determinism, moving well beyond a simple dichotomy (Sewell 2005). Others have asked instead how people develop meaning systems—how they draw from their social circumstances to shape scripts, frames, repertoires, and so forth, rather than how those meaning systems determine their poverty or wealth.

Early approaches such as Lewis's also reflected a Parsonian conception of culture, whereby culture is a unitary and internally coherent set of attributes that characterizes a social group, such as inner-city African Americans or the Japanese. No consensus conception of culture has replaced Parsons' because different scholars focus on different social processes and use different metaphors to describe and explain what they observe. However, most would disagree with the Parsonian conception that emphasizes how one is socialized into values that then shape behaviors (Sewell 2005, chapter 3). Many contemporary scholars have been influenced by Clifford Geertz (1973), who said: "Believing, with Max Weber, that man is an animal suspended in webs of significance he himself has spun, I take culture to be those webs" (1973, 5). In this conception, as well as in the more practice-oriented approaches, culture refers to the meaning that human beings produce and mobilize to act on their environment (Ortner 1984). Instead of having a culture, individuals exist in the midst of, respond to, use and create cultural symbols.

In this respect, we fundamentally agree. The idea that races or ethnic groups have a culture—for example, that there is an Anglo American culture that differs from Asian culture or Afro American culture—is unhelpful to the study of racial differences in poverty. Intragroup differences are often larger than intergroup differences. Consequently, our understanding of racial disparities in poverty does not account for these as a function of inherent ethnic cultures. Instead of imputing a shared culture to groups, we study empirically how individuals make sense of their lives.

CULTURE AND POVERTY TODAY

In what follows, we examine six ways culture has been conceived and examined—as frames, repertoires, narratives, cultural capital, symbolic boundaries, institutions—and assess what researchers studying poverty have uncovered by using each conception, and what differences it makes to use these concepts for our understanding of poverty. Some of the researchers we cover think of culture as an independent variable and poverty as the outcome. Others think of culture as the outcome. Others use neither as a causal outcome, producing instead descriptive accounts of the operation of both variables. Still others abandon the variable-based approach altogether. This heterogeneity is part of the strength of this body of work. Each approach is a lens through which to capture different dimensions of the causal processes that produce inequality and poverty. As such, they can be combined, or used independently of one another. Together, they speak to how factoring in meanings can result in more comprehensive explanations of poverty.

Culture as Frames

Building on insights from Alfred Schütz (1962), Peter Berger and Thomas Luckman (1966), Erving Goffman (1963), and others, some cultural sociologists ask how individuals cognitively perceive the world around them. Whereas normative conceptions focus on how we evaluate good and bad, cognitive ones ask how something is perceived as real. The philosophical underpinnings of this work stem from Immanuel Kant (1781/1982), whose distinction between the noumenal and phenomenal worlds introduced the idea that the world as it truly is differs from the world we represent to ourselves, and that as people, we only have access to the latter.

Sociologists in this tradition assume that no one simply sees things as they are. Instead, every individual's perception of the social world—of social relations, the class system, race, the neighborhood, organizations—is filtered through cultural frames that highlight certain aspects and hide or block others.

The most prominent empirical application of the conception of culture as frames stems from the social movements literature. David Snow and Robert Benford defined a frame as "an interpretive [schema] that simplifies and condenses the 'world out there' by selectively punctuating and encoding objects, situations, events, experiences, and sequences of actions within one's present or past environment" (1992, 137). Much of this literature evolved in response to the resource mobilization perspective on social movements, which focused on the material resources that leaders could access and mobilize for their cause. The framing perspective's critique of resource mobilization theory is that cultural or symbolic elements are essential for the possibility of action. Regardless of resources, activists will be unable to mobilize potential participants without transforming their perceptions, by framing their situation in such a way that mobilization appears necessary (Small 2002, 23).

This perspective has been applied to the study of how people respond to neighborhood poverty. Mario Small's *Villa Victoria* (2004) analyzes local participation in a Latino housing project in Boston created as a response to political mobilization. He examined why residents, thirty years later, differed in their level of local community participation. Contrary to culture-of-poverty expectations, he found that differences in participation bore little relation to their expressed values, and more to differences in their (cognitive) framing of the neighborhood. When asked to describe their neighborhood (and thus, to reveal how they framed it), the two groups differed in whether they included the neighborhood's history in their description and whether they used *community* or *projects* to describe it. Those who perceived themselves as living in a neighborhood with a significant history of political and social involvement continued that tradition by participating in local activities. Those who perceived the neighborhood as little more than the projects, a low-income area with no especially notable history, did not. Those few who increased their participation level over time had first adopted frames consistent with those of other participants, learning from the latter, for example, the history of the political mobilization that led to the creation of the neighborhood.

David Harding (2005, 2007) also examined how framing influences the response to poverty. Whereas Small looked at how individuals frame their neighborhood, Harding focused, among other things, on how they frame the idea of pregnancy. He found that adolescents in disadvantaged neighborhoods in Boston exhibit greater heterogeneity of frames than those in other neighborhoods—for example, in response to whether being pregnant as a teen would be "embarrassing" or "not all that bad." As a result, adolescents in disadvantaged neighborhoods have more options for conceiving their circumstances, including both mainstream and alternative conceptions of the world.

This literature improves on the culture of poverty perspective in two respects. Whereas by definition the culture of poverty expects a single set of cultural responses to arise from conditions of structural poverty, both Small and Harding made clear that heterogeneity is common and salient. Both found little support for the notion of a collective ghetto culture shared universally by residents in high poverty, and show important within-neighborhood differences in cultural frames. By extension, both suggested that studies of racial differences in poverty looking for explanations in values are unlikely to find much.

A second contribution of this work is to redefine the relation between culture and behavior. The norms-and-values perspective posited a cause-and-effect relationship between values and behaviors, whereas the frame perspective tends to posit what Small (2002, 2004) has called a constraint-and-possibility relationship. Frames do not cause behavior so much as make it possible or likely. However, a consequence of this redefinition is that cultural frames are, by design, insufficient explanations of behavior; they may be thought of as necessary but insufficient conditions.

Culture as Repertoires

Scholars have also conceived of culture as a repertoire of practices, beliefs, and attitudes that individuals call forth at the time of action. One of the most widely cited scholars in this tradition is Ann Swidler (1986), who approached culture as a tool kit that individuals open in unsettled times. She argued that "culture influences action not by providing the ultimate values toward which action is oriented but by shaping a repertoire or 'tool kit' of habits, skills, and styles from which people construct 'strategies of action'" (1986, 273). Whereas a metaphor in the frames perspective might be that culture is the particular tint of the glasses through which individuals see the world, in the repertoires perspective it is the set of tools individuals have at their disposal to manage the social world.

For Swidler, it was less important whether individuals are shaped by their values than what repertoires of action are available to them in their figurative toolkits. Different toolkits contain different repertoires of action, and the toolboxes of some have more repertoires than those of others. The notion of strategies of action, which she defined as "persistent ways of ordering action through time" (1986, 273), is important. Speaking explicitly about a perennial issue in the urban poverty literature, Swidler explained that asking whether the poor share the values of the middle class will yield very little:

> The irony of this debate is that it cannot be resolved by evidence that the poor share the values and aspirations of the middle class, as indeed they seem to do. In repeated surveys, lower-class youth say that they value education and intend to go to college. . . . People may share . . . aspirations while remaining profoundly different in the way their culture organizes their overall pattern of behavior.

The root of those differences lies in their toolboxes. Thus

> culture in this sense is more like a style or a set of skills than a set of preferences or wants. If one asked a slum youth why he did not take steps to pursue a middle class path to success (or indeed asked oneself why one did not pursue a different life direction) the answer might well be not "I don't want that life," but instead "Who, me?" One can hardly pursue success in a world where the accepted skills, style, and informal know-how are unfamiliar. One does better to look for a line of action for which one already has the cultural equipment. (Swidler 1986, 275)

This perspective views culture as a heterogeneous set of attributes, rather than a single, coherent system. It allows for cultural differentiation and contradictions within a group. Preceding Swidler, Ulf Hannerz's classic but often overlooked *Soulside* (1969/2004) argued that ghetto residents have access to a repertoire that included both ghetto-specific and mainstream behavior. William Julius Wilson (1996) extended this idea by arguing that under conditions of high joblessness, many mainstream forms of behavior are difficult to implement. In *Flat Broke with Children* (2003), Sharon Hays showed that low-income mothers use of the alternative strategies of action available to them, and that these often contradict one another. She found that the notions of responsibility and financial self-sufficiency are clearly part of low-income women's cultural toolkits. When examining differences in poverty by race, this work leads to questions about the availability of strategies for acting in accordance with mainstream versus alternative values. Wilson's work suggests, for example, that the repertoire of strategies available is constrained by neighborhood (and not just individual) poverty. Blacks have been shown to be much more likely than whites or Latinos to live in high poverty neighborhoods (Jargowsky 1997; Massey and Denton 1993). This would lead one to expect racial differences in repertoires, even if there are few racial differences in values.

As with the frame perspective, the added value of the culture as repertoire perspective is that it leaves room for accounts of diversity within groups and for a multiplicity of perspectives within a single actor. Because individuals can and do resort to different repertoires in the course of action, this perspective makes it possible to understand what to outsiders may appear as inconsistencies—for example, between a reported belief in the sanctity of marriage and a birth out of wedlock. In addition, it helps identify which actions are unlikely: if the strategies for obtaining a college degree or for sustaining a long-term marriage are not part of one's toolkit, one is not likely to pursue either course of action. Today, the strategies for entering a competitive college include contacting the Educational Testing Service and registering for the SAT, obtaining study materials or enrolling in a preparatory course, indicating to which colleges one wants the grades sent, and many others. If a seventeen-year-old does not know to do these things, it is unlikely he or she will pursue a college education in a competitive institution even if, in theory, going to college seems like a rational thing to do. The poor often need multiple repertoires to get out of poverty, such as knowledge of how to enroll in two- or four-year colleges, how to acquire technical skills, how to demonstrate street savvy, and how to avoid being drawn into street violence. Understanding their acquisition and use of these repertoires is critical to understanding the path out of poverty.

As Michèle Lamont (1992, chapter 7) argued, the toolkit perspective presents problems, particularly in that it does not explain why some repertoire choices are followed in a course of action. In a sense, it is concerned with the supply side of culture, but not with the factors that influence the likelihood of access to, or of the use of, one set of tools (for example, how to get access to a college education) rather than another. The choice depends on opportunities and structural constraints that are shaped by cultural and noncultural factors. In addition, Swidler allowed a slippage among the terms *strategies*, *repertoires*, *skills*, *styles*, and *habits*, which weakens the powerful simplicity of the toolkit concept. Nevertheless, this approach does address many of the weaknesses of some earlier paradigms, notably, their incapacity to deal with heterogeneity or contradiction.

Culture as Narratives

Although frames, repertoires, and narratives all cognitively shape people's understanding of their social world, only narratives are stories; they often present a beginning, middle, and end, and are clearly identifiable as a chunk of discourse (Polletta 2006; Ewick and Silbey 2003). Narratives of personal experience have informed the study of social class since the pioneering work of William Labov on the African American vernacular (1997; see also Bertaux and Kohli 1984). Although the term *narrative* is generally used very loosely and one finds many variations in how narrative analysis is practiced, in general it suggests that people develop an understanding of themselves, their environment, and others that shape their actions (Somers 1994). This approach posits that, when faced with two courses of action concerning, for instance, their project of social mobility, individuals are likely to pursue the one most consistent with their personal narrative, rather than one that might seem most rational to an outsider (for example, Abelmann 2003 on gendered projects of upward mobility in South Korea).

Whether scholars use the concept of narrative explicitly or not, they often argue that the stories people tell themselves influence how they make sense of their lives and of their difficulties. For example, Alford Young (2004) found that the black low-income residents of a Chicago public housing project placed little emphasis on racial prejudice in their account of the limitations and possibilities they encountered. The residential segregation they experienced meant that they rarely interacted with whites, and, as a consequence, that whites were not salient in their causal explanations. For their part, in their book *Legacies* (2001), Alejandro Portes and Rubén Rumbaut revealed radically diverse narratives about the immigrant experience among immigrant families in Miami and San Diego, from places as diverse as Jamaica, the Philippines, Cuba, Mexico, Cambodia, Colombia, and Haiti. These narratives help make their choices, notably concerning education and social mobility, more comprehensible (on differences in the cultural orientation of second generation immigrants from various ethnic and racial groups, see also Kasinitz, Mollenkopf, and Waters 2006).

The narrative perspective is particularly useful in demonstrating how self-conception, including one's sense of self-limitations and responsibility toward others, influences action—for instance, how one goes about passing on resources to one's children (for example, Abelmann 2003; Steedman 1987). This perspective has enormous potential and should be more fully explored in the American context. It shows that action is not an automatic response to incentive: it is made possible within the context of narratives around which people make sense of their lives. Qualitative methods are well suited to obtain the stories actors have about their lives. However, narratives can also be studied through discourse and content analysis, surveys, cognitive mapping, and other techniques that are amenable to quantification (Abdelal et al. forthcoming; Jepperson and Swidler 1994).

Culture as Symbolic Boundaries

Symbolic boundaries are conceptual distinctions between objects, people, and practices that operate as a "system of rules that guide interaction by affecting who comes together to engage in what social act" (Lamont and Fournier 1992, 12). Boundaries distinguish between those who are worthy and those who are less so, from the standpoint of morality, economic success, cultural sophistication, and so forth. They are a necessary but insufficient condition for the creation of social boundaries manifested in spatial segregation, labor market segregation, and patterns of intermarriage (Lamont and Molnár 2002). These consequences show the importance of paying heed to the boundaries that members of various groups draw, their relative porousness (the extent to which boundaries are policed), the criteria used to draw and justify them, and the groups they exclude or stigmatize. They reveal how individuals implicitly and explicitly characterize members of various classes, and particularly what they view as the characteristics and flaws of groups, including the poor. Thus, in the United States, workers' self-definitions stress hard work, responsibility, and self-sufficiency. In valuing their own attributes, they draw strong moral boundaries against the poor, whom they view as lazy and as taking advantage. In France, by contrast, workers are more likely to see the poor as fellow workers temporarily displaced by the forces of capitalism, and thus worthy of support. This view is sustained by cultural repertoires—a strong socialist tradition, Catholicism, and Republicanism—that make notions of solidarity widely available (Lamont 2000; Lamont and Thévenot 2000).[8] This cross-national contrast corresponds to wider patterns in redistributive policies toward the poor in France than in the United States (see also Gallie and Paugam 2000; Katz 1989; Silver 1993). Cultural categories of worth, which include widely shared views of the poor, figure prominently among the conditions explaining such policies in the United States (Steensland 2006) or comparatively (Dobbin 1994; Sato 2008).

Boundary work (the separation of Us and Them) is critical to the making of groupness. It is part of the process of construction of collective identity: individuals differentiate themselves from others by drawing on criteria of common traits and experiences and a sense of shared belonging. They must be recognized by outsiders as distinct for their collective identity to crystallize (Cornell and Hartman 1997, chapter 4; Jenkins 1996, chapter 4). Social identity theory, elaborated by social psychologists, suggests that "pressures to evaluate one's own group positively through in-group/out-group comparison lead social groups to attempt to differentiate themselves from each other" (Tajfel and Turner 1985, 16–17 Hogg and Abrams 1988). This process of differentiation aims "to maintain and achieve superiority over an out-group on some dimension" (Tajfel and Turner 1985, 16–17). Hence, in-group favoritism, manifested in stereotyping, is common, especially among high-status groups (for a review, see Sidanius and Pratto 1999; see also chapter 3, this volume). Understanding this process affects how we account for people's success and failures—with external-environmental as opposed to internal-individual and self-blaming explanations (Crocker, Major, and Steele 1998).

Studies of boundary work and identity among the poor have focused on how the poor self-define (as workers, good parents, or moral beings), rather than assigning them an identity by isolating specific cultural patterns as central and enduring aspects of a culture of poverty. These studies also consider whether, how, and by whom such self-identifications are validated, and whether they can crystallize as social categories and in turn affect behavior. For instance, in *No Shame in My Game*, Katherine Newman (1999) studied how the black and Latino working poor of Harlem who are employed in the fast-food industry contrast themselves with the unemployed poor. They develop a sense of their identity as workers in contrast to that of the unemployed poor, and create a status hierarchy that echoes the dominant social hierarchy and the dominant narrative of the American dream. Similarly, in *The Code of the Street*, Elijah Anderson (1999) analyzed intraracial boundaries that separate "decent" from "street" poor African Americans, and examines how the latter develop behavioral traits and identity defined in opposition to those of whites. Nathan Fosse (2008) showed how low-income black men define women as *stunt* and *wifey*, and how these categories are associated with different moral constructs concerning trustworthiness, which in turn affects the prevalence of single-parent families. In *My Baby's Father*, Maureen Waller (2002) showed how unmarried poor men understand their identities as fathers and describes the emotional contributions they make to the lives of their children (contra governmental programs that focus only on their material contributions). She contrasted her approach with earlier ones: "rather than examining whether low-income unmarried parents adopt sub-cultural values that contrast with those in the rest of society, [the] analysis [shows] that these parents draw their ideas, justifications, and practices regarding fatherhood from various sources, including their families, communities, other institutions, and general culture" (45). Thus, these men define themselves in opposition to the deadbeat dads targeted by government child-support enforcement programs. Focusing on their self-concept through boundary work captures conditions that make the choices they make possible, helping social scientists move beyond a view of their lives as aberrational. Without such a focus, analysts would miss important explanations for the choices the poor make.

Ethnic and racial differences, which in the United States overlap with the boundary between the poor and the nonpoor, are often defended and contested by, among others, parents who reinforce ethnic identity to prevent their children from assimilating downward (Noh and Kaspar 2003). This daily boundary work contributes to both the reproduction of racial stereotypes and the policing of racial group boundaries. Policies created to address racial disparities in poverty need to clearly dissociate poverty from race and ethnicity—primarily African American, Native American, and Latino—if they are to avoid reinforcing stereotypical views of racial differences.

Culture as Cultural Capital

Cultural capital refers to the "institutionalized, i.e. widely shared, high status cultural signals" used to exclude others in various contexts (Lamont and Lareau 1988, 56). This concept has become widely used as an analytical device to understand how differences in lifestyles and taste contribute to the reproduction of inequality. It illuminates how middle and upper-middle class adults (professionals and managers) pass on advantages to their children, mostly by familiarizing them with cultural habits and orientations valued by the educational system. The early American literature on this topic tended to focus primarily on familiarity with high culture (for example, DiMaggio 1982), more recent work has tended to focus on a wider range of high status signals.

According to Pierre Bourdieu's and Jean-Claude Passeron's original framework (1977), children of poor and working class families are handicapped by a schooling system that systematically uses criteria of evaluation biased in favor of middle class culture—for instance, use of a wide vocabulary (Bernstein 1993). For these children, this bias frequently results in overselection, self-exclusion, and "relegation" or marginalization (Lamont and Lareau 1988). The living conditions of poor and working class children often lead them to internalize the notion that upper-middle and middle class culture is superior. Thus, they are also victims of a symbolic violence that leads them to downplay the value of their own class culture and to evaluate themselves through the prisms of standards that favor the middle class.[9]

One of the issues raised by students of cultural capital is whether various types of capital operate in different environments, and whether women, ethnic groups, the poor, or the working class have relatively autonomous understandings of what counts as cultural capital (Erikson 1996; Hall 1991; Lamont and Lareau 1988). Thus, forty years after the publication of *Reproduction*, sociologists are studying various coinages that operate across social worlds and the resources they provide. For instance, in *Keeping it Real*, Prudence Carter (2005) wrote about nondominant forms of cultural capital (NDCC) that she contrasted with theories of oppositional culture and reactive assimilation (also Tyson, Darity, and Castellino 2005). She challenged the acting white thesis that suggests that poor African Americans reject education. Drawing on ethnographic data, she documented a wider range of attitudes that poor minority students have toward education and school culture. Foremost in her argument is the importance that students attach to educational achievement and the maintenance of cultural authenticity in schools. The latter requires involvement with, and admiration for, nondominant forms of cultural capital associated with African American youth culture, through which students gain peer respect, but which may be read by teachers as disrespecting school values. Carter thus located students in the broader cultural contexts in which they live, and showed the dynamics between multiple types of cultural coinage that are valued in their environment—not only those that are institutionally sanctioned. She also showed that meaning-making concerning the self should be factored into any explanation of school failure among urban youth.

Annette Lareau's (2004) *Unequal Childhoods* shows that middle class parents on the one hand, and working class and poor parents on the other, manage the extracurricular activities of their children differently. This provides them with different endowments or assets of cultural capital. Drawing on ethnographic fieldwork in a small number of poor, working class, and middle class families, Lareau found that the middle class people she interviewed favored "purposeful cultivation" and organized numerous extracurricular activities for their children. By contrast, her working class and poor interviewees favored "natural growth" and were much less involved in managing their children's lives than their middle class counterparts are (see also Farkas, chapter 5, this volume). The leisure time of the working class and poor in her study was relatively unstructured and did not contribute to teaching children skills that middle class children learned and that would prepare them for professional life (self-directiveness, multitasking, leadership, and so on). Thus, Lareau showed how the use of free time contributes to the reproduction of class inequality, even beyond differences that can be explained simply by class differences in time and money. Among her interviewees, class differences were greater than differences within racial groups; for instance, the black and white middle class parents resembled each other in how they manage children's leisure time. Parents pass on different cultural references, orientations, and habits of the mind (or habitus) to their children, and the relative advantages that some of these confer within a particular social context perpetuate class and racial inequality.[10] This study demonstrates that a cross-class analysis illuminates aspects of social processes of exclusion that remain invisible to studies that focus exclusively on the cultural world of the poor.

Studies of cultural capital qua cultural consumption help us understand how culture contributes to poverty by documenting patterns of cultural differentiation and segmentation across classes. For instance, drawing on the General Social Survey, Bryson (1996) found that the middle class distinguishes itself from other groups by its omnivorous musical tastes, from pop to jazz and classical music. She also showed that members of the middle class appreciate "anything but heavy metal," that is, they most dislike the musical tastes associated with groups socially and culturally most distant from their own—the working class and the poor). Thus, building on Pierre Bourdieu (1984), she showed that shared dislikes are as crucial to understanding boundary work as patterns of cultural similarities. Meanwhile, the poor and the working class in her study appreciated a smaller range of musical genres, and their narrowness acts as a class marker in a cultural universe that values cultural breadth. Bethany Bryson (1996) proposed that cultural tolerance constitutes a multicultural capital more strongly concentrated in the middle and upper classes than in the lower classes. In our view, such shared patterns of distastes and tastes result in culturally isolating practices for the privileged and poor alike, which work in conjunction with class- (and often race-) segregating institutions (housing, schools, families, cities) to create pervasive us-them boundaries. Such insights must be incorporated in the literature on poverty if we are to develop a more encompassing understanding of the conditions that sustain the social isolation of the poor, and inequality more generally. Institutional discrimination may have a multiplier effect against this background of cultural differences. One of the challenges ahead is to tackle the cascading and compounding effects of cultural templates and institutions working together.

Finally, this literature also offers a response to theorists who have argued that if culture is heterogeneous, then it is epiphenomal, and not useful as a causal explanation. Cultural sociologists have demonstrated patterns of cultural likes and dislikes that are differentiated across classes and racial groups (see Peterson 2005). A wide international literature demonstrates how many institutions, such as schools, are biased in favor of middle class tastes, which has indirect effect on working class and low-income populations. Such research offers a powerful counterweight to a view that cultural differences are haphazard and without explanatory power.

Culture as Institution

The growing literature on institutions has become preoccupied with analyzing precisely how institutional channels have cascading effects on individual attitudes. These channels are germane to understanding mechanisms and opportunities for incorporation and exclusion. Institutions can be defined robustly, as formal and informal rules, procedures, routines, and norms (Hall and Taylor 1996), as socially constructed shared cognitive and interpretive schemas (Meyer and Rowan 1991), or more narrowly yet, as formal organizations. In all of these definitions, however, they enable or constrain shared definitions and experiences of race, class, and gender, which in turn affect poverty. Thus, institutions are the last culture-related analytical device to which we turn. They are particularly salient when one considers how cultural constructs feed into poverty-related policy, as when the latter resonates with institutionalized, taken-for-granted boundaries.

Examining guaranteed annual income proposals in the 1960s and 1970s, Brian Steensland (2006) analyzed the role of culture in the schematic, discursive, and institutional mechanisms leading to policy outcomes. Explanations in previous research, he suggested, centered on the impact of social movements, state autonomy, and business interests, but "the role of culture is recognized empirically, but disappears theoretically" (1280, n.8). He, however, emphasized interpretive feedback mechanisms, showing that supporters and opponents of guaranteed annual income proposals "use language that buttressed cultural categories of worthiness" (for example, welfare recipients versus the working poor, or "income supplement" versus "welfare support"), that in turn influence the shape of policies; this illustrates how templates for categorization (or boundaries) encounter discursive opportunity structures (or institutions) that influence the likelihood that specific schemas will diffuse, become institutionalized in policy, and affect who gets what. Moreover, "categories of worth exert institutional influence when they interlock with patterned practices in ways that channel routinized action" (1287). In other words, through feedback or loop effects, boundaries become institutionalized, that is, largely taken for granted and embedded in policies, in informal organization, and in cultural practices. Institutional arrangements come to reproduce themselves and result in systematic exclusion of some categories of the population.

Such processes have consequences for how the poor are incorporated and "dealt with" across advanced industrial societies. For instance, Hilary Silver (2006) contrasted French, British, and other European policies of social inclusion (and their desire to avoid social exclusion) with American approaches that isolate the poor, namely through means-tested (as opposed to universal) welfare programs (Silver 1993). Such cultural qua institutional processes help explain patterns of racial incorporation (for instance, through laws against employment discrimination, or through social security and welfare) in these different contexts. Robert Lieberman (2005) analyzed different configurations of "institutions, group-state linkages, and cultural repertoires" (25) that result in the unintentional but systemic exclusion of blacks in favor of whites in the United States, mediated by labor market access and state structure. This exclusion is then compounded by the efforts of individuals to make sense of their place in the world, as those efforts draw upon the status quo as starting point. Similarly, by contrasting recipients of welfare and disability insurance, Joe Soss (2005) described how the two programs' regulations and organization of casework result in different recipient understandings of their client status and of the potential effectiveness of collective action (see also, on the framing of membership, Jenson and Papillon 2001; Soss and Mettler 2004).

Investigating such institutionalized processes requires reframing poverty knowledge within a broader perspective. It requires focusing less on individuals and more on structures and institutions, including the cultural and social mechanisms that maintain classification systems that demarcate the poor from Us (O'Connor 2001). Cultural approaches to the study of poverty thus have to focus on poverty policies, as well as on the poor.

REMAINING CHALLENGES

We have not argued here that scholars of poverty and racial inequality should concern themselves only with culture. We would not expect, for example, that concentrated urban poverty would be explainable solely by a shift in certain repertoires of action among a population or by a secular decline in the belief in meritocracies. Rather, our goal has been to introduce alternative ways of thinking about culture and to suggest that culture, in its many forms, may interact with structure in ways other than those so far proposed by much of the scholarship on poverty and racial inequality.

Meaning is multifaceted; it may intervene differently at various points in the causal chain that determines whether members of different racial or ethnic groups end up in poverty. Its role will not be the same in all settings. For example, determining whether poor Native Americans born in reservations are likely to escape poverty may call for different cultural tools and analytical strategies, than determining why equally poor people of different racial groups differ in their use of traditional banking (Bertrand, Mullainathan, and Shafir 2006). Thus, breaking down culture into many components is essential if we are to better understand its role in channeling racial disparities.

For this reason, we have not attempted to adjudicate among the six analytical tools we have presented except to suggest that they each can illuminate different processes through which meaning contributes to the uneven distribution of poverty across racial and ethnic groups. These processes cannot be captured by the culture of poverty thesis and its many implicit descendants. Some of these processes concern microlevel processes of meaning making and decision making among the poor—for example, how low-income individuals' framing their neighborhoods shapes their actions, how the narratives of different racial or ethnic groups affects their perceptions of the path to a good life, how the working poor use the poor to help define who they themselves are. Others relate to society-wide cultural representations about groups that impact the policies and institutions that regulate them—for example, the cultural assumptions of policy makers and politicians about the motivations of unwed mothers that cause poverty. The emerging picture is far more complex and multidimensional than that generated by the assumption that living in poverty creates self-perpetuating and pernicious cultural orientations. Again, only by considering a range of culture-related concepts that point to different aspects of an hypothesized causal process—as opposed to culture broadly defined—can a fuller and more fine-tuned understanding of the relevant aspects be brought to light.

For research on racial differences in poverty to produce work that builds on and improves on the literature just described, several changes will be necessary.[11] First, such research should accommodate a broader understanding of how various disciplines accumulate empirical evidence. Certainly some of the ideas discussed here can be examined through quantitative, survey-based methods. Nevertheless, many are best studied through other data-gathering techniques. Inductive research and field-based methods are a sine qua non if we are to capture the distinctive frames or narratives through which the poor make sense of their lives. These methods are also especially well suited to capture path-dependent processes and to perform process-tracing more generally. Familiarity with a variety of methods is probably a requirement for fulfilling the promise of the field.

Second, concerns with endogeneity should not stop researchers from considering how culture-related phenomena figure in the production and reproduction of inequality. Indeed, although the question of what is cause and consequence is critical for research that aims at assessing the relative significance of various factors in multivariate models, it is much less relevant in studies concerned with process-tracing, where loop-back effects and other similar patterns are common. This should be stressed because problems of endogeneity have often deterred quantitatively inclined social scientists from considering the causal role of culture.

Third, we need more heterogeneous views about how culture and poverty are causally related: cultural practices may shape responses to poverty, cultural repertoires may be limited by poverty, cultural frames may be expanded by neighborhood poverty, cultural narratives may change irrespective of poverty, and so on. Whether cultural change leads to structural change is a counterproductive question. Much more useful is to ask when, where, and how cultural change leads to structural change. It is imperative that the terms of the debate be changed to make room for conceptions of culture that go beyond thin accounts of preferences.

A few recent poverty studies show the promise and potential pitfalls of rethinking how culture is examined. In *Promises I Can Keep*, Kathryn Edin and Maria Kefalas (2005) painted a convincing picture of how poor single mothers understand the place of fathers, husbands, and children in their lives. Their respondents give positive meanings to aspects of their lives that many poverty researchers condemn, including marriage, children, and autonomy. If women do not marry, it is because they hold marriage in very high regard and wish to avoid divorce. If women do not postpone childbearing, it is because having a child is a source of self-esteem, given their low labor-market prospects. If they hold off from marriage, it is in part to protect their independence from men through financial security. These cultural orientations, and others, intersect with the structural factors that William Julius Wilson (1987) discussed, such as high male unemployment, to explain the high rate of nonmarital birth among the poor. What is missing, however, is an explicit account of how one meaning is connected to another, and the processes through which women come to give a particular issue a given mean-ing—for example, whether tropes available from feminism, entertainment televi-sion, or Catholicism (especially among the Latina respondents) converge to pro-duce the distinct meanings these women give to autonomy. Though Edin and Kefalas documented in detail how poor white, black, and Latina women living in Philadelphia accounted for their lives, they did not spell out how these accounts feed into the reproduction of poverty. Being clearer about such processes would lead to explicit and more detailed information about the relationship between cul-ture and poverty, and would help us compare processes from case to case and from setting to setting.

Another example is Alford Young's *The Minds of Marginalized Black Men* (2004), based on interviews with twenty-six young, low-income African American men. Young's respondents clearly aspire to a college education, without knowing how to achieve it in part because they are not in frequent contact with the college edu-cated. Their isolation from the middle class makes it difficult to engage in prac-tices likely to lead to higher educational attainment. Their firm belief in educa-tional achievement thus cannot be easily translated into behavior.[12] Just as these respondents value going to college but do not have a cultural template of how to get there, Edin and Kefalas's respondents valued marriage, but viewed it as nearly unattainable because to them it required "the white picket fence lifestyle" (2005, 74, 111). The parallel between the findings of these two studies is striking and cries for further exploration of the disjuncture between the cultural toolkits made available by the American dream, the disconnect between these toolkits and the lives of some Americans, and the resulting institutionalization of popular repertoires among the poor that may, from the perspective of social incorporation, be dysfunctional.

We hope our discussion has made it clear that researchers are unlikely to under-stand racial disparities in poverty by looking at racial or ethnic cultures, in the sense of sets of values or attitudes that all or most members of a racial, ethnic, or class group share. This idea was ineffective in its culture of poverty incarnation, and has recently been shown to be of limited value in other realms as well—see, for instance, the criticisms of the oppositional culture thesis (Ainsworth-Darnell and Downey 1998; Cook and Ludwig 1998; Fordham and Ogbu 1986; Ogbu 1978). The concepts we have discussed all locate cultural processes in individuals or in relations between individuals, rather than in groups. This suggests that the most promising venues for understanding racial disparities through cultural concepts lie in how individuals of different racial backgrounds face differential discrimina-tion, access to structural opportunities, wealth advantages, social capital, and other opportunities and constraints. Cultural factors are more likely to operate in conjunction with these factors, not independently of them.

A proper framing of the role of culture in producing racial disparity in poverty should lead to more appropriate policy recommendations, based on more accu-rate and encompassing understandings of the social worlds that the poor in-habit.[13] For instance, one may imagine that a better understanding of the narra-tives that white, black, and Latino unwed mothers use to make sense of their experience would result in more adequate programs to reduce out-of-wedlock childbirth. Programs to combat poverty among the elderly should be shaped by a more detailed understanding of the frames used to define moral boundaries around family responsibilities among Asians, Latinos, blacks, and whites (Espiritu 1997). Similarly, programs to address prisoner recidivism should take into account that being arrested or having been imprisoned may carry different meanings among different ethnic groups and in different neighborhoods (see Winship and Berrien 2003).

Of course, culture cannot be easily manipulated or changed through policies. However, institutions can be more effective as policy levers if they are based on a fuller understanding of the environment they aim to engineer, and of changes that are in sync with shared understandings. Policies can stimulate cultural responses or exacerbate cultural tensions. An adequate comprehension of contexts, including shared definitions of the situation, are essential to produce successful policy implementation, and to avoid pernicious unintended consequences (on this point, see Swidler forthcoming).

There are many issues we have ignored and much work we have not covered in this chapter—for example, (Patterson 1997, 2000) has attempted to demonstrate the long-term cultural impact of the experience of slavery on African Americans. Although this and other studies are in some senses couched in older conceptions of culture, they nevertheless introduce a concern with meaning that has too often been neglected by poverty scholars. What remains is to enrich this literature with the conceptual tools produced in other terrains more traditionally hospitable to cultural analysis, so as to move toward a richer understanding of the cultural mechanisms involved in the production of poverty. Without this effort, a good part of the puzzle will remain unsolved.

We thank the coeditors of this volume, Ann Lin and David Harris, as well as Lydia Bean, Suzanne Berger, Rebecca Blank, Sheldon Danziger, Joshua Guetzkow, David Harding, Christopher Jencks, Annette Lareau, Katherine Newman, Alice O'Connor, Maureen Waller, Bill Wilson, and Christopher Winship for their useful comments on an earlier draft of this paper. All its shortcomings are our own.

NOTES

1. A straightforward indicator of the messiness of culture research among poverty scholars is its failure to distinguish attitudes from behavior. For instance, failure to marry (a pattern of behavior) does not necessarily indicate an anti-marriage attitude, just as infidelity does not signal the belief that adultery is acceptable. In a recent study of the differences between what employers say concerning their willingness to hire ex-convicts and what they actually do, Devah Pager and Lincoln Quillian (2005) rightfully

noted that "the resolution of these differences represents an important focus of socio-logical investigation in its own right. Although low correlations between attitudes and associated behaviors are often viewed as a purely methodological test of survey questions, in many cases, these discrepancies actually may provide clues for a better substantive understanding of the cognitive-emotional basis for action" (372).

2. Even scholars deep in the sociological tradition who believe cultural factors are im-portant often argue that culture itself stems from economic or structural conditions. For instance, William Julius Wilson (1987) argued that the social isolation fostered by concentrated poverty influences one's cultural orientation (through the scarcity of conventional role models). This model stresses adaptations to constraints and oppor-tunities. However, Robert Sampson and William Julius Wilson (1995) describe com-munity contexts as "cognitive landscapes" concerning behavioral norms (for a focus on culture as repertoire, see also Wilson 1996; Hannerz 1969/2004).

3. The reception of a few works—such as Katherine Newman's *No Shame in My Game* (1999), Elijah Anderson's *Code of the Street* (1999), and Kathryn Edin and Maria Ke-falas's *Promises I Can Keep* (2005)—is an exception.

4. This is not the venue for an extended discussion of methodology. We proceed on the assumption that social science requires multiple methods, because some questions are only or best addressed through particular methods. Still, we believe that culture may be studied through multiple methods, including quantitative methods.

5. Certainly, authors may believe that the welfare system should require work, but stat-ing that *Americans* believe this idea requires empirical substantiation. For example, criticizing Charles Murray's critique of AFDC programs during the 1980s, David Ell-wood (1988) wrote: "But what is often missed in this frenzy is that although Murray is almost certainly wrong in blaming the social welfare system for a large part of the predicament of the poor, he is almost certainly correct in stating that welfare does not reflect or reinforce our most basic values" (6). What are these basic values? Ellwood acknowledges the difficulty of answering this question, but tries anyway: "I have yet to find a definitive and convincing statement of our fundamental American values. The work of philosophers is often esoteric and the results of surveys are difficult to distill. Yet, I see recurring themes in public and academic discussion of what it is Americans believe. Four basic tenets seem to underlie much of the philosophical and political rhetoric about poverty" (1988, 16). Ellwood's "four value tenets" are the au-tonomy of the individual, the virtue of work, the primacy of the family, and the desire for and sense of community. Thus, the author presents a major statement about the characteristics of "American culture" based on no empirical data.

6. More specifically, the culture of poverty perspective argued that the poor remained in poverty not merely as a result of their economic conditions but also because of cul-tural values and practices they had developed from poverty. This perspective, as ex-emplified by Oscar Lewis (1969) and Edward Banfield (1974), argued that culture con-stituted a set of norms and values that guided the behavior of individuals. They also, however, conceived of culture as a lifestyle, at times called a worldview, which made the escape from poverty difficult or impossible. Both authors catalogued a series of characteristics that defined this culture. These included an orientation toward the present and instant gratification, a preference for happiness over work, a tendency to

value familial ties over moral considerations of right or wrong, engaging in sex with multiple partners over the life course, and others. There were several problems with the culture of poverty conception: it assumed that individuals' practices were caused by their values, largely ignoring that many people, rich or poor, constantly act in violation of their values; despite this, its catalogue of the culture of poverty included both values and behaviors, leading to an often circular argument (people have multiple sexual partners because they have a culture characterized by the presence of multiple sexual partners); it assumed that a single culture categorized very diverse people; it assumed that people's culture is fundamentally static and does not change over their lifetimes, as though people play little role in the creation of their own culture or practices (for a related perspective, see Rainwater 1970; for a critique, see Small and Newman 2001).

7. Others, such as Elliot Liebow (1967), attempted to redefine the terrain by proposing the notion of "value stretch." Carol Stack's *All our Kin* (1970) was also a particularly influential critique of Lewis's thesis.

8. Maria Kefalas (2001) analyzes how white working class people in Chicago define and defend their identities largely against blacks who they code as the poor, in what they perceive to be an imperiled environment. They defend themselves through the care with which they keep their homes clean, cultivate their gardens, maintain their property, defend the neighborhoods, and celebrate the nation. In both studies, the meanings given by workers to the poor are closely tied to their own identities as responsible, hard-working, moral people.

9. More specifically, in *Reproduction in Education, Society and Culture*, Pierre Bourdieu and Jean-Claude Passeron (1977) proposed that the lower academic performance of working class children is accounted for not by lower ability but by institutional biases. They suggest that schools evaluate all children on the basis of their familiarity with the culture of the dominant class (or cultural capital), thus penalizing lower class students. Extensive vocabulary, wide-ranging cultural references, and command of high culture are valued by the school system, and students from higher social backgrounds are exposed to this class culture at home. Hence, children from other classes, including the poor, are overselected by the educational system. They are not aware of it, as they remain under the spell of the culture of the dominant class. They blame themselves for their failure, which leads them to drop out or to sort themselves into lower prestige educational tracks.

This work can be read as a direct extension of Karl Marx's and Friedrich Engels's (1845/1979) dominant ideology thesis, which centers on the role of ideology in cementing relations of domination by camouflaging exploitation and differences in class interests. However, the control of subjectivity in everyday life through the shaping of common sense and the naturalization of social relations is the focus of their attention. Bourdieu and Passeron broadened Marx and Engels by suggesting that crucial power relations are structured in the symbolic realm proper and are mediated by meaning. They de facto provide a more encompassing understanding of the exercise of hegemony by pointing to the incorporation of class-differentiated cultural dispositions mediated by both the educational system and family socialization.

In *Distinction* (1984), Bourdieu applied this analysis to the world of taste and cultural practice at large. He showed how the logic of class struggle extends to the realm of taste and lifestyle, and that symbolic classification is key to the reproduction of class privileges: dominant groups define their own culture and ways of being as superior (opposing refined food to heavy food, linen to polyester, tennis to bingo, and so on). Thereby they exercise symbolic violence, that is, impose a specific meaning as legitimate while concealing the power relations that are the basis of its force (Bourdieu and Passeron 1977). They defined legitimate and dominated cultures in opposition: the value of cultural preferences and behaviors are defined relationally around binary oppositions (or boundaries) such as high-lower, pure-impure, distinguished-vulgar, and aesthetic-practical (245). The legitimate culture they thereby defined is used by dominant groups to mark cultural distance and proximity, monopolize privileges, and exclude or recruit new occupants for high status positions (31). Through the incorporation of habitus, or cultural dispositions, cultural practices have inescapable and unconscious classificatory effects that shape social positions. Thus this framework accounts for how the cultural marginalization of the poor is central to processes of domination and to the reproduction of inequality.

10. In *Outline of a Theory of Practice* , Bourdieu (1977) defined habitus as "the durably installed generative principle of regulated improvisations" (78). Repeated exposure to similar social conditions leads individuals to develop a set of *dispositions* toward action that are class-specific, or to simplify, specific to the distance toward material necessity that is characteristic of each class. One of the most successful applications of the concept has been MacLeod's *Ain't No Makin' It* (1995), in which the author studied two small groups of adolescent boys (whites and blacks) as they develop their aspirations in a housing project. He showed that as working class children, the white boys had developed a habitus (a set of rules about their own lives) through which they expected no more than working class lives. To speak of their habitus is to invoke the habitual element of their culture, whereby they expected a working class life because it had never occurred to them or their parents that another life was reasonably possible. In contrast, the high aspirations of the black boys stemmed, in part, from what they saw as the reduction in racial injustice that resulted from the civil rights struggles of their parents' generation—thinking that their own opportunities would be greater than their parents', their aspirations were appropriately higher.

11. The poverty literature is hardly unique in its use of a rather thin conception of culture. Indeed, building on Kornhauser (1978), social scientists studying crime and deviance are also leaving unexamined the impact of cultural mechanisms on their object (Sampson and Bean 2005), and those studying sexuality among the poor have also tended to use a theoretically impoverished model to understand patterns of behavior across a population (Fosse 2008).

12. It is also the case that professing faith in these ideals is a means of acquiring cultural citizenship in a context of acute social exclusion, an issue Lamont has discussed elsewhere (2000; Lamont and Molnár 2002).

13. From our analysis, one should not conclude that no cultural traits or orientations exist that are concentrated among various categories of poor people. There may be large differences in the types of verbal interaction and the words used among professional, working class, and low-income parents when talking with their children. Betty Hart

and Todd Risley (1995), for example, counted class differences in numbers of words employed with children—in the tens of millions by as early as age three (see also Farkas 2003). However, we suggest that such differences should be understood not through the prism of essential or permanent differences between class norms or attitudes, but as elements in a broader account that employs multiple analytical tools to examine the problem.

REFERENCES

Abdelal, Rawi, Yoshiko Herrera, Alastair Iain Johnston, and Rose McDermott, editors. Forthcoming. *Measuring Identity: A Guide for Social Scientists*. Cambridge: Cambridge University Press.

Abelmann, Nancy. 2003. *Melodrama of Mobility: Women, Talk, and Class in Contemporary South Korea*. Honolulu, Hi.: University of Hawaii Press.

Ainsworth-Darnell, James W., and Douglas B. Downey. 1998. "Assessing the Oppositional Culture Explanation for Racial/Ethnic Differences in School Performance." *American Sociological Review* 63(4): 536–53.

Anderson, Elijah. 1999. *Code of the Street. Decency, Violence, and the Moral Life of the Inner City*. New York: W.W. Norton.

Bail, Christopher. 2008. "The Configuration of Symbolic Boundaries against Immigrants in Europe." *American Sociological Review* 73(1): 37–59

Banfield, Edward. 1974. *The Unheavenly City Revisited*. Long Grove, Ill.: Waveland Press.

Bennett, Andrew, and Alexander George. 2005. *Case Studies and Theory Development in the Social Sciences*. Cambridge, Mass.: The MIT Press.

Benson, Rodney, and Abigail C. Saguy. 2005. "Constructing Social Problems in an Age of Globalization: A French-American Comparison." *American Sociological Review* 70(2): 233–59.

Berger, Peter L., and Thomas Luckmann. 1966. *The Social Construction of Reality: A Treatise in the Sociology of Knowledge*. Garden City, N.Y.: Doubleday.

Bernstein, B. 1993. *Class, Codes and Control, vol. 4. The Structuring of Pedagogic Discourse*. London: Routledge and Kegan.

Bertaux, Daniel, and Martin Kohli. 1984. "The Life Story Approach: A Continental View." *Annual Review of Sociology* 10: 215–37.

Bertrand, Marianne, Sendhil Mullainathan, and Eldar Shafir. 2006. "Behavioral Economics and Marketing in Aid of Decision Making Among the Poor." *Journal of Public Policy & Marketing* 25(1): 8–23.

Borjas, George J. 2001. *Heaven's Door: Immigration Policy and the American Economy*. Princeton, N.J.: Princeton University Press.

Bourdieu, Pierre. 1977. *Outline of a Theory of Practice*. New York: Cambridge University Press.

———. 1984. *Distinction: A Social Critique of the Judgment of Taste*. Cambridge, Mass.: Harvard University Press.

Bourdieu, Pierre, and Jean-Claude Passeron. 1977. *Reproduction in Education, Society and Culture*. Beverly Hills, Calif.: Sage Publications.

Bryson, Bethany. 1996. "Anything But Heavy Metal: Symbolic Exclusion and Musical Dislikes." *American Sociological Review* 61(5): 884–99.

Carter, Prudence. 2005. *Keepin' It Real: School Success Beyond Black and White*. New York: Oxford University Press.

Cook, Phillip, and Jens Ludwig. 1998. "The Burden of 'Acting White': Do Black Adolescents Disparage Academic Achievement?" In *The Black-White Test Score Gap*, edited by Christopher Jencks and Meredith Phillips. Washington, D.C.: The Brookings Institution.

Cornell, Stephen E., and Douglas Hartman. 1997. *Ethnicity and Race: Making Identity in a Changing World*. Thousand Oaks, Calif.: Pine Forge Press.

Crocker, Jennifer, Brenda Major, and Claude Steele. 1998. "Social Stigma." In *Handbook of Social Psychology*, edited by Daniel T. Gilbert, Susan T. Fiske, and Gardner Lindzey. Boston, Mass.: McGraw-Hill.

DiMaggio, Paul. 1982. "Cultural Capital and School Success: the Impact of Status Culture Participation of the Grades of U.S. High School Students." *American Sociological Review* 47(2): 189–201.

Dobbin, F. 1994. *Forging Industrial Policy: The United States, Britain, and France in the Railway Age*. Cambridge: Cambridge University Press.

Edin, Kathryn, and Maria Kefalas. 2005. *Promises I Can Keep: Why Poor Women Put Motherhood before Marriage*. Berkeley, Calif.: University of California Press.

Ellwood, David. 1988. *Poor Support: Poverty in the American Family*. New York: Basic Books.

Ellwood, David, and Christopher Jencks. 2004. "The Uneven Spread of Single Parent Families: What Do We Know? Where Do We Look for Answers?" In *Social Inequality*, edited by Kathryn Neckerman. New York: Russell Sage Foundation.

Erikson, Bonnie H. 1996. "Culture, Class and Connections." *American Journal of Sociology* 102(1): 217–51.

Espiritu, Yen Le. 1997. *Asian American Women and Men: Labor, Laws, and Love*. Thousand Oaks, Calif.: Sage Publications.

Ewick, Patrick, and Susan Silbey. 2003. "Narrating Social Structure: Stories of Resistance to Legal Authority." *American Journal of Sociology* 108(6): 1328–72.

Farkas, George. 2003. "Cognitive Skills and Noncognitive Traits and Behaviors in Stratification Processes." *Annual Review of Sociology* 29: 541–62.

Fordham, Signithia, and John U. Ogbu. 1986. "Black Students' School Success: Coping with the Burden of 'Acting White'." *The Urban Review* 18(3): 176–206.

Fosse, Nathan. 2008. "Sex, Self-Worth and the Inner City: Procreation and 'Boundary Work'' Among the Truly Disadvantaged." Working paper, Culture and Social Analysis Workshop. Cambridge, Mass.: Harvard University.

Furstenberg, Frank F. 2007. "The Making of the Black Family: Race and Class in Qualitative Studies in the Twentieth Century." *Annual Review of Sociology* 33: 429–48.

Gallie, Duncan, and Serge Paugam. 2000. *Welfare Regimes and the Experience of Unemployment in Europe*. Oxford: Oxford University Press.

Geertz, Clifford. 1973. *The Interpretation of Cultures*. New York: Basic Books.

Goffman, Erving. 1963. *Stigma*. Englewood Cliffs, N.J.: Prentice-Hall.

Guetzkow, Joshua. 2006. "Common Cause? A Cultural Analysis of the Links Between Welfare and Criminal Justice Policies, 1960-1996." Berkeley, Calif.: University of California, Center on Institutions and Governance.

Hall, John R. 1991. "The Capital(s) of Cultures: A Non-Holistic Approach to Status Situations, Class, Gender, and Ethnicity." In *Cultivating Differences: Symbolic Boundaries and the Making of Inequality*, edited by Michèle Lamont and Marcel Fournier. Chicago, Ill.: University of Chicago Press.

Hall, Peter A., and Rosemary C. R. Taylor. 1996. "Political Science and the Three New Institutionalisms." *Political Studies* 44(5): 936–57.

Hannerz, Ulf. 1969/2004. *Soulside: Inquiries into Ghetto Culture and Community*. New York: Columbia University Press.

Harding, David J. 2005. "Mechanisms of Neighborhood Effects: Linking Culture and Structure to Adolescent Outcomes in Poor Neighborhoods." Ph.D. dissertation, Harvard University.

———. 2007. "Cultural Context, Sexual Behavior, and Romantic Relationships in Disadvantaged Neighborhoods." *American Sociological Review* 72(3): 341–64.

Hart, Betty, and Todd R. Risley. 1995. *Meaningful Differences in Everyday Experiences of Young American Children*. Baltimore, Md.: Brookes Publishing.

Hays, Sharon. 2003. *Flat Broke with Children: Women in the Age of Welfare Reform*. New York: Oxford University Press.

Hogg, Michael A., and Dominic Abrams. 1988. *Social Identification*. London: Routledge.

Jargowsky, Paul A. 1997. *Poverty and Place: Ghettos, Barrios, and the American City*. New York: Russell Sage Foundation.

Jenkins, Richard. 1996. *Social Identity*. London: Routledge.

Jenson, Jane, and Martin Papillon. 2001. *The Changing Boundaries of Citizenship. A Review and a Research Agenda*. Ottawa: Canadian Policy Research Networks.

Jepperson, Ronald L., and Ann Swidler. 1994. "What Properties of Culture Should We Measure?" *Poetics* 22(4): 359–71.

Kant, Immanuel. 1781/1982. *Critique of Pure Reason*. Aalen: Scientia.

Kasinitz, Philip, J. H. Mollenkopf, and Mary C. Waters, editors. 2006. *Becoming New Yorkers: Ethnographies of the New Second Generation*. New York: Russell Sage Foundation.

Katz, Michael. 1989. *The Undeserving Poor: From the War on Poverty to the War on Welfare*. New York: Pantheon.

Kefalas, M. 2001. *The Last Garden: Culture and Place in a White Working Class Chicago Neighborhood*. Berkeley, Calif.: University of California Press.

Kornhauser, Ruth. 1978. *Social Sources of Delinquency: An Appraisal of Analytic Models*. Chicago, Ill.: University of Chicago Press.

Labov, William. 1997. "Some Further Steps in Narrative Analysis." *Journal of Narrative and Life History* 7(1–4): 3–38.

Lamont, Michèle. 1992. *Money, Morals and Manners: The Culture of the French and American Upper-Middle Class*. Chicago, Ill.: University of Chicago Press

———. 2000. *The Dignity of Working Men: Morality and the Boundaries of Race, Class, and Immigration*. Cambridge, Mass.: Harvard University Press.

Lamont, Michèle, and Marcel Fournier, editors. 1992. *Cultivating Differences: Symbolic Boundaries and the Making of Inequality*. Chicago, Ill.: University of Chicago Press.

Lamont, Michèle, and Annette Lareau. 1988. "Cultural Capital: Allusions, Gaps, and Glissandos in Recent Theoretical Developments." *Sociological Theory* 6(2): 153–68.

Lamont, Michèle, and Viràg Molnár. 2002. "The Study of Boundaries Across the Social Sciences." *Annual Review of Sociology* 28: 167–95.

Lamont, Michèle, and Laurent Thévenot, editors. 2000. *Rethinking Comparative Cultural Sociology: Repertoires of Evaluation in France and the United States*. London and Paris: Cambridge University Press and Presses de la maison des sciences de l'homme.

Lareau, Annette. 2004. *Unequal Childhoods: Class, Race, and Family Life*. Berkeley, Calif.: University of California.

Lewis, Oscar. 1969. *A Death in the Sanchez Family*. New York: Random House.

Lieberman, Robert C. 2005. *Shaping Race Policy: The United States in Comparative Perspective*. Princeton, N.J.: Princeton University Press.

Liebow, Elliot. 1967. *Tally's Corner: A Study of Negro Streetcorner Men*. Boston, Mass.: Little, Brown.

Lin, Ann C. 1998. "Bridging Positivist and Interpretivist Approaches to Qualitative Methods." *Policy Studies Journal* 26(1): 162–80.

MacLeod, Jay. 1995. *Ain't No Makin' It: Aspirations and Attainment in a Low-Income Neighborhood*. New York: Westview Press.

Marx, Karl, and Friedrich Engels. 1845/1979. *The German Ideology*. London: Lawrence and Wishart.

Massey, Douglas, and Nancy A. Denton. 1993. *American Apartheid: Segregation and the Making of the Underclass*. Cambridge, Mass.: Harvard University Press.

Mead, Lawrence M. 1986. *Beyond Entitlement: The Social Obligations of Citizenship*. New York: Free Press.

Meyer, John W., and Brian Rowan. 1991. *Institutionalized Organizations: Formal Structure as Myth and Ceremony*. Chicago, Ill.: University of Chicago Press

Newman, Katherine S. 1999. *No Shame in My Game: The Working Poor in the Inner City*. New York: Alfred A. Knopf and Russell Sage Foundation.

Noh, Samuel, and Violet Kaspar. 2003. "Perceived Discrimination and Depression: Moderating Effects of Coping, Acculturation, and Ethnic Support." *American Journal of Public Health* 93(2): 232–38.

O'Connor, Alice 2001. *Poverty Knowledge: Social Science, Social Policy, and the Poor in Twentieth-Century U.S. History*. Princeton, N.J.: Princeton University Press.

Ogbu, John U. 1978. *Minority Education and Caste: The American System in Cross-Cultural Perspective*. New York: Academic Press.

Ortner, Sherry B. 1984. "Theory in Anthropology Since the Sixties." *Comparative Studies in Society and History* 26(1): 126–66.

Pager, Devah, and Lincoln Quillian. 2005. "Walking the Talk? What Employers Say Versus What They Do." *American Sociological Review* 70(3): 355–81.

Patterson, Orlando. 1997. *The Ordeal of Integration: Progress and Resentment in America's "Racial" Crisis*. Washington, D.C.: Counterpoint/Civitas.

———. 2000. "Taking Culture Seriously: A Framework and an Afro-American Illustration." In *Culture Matters: How Values Shape Human Progress*, edited by Samuel P. Huntington and Lawrence E. Harrison. New York: Basic Books.

Peterson, Richard A. 2005. "Problems in Comparative Research: The Example of Omnivorousness." *Poetics* 33(5–6): 257–82.

Polletta, Francesca. 2006. *It Was Like a Fever: Storytelling in Protest and Politics*. Chicago, Ill.: University of Chicago Press.

Portes, Alejandro, and Rubén G. Rumbaut. 2001. *Legacies: The Story of the Immigrant Second Generation*. Berkeley, Calif.: University of California Press.

Rainwater, Lee. 1970. *Behind Ghetto Walls: Black Families in a Federal Slum*. New Brunswick, N.J.: Transaction Publishers.

Sampson, Robert J., and Lydia Bean. 2005. "Cultural Mechanisms and Killing Fields: A Revised Theory of Community-level Racial Inequality." In *The Many Colors of Crime: Inequalities of Race, Ethnicity and Crime in America*, edited by Ruth Peterson, Lauren Krivo, and John Hagan. New York: New York University Press.

Sampson, Robert J., and William Julius Wilson. 1995. "Toward a Theory of Race, Crime, and Urban Inequality." In *Crime and Inequality*, edited by John Hagan and Ruth Peterson. Stanford, Calif.: Stanford University Press.

Sato, Kyoko. 2008. "Politics and Meanings of Genetically Modified Food in the United States, Japan and France." Ph.D. dissertation, Princeton University.

Schütz, Alfred. 1962. *Collected Papers*, vol. 1. The Hague: Martinus Nijhoff.

Sewell, William H., Jr. 2005. *Logics of History: Social Theory and Social Transformation*. Chicago, Ill.: University of Chicago Press.

Sidanius, Jim, and Felicia Pratto. 1999. *Social Dominance: An Intergroup Theory of Social Hierarchy and Oppression*. New York: Cambridge University Press.

Silver, Hilary. 1993. "National Conceptions of the New Urban Poverty: Social Structural Change in Britain, France and the United States." *International Journal of Urban and Regional Research* 17(3): 336–54.

———. 2006. "From Poverty to Social Exclusion: Lessons from Europe." In *Poverty and Race in America: The Emerging Agendas*, edited by Chester Hartman. Lanham, Md.: Lexington Books.

Small, Mario L. 2002. "Culture, Cohorts, and Social Organization Theory: Understanding Local Participation in a Latino Housing Project." *American Journal of Sociology* 108(1): 1–54.

———. 2004. *Villa Victoria*. Chicago, Ill.: University of Chicago Press.

Small, Mario L., and Katherine Newman. 2001. "Urban Poverty After The Truly Disadvantaged: the Rediscovery of the Family, the Neighborhood, and Culture." *Annual Review of Sociology* 27: 23-45.

Snow, David, and Robert Benford. 1992. "Master Frames and Cycles of Protest." In *Frontiers in Social Movement Theory*, edited by Aldon Morris and Carol Mueller. New Haven, Conn.: Yale University Press.

Somers, Margaret. 1994. "Reclaiming the Epistemological 'Other': Narrative and the Social Constitution of Identity." In *Social Theory and the Politics of Identity*, edited by C. Calhoun. Cambridge, Mass.: Blackwell Publishers.

Somers, Margaret, and Fred Block. 2005. "Two Hundred Years of Welfare Debate." *American Sociological Review* 70(2): 260–88.

Soss, Joe. 2005. "Making Clients and Citizens: Welfare Policy as a Source of Status, Belief, and Action." In *Deserving and Entitled: Social Constructions and Public Policy*, edited by Anne Schneider and Helen Ingram. Albany, N.Y.: State University of New York Press.

Soss, Joe, and Suzanne Mettler. 2004. "The Consequences of Public Policy for Democratic Citizenship: Bridging Policy Studies and Mass Politics." *Perspectives on Politics* 2(1): 55–73.

Stack, Carol B. 1970. *All Our Kin*. New York: Harper and Row.

Steedman, Carolyn K. 1987. *Landscape for a Good Woman*. New Brunswick, N.J.: Rutgers University Press.

Steensland, Brian. 2006. "Cultural Categories and the American Welfare State: The Case of Guaranteed Income Policy." *American Journal of Sociology* 111(5): 1273–326.

Swidler, Ann. 1986. "Culture in Action: Symbols and Strategies." *American Sociological Review* 51(2): 273–86.

———. Forthcoming. "Responding to HIV/Aids in Sub-Saharan Africa: Culture, Institutions, and Health." In *Successful Societies: How Institutions and Cultural Repertoires Affect Health and Capabilities*, edited by Peter Hall and Michèle Lamont. Toronto: Canadian Institute for Advanced Research.

Tajfel, Henri, and J. C. Turner. 1985. "The Social Identity Theory of Intergroup Behavior." In *Psychology of Intergroup Relations*, edited by Stephen and William G. Austin Worchel. Chicago, Ill.: Nelson-Hall.

Tyson, Karolyn, William Darity, and Domini R. Castellino. 2005. "It's Not 'a Black Thing': Understanding the Burden of Acting White and Other Dilemmas of High Achievement." *American Sociological Review* 70(4): 582–605.

Valentine, Charles A. 1968. *Culture and Poverty: Critique and Counter-Proposals*. Chicago, Ill.: University of Chicago Press.

Waller, Maureen R. 2002. *My Baby's Father: Unmarried Parents and Paternal Responsibility*. Ithaca, N.Y.: Cornell University Press.

Wilson, William Julius. 1987. *The Truly Disadvantaged: The Inner City, the Underclass, and Public Policy*. Chicago, Ill.: University of Chicago Press.

———. 1996. *When Work Disappears: The World of the New Urban Poor*. New York: Random House.

Winship, Christopher, and Jenny Berrien. 2003. "Should We Have Faith in the Churches? The Ten-Point Coalition's Effect on Boston's Youth Violence." In *Guns, Crime, and Punishment in America*, edited by Bernard Harcourt. New York: New York University Press.

Young, Alford A., Jr. 2004. *The Minds of Marginalized Black Men: Making Sense of Mobility, Opportunity, and Future Life Chances*. Princeton, N.J.: Princeton University Press.

Part II

Nonracial Explanations for Racial Disparities in Poverty

Chapter 5

How Educational Inequality Develops

George Farkas

Academic achievement—schooling completed and degrees attained, as well as the skills and capabilities associated with these credentials—is an important determinant of socioeconomic success. Few if any personal characteristics are more strongly and positively related to an individual's later occupational attainment, employment, earnings, home ownership, health, and other measures of a successful life. In addition, as the United States' and other national economies have evolved, technological innovation and globalization have advanced, and labor union strength has declined, the economic return to academic achievement has increased. Thus, for example, in inflation-adjusted, 1999 dollars, the average American male high school dropout earned $13.61 an hour in 1973, and $9.78 an hour in 1999, a decline of 28 percent. By contrast, the earnings of workers with an advanced degree (beyond college) increased by more than 20 percent during the same period (Krueger 2003, 4). A given educational achievement gap between two individuals leads to a larger earnings gap today than it did in the past.

This trend has been particularly disadvantageous for race-ethnic groups such as African Americans and Latinos, whose academic achievement has historically lagged behind that of whites. At the same time, it has benefited Asians, whose academic achievement has equaled and in some areas surpassed that of whites. The great importance of racial-ethnic academic achievement gaps for understanding racial-ethnic earnings gaps is illustrated by the finding that the earnings gap between African American and white men can be fully explained by a calculation that accounts for, among other variables, the educational credentials (years of schooling completed) and cognitive skills (test score) gaps between these groups. Here, the 40 percent of the black-white hourly wage gap accounted for by the cognitive skills gap is four times the size of the portion accounted for by the credentials gap (Farkas and Vicknair 1996, table 1). Thus, the study of racial-ethnic gaps

FIGURE 5.1   /   Predicted Vocabulary, Whites and Blacks, by Black Socioeconomic Status

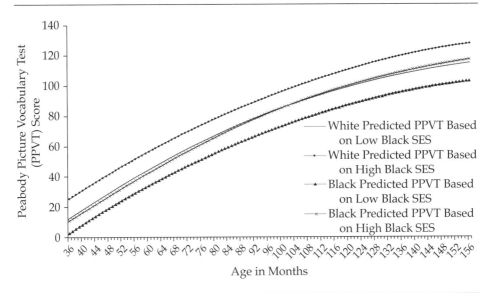

Legend:
—— White Predicted PPVT Based on Low Black SES
—•— White Predicted PPVT Based on High Black SES
—▲— Black Predicted PPVT Based on Low Black SES
—×— Black Predicted PPVT Based on High Black SES

Y-axis: Peabody Picture Vocabulary Test (PPVT) Score

X-axis: Age in Months

Source: Reprinted from *Social Science Research* 33(3), George Farkas and Kurt Beron, "The Detailed Age Trajectory of Oral Vocabulary Knowledge: Differences by Class and Race," pp. 464–97, copyright 2004, with permission from Elsevier.

in academic achievement—test scores and credentials—is central to understanding poverty and income differentials across these groups in America today.

Approximately fifty years after the Brown decision, forty years after the Coleman report, and during a period of intense discussion of *No Child Left Behind*, concern with these gaps is hardly new. What *is* new is recent evidence on the timing and sources of these disparities in the early lives and school careers of children, an example of which is presented in figure 5.1 (originally published in Farkas and Beron 2004). This shows typical growth profiles of oral vocabulary knowledge from three to thirteen years of age for four groups of children—whites and blacks from low and high socioeconomic status (SES) backgrounds. These have been calculated from a regression analysis that separated the effects of race and SES on both the starting value (score at three years) and growth rate of vocabulary knowledge from three to thirteen.

The results show that race and SES each have a distinct effect on oral vocabulary knowledge, with much of these effects occurring before age three. That is, by thirty-six months of age, for two children of otherwise identical SES, the white child has significantly greater oral vocabulary knowledge, and for two children of the same race-ethnicity, the higher SES child has a significantly larger vocabulary, with these effects being of roughly similar magnitude. Thus, the three-year vocabulary knowledge of a lower SES white child is similar to that of a higher SES black child, and the vocabulary gap between a higher SES white child and a lower SES black child is large indeed. The overall effect on white-black differences is increased by the fact that white children tend to be concentrated toward higher SES values, while black children cluster toward lower SES values. Further, these race and SES vocabulary gaps observed at age three remain essentially unchanged through to age thirteen. That is, distinct class and race gaps in oral vocabulary knowledge—a powerful predictor of success in reading and academics generally (Whitehurst and Lonigan 2002; Durham et al. 2007)—date back to before children reach their third birthday.

By contrast, until recently, most nationally representative datasets focused on high school students, at ages beyond the right-hand edge of figure 5.1. Now, however, that data are available covering preschool (the left side of figure 5.1) and elementary school (the middle portion of figure 5.1), we are learning that the roots of unequal outcomes in high school are found in the preschool and early elementary years. The resulting new understanding of the early development of race-ethnic and SES inequalities in educational achievement is the focus of this chapter.

FAMILY RESOURCES AND STRESSORS

A variety of theoretical perspectives, each with its own disciplinary tradition, have been employed to understand how race-ethnicity and low SES or poverty status affect children's schooling outcomes. However, though each of these perspectives has its own particular emphasis, all are essentially grounded in a concern for the resources that parents have available for parenting, and the life stressors that make successful parenting difficult to achieve. These resources and stressors include those stemming from educational, social, economic, cultural, and psychological factors. In general, families with higher social status (measured by education, income, and occupation) and those embedded in stronger networks of social relationships have more resources available for parenting, experience fewer social stressors, and can use their resources to successfully ameliorate the effects of stressors that may occur (McLoyd 1998; Ripke and Huston 2005). By contrast, families closer to the bottom of status hierarchies, and those embedded in fewer or weaker networks of social relationships, have fewer resources available for parenting and dealing with stress, but experience more powerful negative stressors in their daily lives. The evidence shows that families with such multiple risk factors (cumulative disadvantages) are the ones whose children have the least successful school careers and consequently the worst life cycle outcomes.

Family economic status is a common beginning point for analyzing this situation. Economists tend to emphasize the parental economic resources available to be invested in the human capital of their children (Becker 1981). Psychologists and sociologists, as well as some more eclectic economists, have also focused on income, but have been more interested in its absence—families in poverty—as a determinant of the daily life stressors that make parenting difficult (McLoyd 1990; Duncan and Brooks-Gunn 1997; Mayer 1997).

A second resource is whether the child's parents are a coresident married couple. Single-parent households not only tend to have fewer financial resources than two-parent households, but they also have half the time and other parental non-monetary resources (such as social contacts) available for caregiving. It is therefore not surprising that, after statistically adjusting for the effects of other variables, children raised in single-parent households tend to have less positive outcomes than children from two-parent families (McLanahan and Sandefur 1994; McLanahan 1997; Carlson and Corcoran 2001; McLanahan, Donahue, and Haskins 2005).

A third resource is the parents' education level, and related to this, their cognitive skill level, income, and wealth. Well-educated parents tend to have greater financial resources to use in parenting and coping with the stresses of daily life. They also tend to focus more on promoting the cognitive and educational attainment of their children, as well as the skills and knowledge necessary to do so (Lareau 2003). Further, their children are likely to inherit above average cognitive ability from them. Essentially all multivariate empirical studies have found that parents' educational performance and attainment are strongly and positively associated with the performance and attainment of their children (Jencks 1979; Duncan and Brooks-Gunn 1997; Entwisle, Alexander, and Olson 1997; Jencks and Phillips 1998; Duncan and Magnuson 2005).

In addition, parental household structure, education, income, and occupation are correlated with other variables that tend to magnify their effects. Thus, single parents who are high school dropouts and earn little are also more likely to be teenage parents, to suffer from inadequate health care, to be depressed and to have other psychological, behavioral, and health-related problems, to live in unsafe neighborhoods, and to send their children to substandard schools (McLoyd 1990, 1998). When these and related risk factors cumulate, the results for children can be devastating.

These factors are relatively exogenous to parenting. They provide the setting within which parents' time and effort can be directed to help their children develop those cognitive skills and behavioral habits that lead to success in school and subsequent employment. However, different theoretical traditions have emphasized different aspects of parenting as being more or less critical to children's development.

Perhaps the most widely used perspective builds on the work of Robert Bradley and Bettye Caldwell (1984a, 1984b) to conceptualize and measure parenting along three dimensions—the learning environment, the physical environment, and the emotional warmth provided in the home. An additional perspective investigates parental social support, depression, and active behavioral coping (Moos, Cronkite, and Finney 1986). The learning environment and emotional warmth in the home exert positive effects on children's cognitive development, and the learning environment and parents' active behavioral coping reduce child externalizing behavior problems. When included in multivariate studies, these and related variables have also been found to account for large shares of the effects of poverty on child outcomes (Phillips, Crouse, and Ralph 1998; Phillips et al. 1998; Duncan, Brooks-Gunn, and Klebanov 1994; Guo and Harris 2000; Farkas and Beron 2004; Brooks-Gunn and Markman 2005).

Variants of this perspective typically focus on one or another detailed aspect of parenting. One such perspective, derived from developmental psychology and research on the early development of literacy skills, stresses parental oral language and its use with children. Betty Hart and Todd Risley (1995, 1999) showed that better educated parents converse far more with children between one and three years, using a much richer vocabulary, than do less well-educated parents. As a consequence, by age three, the children of the better educated parents had developed far more extensive vocabularies. These social class differences in vocabulary are maintained as the children age from three years to thirteen (Farkas and Beron 2004). Preschool oral vocabulary, as well as other preschool oral language skills, are the primary determinants of reading success in early elementary school (Whitehurst and Lonigan 2002; NICHD Early Child Care Research Network 2005a; Brooks-Gunn and Markman 2005). In addition, early elementary school success—along both cognitive and behavioral dimensions—has schooling effects that carry through to the end of high school, and beyond (Ensminger and Slusarcik 1992; Alexander, Entwisle, and Horsey 1997; Entwisle, Alexander and Olson 1997; Duncan et al. 1998; McLeod and Kaiser 2004).

Research has also shown that higher parental SES, particularly higher levels of education, is positively associated with higher levels of early mathematics skills in their children (Downey, von Hippel, and Broh 2004; Duncan and Magnuson 2005; Farkas and Hibel 2008). Whether this is a result of specific instruction provided by better-educated parents has yet to be ascertained.

In a different, but related, research tradition, Annette Lareau (2003) has reported on how higher SES parents schedule their children for a great many activities, and in general focus on the "concerted cultivation" of their children's skills, abilities, and behaviors. The material to be inculcated is wide ranging, including such disparate subjects as the names for and uses of colors, objects, foods, shapes, numbers, the attitudes to have towards, and the ways to behave, in a wide variety of public social situations, and so on (for supporting quantitative evidence, see Farkas and Hibel 2008; Bodovski and Farkas forthcoming). Lareau observes that by contrast with higher SES parents, lower SES parents view their role as permitting their children to "accomplish natural growth" (2003, 3), which involves far less stimulation of specific, school-relevant skills and behaviors. This connects to the cultural capital research tradition, where higher SES parents transfer school-relevant skills, habits, and styles to their children (Swidler 1986; Lamont and Lareau 1988; Farkas et al. 1990; Farkas 1996; Lamont and Small, chapter 4, this volume).

Finally, another related research tradition demonstrates that the skills and behaviors that higher SES and two-parent families inculcate in their preschool children transfer almost immediately to placement into higher ability groups in elementary school. This in turn raises the student's school engagement and academic performance, setting her or his academic trajectory on a steeper growth

FIGURE 5.2 / Model of the Academic Achievement Process

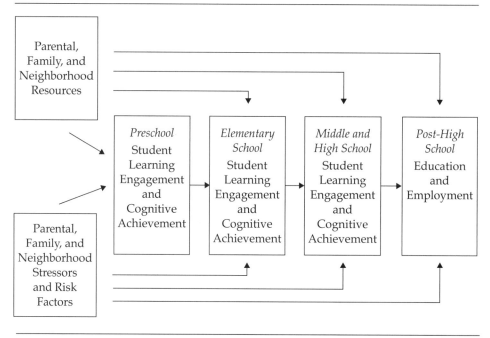

Source: Author's compilation.

slope (Alexander, Entwisle, and Dauber 1993; Pallas et al. 1994; Marks 2000; Carbonaro 2005; Tach and Farkas 2006). Once ability and curriculum group placement are in place to reinforce the higher academic performance and school engagement of more advantaged students, the gap between their performance and that of less advantaged students continues to increase as students move to higher schooling levels (Kerckhoff and Glennie 1999).

Figure 5.2 summarizes the resulting theoretical perspective. Parental and family resources, combined with family and neighborhood stressors and risk factors, determine the child's learning engagement and cognitive achievement during each stage—preschool, elementary, middle, and high school. Learning engagement and cognitive achievement during each of these periods also determine these variables during the one that follows. These cumulate into trajectories of academic achievement, so that, by the end of high school, students from more advantaged backgrounds are advancing much more successfully toward college, advanced degrees, and highly placed and rewarding employment. The model emphasizes the student's engagement with learning in school, as well as actual achievement—measured by test scores—in grades K through 12, because studies have shown that both are highly correlated with course grades during this time period, and that engagement, achievement, and course grades are the primary determinants of high school graduation, college attendance and graduation, the achievement of subsequent educational credentials, and labor market success (Jencks 1979; Farkas 1996, 2003; Entwisle, Alexander and Olson 1997; Rosenbaum 2001).

INEQUALITY IN FAMILY RESOURCES AND STRESS

Children from different racial-ethnic backgrounds are, on average, raised in households with enormously different resources undergoing enormously different levels of stress. These are in many cases so different, and are correlated with so many additional unmeasured variables, as to render our main goal—understanding the determinants of academic achievement differences across race-ethnic groups—quite difficult.

Table 5.1 summarizes some of these differences in family circumstances, using Early Childhood Longitudinal Study, Kindergarten Cohort (ECLS-K) data for children enrolled in kindergarten in 1998. Among Asians, only 10 percent of children are being raised in a single-parent household. Among whites, 15 percent are. Among Hispanics, the proportion rises to 27 percent, and among African Americans to 54 percent. These are large intergroup differences in a characteristic that is negatively correlated with social class, is a powerful indicator of living in poverty, and has been found to have significant negative effects on child outcomes (McLanahan and Sandefur 1994; McLanahan 1997; McLanahan, Donahue, and Haskins 2005). It is perhaps not surprising that the rank order of groups on this characteristic—Asians, whites, Hispanics, and blacks—is also the ordering we shall observe on many child outcomes.

Table 5.1 also shows that fully 42 percent of African American children are being raised in poverty. For Hispanics, the figure is 37 percent, and for whites, 10 percent. Social class is a composite measure taking into account parents' levels of education, occupation, and income. It is constructed to have a mean of zero and a standard deviation of one. As was the case for two-parent families, we find that Asians have the highest average score on this variable, 0.5, with whites coming second, at 0.2. Hispanics average –0.4, and blacks average –0.5. Thus the Asian average is a full standard deviation above that for African Americans, with each group distributed around the group average. Of these distributions, the most spread out is the Asians, with larger shares at both the highest and lowest SES levels. The Hispanic is the narrowest distribution, relatively tightly distributed around its mean. It is not surprising that Asian students, with a higher average SES and percentage of two-parent families than whites, outperform whites in school. Nor is it surprising that, with much lower SES and percentage of two-parent families, African American and Hispanic students have lower school performance than whites.

A major disadvantage for the children of immigrants is the likelihood that their parents are non-English speaking. This is a major challenge to parents' ability to prepare children for and assist them with schoolwork. Significant shares of this

TABLE 5.1 / Disparities in Family Circumstances When Schooling Begins, Selected
Estimates

	White	Black	Hispanic	Asian
Percentage single parent[a]	15	54	27	10
Percentage experiencing poverty[b]	10	42	37	
Average socioeconomic status	0.2	−0.5	−0.4	0.5
(standard deviation)[a]	(1.0)	(1.0)	(0.9)	(1.1)
Percentage non-English household[a]	1	1	31	51
Percentage mother high school dropout[b]	7	18	35	
Percentage teen mother[b]	10	22	19	
Percentage mother depressed[b]	11	20	13	
Percentage low birth weight[b]	6	15	8	
Percentage four or more hardships[b]	4	29	18	
Average number of books[a]	93	40	53	56
Percentage own home computer[a]	66	33	42	65

Source: [a] Lee and Burkam (2002); [b] Duncan and Magnuson (2005).

characteristic are found only among Hispanics (30.7 percent) and Asians (50.5
percent), and can be expected to depress the performance of children from these
groups. Reflecting the high share of immigrants from less developed countries
where educational attainment is low, 35 percent of Hispanic mothers did not complete high school. For African Americans the figure is 18 percent, and for whites it
is 7 percent. Twenty-two percent of African Americans were teenage mothers. For
Hispanics the figure is 19 percent, and for whites, 10 percent.

Physical and mental health differences are also important. As table 5.1 shows,
fully 20 percent of African American mothers have symptoms of depression. For
Hispanics the figure is 13 percent, and for whites, 11 percent. Fifteen percent of
the African American children had low birth weight. This was true of 8 percent of
Hispanics and 6 percent of whites. Low birth weight is associated with health,
cognitive, and behavior problems, and increased chances of learning and emotional disabilities (Reichman 2005). In a wide-ranging review, Janet Currie (2005)
reported on a number of childhood health conditions that likely explain portions
of the lower school readiness of low-income and African American children compared to middle-income and white children. These include ADHD, asthma, lead
poisoning, chronic tooth decay, iron deficiency, and maternal depression. Each of
these conditions is more prevalent among low-income than middle class and
African American than white children, and each has been shown to reduce school
readiness, net of other variables.

When indicators of family hardship multiply, so do the problems experienced
by children. Greg Duncan and Katherine Magnuson (2005) considered the following list of hardships—mother high school dropout, single parent, no or low-pres-
tige job, low-quality neighborhood, three or more siblings, residential instability,
spanking, few children's books, low birth weight, teen mother, and mother depressed—and tabulated, separately by race, the percentage of children experienc-

ing four or more of these. Overall, 29 percent—almost a third—of African American children experienced four or more hardships; comparable figures for Hispanics and whites were 18 percent and 4 percent, respectively. Because the presence of multiple family hardships is one of the most powerful predictors of early school unreadiness (Duncan and Magnuson 2005; Farkas and Hibel 2008), we can expect particularly large readiness gaps among African American children, compared to whites.

Also included in this table are two measures of household material resources likely to impact the child's preparation for, and performance in, school. The first is the number of children's books in the home and available for the child to use. The highest average is found in white households, 93.1 books. Next come Asians, with 55.8, and Hispanics, with 52.5. For African Americans, the average is 39.6. Similarly, 65.7 percent of whites own a computer, 64.8 percent of Asians, 41.5 percent of Hispanics, and 32.9 percent of African Americans. Of course, these are very imperfect measures of the relative resources and effort that parents devote to helping their child prepare to succeed in school. However, they are likely to be positively correlated with those detailed aspects of parent-child interaction and the home environment that have been shown to positively affect school readiness and performance. These include the parents' vocabulary and grammar, and the nature of parent-child verbal and nonverbal interaction. They also include the amount of time the child is read to and the amount of formal and informal instruction the child receives from the parent and other caregivers. Variables such as these have been entered into multivariate regression models and shown to exert unique effects on child outcomes, after other variables are controlled (Hart and Risley 1995, 1999; Duncan and Brooks-Gunn 1997; Jencks and Phillips 1998; Lareau 2003; Hoff 2003; Farkas and Beron 2004; NICHD Early Child Care Research Network 2005b; Brooks-Gunn and Markman 2005; Farkas and Hibel 2008).

In addition to cognitive instruction, behavioral socialization is also important. Indeed, when combined with cognitive skills, these behavioral habits constitute important aspects of the child's cultural and human capital (Farkas 1996, 2003). For a child to be ready to succeed at school, he or she must be able to sit still, pay attention, and concentrate on a task without disturbing others. Some households are much more successful than others in inculcating these skills, habits, and behaviors, and they are the same households that have more abundant parental resources of time, skills, and money (Campbell and von Stauffenberg 2008).

THE PRESCHOOL PERIOD

During the preschool period, unequal parental resources and behaviors produce unequal cognitive and behavioral outcomes for children. The process begins as early as the end of the first year of life, when the child typically utters her or his first words. Between twelve and thirty-six months of age, children work to establish their place within the family conversational culture. They begin barely able to speak, but two years later emerge as full-fledged conversational participants, able to "hold the floor" in conversation with other household members. By this time, they have internalized family vocabulary and speech patterns, as well as the habits of thought and behavior associated with these, which vary enormously by social class background. Central to differential parenting by SES background are the vocabulary and oral language skills parents possess, and their use of these resources with their children. Hart and Risley (1995, 1999) showed that professional parents had addressed more than 30 million words to their children by the time the children were three years old, whereas for low income parents, the comparable figure was below 10 million. Further, better educated parents used a more extensive vocabulary with their children, and involved them in more fully interactive, interrogatory, and direct instructional conversations. As a consequence, Hart and Risley found that by thirty-six months, children differed markedly in their spoken vocabulary, those with professional parents using more than twice as large a vocabulary as children from low-income families (for further evidence, see Hoff 2003). Farkas and Beron (2004) extended this research by using Peabody Picture Vocabulary Test (PPVT) scores from the National Longitudinal Survey of Youth 1979 (NLSY79) data to estimate oral vocabulary growth curves for African American and white children as they aged from three to thirteen. As already shown in figure 5.1, the resulting curves, beginning at three years, match up nicely, by class and race, to those reported by Hart and Risley (for discussion, see Farkas 2004a). Taken together, these studies provide strong evidence of the very early etiology of oral vocabulary differences across class and race groups.

Much research has focused on those preschool and kindergarten skills that best predict the student's success in early elementary school reading performance. The most important are oral vocabulary size, knowledge of the alphabet, letter-sound linkages, and phonological processing skills (sensitivity to, and manipulation of the sounds in spoken words). Stronger skills on the latter two dimensions are often associated with a larger vocabulary size, so that the more extensive and complex linguistic environment of higher SES households serves as a powerful determinant of early school success for these children (Whitehurst and Lonigan 2002; Durham et al. 2007; NICHD Child Care Network 2005a). This language gap between whites and blacks fully explains the reading gap between these groups (Beron and Farkas 2004).

Class and race differences in children's preschool outcomes also occur on the behavioral side. Research has found a greater incidence of child behavior problems reported by lower SES and African American mothers. This is at least partially because these families experience greater adversity and typically have fewer resources to cope with these difficulties, leading to less successful parenting. It may also be associated with the greater use of physical discipline in these families (McLoyd 1990, 1998; Duncan, Brooks-Gunn, and Klebanov1994; McLeod and Nonnemaker 2000; Bradley et al. 2001; McLoyd and Smith 2002), though this issue is controversial (for arguments and evidence that physical discipline is less damaging to African American than to white children, see Deater-Deckard, Dodge, and Sorbring 2005). Low-income families also tend to employ lower quality or a greater quantity of nonmaternal childcare, and a study by the NICHD Early Child

Care Research Network (2003) found more behavior problems in preschool children who experienced such nonmaternal childcare. These researchers also found that, net of such child care, lower SES and African American children show greater behavior problems in the preschool period. These findings may depend on whether such information is collected from a preschool caregiver, a kindergarten teacher, or the child's parent. Douglas Downey and Shana Pribesh (2004) find that, in ECLS-K data, white kindergarten teachers report more behavior problems among black students than black kindergarten teachers do. However, the NICHD study does not report results that control the race of the caregiver or teacher.

Thus, because family child rearing culture is affected by social class, and because different racial-ethnic groups have very different social class distributions, it is not surprising that children from these groups arrive at kindergarten with very different levels of cognitive and behavioral readiness.

SCHOOL READINESS

The cognitive skills that teachers want students to have at the beginning of kindergarten include, on the pre-reading side, oral vocabulary knowledge, letter-sound knowledge, and phonological awareness, particularly the ability to identify the beginning sounds in spoken words. On the pre-mathematics side they include knowledge of shapes, numbers, and simple counting (for a discussion of each, see Farkas 2004b). The NLSY79 and Infant Health and Development Program (IHDP) surveys administered vocabulary tests to preschool children in the 1980s and 1990s. The ECLS-K administered tests of these skills to a national sample of children entering kindergarten in 1998. The results showed that, on average, the highest scores were earned by Asians, followed in order by whites, African Americans, and Hispanics. The magnitudes of the racial gaps are shown in table 5.2.

The gaps are measured in standard deviation units, with whites as the reference category. The largest gaps are found for oral language vocabulary, with the black-white gap being more than one standard deviation. The ECLS-K reading test shows African Americans at 0.40 standard deviation and Hispanics at 0.43 standard deviation below whites. (The Hispanic gap would be larger, but students with very weak oral English language skills were excluded from testing.) Asians begin kindergarten with higher reading and mathematics scores than whites.

Where behavior is concerned, whites score approximately 0.4 standard deviation higher than African Americans on scales measuring approaches to learning and self-control, and 0.3 standard deviation lower on scales measuring externalizing behavior problems. The two groups are close to one another on internalizing behavior problems. Among these behaviors, teachers' judgments of students' approaches to learning—including keeps belongings organized, eagerness to learn new things, works independently, easily adapts to changes in routine, persists in completing tasks, and pays attention well—is the most important, because when

TABLE 5.2 / Reading, Mathematics, and Behavior Gaps When School Begins

	White-Black	White-Hispanic	White-Asian
PPVT-R, NLSY79	1.15		
PPVT-R, IHDP	1.63		
Reading test, ECLS-K	0.40	0.43	−0.34
Math test, ECLS-K[a]	0.64	0.72	−0.15
Approaches to learning, ECLS-K	0.36	0.21	
Self-control, ECLS-K	0.38	0.13	
Externalizing behavior, ECLS-K	−0.31	0.01	
Internalizing behavior, ECLS-K	−0.06	−0.05	

Source: Rock and Stenner (2005); [a] Fryer and Levitt (2004).
Note: Selected estimates in standard deviation units. PPVT-R: Peabody Picture Vocabulary Test—Revised. NLSY79: National Longitudinal Survey of Youth 1979. IHDP: Infant Health and Development Program. ECLS-K: Early Childhood Longitudinal Study—Kindergarten Cohort.

the student behavior variables (approaches to learning, internalizing and externalizing behavior problems, and self control) are included together in an equation to predict later achievement, only the variable measuring approaches to learning shows strong effects (Tach and Farkas 2006; Morgan et al. forthcoming). Further, although Downey and Pribesh (2004) show that the white-black gap on the externalizing behavior scale is significantly higher when the teacher is white rather than black, they find that the gap in approaches to learning is the same whether the teacher is white or black. (In separate calculations, I have found the same result.) There is also a white-Hispanic gap, but of smaller magnitude, on the approaches to learning and self-control scales. The white-Hispanic gap on approaches to learning is explained by SES differences between the groups. However, this is not the case for the white-black gap. After controlling SES, the white-black gap declines only from 0.39 to 0.28 standard deviation, and remains statistically significant (Tach and Farkas 2006, table 4).

Table 5.3 examines race gaps in these behaviors in greater detail, using teacher's responses to three items from the approaches to learning scale—persists at tasks, seems eager to learn, and pays attention.

We see that 81 percent of Asian kindergartners are rated by their teachers as persisting at tasks. Comparable figures are 75 percent for whites, 67 percent for Hispanics, and 61 percent for blacks. Similar race gaps are observed for seems eager to learn and pays attention. These emotional and behavioral maturity measures—key features of school engagement—are quite important for success in school. Indeed, in multivariate growth models I have estimated with the ECLS-K data, the lower performance of blacks compared to whites on these measures of learning-related behavior explains a very significant share of the widening white-black achievement gap as students move up through the elementary school grades.

Let us summarize what we have learned about race gaps in school readiness. On the cognitive side, African Americans and Hispanics begin kindergarten ap-

TABLE 5.3 / Percentage of Students Demonstrating Specific Learning-Related Behaviors When Schooling Begins

	White	Black	Hispanic	Asian
Persists at tasks	75	61	67	81
Seems eager to learn	79	66	72	82
Pays attention	70	56	62	70

Source: West, Denton, and Reaney (2001, table 7).

proximately 0.5 standard deviation below whites and Asians in reading and mathematics. On scales measuring approaches to learning, African Americans begin approximately 0.4 standard deviation below whites; the comparable figure for Hispanics is 0.2. In a comprehensive previous multivariate study, Meredith Phillips et al. (1998) concluded that for blacks, the early cognitive skills gap of 0.5 standard deviation grows to a full standard deviation by twelfth grade, so that approximately half of the final gap occurs in the preschool period, and the other half occurs after students begin schooling. In the following section, I focus on the magnitudes and determinants of achievement growth trajectories after students begin their schooling.

ACHIEVEMENT GROWTH

Table 5.4 shows the magnitude of the reading, mathematics, and science achievement gaps, in standard deviation units, that are observed for the different race-ethnicity groups by the spring of third grade. These have been calculated from the ECLS-K data. The largest gaps are for African Americans: the black score minus the white score is –0.7 standard deviation in reading, –0.9 standard deviation in mathematics, and –1.0 standard deviation in science. By contrast, Hispanics show stronger achievement growth than blacks during this period, so that their gaps with whites are only about half of these magnitudes. Gaps for Asians are much smaller, and are essentially insignificant for reading and mathematics.

How important, in practical terms, are these gaps? One way to gain some perspective on this is to look at achievement on the specific skill measures underlying the composite scales used in the ECLS-K data collection. One such measure is mastery of multiplication and division, from the mathematics assessment. By the spring of third grade, 84 percent of whites, 83 percent of Asians, and 75 percent of Hispanics had achieved such mastery but only 58 percent of African Americans had done so (Rathbun and West 2004). These are the sorts of important gaps in practical skills, occurring for higher level skills at higher grade levels, which underlie the important white-black and white-Hispanic achievement gaps.

Analyzing the ECLS-K data for the same children as they age from the fall of kindergarten through spring of first grade, Douglas Downey, Paul von Hippel, and Beckett Broh (2004) showed that attending school does matter for cognitive

TABLE 5.4 / Reading, Mathematics, and Science Gaps with White Students in Spring, Third Grade (Standard Deviation Units)

	Black	Hispanic	Asian
Reading	−0.70	−0.35	−0.05
Mathematics	−0.89	−0.39	−0.06
Science	−1.04	−0.52	−0.21

Source: Rathbun and West (2004, tables A-4, A-5, A-7, A-8).

achievement. They did so by using multivariate growth models to measure the rate of student academic gains separately for the nine months during which school is in session and for the three summer months when it isn't. All students learn significantly more when school is in session than during the summer. Additionally, individual achievement inequalities tend to increase less when school is in session than during the summer; that is, they are decreased by schooling. As for trends in race-ethnic group achievement gaps as children age, these calculations show that, when school is in session, between approximately September and June, these gaps tend to increase for blacks, decrease for Asians, and change little for Hispanics.

The finding that the black-white cognitive skills gap is not only significant when schooling begins, but also widens substantially as children move up through the grade levels, was first reported by Meredith Phillips, James Crouse, and John Ralph (1998), utilizing a variety of data sets. The ECLS-K calculations presented by Downey et al. further corroborate this result. Both sets of authors also report that the reasons for this finding are somewhat mysterious—most variables show little ability to explain the increasing gap. Yet some variables are obvious candidates for this task. To learn successfully, students need adequate basic skills, a good quantity and quality of instruction, an appropriate level of attentiveness and effort, and parental support. Yet, compared to whites, African American students begin school with lower basic skills and lower evaluations on attentiveness and effort. Their families typically have much lower SES, and they typically go to lower quality schools. At least some of these factors likely account for the lower gains of African American students during grades K through 12. However, Downey and his colleagues report that little of this increasing white-black gap is explained by school-level variables. Further, as Katerina Bodovski and George Farkas (2007) reported, black kindergartners are not disadvantaged by the instruction they receive. Indeed, because full day kindergarten is more common in schools with a high percentage of African American students, these students actually receive, on average, more hours of instruction than white students. An area where school structure does contribute to the white-black gap is ability grouping. Laura Tach and George Farkas (2006), analyzing ECLS-K data, found that, because of the lower reading and mathematics achievement with which black students enter kindergarten, they are placed into lower ability groups than whites, and this placement contributes to the widening white-black achievement gap as students age. Further, in ongoing analyses of the ECLS-K data, I have found that the lower school engagement (approaches to learning) ratings that African American students receive from their teachers explain a significant share of their lower test score growth between kindergarten and third grade.

What about immigrant status and its effect on school achievement and ethnic and racial achievement gaps? This issue can be examined using the National Assessment of Educational Progress (NAEP) test score data collected by the National Center for Education Statistics. These data include information on whether the student is a second-language learner, a major handicap that recent immigrants to the United States often experience. Table 5.5 shows average reading and mathematics test scores for fourth and eighth grade public school students sorted according to their race-ethnicity and second-language learner status in 2005, and the performance gap between each group and white native English speakers. There were too few second language twelfth graders to calculate reliable performance scores for them.

Among white fourth graders, the second-language learner gap is 27 points in reading, and 17 points in mathematics, a pattern consistent with the fact that reading is more language-intensive than mathematics. Among black fourth graders who are proficient in English, we find reading and mathematics gaps of 29 and 26 points, and the gaps for English-proficient Hispanic fourth graders are slightly more than half these magnitudes. When English-language proficiency is not an issue, the greater average resources possessed by Hispanic families produce these differential outcomes. However, the achievement gaps for black second-language learners are similar to those for Hispanic second-language learners. In this case, the additional hardship of being a second-language learner appears to be larger for Hispanics than for blacks. Overall, there is a performance decrement associated with being black or Hispanic, and an additional decrement associated with being a second-language learner. The results are consistent with our overall model of family and individual resource and risk factors—the fewer the resources and the greater the risks, the lower the school performance.

Asian fourth graders with no English deficit show a slight advantage over whites in both reading and mathematics. Differences from the slight Asian disadvantage in table 5.4 are due to different grade levels, years, and databases. This is not surprising, particularly given that, as shown in table 5.1, Asians have a higher average SES and a higher percentage of two-parent families than whites. However, as with the other groups, Asian second-language learners suffer performance deficits, although more in reading than in mathematics. In general, Asian and white second-language learners show quite similar performance levels.

Performance patterns for eighth graders are generally similar. However, particularly large performance gaps are observed for black and Hispanic second-language learners. These students, who, by eighth grade, have not mastered English, have likely missed a great deal of their education, or have been educated in less developed countries where the instructional level is significantly below that of the United States.

What about possible interactions between gender and race? It is typically found

TABLE 5.5 / Test Score Performance by Race-Ethnicity and Whether Student Is
Second-Language Learner

	Reading	Gap	Mathematics	Gap
Fourth grade (2005)				
White				
Second-language learner	201	27	229	17
Not second-language learner	228	—	246	—
Black				
Second-language learner	186	42	208	38
Not second-language learner	199	29	220	26
Hispanic				
Second-language learner	184	44	214	32
Not second-language learner	211	17	232	14
Asian				
Second-language learner	203	25	233	13
Not second-language learner	233	−5	255	−9
Eighth Grade (2005)				
White				
Second-language learner	239	31	261	17
Not second-language learner	270	—	288	—
Black				
Second-language learner	224	46	233	55
Not second-language learner	242	28	254	34
Hispanic				
Second-language learner	220	50	238	50
Not second-language learner	253	17	269	19
Asian				
Second-language learner	240	30	270	18
Not second-language learner	274	−4	299	−11

Source: Author's compilation from National Center for Education Statistics, NAEP Data, calculated for public school students using NAEP data explorer, downloaded on January 2, 2006,
from http://nces.gov/nationsreportcard/nde.

that girls perform better than boys in reading, a pattern that is reversed for mathematics. But do these gender gaps differ across race-ethnicity groups? This question is answered by table 5.6, which uses NAEP data to show the male-female test
score performance gap, separately for each race-ethnicity group.

We see that it is indeed the case that the gender gap favors girls in reading, and
boys in mathematics. However, the male advantage in mathematics is quite small,
whereas the female advantage in reading tends to be substantial across all race
and grade combinations. It is particularly large for twelfth grade whites, due to
the extraordinary high reading performance of twelfth-grade white girls. Al-

TABLE 5.6 / Male-Female Test Score Performance

	White	Black	Hispanic	Asian
Reading				
Fourth grade (2005)	–6	–10	–5	–7
Eighth grade (2005)	–11	–12	–8	–9
Twelfth grade (2005)	–15	–11	–11	–10
Mathematics				
Fourth grade (2005)	3	–1	–6	2
Eighth grade(2005)	1	–1	2	1
Twelfth grade (2000)	3	1	4	2

Source: Author's compilation from National Center for Education Statistics, NAEP Data, calculated for public school students using NAEP data explorer, downloaded on January 2, 2006, and May 14, 2007, from http://nces.gov/nationsreportcard/nde.

though these are simple gender differences, calculated without controlling other variables, multivariate results would likely be similar, because gender is uncorrelated with most other variables.

ACHIEVEMENT GAP TRENDS

Since publication of the papers in *The Black-White Test Score Gap* (Jencks and Phillips 1998), and even more strongly since passage of the No Child Left Behind (NCLB) Act in early 2002, unprecedented attention has been paid to the details of over-time trends in racial gaps in educational inequality. Since passage of the NCLB, most of the more than 16,000 local school districts in the United States have for the first time experienced strong pressures to narrow these gaps. Also, following a report of the National Research Council (Snow, Burns, and Griffin 1998), there has been a nationwide emphasis, led by the U.S. Department of Education, on the implementation of "evidence based reading instruction" in early elementary school. This has been accompanied by efforts to improve the school readiness instruction provided by Head Start and other preschool programs (Whitehurst and Massetti 2004). Are these efforts having any effect in narrowing the white-black and white-Hispanic achievement gaps for K through 12 students? Evidence toward an answer is provided in table 5.7, which is based on results for whites, blacks and Hispanics. Results for Asians were not reported in the historical trends analyses conducted by the National Center for Education Statistics (NCES).

The table reports the results of the long-term trends project conducted by the National Center for Education Statistics, using its uniformly scaled NAEP examination data in reading and mathematics, administered to representative national samples of students from 1973 to 2004. To provide scores that are comparable over time, the NCES has kept the test relatively unchanged since its inception. Nine-year-olds typically score in the 150 to 250 point range, thirteen-year-olds in the

TABLE 5.7   /   Test Score Performance Gaps (Compared with Whites), Historical Trends

	Age Nine		Age Thirteen		Age Seventeen	
	Black	Hispanic	Black	Hispanic	Black	Hispanic
Reading						
1975	35	34	36	30	52	41
1988	29	24	18	21	26	24
1990	35	28	21	24	29	22
1999	35	28	29	23	31	24
2004	26	21	22	24	29	29
Mathematics						
1973	35	23	46	35	40	33
1986	25	21	24	19	29	24
1990	27	21	27	22	21	26
1999	28	26	32	24	31	22
2004	23	18	27	23	28	24

Source: National Center for Education Statistics, NAEP data, Long-Term Trend Reading and Mathematics Assessments, downloaded on January 2, 2006, from http://nces.gov/nationsre portcard/nde.

200 to 300 point range, and seventeen-year-olds in the 250 to 350 point range. I summarize the trends in these scores for three periods: 1973 to 1988, 1988 to 1999, and 1999 to 2004.

Table 5.7 shows that during most of the 1970s and 1980s, the reading and mathematics gaps narrowed at all ages and for both blacks and Hispanics. For example, between 1975 and 1988, the white-black reading performance gap fell from 35 to 29 points among nine-year-olds, from 36 to 18 points among thirteen-year-olds, and from 52 to 26 points among seventeen-year-olds. Similar declines occurred for the white-black mathematics gap, and for the white-Hispanic gaps in each subject. Larry Hedges and Amy Nowell (1998) and David Grissmer, Ann Flanagan, and Stephanie Williamson (1998) undertook extensive analyses in an effort to identify the forces that helped narrow these gaps. Their efforts, however, were relatively fruitless. For example, demographic trends, such as those related to family characteristics, do not explain the trends. Thus far, no clear explanation for these declining white-black and white-Hispanic achievement gaps, supported by detailed data analysis, has emerged. One possibility is that there were at least some gains from school desegregation efforts during this period, but detailed regional analyses fail to connect these decisively to minority achievement (Grissmer, Flanagan, and Williamson 1998).

The 1990s tell a very different story. For both reading and mathematics, for both blacks and Hispanics, and for all age groups, the achievement gap with whites either remained unchanged, or increased somewhat. This is because black and Hispanic scores declined and white scores did not change. The reasons for this abrupt end to the positive trends of the 1970s and 1980s also remain a mystery. The only explanation that Grissmer, Flanagan, and Williamson (1998, 222–23) offered is that black teenage violence was at a particularly high level at the beginning of the 1990s (the period of the crack epidemic). However, it is doubtful that this explanation can explain relative achievement losses at all age groups, and among Hispanics as well as African Americans.

The five years from 1999 to 2004 tell yet another story. As described by the NAEP long-term trend data in table 5.7, achievement gaps began narrowing again after 1999, most strongly and ubiquitously for nine-year-olds, where the trend is observed for both African Americans and Hispanics in both reading and mathematics. African American thirteen-year-olds also narrowed the gap in both reading and mathematics, but Hispanic thirteen-year-olds did not. Finally, among seventeen-year-olds, blacks showed small gains in reading and mathematics. Hispanics did not gain; in fact they appear to have lost ground.

However, there is ambiguity about these findings. In particular, the period-specific NAEP scores (a different set of tests than the NAEP long-term trend data) show little closing of the racial achievement gaps between 2003 and 2005. This has occasioned much debate about whether NCLB led to progress in closing the gaps. One of the few things we can be sure about is that these debates will continue into the foreseeable future.

INTERVENTION PROGRAMS

NCLB aims to improve school performance for all K through 12 students nationwide. Although it contains provisions and policies focused on narrowing achievement gaps for groups defined by race-ethnicity, it can have no effect on the gaps already in place when students begin kindergarten. Narrowing these gaps is the task of compensatory preschool intervention programs. Head Start is the only such program implemented on a large scale.

However, there is evidence that, since its inception in 1966, Head Start has not had a strong enough emphasis on instruction, and that as a result it has achieved at best only modest cognitive gains for participants (Whitehurst and Massetti 2004). Perhaps the best evidence on current magnitudes of Head Start effect is provided by the recent Head Start Impact Study, a designed experiment in which some low-income students were randomly assigned to Head Start but others were not.

The impacts on four-year-olds are shown in table 5.8. We see that of six standardized tests, Head Start had no significant effect on three. For the other three, it did have a significant positive effect, but with an effect size of about 0.2. This means that the program raised students' performance by .2 of a standard deviation on each of these tests. Since preschool white-black cognitive performance gaps are much larger than this, these effects can, at best, narrow the gaps only modestly for three of the tests, and not at all for the other three. Head Start effects

TABLE 5.8 / Significant Effects and Effect Sizes for Four-Year-Olds, Head Start Impact Study, June 2005

Test Scores	
Woodcock-Johnson letter-word ID	.22
Letter naming	.24
McCarthy Draw-A-Design	NS
Woodcock-Johnson spelling	.16
PPVT vocabulary	NS
PPVT color naming	NS
Problem behaviors	
Total behavior problems	NS
Hyperactive behavior	NS
Aggressive behavior	NS
Withdrawn behavior	NS
Social skills and approaches to learning	NS
Social competencies	NS

Source: Head Start Impact Study, June 2005, downloaded on December 1, 2005, from http://www .acf.hhs.gov/programs/opre/hs/impact_study/.
NS = Not significant

will have to increase substantially in size and scope if the program is to substantially narrow white-black and white-Hispanic preschool academic readiness. Unfortunately, this is unlikely to occur as long as Head Start continues to have no national instructional curriculum, and to be viewed primarily as an employment program for relatively unskilled adults in low-income neighborhoods.

As for the effects of Head Start on the problem behaviors, social skills and approaches to learning, or social competencies of four-year-olds, no significant effects were found. Here too, the program will have to improve its performance if it is to play a significant role in reducing poverty and racial-ethnic disparities. Unfortunately, an important recent study finds that children who are placed in childcare for more than thirty hours per week tend to demonstrate elevated levels of problem behavior (NICHD Early Child Care Research Network 2003, 2005b). Further, quality of care matters for both cognitive and behavioral outcomes, and most low-income children are being cared for in relatively low quality facilities.

In efforts to improve on Head Start, a relatively large number of small, experimental preschool intervention prototypes have been tried over the past forty years. Some appear to produce larger effects than Head Start, including effects that persist through to adulthood. However, the findings on these programs are mixed, and sometimes contradictory. Further, most effects become smaller as children age (Brooks-Gunn 2003). Although it is possible to view the evidence on these programs in a positive light (Magnuson and Waldfogel 2005), it is disappointing that forty years of research in this area have not produced greater success in narrowing the school readiness gaps of children from low-income families.

President Johnson's 1964 war on poverty was built around two programs—Head Start, to narrow the preschool achievement gap between poor and nonpoor children, and Title I of the Elementary and Secondary Education Act (of which NCLB was the 2001 reauthorization), to narrow this gap during elementary school. Head Start funding in 2007 was approximately $7 billion; funding for Title I is typically about twice this level. Yet, as noted, the effects of Head Start are, at best, modest. Worse, the effects of Title I have been essentially nonexistent (Farkas and Hall 2000).

Why has Title I been ineffective in raising the elementary school performance of disadvantaged students? As Farkas and Hall discussed, this program has always been more of a funding stream than a structured program. In low-income schools, the lowest performing students were pulled out in groups of three to eight or more students, to work with specially designated teachers. Unfortunately, these teachers had little effective curriculum or training, the students were at different performance levels and had different learning problems, their school engagement was often poor, and the resulting program was stigmatizing and demoralizing. Meanwhile, students in the regular class were moving ahead. Little wonder that the program was largely ineffective.

Beginning around 1990, a number of smaller scale programs began trying to develop more successful intervention models for at-risk elementary school students. Many of these focused on structured curricula, and one-to-one tutoring in reading and language arts. Such programs have been able to show effect sizes in the .25 to .50 standard deviation range (Farkas 1998; Invernizzi 2002; Borman et al. 2005). Now that NCLB has greatly increased funding for supplemental educational services, including tutoring, it seems possible that these services will be deployed on a much larger scale than previously. The expansion of tutoring services under NCLB is only now occurring, as supplementary educational services under Title I, and the evidence on the effects of these services is not yet in. However, what evidence is available is far from promising. This is because these programs are being implemented after school, when student attendance and attention can be a problem, and without close monitoring or meaningful evaluation and with small group tutoring rather than the more effective one-to-one tutoring (Dynarski et al. 2003; Farkas and Durham 2007). As always in program intervention, the quality of the implementation is central to its success. And few if any large-scale educational interventions have ever been well implemented.

This problem aside, what characterizes the best large-scale tutoring programs? Building on my experience with such interventions (Farkas 1998), I believe that to be effective, tutoring programs must begin when the student is very young, must be intensive enough to bring the student up to grade level, and have the resources to provide the extra assistance needed to keep them there, year in and year out, as they move up the grades. To accomplish this, the instructional assistance should be one-to-one, and should provide at least three forty-minute tutoring sessions per week, for approximately thirty weeks during the school year. Thus, each student needs to receive at least ninety forty-minute tutoring sessions, or a total of sixty hours of one-to-one tutoring, per year. Further, the tutors need to be trained in an evidence-based instructional curriculum, and their meetings with students need to be effectively managed. Elsewhere, I have described a program in which scholastically strong local high school students would be used as paraprofessional tutors (Farkas 2000). This would likely encounter political, implementation, and management difficulties. However, if the tutors were paid $10 an hour, it would be relatively inexpensive. Each student could be served for only $600 per year. Thus, assuming they constitute 20 percent of the population, each of the approximately 800,000 low-income first-graders in the nation could be provided with a personal tutor for a total cost of less than $0.5 billion, excluding management costs.

Using a different strategy, Aletha Huston and her colleagues (2005) found positive academic effects for (male) children from New Hope, a program aimed to increase parent employment and reduce poverty. These effects appear to have operated at least partly through the improved ability of participating low-income parents to sustain their family's daily routine. As we continue to struggle to find interventions that can close the preschool and early elementary school achievement gaps, it seems likely that, to be successful, such interventions will need to have a powerful impact on the academic time-on-task of low-income preschool and elementary school students. Improving the ability of low-income parents to maintain an orderly household, including regular mealtimes, homework, and bedtimes for children, while coping with the daily stresses of life, is a very desirable element in any program aimed to improve the school achievement of low-income children.

As for intervention programs to assist middle and high school students with their schoolwork, systematic work on such programs, accompanied by program evaluations with adequate research designs, is just beginning. This is a likely growth area in the years ahead.

CONCLUSION

We have seen that African American and Hispanic students are raised in families that have, on average, many fewer resources than those of white and Asian families. These families and students also experience far more negative stressors than whites and Asians. Multivariate studies have found that, when present simultaneously, these resource and stressor gaps have a dramatic effect in creating relatively large pre-reading, pre-mathematics, and behavioral readiness gaps between the groups during the preschool years (Duncan, Brooks-Gunn, and Klebanov 1994; Phillips et al. 1998; Farkas and Beron 2004; Farkas and Hibel 2008). Thus, the multiple family disadvantages experienced by ethnic minority children, and the associated accumulation of lower levels of skills, knowledge, and behavioral controls from birth to age five, are central to the lower school readiness of these children.

Once school begins, the black-white achievement gaps widen further. However, the Hispanic-white achievement gap does not widen. It seems likely that Hispanics do better than blacks during the schooling years because they overcome their most important risk factor—lack of English-language proficiency. By contrast, the most important problem for African American families may be their high share of single-parent households, and the low resources and high risk factors associated with this. On the other hand, Hispanics have a particularly high rate of school dropout, the determinants of which are poorly understood.

Since comparable data were first collected in the early 1970s, the white-black and white-Hispanic achievement gaps have narrowed. This occurred in three phases, with improvement during the 1970s and 1980s, stagnation during the 1990s, and (perhaps) the resumption of improvement after 1999. Unfortunately, because two different NAEP data series give contradictory answers, we are uncertain whether NCLB has led to a resumption of narrowing in the gaps in the new century, and if so, the detailed factors accounting for any such success. Nor do we know whether black and Hispanic economic progress since 1990, which has been significant, has played any role in improving the academic performance of black and Hispanic children.

The most urgent need is for research and development that can have a practical result in narrowing the white-black and white-Hispanic achievement gaps. Such research will focus on policies, programs, interventions, and other mechanisms for educational improvement, particularly in neighborhoods and schools serving high percentages of low-income African American and Hispanic students. Separate efforts are needed in the areas of preschool, elementary school, and middle and high school. I discuss each of these in turn.

Head Start is by far the largest compensatory preschool program aimed at low-income children. But, as shown in table 5.8, its effects are modest. This is not surprising, given that after almost forty years of operation, the program still has no mandated curriculum. It is imperative that Head Start be reformed to achieve stronger effects. Unfortunately, efforts to do so continue to be embroiled in political struggles (Zigler and Styfco 2004). Given the importance of the preschool period for later school success, improving Head Start should be the top priority for anyone interested in narrowing poverty and racial-ethnic gaps in school performance.

Much effort has been spent on improving literacy instruction in the early elementary grades, and these efforts show success in pilot programs. More work is needed on mathematics instruction in these grades. Whole school improvement and tutoring interventions have been deployed relatively widely, with some success (Borman et al. 2005; Farkas 1998). However, Title I, for the past forty years the principal funding source for compensatory programs in elementary school, has yet to show positive effects. As with Head Start, significant reform is needed.

Relatively less is known and has been undertaken in terms of programs, policies, and interventions for middle and high school students. This area is ripe for future development, particularly because it is at these higher grade levels that we have made the least progress in closing the achievement gaps.

In a recent review of these issues (Farkas 2004a), it was noted that when, in 2003, the Supreme Court ruled in favor of affirmative action by colleges and universities, the majority opinion suggested that special treatment for minorities may no longer be necessary in twenty-five years. But the students who will be applying for college in 2028 will be born in 2010. And the cumulative disadvantages experienced by black and Hispanic families in 2010 will be very similar to what they are now. This does not leave many years in which to meaningfully reform programs such as Head Start or Title I.

APPENDIX

Measurement and Data

The most important measurement instruments in the study of early inequality area have been created by developmental and educational psychologists, and then administered as part of the collection of nationally representative databases. For cognitive development, the central measures include: the Peabody Picture Vocabulary Test—Revised (PPVT-R) administered during the Infant Health and Development Program (IHDP) and National Longitudinal Survey of Youth 1979 (NLSY79) data collection efforts; the reading and mathematics performance measures collected as part of the National Assessment of Educational Progress (NAEP), National Educational Longitudinal Survey (NELS), and Prospects Studies; and the reading, mathematics, and general knowledge measures collected as part of the Early Childhood Longitudinal Study—Kindergarten Cohort (ECLS-K). For learning-related behavior, the central measures have been: items derived from the Behavior Problems Index of the Achenbach Child Behavior Checklist, producing scales of Externalizing and Internalizing Behavior Problems, rated by mothers on the IHDP, NLSY79 and ECLS-K datasets, and by teachers on the ECLS-K data; measures of child behavior in the Early Childcare Network studies; measures of approaches to learning, self-control, and interpersonal skills, rated by teachers on the ECLS-K; and teacher judgments of student learning-related behaviors, as well as student self-reports of these, collected on the NELS.

The cognitive assessments emphasize academic skills that both contribute to and include those taught in school. The PPVT measures one of the earliest-developing of these skills—listening (receptive) oral vocabulary. It is administered one-to-one to children as young as three years of age. A word is said to the child, and she or he must select one of four pictures that best illustrates the word. The number right is a direct measure of vocabulary size. From 1986 to the present, the PPVT-R has been administered to all children born to female members of the NLSY79 sample, as they aged from three to fourteen years. At the end of the 1980s, it was also administered to three- and five-year-olds studied as part of the IHDP, a study of low birth weight children in eight cities.

Reading and mathematics tests, focused on the skills taught in school, are administered on a regular basis to a nationally representative sample of nine, thirteen, and nineteen-year-olds as part of the NAEP assessments. Similar tests were used in the congressionally mandated Prospects Study of Title I Program effectiveness, as well as in the NELS study of a representative sample of eighth, tenth, and twelfth graders.

The ECLS-K study focused on a nationally representative sample of children enrolled in kindergarten in 1998. They were given Item Response Theory (IRT) based tests of reading, mathematics, and general knowledge in kindergarten, first, third, and fifth grade, and will be followed through to twelfth grade. As in the NAEP, NELS, and Prospects studies, these tests are based on standard test items appropriate to the student's grade level in school.

Where behavior is concerned, externalizing behavior problems refer to outward-directed aggressive or disobedient behaviors (survey items include: "cheats or tells lies," "bullies or is cruel or mean to others," "is not sorry for misbehaving," "argues too much," and so on). Internalizing behavior problems refer to inward-directed feelings such as depression or moodiness (items include "is unhappy, sad, or depressed," "feels worthless or inferior," and so on). NLSY79 mothers rated their children age four to fourteen on these behaviors. These scales were also collected on the IHDP, the ECLS-K, and other data sets. Further, the ECLS-K had elementary school teachers rate each student on traits such as attentiveness, task persistence, eagerness to learn, learning independence, flexibility, and organization. When combined into the approaches to learning scale, it is the best behavioral measure in predicting achievement, net of prior achievement.

———

I am grateful to David Harris, Ann Lin, Steven Morgan, Jeff Morenoff, and two anonymous reviewers for their comments on earlier versions of this chapter.

REFERENCES

Alexander, Karl, Doris Entwisle, and Susan Dauber. 1993. "First Grade Behavior: Its Short and Long-Term Consequences for School Performance." *Child Development* 64(3): 801–14.

Alexander, Karl, Doris Entwisle, and C. Horsey. 1997. "From First Grade Forward: Early Foundations of High School Dropout." *Sociology of Education* 70(2): 87–107.

Becker, Gary. 1981. *A Treatise on the Family.* Cambridge, Mass.: Harvard University Press.

Beron, Kurt, and George Farkas. 2004. "Oral Language and Reading Success: A Structural Equation Modeling Approach." *Structural Equation Modeling* 11(1): 110–31.

Bodovski, Katerina, and George Farkas. 2007. "Do Instructional Practices Contribute to Inequality in Achievement: The Case of Mathematics Instruction in Kindergarten." *The Journal of Early Childhood Research* 5(3): 301–22.

———. Forthcoming. "Concerted Cultivation and Unequal Achievement in Elementary School." *Social Science Research.*

Borman, Geoffrey, Robert E. Slavin, Alan C. K. Cheung, Anne M. Chamberlain, Nancy A. Madden, and Bette Chambers. 2005. "The National Randomized Field Trial of Success for All: Second-Year Outcomes." *American Educational Research Journal* 42(4): 673–96.

Bradley, Robert, and Bettye Caldwell. 1984a. "The HOME Inventory and Family Demographics." *Developmental Psychology* 20(2): 315–20.

———. 1984b. "The Relation of Infants' Home Environments to Achievement Test Performance in First Grade: A Follow-Up Study." *Child Development* 55(3): 803–9.

Bradley, Robert H., Robert F. Corwyn, Margaret Burchinal, Harriet Pipes McAdoo, and Cynthia García Coll. 2001. "The Home Environments of Children in the United States. Part II: Relations with Behavioral Development through Age Thirteen." *Child Development* 72(6): 1868–86.

Brooks-Gunn, Jeanne. 2003. "Do You Believe in Magic? What We Can Expect From Early Childhood Intervention Programs." *Social Policy Report (Society for Research on Child Development)* 27(1): 3–16.

Brooks-Gunn, Jeanne, and Lisa Markman. 2005. "The Contribution of Parenting to Ethnic and Racial Gaps in School Readiness." *The Future of Children* 15(1): 139–68.

Campbell, Susan, and Camilla von Stauffenberg. 2008. "Child Characteristics and Family Processes that Predict Behavioral Readiness for School." In *Early Disparities in School Readiness: How do Families Contribute to Successful and Unsuccessful Transitions into School?*, edited by Alan Booth and Ann Crouter. Mahwah, N.J.: Lawrence Erlbaum.

Carbonaro, William. 2005. "Tracking, Students' Effort, and Academic Achievement." *Sociology of Education* 78(1): 27–49.

Carlson, Marcia J., and Mary E. Corcoran. 2001. "Family Structure and Children's Behavioral and Cognitive Outcomes." *Journal of Marriage and the Family* 63(3): 779–92.

Currie, Janet. 2005. "Health Disparities and Gaps in School Readiness." *The Future of Children* 15(1): 117–38.

Deater-Deckard, Kirby, Kenneth A. Dodge, and Emma Sorbring. 2005. "Cultural Differences in the Effects of Physical Punishment." In *Ethnicity and Causal Mechanisms*, edited by Michael Rutter and Marta Tienda. Cambridge: Cambridge University Press.

Downey, Douglas B., and Shana Pribesh. 2004. "When Race Matters: Student/Teacher Racial Matching and Teachers' Evaluations of Students' Behavior." *Sociology of Education* 77(3): 267–82.

Downey, Douglas B., Paul T. von Hippel, and Beckett A. Broh. 2004. "Are Schools the Great Equalizer? Cognitive Inequality during the Summer Months and the School Year." *American Sociological Review* 69(5): 613–35.

Duncan, Greg, and Jeanne Brooks-Gunn. 1997. *Consequences of Growing Up Poor.* New York: Russell Sage Foundation.

Duncan, Greg, Jeanne Brooks-Gunn, and P. K. Klebanov. 1994. "Economic Deprivation and Early Childhood Development." *Child Development* 65(2): 296–318.

Duncan, Greg, and Katherine Magnuson. 2005. "Can Family Socioeconomic Resources Account for Racial and Ethnic Test Score Gaps?" *The Future of Children* 15(1): 35–54.

Duncan, Greg, W. Jean Yeung, Jeanne Brooks-Gunn, and Judith R. Smith. 1998. "The Effects of Childhood Poverty on the Life Chances of Children." *American Sociological Review* 63(3): 406–23.

Durham, Rachel, George Farkas, Carol Scheffner Hammer, and Hugh Catts. 2007. "Kindergarten Oral Language Skill: A Key Variable in the Intergenerational Transmission of Socioeconomic Status." *Research in Social Stratification and Mobility* 25(4): 294–305.

Dynarski, Mark, Linda Rosenberg, Mary Moore, John Deke, Susanne James-Burdumy, and

Wendy Mansfield. 2003. *When Schools Stay Open Late: The National Evaluation of the 21st Century Community Learning Centers Program.* Jessup, Md.: Mathematica Policy Research and U. S. Department of Education.

Ensminger, Margaret, and Anita Slusarcik. 1992. "Paths to High School Graduation or Dropout: A Longitudinal Study of a First-Grade Cohort." *Sociology of Education* 65(2): 95–113.

Entwisle, Doris, Karl Alexander, and Linda Olson. 1997. *Children, Schools, and Inequality.* Boulder, Colo.: Westview Press.

Farkas, George. 1996. *Human Capital or Cultural Capital? Ethnicity and Poverty Groups in an Urban School District.* New York: Aldine de Gruyter.

———. 1998. "Reading One-to-One: An Intensive Program Serving a Great Many Students While Still Achieving Large Effects." In *Social Programs that Work*, edited by Jonathan Crane. New York: Russell Sage Foundation.

———. 2000. "Tutoring for Low-Income Children Via Vouchers to Their Parents." *Journal of Policy Analysis and Management* 19(1): 143–45.

———. 2003. "Cognitive Skills and Noncognitive Traits and Behaviors in Stratification Processes." *Annual Review of Sociology* 29: 541–62.

———. 2004a. "The Black-White Test Score Gap." *Contexts* 3(2): 12–19.

———. 2004b. "School Readiness: Characteristics and Attributes." In *The Encyclopedia of Education*, 2nd ed., edited by James W. Guthrie. New York: Macmillan Reference.

Farkas, George, and Kurt Beron. 2004. "The Detailed Age Trajectory of Oral Vocabulary Knowledge: Differences by Class and Race." *Social Science Research* 33(3): 464–97.

Farkas, George, and Rachel Durham. 2007. "The Role of Tutoring in Standards-Based Reform." In *Standards-Based Reform and the Poverty Gap: Lessons for "No Child Left Behind,"* edited by Adam Gamoran. Washington, D.C.: The Brookings Institution Press.

Farkas, George, Robert P. Grobe, Daniel Sheehan, and Yuan Shuan. 1990. "Cultural Resources and School Success: Gender, Ethnicity, and Poverty Groups in an Urban School District." *American Sociological Review* 55(1): 127–42.

Farkas, George, and L. Shane Hall. 2000. "Can Title I Attain Its Goal?" *Brookings Papers on Education Policy* 2000: 59–103.

Farkas, George, and Jacob Hibel. 2008. "Being Unready for School: Factors Affecting Risk and Resilience." In *Early Disparities in School Readiness: How Do Families Contribute to Successful and Unsuccessful Transitions into School?* edited by Alan Booth and Ann Crouter. Mahwah, N.J.: Lawrence Erlbaum.

Farkas, George, and Keven Vicknair. 1996. "Appropriate Tests of Racial Wage Discrimination Require Controls for Cognitive Skill: Comment on the Paper by Cancio, Evans, and Maume." *American Sociological Review* 61(4): 557–60.

Fryer, Roland G., and Steven D. Levitt. 2004. "Understanding the Black-White Test Score Gap in the First Two Years of School." *Review of Economics and Statistics* 86(2): 447–64.

Grissmer, David, Ann Flanagan, and Stephanie Williamson. 1998. "Why Did the Black-White Score Gap Narrow in the 1970s and 1980s?" In *The Black-White Test Score Gap*, edited by Christopher Jencks and Meredith Phillips. Washington, D.C.: The Brookings Institution Press.

Guo, Guang, and Kathleen M. Harris. 2000. "The Mechanisms Mediating the Effects of Poverty on Children's Intellectual Development." *Demography* 37(4): 431–48.

Hart, Betty, and Todd Risley. 1995. *Meaningful Differences in the Everyday Experience of Young Children.* Baltimore, Md.: Paul Brookes Publishing.

———. 1999. *The Social World of Children Learning to Talk.* Baltimore, Md.: Paul Brookes Publishing.

Hedges, Larry, and Amy Nowell. 1998. "Black-White Test Score Convergence Since 1965." In *The Black-White Test Score Gap,* edited by Christopher Jencks and Meredith Phillips. Washington, D.C.: The Brookings Institution Press.

Hoff, Erika. 2003. "The Specificity of Environmental Influence: Socioeconomic Status Affects Early Vocabulary Development Via Maternal Speech." *Child Development* 74(5): 1368–78.

Huston, Aletha C., Greg J. Duncan, Vonnie C. McLoyd, Danielle A. Crosby, Marika N. Ripke, Thomas S. Weisner, and Carolyn A. Eldred. 2005. "Impacts on Children of a Policy to Promote Employment and Reduce Poverty for Low-Income Parents: New Hope After 5 Years." *Developmental Psychology* 41(6): 902–18.

Invernizzi, Marcia. 2002. "The Complex World of One-on-One Tutoring." In *Handbook of Early Literacy Research,* edited by Susan Neuman and David Dickinson. New York: Guilford Press.

Jencks, Christopher. 1979. *Who Gets Ahead?* New York: Basic Books.

Jencks, Christopher, and Meredith Phillips, editors. 1998. *The Black-White Test Score Gap.* Washington, D.C.: The Brookings Institution Press.

Kerckhoff, Alan C., and Elizabeth Glennie. 1999. "The Matthew Effect in American Education." *Research in Sociology of Education and Socialization* 12: 35–66.

Krueger, Alan B. 2003. "Inequality, Too Much of a Good Thing." In *Inequality in America,* edited by James Heckman and Alan Krueger. Cambridge, Mass.: MIT Press.

Lamont, Michèle, and Annette Lareau. 1988. "Cultural Capital: Allusions, Gaps and Glissandos in Recent Theoretical Developments." *Sociological Theory* 6(2): 153–68.

Lareau, Annette. 2003. *Unequal Childhoods.* Berkeley, Calif.: University of California Press.

Lee, Valerie E., and David T. Burkam. 2002. *Inequality at the Starting Gate: Social Background Differences in Achievement as Children Begin School.* Washington, D.C.: Economic Policy Institute.

Magnuson, Katherine A., and Jane Waldfogel. 2005. "Early Childhood Care and Education: Effects on Ethnic and Racial Gaps in School Readiness." *The Future of Children* 15(1): 169–96.

Marks, Helen. 2000. "Student Engagement in Instructional Activity: Patterns in the Elementary, Middle, and High School Years." *American Educational Research Journal* 37(1): 153–84.

Mayer, Susan. 1997. *What Money Can't Buy.* Cambridge, Mass.: Harvard University Press.

McLanahan, Sara. 1997. "Parent Absence or Poverty: Which Matters More?" In *Consequences of Growing Up Poor,* edited by Greg Duncan and Jeanne Brooks-Gunn. New York: Russell Sage Foundation.

McLanahan, Sara, Elisabeth Donahue, and Ron Haskins. 2005. "Introducing the Issue." *The Future of Children* 15(2): 3–12.

McLanahan, Sara, and Garry Sandefur. 1994. *Growing Up with a Single Parent.* Cambridge, Mass.: Harvard University Press.

McLeod, Jane, and Karen Kaiser. 2004. "Childhood Emotional and Behavioral Problems and Educational Attainment." *American Sociological Review* 69(5): 636–58.

McLeod, Jane, and James Nonnemaker. 2000. "Poverty and Child Emotional and Behavioral Problems: Racial-ethnic Differences in Processes and Effects." *Journal of Health and Social Behavior* 41(June): 137–61.

McLoyd, Vonnie. 1990. "The Impact of Economic Hardship on Black Families and Children: Psychological Distress, Parenting, and Socioemotional Development." *Child Development* 61(2): 311–46.

———. 1998. "Socioeconomic Disadvantage and Child Development." *American Psychologist* 53(2): 185–204.

McLoyd, Vonnie, and Julia Smith. 2002. "Physical Discipline and Behavior Problems in African American, European American, and Hispanic Children: Emotional Support as a Moderator." *Journal of Marriage and the Family* 64(February): 40–53.

Moos, Rudolph H., Ruth C. Cronkite, and John W. Finney. 1986. *Health and Daily Living Form Manual.* Palo Alto, Calif.: Veterans Administration and Stanford University Medical Center.

Morgan, Paul, George Farkas, Paula Tufis, and Rayne Sperling. Forthcoming. "Are Reading and Behavior Problems Risk Factors for Each Other?" *Journal of Learning Disabilities.*

NICHD Early Child Care Research Network. 2003. "Does Amount of Time Spent in Child Care Predict Socioemotional Adjustment During the Transition to Kindergarten?" *Child Development* 74(4): 976–1005.

———. 2005a. "Pathways to Reading: The Role of Oral Language in the Transition to Reading." *Developmental Psychology* 41 (2): 428–42.

———, editors. 2005b. *Child Care and Child Development: Results from the NICHD Study of Early Child Care and Youth Development.* New York: Guilford Press.

Pallas, Aaron, Doris R. Entwisle, Karl L. Alexander, and M. Francis Stluka. 1994. "Ability-Group Effects: Instructional, Social, or Institutional?" *Sociology of Education* 67(1): 27–46.

Phillips, Meredith, Jeanne Brooks-Gunn, Greg J. Duncan, Pamela Klebanov, and Jonathan Crane. 1998. "Family Background, Parenting Practices, and the Black-White Test Score Gap." In *The Black-White Test Score Gap*, edited by Christopher Jencks and Meredith Phillips. Washington, D.C.: The Brookings Institution Press.

Phillips, Meredith, James Crouse, and John Ralph. 1998. "Does the Black-White Test Score Gap Widen After Children Enter School?" In *The Black-White Test Score Gap*, edited by Christopher Jencks and Meredith Phillips. Washington, D.C.: The Brookings Institution Press.

Rathbun, Amy, and Jerry West. 2004. *From Kindergarten Through Third Grade: Children's Beginning School Experiences.* NCES 2004-007. Washington: U.S. Department of Education.

Reichman, Nancy. 2005. "Low Birth Weight and School Readiness." *The Future of Children* 15(1): 91–116.

Ripke, Marika N. and Aletha C. Huston. 2005. "Poverty Consequences for Children." In *Child Psychology: A Handbook of Contemporary Issues*, 2nd ed., edited by Lawrence Balter and Catherine Tamis-LeMonda. New York: Psychology Press.

Rock, Donald, and A. Jackson Stenner. 2005. "Assessment Issues in the Testing of Children at School Entry." *The Future of Children* 15(1): 15–34.

Rosenbaum, James. 2001. *Beyond College for All.* New York: Russell Sage Foundation.

Snow, Catherine, M. Susan Burns, and Peg Griffin, editors. 1998. *Preventing Reading Difficulties in Young Children.* Washington, D.C.: National Academy Press.

Swidler, Ann. 1986. "Culture in Action: Symbols and Strategies." *American Sociological Review* 51(2): 273–86.

Tach, Laura, and George Farkas. 2006. "Learning-Related Behaviors, Cognitive Skills, and Ability Grouping When Schooling Begins." *Social Science Research* 35(4): 1048–79.

West, Jerry, Kristin Denton, and Lizabeth Reaney. 2001. *The Kindergarten Year.* NCES 2001-023R. Washington: U.S. Department of Education.

Whitehurst, Grover, and Christopher Lonigan. 2002. "Emergent Literacy: Development from Prereaders to Readers." In *Handbook of Early Literacy Research*, edited by Susan Neuman and David Dickinson. New York: Guilford Press.

Whitehurst, Grover, and Greta Massetti. 2004. "How Well Does Head Start Prepare Children to Learn to Read?" In *The Head Start Debates*, edited by Edward Zigler and Sally J. Styfco. Baltimore, Md.: Paul Brookes Publishing.

Zigler, Edward, and Sally J. Styfco, editors. 2004. *The Head Start Debates.* Baltimore, Md.: Paul Brookes Publishing.

Chapter 6

Poverty, Migration, and Health

David R. Williams and Selina A. Mohammed

Living and working conditions are important determinants of health because they underscore differential exposure to health risks and resources. Accordingly, poverty and other indicators of socioeconomic status (SES) are important contexts that shape the distribution of health risks and resources. Moreover, SES intersects with race and ethnicity and immigration status and all interact additively and interactively to create cumulative exposure to health risks that contribute to variations in the distribution of illness in the United States. Accordingly, it is vital to include health status in policy initiatives that address poverty. Both researchers and policy makers need enhanced sensitivity to the ways in which a broad range of social policies can have health consequences.

POVERTY AND HEALTH

In the United States, the poor have markedly higher rates of disease disability and death than their more affluent counterparts. One national study concluded that the effect of poverty on increasing the risk of death was comparable to that of cigarette smoking (Hahn et al. 1995). These data are consistent with a larger literature on economic status and health. Socioeconomic status, whether measured by income, education, occupational status or wealth is one of the strongest known determinants of variations in health (Williams and Collins, 1995; Adler et al., 1993; Marmot, Kogevinas, and Elston 1987). This association exists in virtually every society in both the developed and the developing world. In U.S. data, for example, low SES adults have levels of illness in their thirties and forties that are not evident in their highest SES peers until their sixties and seventies (House et al. 1994). The association between SES and health affects all of society, not just certain segments. It is most marked at the low levels of SES but exists throughout the SES hierarchy, with individuals at every level having worse health than their counterparts at higher levels. For example, analysis of the association between income and mortality in the Panel Study of Income Dynamics (PSID) find large reductions in the mortality rate associated with increases of income at low levels of SES, but smaller declines in mortality linked to additional income at higher levels of SES (McDonough et al. 1997).

Why is SES related to health? Socioeconomic deprivation and exposure to poor living and working conditions are central contributors to the poor health of low SES groups. Socioeconomic position is associated with the types and level of stressors to which the individual or the group is exposed, the availability of resources to cope with stress, and the patterned responses and strategies developed over time to manage environmental challenges. Research reveals that those with low SES report elevated levels of stress and are sometimes more vulnerable to the negative effects of stressors than their counterparts. Chronic exposure to stress is associated with altered physiological functioning that may ultimately increase risks for a broad range of health conditions (McEwen 1998).

In addition, virtually all of the behavioral and psychosocial risk factors for common chronic diseases (for example, poor dietary behavior, physical inactivity, cigarette smoking and alcohol abuse) are more prevalent among the poor. Low SES groups are also less likely to reduce high-risk behaviors or to initiate new health enhancing practices. Changes in cigarette smoking over time illustrate this. High SES persons have been markedly more likely to quit cigarette smoking over the last several decades than their lower SES counterparts (Cooper et al. 2000).

Larger social structures and contexts can constrain the ability of those with low SES to cope with unhealthful habits and circumstances. For example, the perception of neighborhood safety is positively associated with getting regular exercise (Centers for Disease Control and Prevention 1999). In addition, neighborhoods differ in the existence and quality of recreational facilities, open spaces and green spaces. Recent research indicates that the presence of trees and vegetation in residential areas have positive effects on physical and psychological well being and can reduce the negative effects of stress on health (Wells and Evans 2003). Similarly, the availability and cost of healthy products in grocery stores vary across residential areas in the United States and the availability of nutritious foods is positively associated with its consumption (Cheadle et al. 1991). Poor residential areas also have a high concentration of billboard advertising for alcohol and tobacco (Hacker, Jacobson, and Jacobson 1987; Moore, Williams, and Qualls 1996). They also typically have elevated levels of multiple sources of stress, including violence, financial stress, family separation, death and family turmoil (Evans and Saegert 2000). In turn, alcohol and tobacco are chemical agents often used to cope with such stress.

Research reveals that the relationship between SES and health status is dynamic and reciprocal. That is, in addition to conditions linked to low SES adversely affecting health, poor health status can also negatively affect SES. Research reveals, for example, that early life illnesses can lead to restricted socioeconomic attainment (Kessler et al. 1995) and major chronic illnesses in adulthood can lead to declines in economic status (Smith 1999). On balance, SES affects health more than health affects SES (House and Williams 2000). The greater knowledge and resources available to high SES persons create fundamental inequalities in health (Link and Phelan 1995; Williams 1990).

RACE AND HEALTH

Race is also a strong predictor of variations in health in the United States and other racially stratified societies (Polednak 1989). Historically, racial categories have been viewed as meaningful indicators of genetic distinctiveness. In contrast, this chapter views race as capturing ethnicity—common geographic origins, ancestry, family patterns, language, cultural norms and traditions—as well as oppression, exploitation and social inequality (American Sociological Association 2003). In the interest of parsimony and economy of presentation, we use the term *race* to refer to all of the Office of Management and Budget (OMB) racial and ethnic categories and the term *ethnicity* to refer to subgroups of these global OMB categories. In addition, in recognition of individual dignity, we use the most preferred terms (Tucker et al. 1996) for the OMB categories (such as black and African American, Hispanic and Latino, American Indian and Native American) interchangeably.

For most of the twentieth century, research on race and health in the United States has centrally focused on the health of blacks compared to that of whites. Earlier research reveals large black-white differences in health. For example, though the magnitude of racial differences in death rates varies by the specific cause of death, African Americans have elevated death rates than whites for twelve of fifteen leading causes of death and the overall death rate for blacks is equivalent to that of whites some twenty to thirty years ago (National Center for Health Statistics 2003). There is broad recognition of the need to give increased attention to the health of indigenous populations (American Indians–Alaska Natives and Native Hawaiians and other Pacific Islanders) and the immigrant groups that are an increasingly large part of the American mosaic (Williams 2005b). Like African Americans, American Indians also have higher age-specific mortality rates than whites, and Hispanics have higher death rates than whites for several causes of death (Williams 2005b).

These racial differences in health largely reflect racial variations in SES (Williams and Collins 1995). There are large SES differences in health within each racial group, and adjusting racial differences in health for SES leads to marked reductions in these disparities. For the most part, SES differences are larger than racial differences. For example, in national data, the differences in health between poor and high income persons (more than $50,000) are more than three times the overall black-white difference in health and more than four times the overall health gap between Hispanics and whites (Pamuk et al. 1998). However, race carries its own burdens for health beyond those associated with socioeconomic disadvantage (Williams 2005b). For example, African Americans generally exhibit worse health outcomes even when compared to whites with statistically equivalent levels of SES. These differences are often largest at the lowest level of SES.

Several explanations have been offered to account for the residual effects of race on health even when SES is controlled. First, some researchers have emphasized the nonequivalence of SES indicators across race. Compared to whites, blacks receive poorer quality education, have lower earnings at equivalent levels of education, less wealth at the same levels of income, and less purchasing power of income due to racial differences in residential environments (Williams and Collins 1995). Institutional discrimination in the form of residential segregation has been viewed as a driving force behind these differences in socioeconomic circumstances (see Pager, chapter 2, this volume).

A second explanatory framework emphasizes that the SES-health relationship should be understood in a life course framework. Current health status is affected by socioeconomic conditions over the life course (Harper et al. 2002). Thus, a complete assessment of the association between SES and health requires a comprehensive and dynamic characterization of exposure to various socioeconomic circumstances over time.

A third set of explanations focus on the ways in which noneconomic forms of discrimination can adversely affect the health of nondominant racial populations. Research suggests that acute and chronic experiences of discrimination are a source of stress adversely related to physical and mental health. National data reveal that 30 percent of the U.S. population report major acute experiences of bias and 60 percent report chronic, everyday discrimination (Kessler, Mickelson, and Williams 1999). Everyday discrimination includes perceptions of being treated with less courtesy than others and receiving poorer service than others in restaurants and stores. Unfair treatment experiences based on race is the most common type of bias in society (Kessler, Mickelson, and Williams 1999), and African Americans and other minorities report much higher levels of racial-ethnic bias than whites (Williams 2000). Discrimination has been linked to poorer physical and mental health for racial groups in the United States, as well as for immigrant groups in Canada and Western Europe (Williams, Neighbors, and Jackson 2003). For example, one study found that reports of chronic discrimination among black women were positively related to the development of subclinical disease in the carotid artery (Troxel et al. 2003). Other research also indicates that perceptions of discrimination make an incremental contribution to explaining the residual effects of race on health after SES is controlled (Williams et al. 1997).

Data on racial differences in access to and especially the quality of medical care illustrate another way in which racial bias can affect health. For example, research reveals systematic racial differences in the kind and quality of medical care received among Medicare beneficiaries (Escarce et al. 1993; McBean and Gornick 1994). In an analysis of racial differences and the rates of procedures performed by hospitals for Medicare beneficiaries in 1992, Marshall McBean and Marion Gornick (1994) found that black Medicare beneficiaries were less likely than their white counterparts to receive all of the sixteen most commonly performed procedures and that the differences appeared largest for referral-sensitive procedures.

McBean and Gornick further examined the Medicare files to ascertain if there were any procedures that black beneficiaries of Medicare received more frequently than their white counterparts, and found that this was true of four non-elective procedures, each of which reflected delayed diagnosis for initial treatment or failure to manage chronic disease. For example, African American Medicare beneficiaries were 3.6 times more likely to have a lower limb amputated (usually as a consequence of diabetes) and 2.2 times more likely to have both testes removed (generally because of cancer) than their white counterparts.

These differences are consistent with a much larger literature that finds consistent and systematic racial differences in the receipt of a broad range of medical procedures. Multiple explanations have been offered for these disparities. It has been argued that they could reflect poor geographic distribution of health resources, racial differences in patient preferences, physiology, economic status, insurance coverage, place of treatment, and trust, knowledge and experience with medical procedures. However, all available evidence suggests that systematic discrimination, some of which may be unconscious, remains a central, plausible explanation (Williams and Rucker 2000; Smedley, Stith, and Nelson 2003).

MIGRATION, SES, AND HEALTH

Efforts to understand the complex associations among poverty, race, and health must also pay attention to immigration. Surprisingly, Hispanics, with a high proportion of immigrants, have relatively low levels of SES but levels of health status that are equivalent and sometimes superior to those of the white population. This better-than-expected profile of Latino health is often referred to as the Hispanic paradox (Franzini, Ribble, and Keddie 2001). This pattern may not be unique. National data reveal that immigrants of all racial groups have lower rates of overall and infant mortality than their native-born counterparts (Singh and Yu 1996; Singh and Miller 2004; Hummer et al. 1999). Nonetheless, a conclusion of superior health for immigrants compared to the native-born may be premature because the health of immigrants appears to vary by the specific indicator of mortality under consideration (Williams 2002). For example, although immigrants have lower levels of infant mortality than nonimmigrants, they have higher rates of maternal mortality (Centers for Disease Control and Prevention 2001). In addition, inadequate attention has been given to measures of illness (Carter-Pokras and Zambrana 2001). For example, in contrast to a pattern of lower overall mortality rates, Hispanics tend to have higher rates of illness than whites for global indicators of morbidity, such as self-rated ill-health (National Center for Health Statistics 2003). Moreover, the very existence of the paradox has been questioned by some given methodological limitations of the available mortality data (Palloni and Morenoff 2001; Palloni and Arias 2004).

We do not yet clearly understand the determinants of the health profile of Hispanics and the ways in which SES and migration might combine to affect health. Moreover, little national data on health status indicators is available for Asians and other numerically small racial populations, so that it is not clear whether patterns observed for Hispanics are generalizable to other groups. Additionally, the Latino and Asian populations are characterized by heterogeneity, with some subgroups varying markedly from others in terms of both SES and health. Research on Hispanics and Asians also suggests that the health of these groups worsen with length of stay in the United States and generational status (Vega and Amaro 1994; Cho and Hummer 2000). These populations also differ dramatically from each other in their levels of SES on arrival in the United States and their trajectories of SES mobility over time. Our current knowledge is limited regarding how immigrant status, race, and ethnicity combine with SES to affect levels of health, and the extent to which the pattern for Latinos compares to that of Asians and varies for subgroups within each of these populations.

THE IMPORTANCE OF HEALTH IN POVERTY POLICY

There are several reasons why it is important for policy makers to be attentive to the association between SES, race, and health. First, volatility in income over the life course affects health. Adjusted for family size, income levels fluctuate with various stages of the life cycle, peaking in the late fifties (McDonough et al. 2000). In addition to these fairly predictable changes, about 40 percent of the U.S. population experience large income gains and losses during their working years. For example, over an eleven-year period of observation, Greg Duncan (1988) found that about 30 percent of the U.S. population experienced a decline in household income by 50 percent or more in consecutive years, and between 20 percent and 35 percent of women aged twenty-five to seventy-five experienced poverty at least once.

These declines in income are closely related to health status. Analysis of economic and health data revealed that individuals who experienced a large income loss had an elevated risk of mortality in the five years that followed, and that this risk was larger for those with middle incomes than for those with low incomes (McDonough et al. 1997). Similarly, individuals who had persistently low incomes had higher mortality risk than those whose low incomes were temporary (McDonough et al. 1997). These findings highlight the importance of researchers and policy makers attending to the potential health consequences of both the level of income and its stability over time.

Second, research reveals widening income inequality in the United States and other industrialized countries in recent decades (Danziger and Gottschalk 1993). In tandem with these trends, socioeconomic inequalities in health in the United States have also widened (Pappas et al. 1993). Similar patterns exist in other countries, with the data for England and Wales being especially striking. Analysis of mortality data by occupational social class for every decade from 1911 to 1981 reveals that despite major changes in the causes of death (from acute, infectious illnesses to chronic degenerative diseases) during the period, the elevated mortality risks for the lower social classes remained large compared to the professional and managerial classes (Marmot 1986). It is especially noteworthy that increases in the quantity and effectiveness of medical care during this period and more equitable access, attributable to the inception of the National Health Service in 1948, appeared to have no effect on eliminating SES inequalities in health.

Third, economic and racial inequalities in health are costly to society. They reflect considerable loss of life during the most economically productive years. National data on survival for 1999 illustrate the magnitude of these differences (Anderson and DeTurk 2002). For every 100,000 black and white females born, some 97,000 white women survive to see their forty-fifth birthday compared to 94,000 black women. Similarly, 87,000 white women but only 78,000 black women survive to age sixty-five. The differences are even larger for males. Of every 100,000 black and white males born in the United States, 5,400 fewer black males than white survive to age forty-five and 16,000 fewer black males live to see sixty-five. Poorer health also affects the level of participation and productivity in the workforce and in income support programs. A recent study found that the higher levels of illness for blacks and American Indians, compared to whites, accounted for a large part of the racial differences in employment rates and in participation in public assistance programs and Social Security, especially among forty-five- to sixty-four-year-olds (Bound et al. 2003).

Fourth, addressing the health status of the poor is central to the success of interventions to improve economic opportunities for poverty populations. For example, a study of women transitioning from welfare to work found that more than 70 percent reported limitations in functioning, more than 60 percent met criteria for major depression or generalized anxiety disorder and 37 percent had a child with a health problem (Corcoran, Danziger, and Tolman 2004). Levels of obesity were also high and served as a barrier to employment and earnings for at least some current and former welfare recipients (Cawley and Danziger 2005). Thus, facilitating the successful transition from welfare to work requires support services that address the barriers that illness can create for success in the labor market.

We will empirically examine the complex ways in which race, poverty and immigrant status relate to each other and combine to produce particular patterns of health by using a unique data source. The 2001 California Health Interview Survey (CHIS) is a two-stage, geographically stratified representative sample of the California population.[1] The CHIS allows for a rare glimpse of the racial and ethnic diversity of the U.S. population with regards to health. In addition to blacks and non-Hispanic whites, it has large samples of Hispanics and Asians, as well as major ethnic subgroups of these populations. It also has much larger than usual samples of American Indians, multiracial persons, and Native Hawaiians and Other Pacific Islanders. No other health survey provides such comprehensive coverage of racial and ethnic groups in the United States.

Another strength of the CHIS data is the availability of multiple measures of health: self-rated ill-health, emotional distress, physical limitations, and chronic conditions. Health is multidimensional and the associations among poverty, race, immigration, and health may vary by the indicator of health status under consideration. Self-rated ill-health is based on a single question in which respondents rate their health on a 5-point scale, with 1 as excellent and 5 as poor. This global indicator of health status is a strong predictor of mortality and changes in physical functioning (Idler and Benyamini 1997; Idler and Kasl 1995). Emotional distress sums the frequency with which the respondent felt calm and peaceful, downhearted and sad and had lots of energy in the past four weeks. Scales of emotional distress can reflect not only clinically significant symptoms of anxiety and depression but also aspects of demoralization that are reflective of stressors and adverse living conditions common in low SES contexts (Link and Dohrenwend 1980). Recent research indicates that mental health problems are among the most common causes of absenteeism from work and reduced productivity at work (Ustun et al. 2004). Physical limitations captures the extent to which respondents reported being limited when climbing stairs, pushing a vacuum cleaner, and at work or in other activities. A high score on the scale is indicative of greater limitations. Finally, chronic conditions is a count of the presence of specific diagnosed illnesses: asthma, arthritis, diabetes, high blood pressure, heart disease or high cholesterol. This measure of health status is at least partly confounded by access to medical care.

The CHIS data can shed light on the following questions:

1. How is SES (poverty and education) related to race, and to ethnic status within racial categories?
2. What is the nature of the association between poverty and health? To what extent is there a threshold effect or a graded association between economic status and health? How generalizable is this association across multiple racial groups, and ethnicity within race categories?
3. To what extent does race and ethnicity predict variations in health? Are observed variations in health consistent across ethnic categories within racial groups and for multiple indicators of health status? How much of the variation in health status by race and ethnicity is accounted for by SES?
4. How does SES (poverty and education) vary by immigrant status for multiple racial and ethnic groups?
5. How does the health of immigrants compare to that of the native-born for multiple racial groups, as well as for subgroups of the Latino and Asian populations? How generalizable is this pattern across multiple indicators of health status?
6. How does the health of immigrants vary by length of stay in the United States? To what extent does this pattern vary by the indicator of health status under consideration?

POVERTY AND HEALTH

The CHIS reveals both high poverty rates for nonwhite racial groups and high variation in income within each group. Compared to a white rate of poverty of 6.1

percent, table 6.1 shows a rate five times higher for Latinos, three times higher for blacks, and twice as high for Pacific Islanders, American Indians, and Asians. Yet both the Hispanic and Asian groups are characterized by considerable hetero-geneity. For example, Mexican and Central Americans have rates of poverty three times as high as that of Puerto Ricans. Similarly, Filipinos, South Asians and Japanese have poverty rates markedly lower than the Asian average and only one-fifth that of the Vietnamese. The variation is very similar to the racial-ethnic patterns at high levels of income. For example, two-thirds of whites and half of all Asians have income levels that are at least three times that of the federal poverty level. In contrast, 41 percent of blacks, 46 percent of Pacific Islanders, and 41 percent of American Indians, but only 22 percent of Hispanics, fall into the two highest income categories. Both the Other Race and multiracial categories have patterns of poverty generally similar to that of whites.

Levels of educational attainment mirror that observed for poverty (data not shown). Hispanics stand out as the most disadvantaged group, with half of all Hispanic adults having less than a high school education. Fully 24 percent of American Indians also fall into this category. But marked variation in formal education is again evident. Mexicans (55 percent) and Central Americans (57 percent) are four times more likely to have less than a high school education than Puerto Ricans (14 percent) and South Americans (14 percent). Asians, blacks, Other Race, and multiracial persons are about twice as likely as whites to have not graduated from high school. Among Asians, Japanese (3 percent) and South Asians (13 percent) have the lowest rates and Vietnamese (30 percent) have the highest rates of not completing high school. Asians (47 percent) and whites (39 percent) have the highest rates of college completion, blacks (24 percent) and Pacific Islanders (22 percent) have intermediate rates, and American Indians (13 percent), and Latinos (8 percent) have very low rates.

For all of our racial and ethnic categories, except Other Race, the poor are more likely to rate their health negatively than the affluent are. The largest effects are at the lower levels of income. Each row of table 6.2 presents the results from a separate regression model in which we examined the association between household income and self-rated ill-health, with very high income as the omitted category. It shows that for whites, blacks, Hispanics, Native Americans, Asians, and multiracial persons, there is a stepwise progression with each higher level of income associated with better health status. T9 + his pattern, however, was not evident for Pacific Islanders, Puerto Ricans, Chinese, Filipinos, and Vietnamese. Of particular interest is that the highest risk of poor health was observed for the penultimate income group among Pacific Islanders. A somewhat similar pattern has been noted for blacks, where for some measures of health status (such as hypertension and suicide), middle class African Americans sometimes have worse health than their lower SES peers (Williams 2003). Future research needs to clearly identify the factors that may be an added pathogenic burden for middle class members of some socially disadvantaged groups and the conditions that give rise to this specific pattern of ill-health.

Our next set of analyses confirm that SES is the most important reason for racial

TABLE 6.1 / Poverty Level by Race-Ethnicity

Race-Ethnicity	N	Poverty (0 to 99 Percent)	Near Poverty (100 to 199 Percent)	Moderate Income (200 to 299 Percent)	High Income (300 to 399 Percent)	Very High Income (400 Percent and Higher)
White	34,383	6.1	14.3	13.7	18.6	47.3
Black	2,498	20.9	21.5	16.3	15.3	26.0
Latino	11,840	32.4	31.1	14.0	10.8	11.6
Mexican	8,304	35.0	32.1	14.3	9.4	9.2
Central American	1,019	37.1	35.3	11.1	9.5	7.0
Puerto Rican	180	12.6	23.9	16.3	20.2	27.0
South American	275	18.4	23.7	17.5	14.9	25.4
Other Latino	788	16.8	22.4	12.0	17.4	31.4
Multiethnic Latino	1,155	19.8	25.9	15.1	18.0	21.2
Pacific Islander	189	11.5	20.8	22.1	20.0	25.6
American Indian	424	15.3	25.8	17.4	17.5	24.0
Asian	4,651	13.5	18.6	15.1	15.1	37.7
Chinese	1,227	14.0	18.0	11.9	12.2	43.8
Filipino	831	6.7	21.2	20.1	21.2	30.9
South Asian	381	4.6	10.6	14.8	11.6	58.4
Japanese	468	6.2	14.2	12.4	16.9	50.3
Korean	789	11.6	21.6	17.3	13.2	36.3
Vietnamese	821	33.0	23.3	13.9	12.1	17.7
Other Asian	281	26.5	17.7	10.7	17.0	28.1
Other race	181	8.3	21.0	16.7	12.8	41.2
Multiracial	2,104	10.4	18.8	14.7	20.5	35.5

Source: Authors' analyses of the California Health Interview Study, 2001.

TABLE 6.2 / Poverty and Self Rated Ill-Health by Race-Ethnicity and National Origin[a]

	Poverty (0 to 99 Percent)	Near Poverty (100 to 199 Percent)	Moderate Income (200 to 299 Percent)	High Income (300 to 399 Percent)	VeryHigh Income (400 Percent and Higher)
White	.830(.03)**	.565(.02)**	.398(.02)**	.262(.02)**	(omitted)
Black	.807(.05)**	.446(.05)**	.321(.06)**	.148(.06)*	(omitted)
Latino	.997(.03)**	.726(.03)**	.494(.03)**	.269(.03)**	(omitted)
Mexican	.998(.03)**	.748(.03)**	.510(.04)**	.287(.04)**	(omitted)
Central American	.953(.11)**	.530(.11)**	.287(.12)+	.148(.13)**	(omitted)
Puerto Rican	.902(.25)**	.205(.20)**	−.019(.22)**	.280(.20)**	(omitted)
South American	.929(.16)**	.997(.15)**	.767(.17)**	.343(.17)+	(omitted)
Other Latino	.875(.11)**	.495(.10)**	.409(.12)**	.264(.11)+	(omitted)
Multiethnic Latino	.614(.09)**	.530(.08)**	.371(.09)**	.175(.09)**	(omitted)
Pacific Islander	.616(.30)+	.430(.25)**	.014(.25)**	1.093(.25)**	(omitted)
American Indian	.772(.19)**	.503(.17)*	.408(.19)+	.081(.19)**	(omitted)
Asian	.837(.04)**	.415(.04)**	.392(.04)**	.224(.04)**	(omitted)
Chinese	.455(.07)**	.228(.06)**	.177(.07)+	.287(.07)**	(omitted)
Filipino	.684(.10)**	.095(.07)**	.379(.07)**	.121(.07)**	(omitted)
South Asian	.962(.16)**	.448(.11)**	.180(.10)**	.220(.11)+	(omitted)
Japanese	.448(.17)*	.552(.13)**	.425(.13)*	.047(.11)**	(omitted)
Korean	.614(.14)**	.538(.11)**	.454(.11)**	.303(.12)+	(omitted)
Vietnamese	.889(.10)**	.786(.11)**	.488(.12)**	.619(.13)**	(omitted)
Other Asian	.948(.13)**	.802(.15)**	.647(.18)**	.195(.15)**	(omitted)
Other race	.325(.30)**	.350(.20)**	.550(.23)+	.327(.24)**	(omitted)
Multiracial	.791(.13)**	.611(.11)**	.336(.12)*	.187(.10)**	(omitted)

Source: Authors' analyses of the California Health Interview Study, 2001.
[a] Adjusted for age and gender.
* p < .01; ** p < .001; + p < .05

disparities in health, but that disparities remain after SES is considered. Table 6.3 presents unstandardized regression coefficients for the association between race-ethnicity and our four indicators of health status. Two models are presented for each outcome. The first model shows the association between race-ethnic status and health, adjusted for gender and age. The second model adds three indicators of SES: poverty levels, years of formal education, and employment status (currently employed versus not employed). Model 1 shows that almost all of the racial-ethnic categories have higher levels of self-rated ill-health, emotional distress and physical limitation than the non-Hispanic white population. Model 2 shows that the consideration of SES markedly reduces these excess levels of ill health, at times to nonsignificance; this is especially true for emotional distress. Only for self-rated ill-health is there a residual effect of race for most groups after SES has been taken into account. But differences from this pattern are instructive. African Americans and those identifying as multiracial also show higher levels of emotional distress and physical limitations, even after controlling for SES. By contrast, Japanese Americans show lower rates of emotional distress and several Asian groups report lower levels of physical limitations than whites. These associations are unchanged or become more, not less, marked when socioeconomic indicators are considered. Factors other than SES, presumably the psychosocial context of mental health and immigration status, may play a role in shaping the health status of these Asian groups.

The final panel of table 6.3 shows the association of race and ethnicity with chronic conditions. Groups with a long history of residence in the United States (African Americans, Puerto Ricans, Pacific Islanders, American Indians, and multiracial persons) report higher levels of chronic health conditions than whites. At the same time, Latino and Asian populations that have a high proportion of immigrants report lower levels of chronic health conditions. As we have already seen, for groups with elevated rates of chronic health conditions, the addition of SES in Model 2 reduces the size of that relationship but does not eliminate it. For those population groups with lower levels of chronic health conditions than whites, the addition of SES generally leaves that association intact.

In sum, table 6.3 reveals a fairly complex pattern of association between race-ethnicity, SES, and health. In general, most nonwhite racial and ethnic populations have higher levels of illness than whites, but the association varies by specific health outcome and by the particular population under consideration. Across all of the health status indicators considered, African Americans and American Indians have elevated levels of poor health. A consistent disadvantage is also evident in these data for persons reporting multiracial status. Our analyses also confirm that racial differences in SES play a large role in accounting for variations in health. Associations between race and health were reduced when socioeconomic variables were considered, but remained robust and significant even in the face of controls for three SES indicators. The CHIS data do not allow for the analysis of the relative contribution of the various race-related factors, reviewed earlier, that have been shown to contribute to an elevated risk of illness after SES is taken into account.

TABLE 6.3 / Race-Ethnicity and Health Conditions

	Self-Rated Ill-Health		Emotional Distress		Physical Limitations		Chronic Health Conditions	
	Model 1	Model 2	Model 1	Model 2	Model 1	Model 2	Model 1	Model 2
Gender (women)	.063 (.01)*	-.030 (.01)*	.516 (.04)*	.380 (.02)*	.451(.02)*	.241 (.02)*	.042 (.01)*	-.003 (.01)*
Age	.013 (.00)*	.010 (.00)*	.003 (.00)*	-.002 (.00)+	.04 (.00)*	.033 (.00)*	.026 (.00)*	.024 (.00)*
White (omitted)								
Black	.387 (.02)*	.216 (.02)*	.361 (.04)*	.159 (.04)*	.498 (.04)*	.246 (.04)*	.276 (.02)*	.231 (.02)*
Latino								
Mexican	.769 (.01)*	.321 (.00)*	.322 (.02)*	-.150 (.03)*	.339 (.03)*	-.252 (.03)*	-.036 (.01)*	-.151 (.01)*
Central American	.776 (.03)*	.328 (.03)*	.482 (.05)*	.003 (.05)*	.336 (.06)*	-.241 (.06)*	-.090 (.02)*	-.200 (.02)*
Puerto Rican	.243 (.07)*	.094 (.07)*	.334 (.14)+	.181 (.14)	.248 (.16)*	.072 (.16)	.139 (.06)+	.108 (.06)*
South American	.245 (.06)+	.116 (.06)+	.102 (.11)*	-.061 (.11)*	.038 (.13)*	-.131 (.12)*	-.155 (.05)*	-.182 (.05)*
Other Latino	.311 (.04)*	.137 (.04)*	.303 (.07)*	.121 (.07)*	.305 (.08)*	.083 (.08)*	.104 (.03)*	.051 (.03)*
Multiethnic Latino	.432 (.03)*	.159 (.03)*	.361 (.06)*	.070 (.06)*	.458 (.06)*	.082 (.06)*	.149 (.02)*	.071 (.02)+
Pacific Islander	.276 (.08)*	.122 (.07)*	.330 (.15)+	.168 (.15)*	.588 (.17)*	.396 (.16)+	.126 (.06)+	.089 (.06)*
American Indian	.476 (.06)*	.251 (.05)*	.228 (.11)+	.073 (.11)*	.600 (.12)*	.328 (.12)+	.359 (.04)*	.303 (.04)*
Asian								
Chinese	.284 (.02)*	.230 (.02)*	-.024 (.05)*	-.103 (.05)+	-.316 (.05)*	-.418 (.05)*	-.237 (.02)*	-.256 (.02)*
Filipino	.133 (.03)*	.122 (.03)*	.075 (.05)*	.033 (.05)*	-.223 (.06)*	-.256 (.06)*	-.048 (.02)+	-.047 (.02)+
South Asian	-.160 (.04)*	-.025 (.04)	-.163 (.08)+	-.069 (.08)*	-.130 (.09)*	-.007 (.09)*	-.177 (.03)*	-.146 (.03)*
Japanese	.031 (.04)*	.051 (.04)*	-.242 (.09)+	-.242 (.08)+	-.322 (.10)*	-.349 (.09)*	-.057 (.03)*	-.063 (.03)*
Korean	.370 (.04)*	.312 (.04)*	-.028 (.08)*	-.148 (.08)*	-.216 (.09)+	-.371 (.09)*	-.241 (.03)*	-.266 (.03)*
Vietnamese	.920 (.04)*	.604 (.04)*	.449 (.07)*	.085 (.07)*	.444 (.08)*	-.016 (.08)*	-.107 (.03)*	-.197 (.03)*
Other Asian	.418 (.05)*	.212 (.05)*	.378 (.10)*	.106 (.10)*	.295 (.11)+	-.055 (.11)*	-.128 (.04)*	-.193 (.04)*
Other Race	.057 (.08)*	-.011 (.08)*	-.129 (.16)*	-.214 (.15)*	.042 (.18)*	-.056 (.17)*	-.003 (.06)*	-.023 (.06)*
Multiracial	.308 (.04)*	.206 (.03)*	.404 (.07)*	.299 (.07)*	.691 (.08)*	.563 (.08)*	.259 (.03)*	.233 (.03)*
Income (poverty levels)		-.123 (.00)*		-.170 (.01)*		-.176 (.01)*		-.022 (.00)*
Education		-.128 (.00)*		-.084 (.01)*		-.125 (.01)*		-.035 (.00)*
Employment (employed)		-.228 (.01)*		-.403 (.02)*		-.798 (.02)*		-.187 (.01)*
Constant	1.597 (.02)	2.963 (.02)	5.52 (.04)	7.17 (.05)	3.02 (.04)	5.40 (.06)	-.530 (.02)	-.034 (.02)
R²	.107	.195	.023	.058	.103	.158	.252	.267

Source: Authors' analyses of the California Health Interview Study, 2001.
* p < .001; + p < .05

For Latinos, the pattern is complex, with higher levels of illness than whites observed for some health outcomes such as self-rated ill-health, emotional distress and physical limitation, but with a lower level of chronic health conditions. At the same time, the consideration of SES markedly reduces and in some cases reverses the elevated levels of ill health for some Latino populations, particularly Mexicans and Central Americans. This may reflect the selective effect of immigration: these two populations are some of the most disadvantaged in SES, but are nonetheless probably selected on the basis of health.

A very complex pattern of association is observed for the Asian population: most Asian groups rate their own health more poorly than whites, but do considerably better than whites on emotional distress, physical limitations, and chronic health conditions. An important take-home message from the results in table 6.3 is the great diversity within the Latino and Asian categories, where patterns vary dramatically depending on the health outcome and the particular group under consideration.

GENDER, RACE, POVERTY, AND HEALTH

Time and space prevent us from fully and systematically attending to variations in the association among race-ethnicity, SES and health by gender. Each of these variables can make an important contribution to disparities in health. Moreover, their effects are additive. David Williams (2005a) shows that national data on life expectancy at age twenty-five for blacks and whites reveal that the most advantaged, in terms of health, are white women at the highest level of income: at age twenty-five, they can expect to live almost fifty-eight more years. The worst off are low-income African American males, who can only expect to live an additional 41.6 years. The life expectancy difference between these two groups (16.2 years) is almost four times as large as the overall black-white difference, more than twice as large as the gender difference for blacks and whites, and almost twice the size of the largest income differences in life expectancy.

Pamela Jackson and Williams (2006) also highlighted the paradoxes of the black middle class. For example, in national data, the highest SES group of African American women show equivalent or higher rates of infant mortality, low birth weight, hypertension, and overweight than the lowest SES group of white women (Pamuk et al. 1998). Among men, although SES is inversely related to the suicide rate for whites, it is positively related to suicide for blacks (Williams 2003). Some evidence suggests these patterns result from differential exposure to social and economic adversity and individual and institutional discrimination over the life course, as well as from different cultural practices and beliefs and the noncomparability of SES indicators across race (Jackson and Williams 2006).

Addressing how migration history and acculturation combine with nativity differences and SES to produce gendered patterns in racial health disparities is beyond the scope of this chapter. Nonetheless, to highlight the importance of attending to gender, we examined the association between poverty levels and self-rated ill-health separately for men and women, in each of the racial categories in the CHIS data. Our analyses, not shown here, reveal a now familiar finding: for most racial groups, for both genders, the largest effect of SES is in the poor and near-poor categories, with a stepwise progression of risk in which each higher level of income is associated with better health. There were two noteworthy exceptions to this pattern. Among Pacific Islanders, poor men have markedly elevated rates of ill-health compared to higher income men, but women with higher incomes (at least three times the poverty level) are almost twice as likely as poor women to report being in poor health. Among American Indians, there was little variation in health by income for men, though poor women were three times more likely to report ill-health than poor men. Some 27 percent of American Indian women in poverty reported their health as fair or poor, substantially higher than that of any other racial-income group in CHIS. Future research needs to elucidate the determinants of the markedly elevated health risks of high income Pacific Island women and poor American Indian women.

MIGRATION, SES, AND HEALTH

The relationship between race-ethnicity and health requires careful attention to the role of migration in shaping patterns in the distribution of health. The impact of immigration is likely to be especially important for Hispanics and Asians because high proportions of these groups are immigrants. Immigrant groups vary dramatically from each other and from their native counterparts in income. Table 6.4 shows that immigrant whites, most of the Latino subgroups, and Pacific Islanders all have higher rates of poverty than their native-born counterparts, and that the opposite pattern is evident for blacks, Puerto Ricans, South Asians, Koreans, Vietnamese, and multiracial persons. For other groups, such as Filipinos, immigrant and native-born rates of poverty are very close. A similar heterogeneity is evident at high levels of income. Levels of high and very high income (300 percent of the federal poverty level or greater) are roughly comparable for immigrants and the native-born for whites, blacks, Filipinos, Japanese and multiracial persons. For some Latino groups (Mexican Americans, Central Americans, South Americans), Pacific Islanders, some Asian groups (Chinese, South Asians, Other Asians), and Other Race persons, the native-born are much more likely to be in the high income categories. However, immigrants from Puerto Rico, Korea, and Vietnam are much more likely to fall into the high income categories than their native-born counterparts.

In the 2000 census, 24 percent of American adults aged twenty-five years and older had a college degree. Analyses in the CHIS sample (not shown) of variations in educational attainment by immigrant status show striking differences across the various racial and ethnic populations. White, black, South American, and Asian immigrants in California have levels of college completion that are twice the U.S. average: the South Asian immigrant rate is especially high (83 percent). Some immigrants also have markedly higher levels of formal education com-

TABLE 6.4 / Poverty Levels by Race-Ethnicity and Nativity Status

Race-Ethnicity	N	Poverty (0 to 99 Percent)	Near Poverty (100 to 199 Percent)	Moderate Income (200 to 299 Percent)	High Income (300 to 399 Percent)	Very High Income (400 Percent or Higher)
White native	38,818	5.9	14.2	13.8	18.7	47.4
White immigrant	2,565	8.1	15.5	12.5	17.4	46.6
Black native	2,373	21.6	21.6	15.3	15.7	25.8
Black immigrant	125	9.5	20.4	30.3	10.4	29.5
Latino native	5,104	18.0	23.2	17.1	17.9	23.8
Latino immigrant	6,736	40.3	35.5	12.4	6.9	4.9
Mexican native	3,171	18.9	22.6	18.8	17.7	22.0
Mexican immigrant	5,133	42.3	36.5	12.3	5.6	3.3
Central American native	106	19.3	33.9	9.2	19.6	18.0
Central American immigrant	913	38.9	35.5	11.3	8.5	5.9
Puerto Rican native	155	13.9	22.6	17.7	18.6	27.2
Puerto Rican immigrant	25	5.3	31.5	8.2	28.8	26.2
South American native	57	8.2	7.9	9.1	21.4	53.4
South American immigrant	218	20.6	27.0	19.3	13.5	19.6
Other Latino native	601	13.5	23.0	12.7	16.8	34.0
Other Latino immigrant	187	25.2	20.8	10.3	19.0	24.8
Multiethnic Latino native	931	17.7	25.1	15.0	18.6	23.5
Multiethnic Latino immigrant	224	27.5	28.6	15.6	15.7	12.6
Pacific Isle native	145	10.4	15.8	24.1	23.0	26.7
Pacific Isle immigrant	44	14.3	33.0	17.3	12.5	22.9

Asian native	879	8.4	14.2	15.3	17.3	44.8
Asian immigrant	3,772	14.9	19.7	15.0	14.5	35.8
Chinese native	275	5.8	9.4	12.3	15.3	57.2
Chinese immigrant	952	15.9	20.0	11.7	11.4	40.9
Filipino native	165	8.6	17.0	21.1	22.9	30.3
Filipino immigrant	666	6.2	22.2	19.8	20.4	31.4
South Asian native	37	8.3	25.8	14.0	10.1	41.8
South Asian immigrant	344	4.3	7.5	15.2	12.0	61.0
Japanese native	341	4.3	13.8	12.8	16.7	52.4
Japanese immigrant	127	12.6	13.8	12.0	15.4	46.1
Korean native	73	20.9	19.8	16.2	4.0	39.1
Korean immigrant	716	10.3	21.9	17.4	14.5	35.8
Vietnamese native	16	38.0	29.6	16.8	13.8	1.8
Vietnamese immigrant	805	32.8	23.1	13.7	12.0	18.4
Other Asian native	58	15.7	7.5	8.2	25.9	42.7
Other Asian immigrant	223	29.6	20.1	11.5	15.1	23.7
Other race native	137	7.1	12.0	21.6	15.5	43.8
Other race immigrant	44	10.6	39.0	7.0	7.5	36.0
Multiethnic native	1,990	10.9	17.9	14.6	20.7	35.9
Multiethnic immigrant	114	6.3	27.6	16.0	18.2	31.9

Source: Authors' analyses of the California Health Interview Study, 2001.

pared to the native-born individuals of their racial group. This is true for whites, blacks, Puerto Ricans, Other Latinos, Pacific Islanders, Other Race, and multiracial persons. The overall levels of education for Asian immigrants and natives are comparable, but some Asian immigrant subgroups (Filipino, South Asian, Korean, Vietnamese, and Other Asians) have higher levels of college completion than their native-born peers. In contrast, college completion rates among Latino immigrants are very low: only 5 percent for all Latinos, and 3 percent for Mexicans.

As noted earlier, research suggests that there should be a general expectation that immigrants, especially Hispanics, would enjoy better health than their native-born counterparts. Table 6.5 provides a careful look at this issue for self-rated ill health and emotional distress. It shows that the expected pattern is true for black, Puerto Rican, and Filipino immigrants. Strikingly, black immigrants in California actually enjoy better health than U.S.-born whites. In contrast, the Hispanic paradox does not hold true for most Latino groups or for Pacific Islanders, Koreans, Other Asians, and persons of multiracial status: these are more likely than their native-born counterparts to report ill health and emotional distress. For still other groups—Vietnamese, Japanese, and Chinese—immigrants and native-born persons report fairly similar levels of self-rated health and emotional distress. Taking SES into account in Model 2 produces few changes to the patterns for self-rated ill health noted in Model 1, but does produce large reductions in the excess risk of emotional distress for immigrants. This suggests that, compared to physical health, immigrant mental health and emotional well being are more affected by stressors linked to migration, adaptation, and SES.

By contrast, physical limitations and chronic conditions display patterns that more closely mirror the general expectations of the literature. Several immigrant groups report lower levels of physical limitations than their native-born counterparts. This is true for whites, blacks, Central Americans, Filipinos, Japanese, and multiracial persons. Adjusting the relationship for SES reduces the association but the underlying pattern persists. At the same time, Pacific Island immigrants and multiethnic Latino immigrants report higher levels of physical limitation than their native-born counterparts; when SES is taken into account, the pattern remains significant for Pacific Islanders but becomes nonsignificant for multiethnic Latinos.

The analyses of chronic conditions most clearly show the effect of immigrant selectivity. Most immigrant populations have lower levels of chronic conditions than their native-born counterparts and adjusting for SES makes this pattern stronger (see table 6.6). The only exception to this pattern is Puerto Ricans, who report a higher level of chronic conditions than their native-born counterparts. In addition, adjustment for SES leaves the fundamental pattern largely unchanged for blacks, whites, Filipinos, and South Asians.

Much of existing research on the health of immigrants has used readily available mortality data. Our analyses reveal that the pattern observed in the mortality data (immigrants have better health than the native-born) is generally true for measures of physical health status as well. On measures that capture emotional

TABLE 6.5 / Immigrant Status and Self-Rated Ill-Health and Emotional Distress[a]

	Subjective Health		Emotional Distress	
	Model 1	Model 2	Model 1	Model 2
White native (omitted)				
White immigrant	-.049 (.02)+	-.018 (.02)	.085 (.04)+	.097 (.04)+
Black native	.419 (.02)*	.249 (.02)*	.381 (.04)*	.169 (.04)*
Black immigrant	-.162 (.07)+	-.197 (.07)+	.188 (.14)	.119 (.14)
Latino				
Mexican native	.412 (.02)*	.164 (.02)*	.155 (.04)*	-.114 (.04)*
Mexican immigrant	.925 (.01)*	.418 (.02)*	.409 (.03)*	-.161 (.03)*
Central American native	.518 (.08)*	.218 (.08)+	.263 (.16)	-.098 (.16)
Central American immigrant	.797 (.03)*	.357 (.03)*	.512 (.05)*	.018 (.05)
Puerto Rican native	.282 (.08)*	.139 (.08)	.332 (.16)+	.171 (.16)
Puerto Rican immigrant	-.003 (.19)	-.123 (.18)	.391 (.37)	.285 (.36)
South American native	-.096 (.14)	-.045 (.13)	.000 (.27)	.032 (.26)
South American immigrant	.311 (.06)*	.155 (.06)*	.131 (.12)	-.071 (.12)
Other Latino native	.344 (.04)*	.185 (.04)*	.325 (.09)*	.148 (.08)
Other Latino immigrant	.213 (.07)+	.030 (.07)	.273 (.14)+	.077 (.13)
Multiethnic Latino native	.393 (.03)*	.150 (.03)*	.323 (.06)*	.050 (.06)
Multiethnic Latino immigrant	.553 (.06)*	.228 (.06)*	.538 (.12)*	.173 (.12)
Pacific Isle native	.248 (.09)+	.104 (.09)	.288 (.18)	.139 (.17)
Pacific Isle immigrant	.328 (.14)+	.183 (.13)	.461 (.28)	.265 (.28)
American Indian	.495 (.06)*	.276 (.05)*	.324 (.11)+	.103 (.11)

TABLE 6.5 / Continued

	Subjective Health		Emotional Distress	
	Model 1	Model 2	Model 1	Model 2
Asian				
Chinese native	.124 (.06)+	.212 (.05)*	.127 (.11)	.196 (.11)
Chinese immigrant	.313 (.03)*	.234 (.03)*	-.047 (.05)	-.157 (.05)+
Filipino native	.349 (.06)*	.244 (.05)*	.057 (.11)	-.089 (.11)
Filipino immigrant	.072 (.03)+	.078 (.03)+	.088 (.06)	.075 (.06)
South Asian native	-.285 (.13)+	-.449 (.13)*	-.252 (.26)	-.517 (.26)+
South Asian immigrant	-.152 (.04)*	.011 (.04)	-.146 (.09)	-.012 (.09)
Japanese native	.022 (.05)	.064 (.05)	-.279 (.10)+	-.245 (.10)+
Japanese immigrant	.047 (.09)	-.001 (.08)	-.100 (.17)	-.196 (.17)
Korean native	.146 (.15)	-.024 (.11)	.349 (.23)	.098 (.23)
Korean immigrant	.395 (.04)*	.356 (.04)*	-.072 (.09)	-.171 (.09)+
Vietnamese native	1.157 (.17)*	.667 (.16)*	.584 (.33)	-.047 (.33)
Vietnamese immigrant	.904 (.04)*	.611 (.04)*	.450 (.07)*	.097 (.07)
Other Asian native	.190 (.11)	.148 (.10)	-.578 (.21)+	-.654 (.21)+
Other Asian immigrant	.473 (.06)*	.235 (.05)*	.645 (.11)*	.320 (.11)+
Other race native	.095 (.10)	.062 (.09)	-.117 (.19)	-.158 (.19)
Other immigrant	-.032 (.14)	-.155 (.13)	-.133 (.27)	-.301 (.27)
Multiethnic native	.296 (.04)*	.202 (.04)*	.421 (.08)*	.318 (.07)*
Multiethnic immigrant	.376 (.12)*	.276 (.11)+	.315 (.23)	.190 (.23)
Poverty		-.117 (.00)*		-.170 (.01)*
Education		-.123 (.00)*		-.086 (.01)*
Employment		-.233 (.01)*		-.404 (.02)*
Constant	1.60 (.02)	2.93 (.03)	5.52 (.04)	7.18 (.05)
R²	.119	.199	.025	.059

Source: Authors' analyses of the California Health Interview Study, 2001.
[a] Adjusted for age and gender.
* p < .001; + p < .05

TABLE 6.6 / Immigrant Status and Physical Limitations and Chronic Conditions[a]

	Physical Limitations		Chronic Conditions	
	Model 1	Model 2	Model 1	Model 2
White native (omitted)				
White immigrant	-.265 (.05)*	-.243 (.05)*	-.159 (.02)*	-.150 (.02)*
Black native	.519 (.04)*	.245 (.04)*	.294 (.02)*	.238 (.02)*
Black immigrant	-.160 (.16)	-.211 (.15)	-.203 (.06)	-.205 (.06)*
Latino				
Mexican native	.300 (.04)*	-.053 (.04)	.079 (.01)*	-.000 (.01)
Mexican immigrant	.327 (.03)*	-.407 (.03)*	-.106 (.01)*	-.264 (.01)*
Central American native	.685 (.18)*	.192 (.18)	-.008 (.07)	-.114 (.06)
Central American immigrant	.277 (.06)*	-.335 (.06)*	-.113 (.02) *	-.243 (.02)*
Puerto Rican native	.239 (.18)	.042 (.17)	.053 (.06)	.013 (.06)
Puerto Rican immigrant	.156 (.41)	.049 (.40)	.540 (.15)*	.516 (.15)*
South American native	-.275 (.30)	-.246 (.29)	.059 (.11)	.067 (.11)
South American immigrant	.079 (.14)	-.142 (.13)	-.216 (.05)*	-.258 (.05)*
Other Latino native	.341 (.10)*	.099 (.09)	.125 (.03)*	.070 (.03)+
Other Latino immigrant	.136 (.15)	-.064 (.15)	.001 (.05)	-.067 (.05)
Multiethnic Latino native	.411 (.07)*	.039 (.07)	.186 (.03)*	.103 (.03)*
Multiethnic Latino immigrant	.534 (.13)*	.088 (.13)	-.046 (.05)	-.151 (.05)*
Pacific Isle native	.309 (.20)	.118 (.19)	.180 (.07)+	.137 (.07)+
Pacific Isle immigrant	1.20 (.31)*	.982 (.30)*	-.053 (.11)	-.094 (.11)
American indian	.622 (12)*	.333 (.12)+	.360 (.04)*	.294 (.04)*

TABLE 6.6 / Continued

	Subjective Health		Emotional Distress	
	Model 1	Model 2	Model 1	Model 2
Asian				
Chinese native	-.268 (.12)+	-.185 (.12)	-.106 (.04)+	-.085 (.04)+
Chinese immigrant	-.353 (.06)*	-.497 (.06)*	-.281 (.02)*	-.310 (.02)*
Filipino native	.097 (.12)	-.124 (.12)	.042 (.04)	-.005 (.04)
Filipino immigrant	-.332 (.06)*	-.320 (.06)*	-.087 (.02)*	-.077 (.02)*
South Asian native	.049 (.29)	-.398 (.28)	-.028 (.11)	-.125 (.10)
South Asian immigrant	-.172 (.10)	.019 (.09)	-.207 (.03)*	-.157 (.03)*
Japanese native	-.288 (.11)+	-.256 (.11)+	-.020 (.04)	-.012 (.04)
Japanese immigrant	-.522 (.19)+	-.711 (.19)*	-.225 (.07)*	-.261 (.07)*
Korean native	-.220 (.26)	-.603 (.25)+	-.122 (.09)	-.203 (.09)+
Korean immigrant	-.240 (.10)+	-.365 (.09)*	-.272 (.03)*	-.291 (.03)*
Vietnamese native	.433 (.37)	-.466 (.36)	.127 (.13)	-.066 (.13)
Vietnamese immigrant	.422 (.08)*	-.032 (.08)	-.132 (.03)*	-.229 (.03)*
Other Asian native	-.357 (.24)	-.471 (.23)+	-.168 (.09)+	-.191 (.08)+
Other Asian immigrant	.447 (.12)*	.023 (.12)	-.132 (.04)+	-.218 (.04)*
Other native	-.085 (.21)	-.151 (.21)	.128 (.08)	.115 (.08)
Other immigrant	.246 (.31)	.073 (.30)	-.302 (.11)+	-.342 (.11)*
Multiethnic native	.773 (.08)*	.645 (.081)*	.275 (.03)*	.246 (.03)*
Multiethnic immigrant	-.333 (.26)	-.501 (.247)+	-.036 (.09)	-.071 (.10)
Poverty		-.187 (.008)*		-.031 (.00)*
Education		-.129 (.008)*		-.038 (.00)*
Employment		-.790 (.022)*		-.179 (.01)*
Constant	3.04 (.14)	5.46 (.06)	-.521 (.02)	.012 (.021)
R²	.105	.161	.257	.274

Source: Authors' analyses of the California Health Interview Study, 2001.
[a] Adjusted for age and gender.
* p < .001; + p < .05

functioning or have a large subjective component, however, many immigrant groups do more poorly than their native-born peers. This pattern of findings suggests the importance of studying multiple indicators of health status: in particular, how stressors linked to migration and adaptation can affect well being and economic productivity. In addition, the variation across race and ethnicity highlight the necessity of understanding the role of culture and acculturation and its effects on health.

LENGTH OF RESIDENCE AND HEALTH

Research suggests that the health advantage of immigrants tends to decline over time as length of stay and acculturation increase. Adaptation to U.S. behavioral norms can lead to the adoption of nutritional, physical, and substance use behaviors that in turn lead to increased risk of common chronic diseases. In addition, increasing exposure to American society can result in experiences of discrimination and other barriers to social and economic opportunity. The resultant feelings of frustration and thwarted aspirations, combined with exposure to elevated levels of acute and chronic stress consistent with life in a modern industrialized society, can lead to increased emotional distress. Research on Latinos reveals that adult mortality, infant mortality, psychiatric disorders, psychological distress, substance use, low birth weight, poor health practices, and other indicators of morbidity all increase with length of stay and acculturation (Finch et al. 2002; Vega and Amaro 1994). Similarly, an analysis of the prevalence of chronic disease in the National Health Interview Survey from 1992 to 1995 show that recent immigrants reported better health than long-term immigrants and the U.S.-born (Singh and Miller 2004). This pattern existed for non-Hispanic whites and blacks, most Asian groups, and Mexicans, Cubans, and Central and South Americans.

This issue has not received as much attention as it should, because sample sizes of immigrants need to be quite large before the effects of length of stay can be measured accurately. In the CHIS, this is true for four groups: Mexicans, Central Americans, Chinese, and Filipinos. In these analyses persons born in the United States are compared to immigrants of one year or less, two to four years, five to nine years, ten to fourteen years, and fifteen or more years. The result, presented in tables 6.7 and 6.8, largely contradict previous findings: for three of the four measures of health, they show worse, not better, health for recent immigrants. They also highlight the importance of controlling for SES to explain the variation in health for the different ethnic groups.

Recent Mexican, Central American, and Chinese immigrants report poorer self-rated health than their native-born counterparts. The coefficients for time in the United States become smaller with increasing lengths of stay, markedly so for Central Americans and Chinese, and adjusting for SES markedly reduces the association between length of stay and self-rated ill-health for all. Hispanic immigrants, especially those most recently arrived, are also are more likely to report emotional distress and physical limitations. Again, adjusting for SES reduces the

TABLE 6.7 / Length of U.S. Residence and Health Conditions for Mexican and Central Americans[a]

	Self-Rated Ill-Health		Emotional Distress		Physical Limitations		Chronic Conditions	
	Model 1	Model 2	Model 1	Model 2	Model 1	Model 2	Model 1	Model 2
Mexican								
U.S.-born (omitted)								
Less than one year	.563 (.06)*	.199 (.06)+	.683 (.14)*	.275 (.12)	.288 (.14)+	-.104 (.14)*	-.115 (.04)+	-.163 (.05)*
Two to four year	.673 (.04)*	.332 (.04)*	.374 (.09)*	-.021 (.10)	.160 (.09)*	-.235 (.09)+	-.125 (.03)*	-.188 (.03)*
Five to nine years	.624 (.03)*	.277 (.03)*	.301 (.07)*	-.118 (.08)	.175 (.07)+	-.264 (.07)*	-.174 (.02)*	-.238 (.02)*
Ten to fourteen years	.563 (.03)*	.248 (.03)*	.324 (.06)*	-.003 (.06)	.007 (.06)*	-.312 (.06)*	-.210 (.02)*	-.263 (.02)*
Fifteen or more years	.393 (.02)*	.146 (.02)*	.130 (.05)+	-.137 (.06)+	-.075 (.05)*	-.304 (.05)*	-.190 (.02)*	-.226 (.02)*
Poverty		-.138 (.01)*		-.176 (.02)*		-.166 (.02)*		-.018 (.01)+
Education		-.138 (.01)*		-.107 (.02)*		-.080 (.02)*		-.022 (.01)*
Employment		-.154 (.02)*		-.412 (.05)*		-.745 (.05)*		-.130 (.02)*
Constant	1.82 (.04)*	2.91 (.05)*	5.12 (.09)*	6.63 (.12)*	3.61 (.08)*	5.47 (.12)*	-.645 (.03)	-.328 (.04)
R²	.102	.171	.031	.055	.068	.110	.276	.281
Central American								
U.S.-born (omitted)								
Less than one year	.485 (.18)+	.235 (.18)	.928 (.42)+	.683 (.42)*	-.101 (.36)*	-.433 (.35)*	-.219 (.11)+	-.254 (.11)+
Two to four year	.703 (.13)*	.320 (.13)+	.822 (.31)+	.400 (.32)*	.662 (.26)+	.160 (.27)*	-.116 (.08)*	-.160 (.08)*
Five to nine years	.243 (.11)*	-.025 (.11)*	.069 (.27)*	-.151 (.27)*	.009 (.23)*	-.274 (.23)*	.091 (.08)*	.087 (.07)*
Ten to fourteen years	.092 (.10)*	-.059 (.10)*	-.145 (.24)*	-.272 (.24)*	-.702 (.20)*	-.850 (.20)*	-.182 (.06)+	-.151 (.06)+
Fifteen or more years	.010 (.10)*	-.035 (.10)*	-.037 (.23)*	-.040 (.23)*	-.650 (.20)*	-.661 (.20)*	-.079 (.06)*	-.043 (.06)*
Poverty		-.245 (.03)*		-.158 (.06)+		-.241 (.05)*		-.037 (.02)+
Education		-.170 (.02)*		-.109 (.06)*		-.087 (.05)*		.013 (.01)*
Employment		-.212 (.06)*		-.348 (.14)+		-.377 (.20)+		-.195 (.04)+
Constant	1.66 (.12)*	2.93 (.15)*	5.00 (.28)*	6.34 (.37)	3.18 (.23)*	4.78 (.31)*	-.598 (.07)	-.272 (.10)*
R²	.084	.172	.044	.057	.104	.132	.197	.209

Source: Authors' analyses of the California Health Interview Study, 2001.
[a] Adjusted for age and gender.
* p < .001; + p < .05

TABLE 6.8 / Length of U.S. Residence and Conditions for Chinese and Filipinos[a]

	Self-Rated Ill-Health		Emotional Distress		Physical Limitations		Chronic Conditions	
	Model 1	Model 2	Model 1	Model 2	Model 1	Model 2	Model 1	Model 2
Chinese								
U.S.-born (omitted)								
Less than one year	.415 (.12)*	.337 (.13)+	-.354 (.25)	-.543 (.25)+	-.314 (.23)	-.524 (.24)+	-.265 (.08)*	-.349 (.08)*
Two to four year	.205 (.09)+	.110 (.09)*	-.043 (.19)	-.234 (.19)*	.269 (.17)	.080 (.18)*	-.124 (.06)+	-.181 (.06)+
Five to nine years	.435 (.08)*	.351 (.09)*	.263 (.17)	.133 (.17)*	.026 (.16)	-.080 (.16)*	-.189 (.05)*	-.198 (.05)*
Ten to fourteen years	.183 (.08)+	.133 (.08)*	-.128 (.15)	-.201 (.15)*	-.041 (.14)	-.098 (.14)*	-.127 (.05)+	-.129 (.05)+
Fifteen or more years	-.024 (.07)*	-.034 (.07)*	-.256 (.13)	-.253 (.13)*	-.217 (.12)	-.197 (.12)*	-.104 (.04)+	-.086 (.04)+
Poverty		-.058 (.02)*		-.066 (.04)*		-.052 (.03)*		.001 (.01)*
Education		-.025 (.02)*		-.044 (.03)*		-.032 (.03)*		.005 (.01)*
Employment		-.067 (.05)*		-.296 (.11)+		-.377 (.10)*		-.198 (.03)*
Constant	1.29 (.10)*	1.84 (.15)*	5.96 (.21)*	6.96 (.30)*	2.63 (.19)*	3.6 (.28)*	-.355 (.07)*	-.124 (.09)
R^2	.120	.132	.015	.025	.139	.150	.232	.246
Filipinos								
U.S.-born (omitted)								
Less than one year	-.624 (.15)*	-.700 (.14)*	-.551 (.30)	-.793 (.30)+	.774 (.30)+	.608 (.28)+	-.069 (.11)*	-.132 (.11)*
Two to four year	-.574 (.11)*	-.447 (.11)*	.169 (.23)	.302 (.23)*	-.438 (.23)*	-.207 (.22)*	-.314 (.09)*	-.262 (.09)+
Five to nine years	-.406 (.10)*	-.412 (.10)*	-.368 (.19)	-.412 (.19)+	-.177 (.19)*	-.171 (.18)*	-.272 (.07)*	-.277 (.07)*
Ten to fourteen years	-.294 (.09)*	-.185 (.09)+	-.071 (.18)	.106 (.18)*	-.746 (.18)*	-.484 (.17)+	-.104 (.07)*	-.039 (.07)*
Fifteen or more years	-.334 (.07)*	-.213 (.07)+	-.221 (.15)	-.002 (.15)*	-.378 (.14)+	-.130 (.14)*	-.288 (.06)*	-.218 (.06)*
Poverty		-.056 (.02)+		-.156 (.04)*		-.059 (.04)*		-.033 (.02)+
Education		-.136 (.02)*		-.119 (.04)*		-.203 (.04)*		-.039 (.01)+
Employment		-.162 (.058)+		-.457 (.120)*		-.606 (.114)		-.169 (.045)*
Constant	2.02 (.10)*	2.85 (.13)*	5.57 (.20)*	7.01 (.26)*	3.71 (.19)*	5.16 (.25)*	-.509 (.08)*	-.093 (.10)*
R^2	.090	.151	.023	.062	.123	.174	.348	.365

Source: Authors' analyses of the California Health Interview Study, 2001.

[a] Adjusted for age and gender.

* p < .001; + p < .05

association for emotional distress to nonsignificance, and tends to reverse the relationship for physical limitations. All of these results show that on most measures, recent immigrants do not enter with a health advantage: their lower SES seems to have the most effect on their health.

The Asian results for emotional distress and physical limitations, by contrast, at first seem to support the literature's findings of better health for immigrants. When adjusted for SES, both Chinese and Filipino immigrants who have spent one year or less in the United States report lower levels of emotional distress than their native-born counterparts. This may reflect an initial effect of a certain level of euphoria and high expectations linked to their successful immigration (Vega and Rumbaut 1991). However, this positive effect is no longer evident with two years or more in the United States, which casts doubt on the literature's more general claim. Recent Chinese immigrants do show lower levels of physical limitations, but only after adjusting for SES, and only then for immigrants of less than a year. For Filipinos, the findings are more complex: immigrants report lower levels of self-rated ill-health than the native-born, and this pattern appears largely independent of SES. Also, Filipino immigrants in the United States ten years or longer report lower levels of physical limitation than the native-born, but those with less than a year report more physical limitations. These associations are reduced but remain significant when adjusted for SES. In total, these results suggest that any health benefit for recent immigrants is generally temporary and contingent on SES, though Filipino immigrants may be an exception.

Chronic conditions are the only health outcomes for which previous expectations about the better health of recent immigrants are confirmed across all groups. For Mexicans, all immigrants report significantly lower levels of chronic conditions than their native-born counterparts. The pattern is somewhat graded, such that the coefficients increase with increasing length of stay in the United States, and adjustment for SES makes the pattern more pronounced. For Central Americans, the very recent immigrants (one year or less) and those in the United States ten to fourteen years, have lower levels of chronic conditions than their native-born counterparts; these relationships remain significant when socioeconomic factors are also considered. Similarly, recent Chinese and Filipino immigrants have lower levels of chronic conditions than their native-born counterparts. This association is largely independent of SES.

Thus, in contrast to our expectation, we found that for three of the four health outcomes, recent Hispanic immigrants report worse health status than their native-born counterparts. Chronic conditions are the only exception. These patterns are more marked for Mexican than Central American immigrants. Research on Central American immigrants has emphasized that many fled conditions of civil war, and thus that Central American immigrants, relative to Mexicans, might be doing much more poorly than their U.S.-born counterparts (Portes and Rumbaut 1996). Our findings suggest, however, that Mexican immigrants may face economic exit conditions or adaptation challenges as harsh or harsher than those for Central Americans.

Perhaps most challenging, the associations between length of residence and health for Asians differed by the indicator under consideration and by the particular immigrant population. Filipinos differed from the Chinese (and Hispanics), with immigrants from this population enjoying better self-rated health than the U.S.-born. Some of the other observed effects of length of residence were less consistent across the two Asian groups, and, whether positive or negative, tended to be prominent primarily for recent immigrants. These analyses document that the association between length of residence in the United States and health status is neither simple nor straightforward. More careful attention is needed to identify the conditions under which particular patterns of association vary by health outcome and by specific population.

DISCUSSION

Our empirical analysis of a large, diverse, multiethnic sample from America's most populous state has several limitations. The generalization of findings to all U.S. immigrants may not be warranted, if immigrants (or the native-born) in California are distinct. In addition, the data are cross-sectional and provide no basis for the temporal ordering of observed associations. There is a need to follow populations over time and monitor changes in their social conditions and health, especially for second- and third-generation immigrants. Nonetheless, the empirical analyses provided a rare and unique glimpse of America's diversity. For example, the analyses provide one of the most comprehensive glimpses of the health of persons who identify as multiracial. Across the four health measures considered, they experience poorer health than whites that is not explained by SES.

Our findings also converge with our review of the literature in important ways and extend it in others. They illustrate that there is no generic minority health model that can be indiscriminately applied to all groups. Instead, they emphasize the importance of paying attention to the unique history—context of migration or conquest—and pattern of incorporation into the United States for each population. Future research needs to more systematically and comprehensively assess how specific risks and resources link to socioeconomic conditions, relate to each other, and cumulate over time. In particular, factors associated with migration history and status, and with the social context of racial oppression and privilege, may interact with SES to create conditions that initiate and sustain elevated health risks. Such investigations must be grounded in the notion that racial effects and interactions are unlikely to be identical across all racial groups, and that ethnic diversity within broad racial categories does predict variation in social circumstances and health.

The evidence considered here reveals that poverty and other socioeconomic indicators are important predictors of variation in health. Policy makers need to give more attention to health status in policy initiatives around poverty. This is especially important given the growing economic inequality and high rates of childhood poverty in the United States. Twenty-three percent of all American children under the age of eighteen—19 percent for whites, 21 percent for Asian and Pacific

Islanders (API), 26 percent for blacks, and 33 percent for Hispanics—are being raised in a poor household (National Center for Health Statistics 1999). Moreover, 43 percent of all children (31 percent for whites, 41 percent for APIs, 68 percent for blacks, and 73 percent for Hispanics) are in economically vulnerable households (annual income less than twice the poverty level). Early childhood is likely to be a strategic intervention point not only for improving child health outcomes but also for establishing a trajectory for enhanced SES and thus health in adulthood.

Effectively addressing the relationship between poverty and health requires initiatives in four domains (Mackenbach and Stronks 2002). First, policies must seek to reduce the levels of poverty in the population. Such strategies could include enhancing educational achievement among poor children, implementing new tax and income support policies to prevent an increase in income inequality, reducing long-term poverty through new programs that assist the chronically unemployed to find paid employment, and providing additional financial resources for very poor families with children. A second category includes policies that reduce the effects of health on SES. This could include modifying work conditions so that the work participation levels of the chronically ill and disabled could be increased, and offering counseling services to low-income populations whose health poses challenges to employment. Third, policies need to reduce the intervening factors between SES and health. An example would be the initiation of health promotion programs targeted to low SES groups. Such initiatives should focus not only on individual behavior but also on environmental measures, such as providing free fruit at elementary schools, increasing tobacco taxes to reduce consumption, and re-engineering work conditions to reduce the physical workload of manual jobs. Finally, policies must improve access to medical care. Specific initiatives include increasing access to care for low SES groups, reducing the shortage of primary care providers in disadvantaged areas, strengthening health care access and quality by deploying more health care professionals and peer educators to implement disease prevention programs, and ensuring the availability of culturally sensitive care to all language groups.

Policy makers also need greater awareness that nonhealth policies can have decisive consequences for the health of economically vulnerable populations. Although a causal relationship has not been established, it is instructive that black-white inequalities in health over the last fifty years have narrowed or widened in tandem with those in income. When the racial gap in income narrowed between 1968 and 1978 as a result of the gains of the civil rights movement, black men and women experienced larger declines in mortality, absolutely and relatively, compared to their white counterparts (Cooper et al. 1981). Similarly, as incomes for blacks declined relative to those of whites during the 1980s, the life expectancy for blacks declined absolutely as well as relative to that of whites (Williams and Collins 1995).

A U.S. task force identified more than 200 community-based interventions that could be used to improve social environments and health (Anderson et al. 2003). These include initiatives to enhance neighborhood living conditions, civic engagement, and collective efficacy, and to increase opportunities for learning, capacity development, community development, and disease and injury prevention. At the same time, rigorous evaluation efforts are needed to identify the conditions under which particular interventions are more or less likely to work and to be cost effective. The task force report concluded that strong evidence supported the effectiveness of only two interventions: early childhood development programs for low-income children and rental assistance programs for low SES families (Anderson et al. 2003). Thus, though there is good reason to believe that improving health depends on increased access to societal resources, much is yet to be learned about how to maximize their effects to eliminate social disparities in health.

The larger sociopolitical context can also have health consequences. A panel study of African Americans from 1979 through 1992 found the lowest levels of chronic health problems, disability, and emotional distress in 1988 (Jackson et al. 1996). That year also marked the lowest level of racial discrimination and the highest level of optimism about race relations. Given that 1988 was the year that Jesse Jackson, an African American male, was running the most successful presidential campaign by a black person in American history, the researchers suggested a spillover effect from the larger political climate to health and dubbed it the Jesse Jackson effect (Jackson et al. 1996). There is similar evidence of a post-election euphoria in South Africa after the election of Nelson Mandela in 1994, with marked increases in happiness and life satisfaction among black South Africans and the elimination of black-white differences on these measures of psychological well being (Moller 1998). However, this improvement was no longer evident at the next data collection point, only eighteen months later. A recent study provides another example: the increased threat of discrimination and harassment for Arab Americans after the terrorist attacks in 2001 appears to have created an environment that adversely affected health. An analysis of birth outcomes in the state of California, six months before and six months after September 11, 2001, revealed that Arab American women were the only group of California women to experience an increased risk of low birth weight and preterm birth in the post–September 11 period (Lauderdale 2006).

These studies raise the intriguing possibility that anti-immigrant initiatives in California could have affected the levels of health observed for immigrants. In contrast to earlier research using both national and California data (Burnham et al. 1987; Singh and Miller 2004; Vega and Rumbaut 1991), our analyses of the CHIS data reveal that many immigrant groups, including Mexican immigrants, report poorer health than the native-born, especially for indicators of health status that have a large emotional component. The CHIS data were collected in 2001, a time of considerable anti-immigrant sentiment in California. First, as reported in the *San Diego Tribune* on March 19, 2000, there was a movement to resurrect Proposition 187, which had been overturned in 1998 (Ed Mendel, "Proposition 187 Backers Faltering: Anti-Immigrant Tone Moderated," A3). Proposition 187, initially passed in 1994, would have limited undocumented immigrants' access to a range of social services, including medical care and public school education. It also required law enforcement officials and public employees to report those they suspected of being undocumented to the immigration authorities. Second, in October 2001, the governor of California, Gray Davis, vetoed two bills that would have provided some rights to immigrants who were waiting for their applications for legal residency to be approved. One bill would have allowed immigrants to obtain a temporary driver's license, and the other would have allowed students who had graduated from a state high school to be eligible for the more affordable in-state tuition at California's colleges and universities (Hahn Kim Quach, "Immigrant Aid Bills Rejected," *The Orange County Register*, October 1, 2000, A4). It is possible that the anti-immigrant rhetoric and fear of impending policies adversely affected immigrants' levels of self-rated ill health and emotional distress.

Health is closely tied to the social conditions in which groups live and work. Poverty and migration status are important contexts in this regard. Individuals in poverty and other economically vulnerable populations have elevated risks of disease, disability, and early death. Their health problems can serve as a barrier to their ability to benefit from initiatives designed to improve their SES. Accordingly, strategies to improve the mental and physical health of the poor should be considered as a component of any comprehensive poverty policy. Policy makers also need to be aware that policies in domains far removed from traditional health policy (such as taxes, education, employment and workplace design) can impair or enhance health.

Preparation of this paper was supported in part by grant R01 MH 59575 from the National Institute of Mental Health, grant 1-T32-NRO7965-03 from the National Institute of Health, and the John D. and Catherine T. McArthur Foundation Research Network on Socioeconomic Status and Health. We wish to thank John Sonnega for assistance with the data analysis and Car Nosel and Kristine Lee for assistance with the preparation of the manuscript.

NOTES

1. The CHIS used a random digit-dial telephone survey of 55,428 households in California with oversamples of Asian ethnic groups and rural and urban American Indian–Alaska Natives. It sampled one adult in each household. Interviews were conducted in English, Spanish, Chinese (Mandarin and Cantonese dialects), Vietnamese, Korean, and Khmer. Up to fourteen attempts were made to reach telephone numbers that were repeatedly busy, not answered, or had answering machines. The cooperation rate (ratio of completed interviews over the sum of completed interviews and refusals of selected respondents) was 77.1 percent, but the weighted response rate was 43.3 percent, comparable to that of other statewide surveys (California Health Interview Survey 2003).

REFERENCES

Adler, Nancy E., Thomas Boyce, Margaret A. Chesney, Susan Folkman, and S. Leonard Syme. 1993. "Socioeconomic Inequalities in Health: No Easy Solution." *Journal of the American Medical Association* 269(24): 3140–45.

American Sociological Association. 2003. *The Importance of Collecting Data and Doing Social Scientific Research on Race*. Washington, D.C.: American Sociological Association.

Anderson, Laurie M., Susan C. Scrimshaw, Mindy T. Fullilove, Jonathan E. Fielding, and Task Force on Community Preventive Services. 2003. "The Community Guide's Model for Linking the Social Environment to Health." *American Journal of Preventive Medicine* 24(3S): 12–20.

Anderson, Robert N. and Peter B. DeTurk. 2002. *United States Life Tables, 1999*. National Vital Statistics Reports, Vol. 50, No. 6. Hyattsville, Md.: National Center for Health Statistics.

Bound, Jeffery, Timothy Waidmann, Michael Schoenbaum, and Jeffery B. Bingenheimer. 2003. "The Labor Market Consequences of Race Differences in Health." *The Milbank Quarterly* 81(3): 441–73.

Burnham, Audrey, Marvin Karno, Richard L. Hough, Javier I. Escobar, and Cynthia Telles. 1987. "Acculturation and Lifetime Prevalence of Psychiatric Disorders Among Mexican Americans in Los Angeles." *Journal of Health and Social Behavior* 28(1): 89–102.

California Health Interview Survey. 2003. "The CHIS Sample: Response Rate and Representativeness." Technical Paper No. 1. Los Angeles, Calif.: UCLA Center for Health Policy Research.

Carter-Pokras, Olivia, and Ruth E. Zambrana. 2001. "Latino Health Status." In *Health Issues in the Latino Community*, edited by Marilyn Aguirre-Molina, Carlos W. Molina, and Ruth E. Zambrana. San Francisco, Calif.: Jossey-Bass.

Cawley, John, and Shai Danziger. 2005. "Morbid Obesity and the Transition From Welfare to Work." *Journal of Policy Analysis and Management* 24(4): 727–43.

Centers for Disease Control and Prevention. 1999. "Neighborhood Safety and the Prevalence of Physical Inactivity-Selected States, 1996." *Morbidity and Mortality Weekly Report* 48(7): 143–46.

———. 2001. "Pregnancy-Related Deaths Among Hispanic, Asian/Pacific Islander and American Indian/Alaska Native Women—United States, 1991–1997." *Morbidity and Mortality Weekly Report* 50(18): 361–64.

Cheadle, Allen, Bruce M. Psaty, Susan Curry, Edward Wagner, Paula Diehr, Thomas Koepsell, and Alan Kristal. 1991. "Community-Level Comparisons Between the Grocery Store Environment and Individual Dietary Practices." *Preventive Medicine* 20(2): 250–61.

Cho, Youngtae and Robert A. Hummer. 2000. "Disability Status Differentials Across Fifteen Asian and Pacific Islander Groups and the Effect of Nativity and Duration of Residence in the U.S." *Social Biology* 48(3–4): 171–75.

Cooper, Richard, Jeffrey Cutler, Patrice Desvigne-Nickens, Stephen P. Fortmann, Lawrence Friedman, Richard Havlik, Gary Hogelin, John Marler, Paul McGovern, Gregory Morosco, Lori Mosca, Thomas Pearson, Jeremiah Stamler, Daniel Stryer, and Thomas Thom.

2000. "Trends and Disparities in Coronary Heart Disease, Stroke, and Other Cardiovascular Diseases in the United States: Findings of the National Conference on Cardiovascular Disease Prevention." *Circulation* 102(25): 3137–47.

Cooper, Richard S., Michael Steinhauer, Arthur Schatzkin, and William Miller. 1981. "Improved Mortality Among U.S. Blacks, 1968–1978: The Role of Antiracist Struggle." *International Journal of Health Services* 11(4): 511–22.

Corcoran, Mary, Sheldon K. Danziger, and Richard Tolman. 2004. "Long-Term Employment of African American and White Welfare Recipients and the Role of Persistent Health and Mental Health Problems." *Women and Health* 39(4): 21–40.

Danziger, Sheldon. and P. Gottschalk, editors. 1993. *Uneven Tides: Rising Inequality in America*. New York: Russell Sage Foundation.

Duncan, Greg J. 1988. "The Volatility of Family Income Over the Life Course." In *Life Span Development and Behavior*, edited by Paul Bates, David. Featherman, and Richard M. Lerner. Hillsdale, N.J.: Lawrence Erlbaum.

Escarce, Jose J., Kenneth R. Epstein, David C. Colby, and J. Sanford Schwartz. 1993. "Racial Differences in the Elderly's Use of Medical Procedures and Diagnostic Tests." *American Journal of Public Health* 83(7): 948–54.

Evans Gary W., and Susan Saegert . 2000. "Residential Crowding in the Context of Inner City Poverty." In *Theoretical Perspectives in Environment-Behavior Research*, edited by Seymour Wapner, Jack Demick, Takji Yamamoto, and Hiroufmi Minami. New York: Kluwer Academic/Plenum Publishers.

Finch, Brian K., Robert A. Hummer, Maureen Reindl, and William A. Vega. 2002. "Validity of Self-Rated Health Among Latino(a)s." *American Journal of Epidemiology* 155(8): 755–59.

Franzini, Luisa, John C. Ribble, and Arlene M. Keddie. 2001. "Understanding the Hispanic Paradox." *Ethnicity and Disease* 11(3): 496–518.

Hacker, George R., Collins Jacobson, and Michael Jacobson. 1987. *Marketing Booze to Blacks*. Washington, D.C.: Center for Science in the Public Interest.

Hahn, Robert A., Elaine Eaker, Nancy D. Barker, Steven M. Teutsch, Waldemar Sosniak, and Nancy Krieger. 1995. "Poverty and Death in the United States—1973 and 1991." *Epidemiology* 6(5): 490–97.

Harper, Sam, John Lynch, Wan-Ling Hsu, Susan A. Everson, Marianne M. Hillemeier, Trivellore E. Rhaghunatian, Jukka T. Salonen, and George A. Kaplan. 2002. "Life Course Socioeconomic Conditions and Adult Psychosocial Functioning." *International Journal of Epidemiology* 31(2): 395–403.

House, James S., James M. Lepkowski, Ann M. Kinney, Richard P. Mero, Robert C. Kessler, and A. Regulla Herzog. 1994. "The Social Stratification of Aging and Health." *Journal of Health and Social Behavior* 35(3): 213–34.

House, James S., and David R. Williams. 2000. "Understanding and Reducing Socioeconomic and Racial-ethnic Disparities in Health." In *Promoting Health: Intervention Strategies from Social and Behavioral Research*, edited by B. D. Smedley and S. L. Syme . Washington, D.C.: National Academy of Sciences Press.

Hummer, Robert A., Richard G. Rogers, Charles B. Nam, and Felicia B. LeClere. 1999. "Race/Ethnicity, Nativity, and U.S. Adult Mortality." *Social Science Quarterly* 80(1): 136–53.

Idler, Ellen L., and Yael Benyamini. 1997. "Self-Rated Health and Mortality: A Review of Twenty-Seven Community Studies." *Journal of Health and Social Behavior* 38(1): 21–37.

Idler, Ellen L., and Stanislav V. Kasl. 1995. "Self-Ratings for Health: Do They Also Predict Change in Functional Ability." *Journals of Gerontology Series B-Psychological Sciences and Social Sciences* 50(6): S344–53.

Jackson, James S., Tony N. Brown, David R. Williams, Myriam Torres, Sherill L. Sellers, and Kendrick Brown. 1996. "Racism and the Physical and Mental Health Status of African Americans: A Thirteen Year National Panel Study." *Ethnicity and Disease* 6(1–2): 132–47.

Jackson, Pamela B., and David R. Williams. 2006. "The Intersection of Race, Gender, and SES: Health Paradoxes." In *Gender, Race, Class and Health*, edited by A. Shulz and L. Mullings. San Francisco, Calif.: Jossey-Bass.

Kessler, Ronald C., Kristin D. Mickelson, and David R. Williams. 1999. "The Prevalence, Distribution, and Mental Health Correlates of Perceived Discrimination in the United States." *Journal of Health and Social Behavior* 40(3): 208–30.

Kessler Ronald C., Cindy L. Foster, William B. Saunders, and Paul E. Stang. 1995. "Social Consequences of Psychiatric Disoders I: Educational Attainment." *American Journal of Psychiatry* 152(7): 1026–32.

Lauderdale, Diane S. 2006. "Birth Outcomes for Arabic-Named Women in California Before and After September 11." *Demography* 43(1): 185–201.

Link, Bruce G., and Bruce P. Dohrenwend. 1980. "Formulation of Hypotheses About the True Prevalence of Demoralization." In *Mental Illness in the United States: Epidemiological Estimates*, edited by Bruce P. Dohrenwend. New York: Praeger.

Link, Bruce G., and Jo Phelan. 1995. "Social Conditions as Fundamental Causes of Disease." *Journal of Health and Social Behavior* 35(Extra Issue): 80–94.

Mackenbach, Johan P., and Karien Stronks. 2002. "A Strategy for Tackling Health Inequalities in the Netherlands." *British Journal of Medicine* 325(7371): 1029–32.

Marmot, Michael G. 1986. "Social Inequalities in Mortality: The Social Environment." In *Class and Health: Research and Longitudinal Data*, edited by Richard G. Wilkinson. London: Tavistock.

Marmot, Michael G., M. Kogevinas, and M. A. Elston. 1987. "Social/Economic Status and Disease." *Annual Review of Public Health* 8: 111–35.

McBean, A. Marshall, and Marian Gornick. 1994. "Differences by Race in the Rates of Procedures Performed in Hospitals for Medicare Beneficiaries." *Health Care Financing Review* 15(4): 77–90.

McDonough, Peggy, Greg J. Duncan, David R. Williams, and James House. 1997. "Income Dynamics and Adult Mortality in the U.S., 1972–1989." *American Journal of Public Health* 87(9): 1476–83.

———. 2000. "The Impact of Income Dynamics on Mortality in the United States." In *The Mortality Crisis in Transitional Economies*, edited by Giovanni A. Cornia and Renato Paniccia. New York: Oxford University Press.

McEwen, Bruce S. 1998. "Protective and Damaging Effects of Stress Mediators." *New England Journal of Medicine* 338(3): 171–79.

Moller, Valerie. 1998. "Quality of Life in South Africa: Post-Apartheid Trends." *Social Indicators Research* 43(1–2): 27–68.

Moore, David J., J. D. Williams, and W. J. Qualls. 1996. "Target Marketing of Tobacco and Alcohol-Related Products to Ethnic Minority Groups in the United States." *Ethnicity and Disease* 6(1–2): 83–98.

National Center for Health Statistics. 1999. *Health, United States, 1999 with Health and Aging Chartbook.* Hyattsville, Md.: U.S. Government Printing Office.

———. 2003. "Health United States 2003, Department of Health and Human Services, Centers for Disease Control and Prevention." Hyattsville, Md.: U.S. Government Printing Office.

Palloni, Alberto, and Elizabeth Arias. 2004. "Paradox Lost: Explaining the Hispanic Adult Mortality Advantage." *Demography* 41(3): 385–415 .

Palloni, Alberto, and Jeffery D. Morenoff. 2001. "Interpreting the Paradoxical in the Hispanic Paradox: Demographic and Epidemiologic Approaches." In *Population Health and Aging: Strengthening the Dialogue Between Epidemiology and Demography.* New York: New York Academy of Sciences.

Pamuk, Elsie R., Diane M. Makuk, Katherine E. Heck, Cynthia Reuben, and Kimberly Lochner. 1998. *Health, United States, 1998, with Socioeconomic Status and Health Chartbook.* Hyattsville, Md.: National Center for Health Statistics.

Pappas, Greg, Susan Queen, Wilbur Hadden, and Gail Fisher S. 1993. "The Increasing Disparity in Mortality Between Socioeconomic Groups in the United States, 1960 and 1986." *New England Journal of Medicine* 329(2): 103–9.

Polednak, Anthony P. 1989. *Racial and Ethnic Differences in Disease.* New York: Oxford University Press.

Portes, Alejandro, and Rubén G. Rumbaut. 1996. *Immigrant America: A Portrait.* Berkeley, Calif.: University of California Press.

Singh, Gopal K., and Barry A. Miller. 2004. "Health, Life Expectancy, and Mortality Patterns Among Immigrant Populations in the United States." *Canadian Journal of Public Health* 95(3): I14–I21.

Singh, Gopal K., and Stella M. Yu. 1996. "Adverse Pregnancy Outcomes: Differences Between US-and Foreign-Born Women in Major US Racial and Ethnic Groups." *American Journal of Public Health* 86(6): 837–43.

Smedley, Brian D., Adrienne Y. Stith, and Alan R. Nelson, editors. 2003. *Unequal Treatment: Confronting Racial and Ethnic Disparities in Health Care.* Institute of Medicine. Washington, D.C.: National Academies Press.

Smith, James P. 1999. "Healthy Bodies and Thick Wallets: The Dual Relation Between Health and Economic Status." *Journal of Economic Perspectives* 13(2): 144–66.

Troxel, Wendy M., Karen A. Matthews, Joyce T. Bromberger, and Kim Sutton-Tyrrell. 2003. "Chronic Stress Burden, Discrimination, and Subclinical Carotid Artery Disease in African American and Caucasian Women." *Health Psychology* 22(3): 300–309.

Tucker, Clyde, Ruth McKay, Brian Kojetin, Roderick Harrison, Manuel de la Puente, Linda Stinson, and Ed Robison. 1996. "Testing Methods of Collecting Racial and Ethnic Information: Results of the Current Population Survey Supplement on Race and Ethnicity." *Bureau of Labor Statistical Notes* No. 40. Office of Research and Evaluation, Bureau of Labor, Washington, D.C.

Ustun, T. B., J. L. Ayuso-Mateos, S. Chatterji, Colin Mathers, and C. J. Murray. 2004. "Global

Burden of Depressive Disorders in the Year 2000." *British Journal of Psychiatry* 184(5): 386–92.

Vega, William A., and Hortensia Amaro. 1994. "Latino Outlook: Good Health, Uncertain Prognosis." *Annual Review of Public Health* 15: 39–67.

Vega, William A., and Rubén G. Rumbaut. 1991. "Ethnic Minorities and Mental Health." *Annual Review of Sociology* 17: 351–83.

Wells, Nancy M., and Gary W. Evans. 2003. "Nearby Nature: A Buffer of Life Stress Among Rural Children." *Environment and Behavior* 35(3): 311–30.

Williams, David R. 1990. "Socioeconomic Differentials in Health: A Review and Redirection." *Social Psychology Quarterly* 53(2): 81–99.

———. 2000. "Race, Stress, and Mental Health: Findings from the Commonwealth Minority Health Survey." In *Minority Health in America: Findings and Policy Implication from the Commonwealth Fund Minority Health Survey*, edited by Carol Hogue, Martha Hargraves, and Karen Scott-Collins. Baltimore, Md.: Johns Hopkins University Press.

———. 2002. "Racial-Ethnic Variations in Women's Health: The Social Embeddedness of Health." *American Journal of Public Health* 92(4): 588–97.

———. 2003. "The Health of Men: Structured Inequalities and Opportunities." *American Journal of Public Health* 93(5): 724–31.

———. 2005a. "Patterns and Causes of Disparities in Health." In *Policy Challenges in Modern Health Care*, edited by David Mechanic, Lynn B. Rogut, David C. Colby, and James R. Knickman. Piscataway, N.J.: Rutgers University Press.

———. 2005b. "The Health of U.S. Racial and Ethnic Populations." *Journals of Gerontology* Series B 60B(Special Issue II): 53–62.

Williams, David R., and Chiquita Collins. 1995. "U.S. Socioeconomic and Racial Differences in Health: Patterns and Explanations." *Annual Review of Sociology* 21: 349–86.

Williams, David R., Harold W. Neighbors, and James S. Jackson. 2003. " Racial-ethnic Discrimination and Health: Findings from Community Studies." *American Journal of Public Health* 93(2): 200–208.

Williams, David R., and Toni D. Rucker. 2000. "Understanding and Addressing Racial Disparities in Health Care." *Health Care Financing Review* 21(4): 75–90.

Williams, David R., Yan Yu, James Jackson, and Norman Anderson. 1997. "Racial Differences in Physical and Mental Health: Socioeconomic Status, Stress, and Discrimination." *Journal of Health Psychology* 2(3): 335–41.

Chapter 7

Can Social Capital Explain Persistent Racial Poverty Gaps?

Lincoln Quillian and Rozlyn Redd

ocial capital has recently become one of the most widely used concepts in sociology and social science. No fewer than four monographs (Lin 2001; Aberg and Sandberg 2003; Feld 2003; Halpern 2005), ten edited volumes, and 900 social science articles (Halpern 2005, figure 1.1) on social capital have been published since 2001. The term has been one of sociology's most successful exports, finding its way into political science, economics, and anthropology. Broadly encompassing the personal relationships that aid in achieving goals, social capital is not a single explanation or variable, but rather points toward a variety of explanations of how informal human social relationships are important for human behavior.

A number of social capital explanations have been proposed for the persistence of major disparities in poverty rates among racial and ethnic groups. Many of these explanations are long-standing and actually predate the term *social capital*. William Julius Wilson's social isolation thesis in *The Truly Disadvantaged* (1987), for instance, argues that the isolation of poor urban minorities from social contact with middle class persons contributes to their persistent poverty. Likewise, the Coleman report's (1966) finding that socioeconomic status of school peers predicts school success, and that minority students have peers of lower socioeconomic standing, suggests a social capital explanation. In most social capital explanations of racial poverty gaps, a disadvantaged racial or ethnic group's structural position in social networks results in a reduced stock of a type of social capital, contributing to higher rates of group poverty. Less commonly, some explanations focus on the potential negative consequences of social relationships as a form of negative social capital.

Here we consider whether several leading social capital theories can explain persistent disparities in poverty rates across racial groups. We begin with the definition of social capital and then move on to the relevance, for social capital, of high levels of segregation or homophily on the basis of race and ethnicity. In many situations, segregation or homophily combines with racial inequality to create contextual disadvantages for members of disadvantaged racial groups. The consequences of segregation or homophily, however, are not necessarily negative: segregation or homophily can also facilitate developing denser or stronger social networks by grouping like individuals together, contributing to community institutions and social control.

A wide variety of theories can be described as social capital theories (Portes 1998; Small 2004; Halpern 2005) and we focus on four of the most promising social capital explanations of racial differences in poverty outcomes. One is that employment and wage gaps of nonwhite jobseekers can be explained by exclusionary job networks. Another is that lower-income nonwhites often reside in urban neighborhoods with low levels of collective efficacy, reducing their ability to control delinquency and crime. A third is that coethnic social capital contributes to lower poverty rates among certain immigrant groups and their offspring. The fourth is that endogenous friend effects in peer networks are a source of educational disadvantage. At points we supplement our review of the literature with analysis of data on peer social capital from the National Longitudinal Study of Adolescent Health (Add Health). We conclude that the evidence for these explanations is mixed, but that the stronger evidence supports the contextual disadvantages from disadvantaged neighborhoods and peer groups, which contribute especially to crime and delinquency problems in minority communities. We also suggest that social capital among coethnics aids the incorporation of new immigrants and can facilitate the school achievement of second generation immigrant youth.

WHAT IS SOCIAL CAPITAL?

Although the term social capital has been invented independently by several scholars (Loury 1977; Bourdieu 1985), the widespread modern use of the term was initiated by James Coleman's (1988) seminal discussion of social capital in the creation of human capital. Coleman defines social capital as encompassing two features: that it consists "of some aspect of social structures" and that it "facilitates certain action of actors—whether persons or corporate actors—within the structure." Robert Putnam, in an equally influential discussion, defined social capital as "features of social life—networks, norms, and trust—that enable participants to act together more effectively to pursue shared objectives" (1995, 664–65).

Since Coleman's discussion, a number of books and reviews have attempted to clarify the concept. Nan Lin (2001), for instance, stressed the connection of social capital to social networks in his definition: "social capital may be defined operationally as resources that are embedded in social networks and accessed and used by actors for actions. Thus, the concept has two important components: it represents resources embedded in social relations rather than individuals, and access and use of such resources reside with actors" (24–25).

Alejandro Portes described social capital as "the ability of actors to secure benefits by virtue of membership in social networks or other social structures" (1998, 6). Steven Durlauf and Marcel Fafchamps succinctly encapsulated it as "community relations that affect personal interactions" (2004, 1). David Halpern defined it as encompassing three elements, "a network; a cluster of norms, values and expectancies that are shared by group members; and sanctions—punishments and rewards—that help to maintain the norms and network" (2005, 10).

Applying these definitions to research in sociology, a great many of the books and articles that have been written by sociologists since the earliest years of the discipline could be described as studies of social capital. Thus Portes noted that social capital "does not embody any idea really new to sociologists" (1998, 2); sociology as a discipline has long pointed to the importance of social context and social ties for understanding human behavior. Rather than representing a new theory, the usefulness of the social capital concept has been its heuristic value in helping social scientists connect literatures in diverse areas and in providing a language to consider the importance of social context and social ties across many settings.

Corresponding to the multifaceted definitions of social capital are many measures of it. Empirical studies have principally used three. The first approach has been to measure social relations directly: assessing the number, structure, or properties of relationships among individuals. This includes measuring the intensity of contact or frequency of interaction, the structural characteristics of a whole social network, or the characteristics of persons in contact with an individual or group. This form of measurement is often most appropriate for explanations that emphasize the transmission of information across networks or the social pressures that result from overlapping or intense contacts. Jay Teachman, Kathleen Paasch, and Karen Carver (1996), for instance, used the frequency of conversations between parents and their eighth grade children about their school experiences and their plans for high school and college to measure parental academically related social capital.

The second approach is based on individuals' beliefs about their relationships with others. The most often measured attitude or expectation is trust. Pamela Paxton (1999), for instance, relied on questions from national survey data about the level of trust in other people and in major social institutions to examine changes in levels of social capital over time.

The third approach uses measures of membership in certain voluntary organizations to assess the level of social capital. Often, membership in voluntary organizations is treated as an indirect measure of social ties believed to be fostered by voluntary organizations, and is used because direct measures of social ties are not available. Putnam's (1995) use of memberships in clubs like bowling leagues is the most influential example of this approach to measuring social capital.

Although these definitions of social capital focus on the positive potentials of social relationships, social relationships may also have negative consequences. If social capital is a resource to achieve goals, then it can also be used to achieve goals that are negative from the perspective of the wider society. Criminal networks are one of the clearest examples of social capital employed for socially dysfunctional ends. In some cases, dense networks can create pressures for conformity that stifle individuality (Portes 1998).

Even in cases where the direct consequences of a network are to facilitate production of a valued good, the exclusionary nature of social networks raises equity issues. To take one example, social capital may facilitate improvements in reading by the members of a group, thus developing their human capital. Although everyone can learn to read better, some scarce goods are allocated in part based on ranking skills in a queue, meaning that gains by one group necessarily trade off with other groups. Positions in elite colleges, for instances, are awarded to a fixed number of students based in part on ranking of reading scores. For outcomes with limited positions, when one group gains, another group necessarily loses.

A useful aspect of the social capital metaphor is that it points out the instrumental use of social ties in everyday life: for most individuals, social networks provide a valuable and useful resource. At the same time, social relationships can have negative consequences for participants, and relationships that advantage one group often disadvantage another. These points are especially relevant in understanding how social capital relates to social stratification and poverty.

SEGREGATION, HOMOPHILY, AND SOCIAL CAPITAL

Most arguments about how social capital may contribute to inequality among racial and ethnic groups follow the same general logic. This argument is very similar to a general logic showing how segregation or homophily in social life tends to advantage members of advantaged groups and disadvantage members of disadvantaged groups. Peter Blau's *Inequality and Heterogeneity* (1977) spells out several parts of this logic; Douglas Massey (1990) provided a worked-out application in the specific case of neighborhood segregation. Segregation and homophily are both terms that imply that persons with similar social characteristics associate with each other, though *homophily* is more often viewed as voluntary choice whereas *segregation* is more often viewed as mandated or forced group separation. By grouping like with like, segregation or homophily increases the average contact of members of advantaged groups with advantaged associates, and decreases their contact with members of disadvantaged groups. To the extent that having advantaged social contacts or exposure to advantaged social contexts is itself of benefit in generating positive stratification outcomes, homophily or segregation then contributes to the advantage of the advantaged and the disadvantage of the disadvantaged.

A few examples may help to clarify this logic as it applies to many social capital explanations. Many argue that job placement networks may bring greater advantage if others in the network have high-status jobs themselves, since these persons are more likely to be able to provide information and influence in obtaining high-status and high-pay jobs (Lin 1999). The combination of racial segregation in job networks, and the higher average job status of whites, will then tend to increase the average status of job contacts for whites and decrease it for blacks. Likewise, as many parents have long believed, a like-begets-like influence among adolescent peers means that having peers with high grade point averages (GPA) increases school achievement. Racial homophily in adolescent peer networks, combined with racial gaps in GPA, imply that white students will (on average) tend to have friends with higher GPA than black students.[1] If high-GPA friends are an advantage, then white students benefit from high-GPA associates.

The extent to which segregation or homophily advantages the advantaged group depends on the extent of racial inequality between the advantaged and disadvantaged racial groups, the strength of racial homophily (or segregation) in the relevant context, the strength of homophily (or segregation) on other non–race-based criteria, and finally the advantage that comes from having an advantaged network or social context. Although the argument outlined here can apply to any characteristic—not just race and ethnicity—that distinguishes an advantaged from a disadvantaged group, it applies especially strongly to race and ethnicity because these tend to be among the strongest bases for homophily or segregation. In American society, segregation or homophily on the basis of race is stronger than socioeconomic status homophily within racial groups (on residential segregation, see White 1987; on friendship homophily, see Quillian and Campbell 2003).

A different line of argument, more commonly applied to situations of homophily than segregation, argues that under certain conditions segregation or homophily can be of assistance to the disadvantaged group. Unlike the arguments about how segregation or homophily concentrates advantage or disadvantage, which consider the characteristics of social network members as the outcome, the potential benefit of grouping like-with-like is that it can increase the number and intensity of social ties within the group (Quillian and Campbell 2003). Dense social ties then contribute to building local institutions and to networks that connect across multiple settings, such as school and church. Because behavior in one setting has consequences for other settings, grouping like-with-like in certain circumstances can build group solidarity and harness it in pursuit of group goals (Krohn 1986). The most common situation is immigrant ethnic grouping, including both ethnic spatial groupings (enclaves) and high ethnic concentration in particular businesses (ethnic niches or economies). In these situations, grouping like-with-like is thought to help coethnic members form institutions and use collective control to help motivate community members to achieve socially valued goals.

These two influences of grouping like-with-like can operate simultaneously. Whether grouping like-with-like hurts or helps disadvantaged groups overall is a question that must be resolved empirically, one outcome at a time. These processes can also have implications for inequality within a disadvantaged racial or ethnic group. For instance, the categorical refusal to hire non-coethnics might help advantage coethnic employers, but disadvantage coethnic workers by creating a surplus of disadvantaged ethnic labor within an ethnic enclave.

DIFFICULTIES OF TESTING SOCIAL CAPITAL THEORIES

With appropriate survey data, it is straightforward to establish racial differences in the average characteristics of network peers or other measures of social capital. What is less straightforward is determining confidently how important an advantaged social context is in influencing individual outcomes (for discussions, see Manski 1993; Moffitt 2001; Durlauf and Fafchamps 2004; Mouw 2006). The simplest approach is to measure the similarity on an outcome among individuals who share a social capital influence (for example, are in the same social network) after controlling for causes of similarity on the outcome on other measured (nonsocial capital) characteristics. The problem with this approach is that there are often other reasons to expect similarity among persons who are friends and associates other than any causal social capital effect on outcomes. Persons usually have some ability to select the social context they experience (and thus their level of social capital) and they tend to select contexts populated by persons like themselves. This selection tends to result in overestimation of the effect of social capital. An additional problem in evaluating peer effects is the what Charles Manski calls the "reflection problem" (1993, 32): if group members' behaviors mutually influence each other, as proposed by social capital, it becomes difficult to estimate the magnitude of the influence of any one person on any others.

Too often the empirical literature on social capital has minimized or ignored these problems, resulting in likely overestimation of social capital effects. Cross-sectional data with controls alone is not enough to overcome these problems. Better approaches are available to assess the effects of social capital, but generally involve examining data carefully to find natural experiment situations in which individuals do not choose their own contexts.

Although anecdotes and intuition strongly suggest that social capital has some influence on stratification outcomes, the difficult issue is to isolate the specific social capital explanations that may have an important impact on racial stratification and measure their influence. Because social capital is a not a single theory, but rather a wide variety of explanations with the shared element of stressing the importance of social relationships, the range of explanations that can be included as social capital is enormous. For an explanation to have a major impact on racial differences in poverty there must be a substantial racial difference in that dimension of social capital and a strong influence of that form of social capital on outcomes linked to poverty.

We explore four of the most heavily discussed and researched social capital explanations in connecting to issues of race and inequality. In all of these cases, the explanation is based on the idea that grouping like-with-like creates disadvantage or advantage in social contacts and settings. Generally, these explanations propose to explain outcomes related to race and ethnic differences in poverty by the amount and forms of social capital held by members of different racial and ethnic groups.

The theories we consider emphasize job search networks, neighborhood social capital as a source of social control, social capital among first- and second-generation ethnic group members (ethnic capital) as a source of advantage, and the influence of friendships on youth academic achievement. There are several other social capital explanations in the literature that may contribute to understanding racial differences in poverty rates (for example, see Briggs 1998; Morgan and Sorensen 1999; Stanton-Salazar and Dornbusch 1995; Cohen 2001), but they have received much less research attention than the four we consider. Although we briefly discuss Wilson's (1987) social isolation thesis—that the minority urban poor are socially isolated from the middle class—our view is that much of Wilson's discussion is subsumed in our discussion of the four specific theories of social capital we consider here.

Closely related to social capital effects are studies of the influence of contextual effects on outcomes, the best known of which are the extensive literatures on neighborhood effects (for a review, see Duncan and Raudenbush 1999) and school effects (see Rumberger and Palardy 2005). Contextual effects look at the total influence of a social context on outcomes without, in most instances, identifying the mechanism. Contextual effects studies include social capital effects as potential mechanisms by which the contextual effects operate, but contextual effects could also capture other mechanisms that are not thought of as social capital, such as inequalities in the qualities of services delivered by local institutions (such as schools) or effects of physical infrastructure (such as broken windows). We consider only one contextual effect theory because it clearly specifies a social capital mechanism. It is important to keep in mind, however, that social contexts tend to have a strong influence on social relations. Individuals cannot make friends or marry persons they are not in contact with, and frequency of incidental contact strongly predicts the formation of friendships and other significant relationships (Festinger, Schachter, and Back 1950; Quillian and Campbell 2003).

JOB NETWORKS AND SOCIAL CAPITAL

One important social-capital-based explanation of racial differences in poverty focuses on racial differences in employment and earnings. Job search networks serve as a source of information about available jobs and may influence employers to hire a connected applicant. If many black and Hispanic job seekers have job networks that provide less information and influence toward acquiring a job than the networks of white job seekers, and these connections are an important advantage in gaining employment, then it could be that job networks are an important factor contributing to racial gaps in employment. Correspondingly, a high-quality job network might also improve the quality of the job obtained, which in the empirical literature has usually been measured by earnings or wages. Other things equal, if network size or network quality is helpful for gaining jobs, a larger or higher quality network should lead to more information about openings, allowing the job candidate to choose from more offers and thus securing a higher quality job.

In addition to a compelling intuitive logic, several stylized facts support the importance of job networks. First, social network contacts are widely used in job searches. Retrospective surveys indicate that 25 to 50 percent of workers acquire their jobs through personal networks (Granovetter 1995). Low-wage jobs are especially likely to be filled by informal personal contacts (Holzer 1987). Second, job contacts are mostly racially homogeneous: more than 85 percent of network contacts are the same race as the job seeker (Mouw 2002; Reingold 1999). Many qualitative studies also suggest job networks are important (for example, Kasinitz and Rosenberg 1996; Royster 2003; Waldinger 2003).

Corresponding to segregation in job networks, whites also tend to have contacts with somewhat higher average rates of employment, occupational prestige, and earnings compared to black or Hispanic job seekers (Lin 1999; Reingold 1999). This is an example of advantaged contacts accruing to advantaged groups as a result of homophily in job contact networks. On the other hand, many studies find smaller differences on the basis of race and class than Wilson's discussion of social isolation indicates. Whites and blacks appear to use job networks about equally for job search, with higher use by Latinos (see Mouw 2002; Holzer 1987; Reingold 1999; Green, Tigges, and Diaz 1999; but see Korenman and Turner 1996). The equal or greater use of contacts by nonwhite job seekers suggests that there is not a large racial gap in availability of job contacts. Several studies focusing on poor, urban African Americans find that they have social networks of size comparable to nonpoor blacks and that their networks include employed and middle class persons (Oliver 1988; Fernandez and Harris 1992; Reingold 1999; Smith 2005). Sandra Smith concluded from reviewing the social networks literature that "the extent of the poor's disengagement from the mainstream has been overestimated" (2003, 1032). Mario Small (2004) likewise called into question the social isolation of Latinos in a Boston housing project, though job networks in particular are not his focus. Our review leads us to agree with Smith and Small that nonwhites have networks that are comparable in size to whites and that include many employed persons, contrary to any extreme form of social isolation. But we also conclude that whites tend to have contacts with somewhat better jobs on average than nonwhites.

Recently, Smith (2005) argued that though poor blacks do have job contacts with people who are employed, their contacts are often reluctant to recommend them to current employers out of fear that the worker they recommend will do a poor job, reflecting badly on them. Smith concluded that the black poor may have extensive networks, but that they have difficulty activating support through networks to their job search benefit. She redirected the emphasis in the job networks discussion toward the willingness of network members to help rather than the size or composition of networks. Her argument was innovative and evidence from her interview study is convincing. There remains little evidence, however, that job outcomes would be substantially different were the black poor able to activate their social capital successfully. Employer attitudes, human capital deficiencies, and perhaps poor work habits (if their job contacts' fears are correct) might mean that better job referrals would result in little net gain in employment.

Racial gaps in the quality of job networks or in the willingness of contacts to provide recommendations are largely irrelevant if job networks provide little advantage relative to other methods of job search. The second major question we must then consider is whether job networks provide a significant benefit in getting a good job in modern American labor markets. The literature that addresses this question is decidedly mixed.

Among surveys of individuals, most studies find that the use of personal contacts does not appear to be associated with advantage in job quality of jobs obtained (higher wages or earnings) relative to other methods of job search (Lin 1999; Marsden and Gorman 2001; Mouw 2003). Nor do individuals who obtained their jobs by personal contacts tend to have shorter jobless spells than individuals who use other methods (Mouw 2003). Timothy Conley and Giorgio Topa (2002) examined spatial patterns of unemployment in Chicago for evidence of social interaction effects, but find little correlation in unemployment rates after accounting for a basic set of tract population characteristics. These studies suggest no substantial benefits to use of networks contacts in job search.

Supporters of the importance of job networks point to two other lines of research in support of the significance of job network quality for job search outcomes. First, studies of hiring by a single large employer find applicants with a personal contact at the company were much more likely to receive an offer than those without a personal contact, controlling for other applicant characteristics (Fernandez and Weinberg 1997; Fernandez, Castilla, and Moore 2000). Their results indicate that applicants with contacts have a substantial advantage, although this could reflect a particular practice of the one employer studied. Second, several studies find that the occupational prestige of contacts in a seeker's job network is predictive of the occupational prestige of the job attained by the seeker (Lin 1999). This finding has led Lin (1999) and others to argue that there is a benefit of the status of the contacts in the searcher's network for obtaining high-status jobs.

Recently, Ted Mouw (2003) argued that these two findings do not—in light of others—provide convincing evidence of the benefits of job networks. He maintained that the association between network contacts status and status of job obtained or unemployment duration may reflect the fact that individuals in high-status jobs tend to have high-status friends (homophily) rather than any causal effect of high-status contacts on obtaining high-status jobs. Following James Montgomery (1992), Mouw pointed out ambiguities in drawing conclusions from prior empirical tests of job networks. He proposed an alternative test: if the effect of contact status on job quality or employment probability is causal, then individuals with high-status persons in their networks should be more likely to use networks to find jobs than those who do not. Using four sources of data, he found no evidence that this is the case. Overall, he concluded that the evidence of a strong causal effect of networks on wages or employment probability is weak. He argued that applicants may have advantages in getting jobs for certain specific employers with which they have contacts, but this results more in matching individuals with specific employers than in improving the overall quality of their jobs. Likewise, Mouw (2002) found evidence that racial segregation in employment networks contributes significantly to racial segregation in employment among firms, but not that it significantly decreases the wages or increases the time unemployed of black job seekers. Ultimately, Mouw concluded that the evidence does not disprove the possibility that workers who receive jobs through contacts could have done as well if they used other job search methods.

Mouw's arguments provide a cogent reconciliation of several findings in support of the conclusion that a high-quality job network is not of much benefit because other methods of job search may be equally effective. In this case, racial and ethnic differences in access to employment networks may not, then, be a major explanatory factor in racial gaps in the probability of employment or earnings.

Two limits of existing quantitative studies are important to note in highlighting the weakness of the evidence of network benefits for job seekers. The first is that it remains plausible that quantitative studies have not measured the properties of job networks that matter most for obtaining jobs. For instance, no study has measured the average influence of a contact over hiring decisions at the destination company, which could be the property of a job contact that is most significant for a job seeker. Indeed, all current quantitative tests may be wrong because they are measuring the wrong network qualities. Second, job networks may be more important for subgroups of workers not heavily represented in general labor market surveys. There is good reason, for instance, to believe that job networks are especially important for immigrants, as discussed in the ethnic capital section.

Several studies find that those who use personal networks do not end up with jobs with higher wages or occupational prestige (or shorter unemployment times) than those who use other methods. This fact has been especially difficult to square with claims about the benefits of job search networks. Yet because of the intuitive appeal of this explanation, and because job contacts seem important in qualitative interview studies of hiring (Royster 2003; Waldinger 2003) and the single employer studies (Fernandez and Weinberg 1997), active debate and interest surrounding this explanation will continue. Current research, however, contains very mixed findings about the benefits to job network use for job search, with many results suggesting little benefit to search through job networks.

SOCIAL CAPITAL AND NEIGHBORHOOD COLLECTIVE EFFICACY

Most studies in the neighborhood effects literature estimate the total effect of neighborhood poverty or neighborhood affluence on later life outcomes for children without identifying the mechanism behind the effect of neighborhood poverty or affluence. Neighborhood effect studies thus include advantages that may come from social capital in more affluent neighborhoods, but also include many effects that are not social capital, such as better instruction at local schools.

One major line of neighborhood research that specifies and measures a social capital mechanism involves the role of neighborhood collective efficacy in violent crime (Sampson, Raudenbush, and Earls 1997; Sampson, Morenoff, and Earls 1999; Sampson, Morenoff, and Raudenbush 2005). Collective efficacy is the shared willingness of residents of a neighborhood to intervene to maintain social order and control crime and delinquency. Robert Sampson and his colleagues measured collective efficacy through a series of survey questions that evaluate the willingness of neighborhood residents to intervene and stop delinquency, the residents' expectations that others will likewise act to stop delinquency, and the level of trust among neighbors. In their results, collective efficacy strongly predicted the level of neighborhood violence, even controlling for a number of measures of neighborhood structural conditions.[2]

Closely related to the concept of collective efficacy is Elijah Anderson's (1999) work on factors leading to a breakdown in community order and a "code of the street" in some poor urban communities. Based on extensive ethnographic work, Anderson argued that a combination of a lack of jobs and poor police protection can result in the breakdown of basic trust among community members and violence, or the threat of violence, becoming the main means of neighborhood social control. In this situation, the code of the street takes hold and even law-abiding residents must then project a tough image to avoid victimization. Anderson's work can to a significant degree be viewed as an analysis of neighborhoods in which an extreme lack of social efficacy contributes to a breakdown in the basic norms and rules that govern social interaction in less crime-ridden neighborhoods.

Although neighbor networks are one element of collective efficacy, they are not enough to produce collective efficacy as Sampson defined it. In fact, neighbor networks can support certain forms of crime as well as suppressing crime—especially in situations in which neighborhood criminal networks are rich in resources relative to non-criminal neighbor networks. Susan Popkin (2000) and Sudhir Venkatesh (1997), for instance, described how gang networks overlap and connect with the friend and family networks of individuals not associated with gangs in Chicago public housing. Mary Pattillo (1999) described a less extreme but somewhat similar case in a middle class African American neighborhood. In these cases, residents become reluctant to call police because they have strong familial or personal connections to gang members and because they fear retaliation for cooperating with the police. Gangs also command loyalty because they take on certain community organizing roles and provide resources, such as providing funding for neighborhood social events. When the resources available to criminal networks are substantial enough to compete with noncriminal neighbor networks, social capital may operate as strongly through street networks that promote certain forms of criminal activity as through decent networks that counteract it.

No scholar has drawn out the implications from this literature to racial or neighborhood disparities in poverty or other stratification outcomes, but it is clear that connections are present. On average, there are very large racial gaps in neighborhood poverty and affluence, which follow from the logic that segregation plus inequality generate inequality in contextual conditions. Racial gaps in neighborhood affluence contribute to large racial gaps in neighborhood collective efficacy

(Sampson, Morenoff, and Earls 1999). These conditions are likely to be an important factor in explaining large racial disparities in participation in criminal activity and contact with the criminal justice system (Petit and Western 2004; Sampson, Morenoff, and Earls 2005; Wheelock and Uggen, chapter 10, this volume). Prison is highly deleterious to income and employment prospects, with studies showing an enormous negative impact on the life chances of the most affected group, African American men (Pager 2003; Oliver et al. 2005; Wheelock and Uggen, chapter 10, this volume). To be sure, disparities in sentencing for type of crime and racial bias in arrest are also very important in the racially disproportionate impact of the criminal justice system, but racial disparities in involvement in crime are also a factor (see Sampson, Morenoff, and Raudenbush 2005).

Although the social efficacy literature is promising, it is also saddled with a few notable limitations. One is the emphasis on the link between collective efficacy and violent crime; the relationship of efficacy to property and drug crimes, which constitute most crime and are the basis for most arrests, is less well established. A second important limitation is that collective efficacy measures may capture some other social process at the neighborhood level that jointly determines efficacy and violent crime, though the extensive set of neighborhood controls these studies use reduces the extent of this problem. Finally, the literature has been tested using only one source of data and by one group of researchers, albeit a very competent one. The literature lacks the testing and external validation that can only come from other data sets analyzed by a wider group of researchers.

IMMIGRANTS, ETHNICITY, AND SOCIAL CAPITAL

On average, immigrants to the United States are socioeconomically disadvantaged. The poverty rate among immigrants is about 18 percent, versus about 13 percent among natives. This statistic, however, conceals tremendous variability in socioeconomic status across national origin groups. Immigrants from Mexico, Latin America, Cambodia, Laos, Vietnam, Haiti, the Dominican Republic, and the former Soviet Union have poverty rates ranging from 20 to 40 percent. Immigrants from most other Asian countries and Europe have rates below 16 percent, with some even lower than the native 13 percent (Portes and Rumbaut 1996, 78–79). To a large extent, these differences reflect differences in immigrant flows, especially in human capital level. Evidence is much sketchier on the second generation because the second generation, unlike their parents, cannot routinely be identified in census statistics. Studies find, however, that many of these patterns are reproduced in the academic achievement of the second generation, with Asian students doing well and students of Mexican, Latin American, and Caribbean descent doing less well. These patterns of unequal backgrounds persist after controls for family socioeconomic status (Portes and Rumbaut 2001).

Several basic features of migration promote the formation of social capital along ethnic immigrant lines. The importance of social networks in facilitating migration, both through social processes and U.S. immigration law, gives many immigrants a ready kin network on arrival in this country (Portes and Rumbaut 1996). Common culture, history, language, and outlook provide a common bond among coethnics (Bankston 2004). On arrival also, the salience of ethnicity is greatly accentuated by reactive ethnicity, or the greater salience that ethnic identity and culture take on in reaction to the culture of the host society, especially if the immigrant group receives a hostile reception.

The high stock of social capital held by immigrant ethnics is frequently invoked in attempts to understand immigrant adaptation in general and the relative economic and schooling success of certain immigrant groups in particular. Social capital explanations have dominated explanations of three major patterns of immigrant incorporation: the tendency of ethnic employees to dominate certain employment sectors, or ethnic niches; the high rate of entrepreneurship among certain new immigrant groups, or ethnic entrepreneurship; and the spatial clustering of ethnic group members, or ethnic enclaves (Light and Gold 2000).

Ethnic niches, or employment sectors dominated by a particular ethnicity, are a major feature of immigrant labor market incorporation. Most accounts explain niching as a result of ethnic employment networks in hiring and shared information about opportunities (Waldinger 1996, 2003; Wilson 2003). The arguments are very similar to those made in the broader literature on the benefits of employment networks, that job networks provide information about jobs and influence with hiring agents in obtaining jobs. Although we argue that the evidence supporting the superiority of information networks for job search in general is inconclusive, there is reason to think that network job search methods are especially important and useful for job matching among immigrants. Immigrants are less able to use formal methods of job search than natives because of their relative unfamiliarity with American labor market institutions and their limited English. Networks are an efficient way to match ethnic immigrant workers with employers who tolerate limited English and who do not discriminate blatantly against the ethnic target group. Correspondingly, ethnographic studies document the especially extensive use of networks in hiring immigrants (Waldinger 2003). We know of no quantitative studies of immigrants' job networks, but quantitative studies have found higher use of networks by Latinos, a high share of whom are immigrants.

A second line of social capital argument stresses the advantages of ethnic social capital for developing immigrant businesses (Aldrich and Waldinger 1990). On average, immigrants have a higher rate of self-employment than natives, but this average obscures great variation in rates of self-employment by national origin (Light 1979; Borjas 1990). Ethnic social capital contributes to the development of immigrant businesses through several mechanisms. First, ethnic cooperative credit associations help make capital available to ethnic group members who could otherwise not gain it. Debate continues, however, about whether the amount of money available through this mechanism is enough to support significant business development or expansion (Light 1972; Min 1996; Park 1997). Ethnic enterprises may also benefit from a ready network of coethnic business contacts, especially in enclave areas. In some cases, ethnic entrepreneurs benefit from international networks, such as those linking productions sites in foreign countries to retail outlets in America. Finally, ethnic enterprise may be facilitated by dense network connections with coethnics in helping to find and recruit labor.

Some of the literature in the area of ethnic entrepreneurship and labor goes beyond the benefits of ethnic social capital in founding ethnic businesses to argue that ethnicity also provides efficiencies unavailable to nonethnic employers—that ethnicity gives ethnic businesses lasting advantages over nonethnic ones. Kenneth Wilson and Allan Martin (1982) suggested that ethnic ties allow small businesses to increase profits by vertical and horizontal integration, providing better jobs than the typical small business opportunities available in the non-ethnic economy. Thomas Bailey and Roger Waldinger (1991) argued that coethnic hiring through networks is beneficial for employers because it engenders mutual obligation, reducing the chance that trained employees are likely to leave their employer. Several authors have suggested that contacts with coethnics in ethnic communities help create trust, mutual expectations, and enforceable sanctions, because both parties are in the same community and a bad business reputation can spread along the coethnic network. Wilson and Portes (1980) and Portes and Robert Bach (1985) extended arguments about ethnic economy benefits to workers, whom they maintained receive higher wages in immigrant enclave businesses than in majority sector businesses, making ethnic economy jobs more desirable than comparable jobs among small firms in the nonethnic economy.

Claims about the greater efficiency of ethnic enterprise, however, have been contested in the empirical literature. Studies of self-employed immigrants, for instance, have found that the immigrants have incomes slightly below those of native workers with similar characteristics who are not self-employed (Borjas 1990; Sanders and Nee 1987). Portes' initial results suggesting higher job quality in enclaves have been disputed by Jimy Sanders and Victor Nee (1987), and solid evidence in favor of the idea that ethnic enclaves produce specific functional benefits for ethnic business has been elusive (see also Zhou and Logan 1989; Evans 1989). Fundamentally, studies that claim unique efficiency benefits to ethnic business have usually not involved direct comparisons of immigrants and native businesses. When such direct comparisons are made, they provide little evidence that ethnic businesses function better than similar nonethnic businesses.

The third advantage of ethnic social capital accrues to the children of immigrants, and possibly also later generations of enclave ethnics. Several scholars have argued that social capital among immigrants can help adults maintain social control of the community's youth, reducing delinquency and maintaining an orientation that encourages school achievement (Portes and Zhou 1993). This argument is most convincingly made by Min Zhou and Carl Bankston in their study of Versailles Village, a Vietnamese community in New Orleans (1998). They documented the success of second-generation Vietnamese students in school, arguing that ethnic social capital has been an important contributor to the children's success. The Vietnamese community had high social capital through strong extended family structures, in part because post-war government relocation assistance for Vietnamese refugees allowed entire families to relocate. Their arguments are made more persuasive by the disadvantages the children of Versailles Village faced on dimensions other than social capital: Vietnamese immigrants held little human capital before arrival, and after arrival experienced high rates of poverty and welfare receipt and lived in a high-poverty African American area.

Zhou and Bankston (1998) argued that dense social networks in the community provide a series of supports and constraints that help Vietnamese families maintain elements of Vietnamese culture, and that these in turn aid in successful adaptation to American society. The dense and overlapping community networks cross multiple contexts such as church, community, and work. The result is pervasive community observation and control. Deviance is punished by poor reputation; positive achievements in school and the community are celebrated as public events.

As Zhou and Bankston (1998) pointed out, the second generation in Versailles Village define themselves in part by contrast with the low-income, minority community surrounding them: they compare studious immigrants (selves) against hedonistic natives (others). Their definition is consistent with cultural images of Asian Americans as model minorities. This provides an interesting contrast to the children of West Indian immigrants that Mary Waters discussed (1999). What emerges most clearly from her study is the way in which the white world's attribution of West Indians as black, with all that entails in terms of stereotypes and discrimination, facilitates adoption of a black identity that incorporates oppositional elements among many in the second generation. Differences in the level of social capital available to West Indian and Vietnamese immigrants may also play a role, though that was not Waters's focus. In the West Indian case, the contrast of studious immigrant versus hedonistic American is undercut by cultural images of blacks and treatment by whites that together often place West Indians and other African Americans in the same category.

The literature on ethnic economies has documented the importance of networks and other forms of social capital within ethnic enclaves and ethnic economies. Ethnic economies provide a secondary market in which deficits immigrants face in the labor market and in business, especially limited English proficiency, are less of a handicap. These ethnic markets, enclaves, and economies thus provide an important submarket without which immigrants would be worse off. Zhou and Bankston (1998) also made a convincing case that social capital plays a role in helping to maintain achievement orientations and social control among second-generation Vietnamese Americans.

SOCIAL CAPITAL AND FRIENDS

The Coleman report (1966) is one of the earliest examples of a study that emphasized the role of peers in explaining racial differences in academic achievement. Coleman concluded that peers were important based on the strong association between average characteristics of school populations and academic achievement outcomes. Friend influences were subsequently included in early models of status attainment through the influence of friends' educational aspirations on the respondent's educational aspirations (Duncan, Haller, and Portes 1968; Hauser 1972; Sewell and Hauser 1975; see also Hallinan and Williams 1990). Most of these studies found relatively large friend influences on educational aspirations. Groups of high-achieving friends may tend to motivate each other's academic achievement through internal group competition, or may directly help each other to learn more. High-achieving groups of friends might also encourage taking more advanced and difficult classes.[3]

These early studies take the total similarity between friends after controls as an estimate of the friend effect on outcomes. Because total similarity captures both the influence of friends on each other as well as homophily in friend selection—the tendency of like persons to become friends—these estimates overestimate the causal effect of friends. Later studies have attempted to separate homophily and causal effects by using longitudinal data to estimate friend influence with initial similarity controlled (Kandel 1978; Cohen 1983) or by attempting to isolate variation in friendships driven by factors unrelated to students' own choices. Often this involves finding a situation with certain qualities similar to experiments, such as random assignment. For example, recent studies have examined mutual influences among roommates at colleges that assign roommates randomly (Sacerdote 2001; Zimmerman 2003; Duncan et al. 2005). Other studies have estimated peer effects by using variation in average peer characteristics in classrooms that are (arguably) independent of the contaminating influence of contextual choice, such as small variations in class, gender, and race across grades in a school district (Hoxby 2000), or variation in rates of names linked to teasing among students (Figlio 2005).

The finding of both longitudinal and natural-experiment studies is that there is a like-begets-like influence among friends. Denise Kandel (1978), for instance, found that of total friend similarity in marijuana use, educational aspirations, and delinquent activity, about half results from friend influence, with the other half resulting from friend selection (homophily). Bruce Sacerdote (2001) and David Zimmerman (2003) each found somewhat smaller effects, though they were really examining roommate rather than friend effects (roommates are not necessarily friends), and they use special subsamples of students at elite colleges. Duncan and his colleagues (2005) found evidence of roommate effects on binge drinking among male students, but not for female students nor for sexual behavior or marijuana use. Hoxby (2000) found rather large peer effects on academic achievement, and David Figlio (2005) found evidence that disruptive classroom behavior reduces academic learning among all students in class. Mouw (2006) also described several other recent analyses (many unpublished) of roommate assignment on several social outcomes. In an analysis that uses total cluster correlations to estimate upper bounds for neighborhood, peer, schoolmate, and family effects, Greg Duncan, Johanne Boisjoly, and Kathleen Harris (2001) found that friend correlations (after adjustments for other covariates) are second in magnitude only to sibling correlations and are far larger than adjusted correlations among neighbors or schoolmates. If we can apply Kandel's (1978) result that roughly half of total similarity among friends results from friend influence (a stretch, because Kandel did not study exactly the same outcomes as Duncan and his colleagues), then friend effects would be important to understanding socioeconomic inequality.

The remaining issue is whether racial and ethnic differences in peer characteristics relevant to stratification are large enough to have a substantial influence on stratification outcomes. Race is a very strong basis for friend homophily (Moody 2001; Quillian and Campbell 2003). Indirectly, racial homophily in friendship creates differences in the average characteristics of friends on characteristics correlated with race, like grade point average and socioeconomic background. We know of no studies, however, that have systematically examined the magnitude of achievement-relevant differences in peer characteristics across race.

To investigate further, we use data from the National Longitudinal Study of Adolescent Health (Add Health), a large school-based study of students in grades six through twelve conducted in 1994 and 1995. The Add Health data provides the most comprehensive data on friendship networks for any large group of individuals in the United States. Students were asked to name up to five friends of each gender. Following Quillian and Campbell (2003), we focus on same-sex friends only, because the survey does not separate other-sex friends from romantic relationships.

Table 7.1 shows the characteristics of peers on three dimensions, all available from the Add Health in-school survey, that past studies suggest are relevant for understanding peer influence and school-relevant social capital: the average GPA of friends, the percentage of friends with at least one parent with a college degree, and the percentage of friends for whom neither parent graduated from high school. The left columns show results for all respondents by race; the right columns show results for respondents whose parents lack high school diplomas. Parental education is the best measure of parental socioeconomic status on the in-school survey.

The results indicate that black and Hispanic students have friends who, on average, have lower GPAs and less educated parents. The differences are large enough to have some impact. Whites students' friends have GPAs that are on average about 0.3 higher (on a 1-4 scale) than black or Hispanic students, a difference of about .4 of a standard deviation. More than 50 percent of the friends of white students' parents have a college degree, contrasted to 30 to 35 percent of black and Hispanic students. Asian students have friends with high GPAs and parental education. When we examine only students from relatively disadvantaged backgrounds—in this case students with parents who did not graduate from high school—racial differences are smaller. Homophily in friend selection depresses the GPAs of friends of black and Hispanic students with high GPAs, relative to white students with high GPAs (Redd 2004). We also do not find evidence of true social isolation from the middle class. Of the black and Hispanic students whose parents do not have high school diplomas, more than 25 percent of their friends have a parent with a college degree, and the large majority of their friends have a parent with a high school diploma. This results from reasonably high levels of SES-mixing in friendship formation (Quillian and Campbell 2003).

Table 7.2 uses this data to estimate crude models of friend influence. Like the earlier status attainment literature, these models do not attempt to separate friend

TABLE 7.1   /   Average Characteristics of Named Friends by Race

Student Race	All Students	N	Students Without a High School Graduate Parent	N
GPA of named friends				
White	2.97	30,873	2.74	1,282
Black	2.65	7,382	2.51	475
Hispanic	2.62	7,474	2.56	1,711
Asian	3.15	2,465	3.12	108
Named friends with a parent with a college degree				
White	41.0%	30,873	30.9%	1,282
Black	34.1	7,382	28.9	475
Hispanic	31.9	7,474	30.0	1,711
Asian	45.7	2,465	40.7	108
Named friends not living with a parent with a high school degree				
White	5.5%	30,873	9.4%	1,282
Black	8.2	7,382	9.6	475
Hispanic	12.5	7,474	14.8	1,711
Asian	7.7	2,465	8.3	108

Source: Authors' compilation; Add Health in School Sample 1994–1995.
Note: Students of other races and multiracial students not included.

influence from friend homogamy—a project that requires longitudinal data or exogenous instrumental variables. We instead use this simple OLS regression of respondent GPA on friends' average GPA, though we improve on the early status attainment literature by adding fixed effect variables for schools.[4] Following the loose rule of thumb from Kandel (1978) and Cathy Cohen (1983), we estimate that friend influence is half of what we find here, translating to an increase in respondent GPA of .19 to .22 with a one unit increase in the average GPA of friends.

Finally, table 7.3 uses this data to compare estimates of the GPA effects of friends, or roommates in Bruce Sacerdote's study (2001), to derive estimates of the extent of racial difference in GPA that can be explained by average GPA of friends. The Sacerdote estimates we present are likely too low for our sample, because we believe roommate influences are likely weaker than friend influences. Xu Lin (2005) used the Add Health friendship data to estimate peer effects based on an econometric model that borrows from the literature on estimating spatial effects. His estimates varied greatly depending on controls in the model. Lin's weaker effects are similar to the effects we find, based on coefficients estimated from table 7.2 and multiplied by .5 to represent an influence of homophily. Most of these estimates suggest friend effects account for about 15 to 20 percent of the

TABLE 7.2 / Regression of Respondent's GPA on Friends' GPA, Parental Characteristics, and School Characteristics

Variable	No School Fixed Effects				With School Fixed Effects			
	Baseline		GPA of Friends		Baseline		GPA of Friends	
	Coefficient	Standard Error	Coefficient	Standard Error	Coefficient	Standard Error	Coefficient	Standard Error
Race								
White	(reference)		(reference)		(reference)		(reference)	
Black	−0.33	0.01***	−0.19	0.01***	−0.29	0.01***	−0.20	0.01***
Hispanic	−0.29	0.01***	−0.17	0.01***	−0.25	0.01***	−0.17	0.01***
Asian	0.22	0.02***	0.13	0.01***	0.21	0.02***	0.14	0.02***
Mother's grades in school completed	0.04	0.00***	0.03	0.00***	0.04	0.00***	0.03	0.00***
Neither parent has a high school degree	(reference)		(reference)		(reference)		(reference)	
At least one parent high school, neither college	0.04	0.01**	0.03	0.01*	0.07	0.01***	0.05	0.01***
At least one parent has college degree	0.22	0.02***	0.15	0.02***	0.23	0.02***	0.18	0.02***
Mother not in a professional occupation	(reference)		(reference)		(reference)		(reference)	
Mother in a professional occupation	0.03	0.01***	0.02	0.01**	0.03	0.01***	0.02	0.01**
Gender								
Female	(reference)		(reference)		(reference)		(reference)	
Male	−0.15	0.01***	−0.08	0.01***	−0.17	0.01***	−0.10	0.01***
Born in United States	(reference)		(reference)		(reference)		(reference)	
Foreign-born	−0.01	0.01	0.02	0.01	0.06	0.01***	0.06	0.01***
Average GPA of friends			0.45	0.01***			0.38	0.01***
School fixed effects	No		No		Yes		Yes	
N	46,980		46,980		46,980		46,980	

Source: Authors' compilation.
Note: All models estimated with a constant but constant not shown.
* = p < .05; ** = p < .01; *** = p < .001

TABLE 7.3 / Alternative Estimates of Peer GPA Effect

Author	Estimate	Percentage of White-Black Difference Explained	Percentage of White-Hispanic Difference Explained	Explanations
Sacerdote (2001)	0.125	11.3	10.4	GPA roommate effect among students at Williams College. Based on random roommate assignment.
Lin (2005)	.840; .221	76.2; 20.1	70.2; 18.5	Spatial Autoregressive Statistical Model using Add Health data. Second estimate incorporates school by grade fixed effects and is not statistically signficant.
Quillian and Redd, table 7.2	.225; .190	20.4; 17.2	18.8; 15.9	Assumes half of peer effect spurious, following Kandel (1978). Second estimate incorporates school fixed effects.

Source: Authors' compilation.

racial difference in GPA between white and black students and white and Hispanic students.

Combined with the evidence from many studies that like-beget-like peer effects exist and may be reasonably important, the differences in average peer characteristics across race that we observe here are large enough to be a contributing factor to racial differences in school achievement. Our analysis suggests that peer effects matter, though they are far from a complete explanation of racial differences in schooling-related outcomes.

CONCLUSION

Social capital has become a catchphrase for the myriad ways in which social interactions matter. The broad social capital framework has been useful in many respects, but really understanding the importance of social capital involves going beyond the metaphor to assess specific processes and explanations.

Social capital explanations that contribute to understanding racial poverty gaps have tended to follow one of two logics. The first and more commonly used logic explains racial poverty gaps by references to social capital deficits of disadvantaged racial groups relative to advantaged groups. Inequalities in social capital result primarily from the combination of racial inequality with racial segregation or racial homophily, which results in relatively advantaged associates for members of advantaged groups and less advantaged associates for members of disadvantaged groups. To the extent that advantaged associates are of benefit in generating positive stratification outcomes, differences in social networks then increase the advantage of the advantaged. In the second logic, homophily or segregation facilitates the development of dense social ties and common orientation among coethnics, which acts as a resource in generating positive stratification outcomes.

We have focused on four social capital explanations that follow these logics. Three follow the first logic of segregation plus inequality leading to social contextual disadvantage for disadvantaged racial groups, while one (ethnic social capital) follows the opposite logic of beneficial social capital arising from homophily or segregation. Table 7.4 provides a summary of our conclusions. For a social capital explanation to be important in understanding racial poverty gaps, there must be a large racial gap associated with the form of social capital considered by the explanation, and that form must have a large effect on outcomes related to poverty. Our review leads us to conclude that neighborhood collective efficacy, ethnic social capital, and school friendship networks are explanations for which good evidence supports their importance in understanding racial poverty gaps. For job finding networks, the evidence is weaker, largely because studies of the benefits of job networks relative to other methods of job search are mixed.

We conclude that the term social capital, then, covers several processes important for understanding racial disparities in poverty. On the other hand, we do not find reason to privilege social capital explanations over a variety of other processes, such as discrimination, that we believe to be equally or more important. We also find that the evidence is often not as strong as a careful scholar might hope, because studies have too often failed to account for the confounding influence of selection in social context. This is an especially large problem in the ethnic social capital literature, where no natural-experiment studies are available.

We find the evidence linking racial inequality to social capital disadvantages resulting from disadvantaged neighborhoods especially compelling. Racial gaps in neighborhood conditions are very large. In the year 2000, for instance, a black or Hispanic family with income below the federal poverty line was about three times as likely to be living in a high-poverty neighborhood as a white family with income below the poverty line (Jargowsky 2003). Racial gaps in neighborhood conditions experienced by members of different racial groups are larger than differences in most measures of economic or social status. Research on neighborhood collective efficacy suggests that gaps in neighborhood conditions are linked to differences in rates of criminal victimization and offending. In impoverished neighborhoods with poor community social control, the temptation for youth to seek criminal means of social mobility rather than legitimate means are strong, with

TABLE 7.4 / Summary of Four Social Capital Theories of Racial Poverty Gaps

Explanation	Racial Difference	Effect on Stratification Outcomes	Overall Effect on Racial Poverty Disparities
Job-finding networks	moderate	small	small increase
Neighborhood collective efficacy	large	moderate to large	moderate to large increase
Ethnic social capital among immigrants	large for immigrants versus natives	moderate	moderate reduction
School friendship networks	small to moderate	moderate	small to moderate increase

Source: Authors' compilation.

the high risk of becoming involved in the criminal justice system and the diminished legitimate career prospects that follow from this involvement. The increasingly long sentences for nonviolent drug crimes further contribute to the likely importance of this explanation for racial disparities in poverty outcomes. Ongoing research on this topic should help to better clarify the part that neighborhood social capital plays in the nexus of crime, criminal justice, and racial inequality.

Our thanks to David R. Harris, Ann Chih Lin, Stephen Morgan, and Jeffrey Morenoff for helpful comments on an earlier draft.

NOTES

1. This logic will not work in the special case of perfect or near perfect friendship homophily on GPA, but in practice homophily on non-race characteristics is almost never strong enough to undercut the logic of this argument.
2. Robert Sampson, Jeffrey Morenoff, and Stephen Raudenbush, however, do not find that collective efficacy accounts for racial disparities in committing violence—a distinct measure from local area crime rates—although they find that other neighborhood social conditions can account for these disparities (2005).
3. Another potentially important peer effect for racial differences in poverty results from the peers that recruit individuals into delinquency. We view this argument as somewhat subsumed by our earlier discussion of neighborhood efficacy, a major factor in controlling local adolescent peer groups. Peers play an important role in the microprocess of participation in delinquency.

4. Fixed effects include a dummy variable for each school, allowing the model to control for all average differences between schools. This provides a control for school-level characteristics. In models with school fixed effects, differences in GPA and friendship networks between schools do not contribute to the estimate of the effect of friendship network GPA on student GPA.

REFERENCES

Aberg, Martin, and Mikael Sandberg. 2003. *Social Capital and Democratisation: Roots of Trust in Post-Communist Poland and Ukraine*. Burlington, Vt.: Ashgate Publishing.

Aldrich, Howard, and Roger Waldinger. 1990. "Ethnicity and Entrepreneurship." *Annual Review of Sociology* 16: 111–35.

Anderson, Elijah. 1999. *The Code of the Streets: Decency, Violence, and the Moral Life of the Inner City*. New York: W. W. Norton.

Bailey, Thomas, and Roger Waldinger. 1991. "Primary, Secondary, and Enclave Labor Markets: A Training Systems Approach." *American Sociological Review* 56(4): 432–45.

Bankston, Carl L. 2004. "Social Capital, Cultural Values, Immigration, and Academic Achievement: The Host Country Context and Contradictory Consequences." *Sociology of Education* 77(2): 176–79.

Blau, Peter. 1977. *Inequality and Heterogeneity: A Primitive Theory of Social Structure*. New York: The Free Press.

Borjas, George. 1990. *Friends or Strangers: The Impact of Immigrants on the U.S. Economy*. New York: Basic Books.

Bourdieu, Pierre. 1985. "The Forms of Capital." In *Handbook of Theory and Research for the Sociology of Education*, edited by J. G. Richardson. New York: Greenwood.

Briggs, Xavier de Souza. 1998. "Brown Kids in White Suburbs: Housing Mobility and the Many Faces of Social Capital." *Housing Policy Debate* 9(1): 177–221.

Cohen, Cathy J. 2001. "Social Capital, Intervening Institutions, and Political Power." In *Social Capital and Poor Communities*, edited by Susan Saegert, J. Phillip Thomson, and Mark Warren. New York: Russell Sage Foundation.

Cohen, Jere. 1983. "Peer Influence on College Aspirations with Initial Aspirations Controlled." *American Sociological Review* 48(5): 728–34.

Coleman, James. 1988. "Social Capital in the Creation of Human Capital." *The American Journal of Sociology* 94(S1): S95–120.

Coleman, James, E. Q. Campbell, C. J. Hobson, J. McPartland, A. M. Mood, F. D. Weinfeld, and R. L. York. 1966. *Equality of Educational Opportunity*. Washington, D.C.: Government Printing Office.

Conley, Timothy, and Giorgio Topa. 2002. "Socio-Economic Distance and Spatial Patterns in Unemployment." *Journal of Applied Econometrics* 17(4): 303–27.

Duncan, Greg J., Johanne Boisjoly, and Kathleen Harris. 2001. "Sibling, Peers, Neighbor, and Schoolmate Correlations as Indicators of the Importance of Context for Adolescent Development." *Demography* 38(3): 437–47.

Duncan, Greg J., Johanne Boisjoly, Michael Kremer, Dan M. Levy, Jacque Eccles. 2005. "Peer Effects in Drug Use and Sex Among College Students." *Journal of Abnormal Child Psychology* 33(3): 375–85.

Duncan, Greg J., and Stephen Raudenbush. 1999. "Assessing the Effects of Context in Studies of Child and Youth Development." *Educational Psychologist* 34(1): 29–41.

Duncan, Otis Dudley, Archibald Haller, and Alejandro Portes. 1968. "Peer Influences on Aspirations: A Reinterpretation." *The American Journal of Sociology* 74(2): 119–37.

Durlauf, Steven, and Marcel Fafchamps. 2004. "Social Capital." Social Systems Research Institute Working Paper 2004-12. Madison, Wisc.: University of Wisconsin.

Evans, Mariah. 1989. "Immigrant Entrepreneurship: Effects of Market Size and Isolated Labor Pool." *American Sociological Review* 54(6): 950–62.

Feld, John. 2003. *Social Capital*. New York: Routledge.

Fernandez, Roberto, Emilio Castilla, and Paul Moore. 2000. "Social Capital at Work: Networks and Employment at a Phone Center." *The American Journal of Sociology* 105(5): 1288–356.

Fernandez, Roberto, and David Harris. 1992. "Social Isolation and the Underclass." In *Drugs, Crime, and Social Isolation*, edited by Adele Harrell and George Peterson. Washington, D.C.: Urban Institute Press.

Fernandez, Roberto, and Nancy Weinberg. 1997. "Personal Contacts and Hiring in a Retail Bank." *American Sociological Review* 62(6): 883–902.

Festinger, Leon, Stanley Schachter, and Kurt Back. 1950. *Social Pressures in Informal Groups: A Study of Human Factors in Housing*. Stanford, Calif.: Stanford University Press.

Figlio, David. 2005. "Boys Named Sue: Disruptive Children and their Peers." NBER Working Paper 11277. Cambridge, Mass.: National Bureau of Economic Research.

Granovetter, Mark. 1995. *Getting a Job: A Study of Contracts and Careers*, 2nd ed. Chicago, Ill.: The University of Chicago Press.

Green, Gary P., Leann Tigges, and Daniel Diaz. 1999. "Racial and Ethnic Differences in Job Search Strategies in Atlanta, Boston, and Los Angeles." *Social Science Quarterly* 80(2): 263–78.

Hallinan, Maureen, and Richard Williams. 1990. "Students' Characteristics and the Peer Influence Process." *Sociology of Education* 63(2): 122–32.

Halpern, David. 2005. *Social Capital*. Malden, Mass.: Polity Press.

Hauser, Robert. 1972. "Disaggregating a Social-Psychological Model of Peer Attainment." *Social Science Research* 1(2): 159–88.

Holzer, Harry J. 1987. "Informational Job Search and Black Youth Unemployment." *The American Economic Review* 77(3): 446–52.

Hoxby, Caroline. 2000. "Peer Effects in the Classroom: Learning from Gender and Race Variation." NBER Working Paper No. 7867. Cambridge, Mass.: National Bureau of Economic Research.

Jargowsky, Paul. 2003. "Stunning Progress, Hidden Problems: The Dramatic Decline of Concentrated Poverty in the 1990s." Living Census Series. Washington, D.C.: The Brookings Institution Press.

Kandel, Denise. 1978. "Homophily, Selection, and Socialization in Adolescent Friendships." *The American Journal of Sociology* 84(2): 427–36.

Kasinitz, Philip, and Jan Rosenberg. 1996. "Missing the Connection: Social Isolation and Employment on the Brooklyn Waterfront." *Social Problems* 43(2): 180–96.

Korenman, Sanders, and Susan Turner. 1996. "Employment Contacts and Differences in Wages Between Minority and White Youths." *Industrial Relations* 35(1): 106–22.

Krohn, Marvin D. 1986. "The Web of Conformity: A Network Approach to the Explanation of Delinquent Behavior." *Social Problems* 33(6): S81–93.

Light, Ivan. 1972. *Ethnic Enterprise in America: Business and Welfare Among Chinese, Japanese, and Blacks*. Berkeley, Calif.: University of California Press.

———. 1979. "Disadvantaged Minorities in Self-Employment." *International Journal of Comparative Sociology* 20(1/2): 31–45.

Light, Ivan, and Steven Gold. 2000. *Ethnic Economies*. San Diego, Calif.: Academic Press.

Lin, Nan. 1999. "Social Networks and Status Attainment." *Annual Review of Sociology* 25: 467–87.

———. 2001. *Social Capital: A Theory of Social Structure and Action*. Cambridge: Cambridge University Press.

Lin, Xu. 2005. "Peer Effects and Student Academic Achievement: An Application of Spatial Autoregressive Model with Group Unobservables." Paper presented at the meeting of the Canadian Economics Association, Hamilton, Ontario, May 27–29, 2005.

Loury, Glenn. 1977. "A Dynamic Theory of Racial Income Differences." In *Women, Minorities, and Employment Discrimination*, edited by Phyllis A. Wallace and Annette M. LaMond. Lexington, Mass.: Lexington Books/DC Heath.

Manski, Charles. 1993. "Identification of Endogenous Social Effects: The Reflection Problem." *Review of Economic Studies* 60(3): 531–42.

Marsden, Peter, and Elizabeth Gorman. 2001. "Social Networks, Job Changes, and Recruitment." In *Sourcebook on Labor Markets: Evolving Structures and Processes*, edited by Ivar Berg and Arne L. Kalleberg. New York: Kluwer/Plenum.

Massey, Douglas. 1990. "American Apartheid: Segregation and the Making of the Underclass." *The American Journal of Sociology* 96(2): 329–57.

Min, Pyong-Gap. 1996. *Caught in the Middle: Korean Communities in New York and Los Angeles*. Berkeley, Calif.: University of California Press.

Moffitt, Robert A. 2001. "Policy Interventions, Low-Level Equilibria, and Social Interactions." In *Social Dynamics*, edited by Steven N. Durlauf and H. Peyton Young. Washington, D.C.: The Brookings Institution Press.

Montgomery, James. 1992. "Job Search and Network Composition: Implications of the Strength-of-Weak-Tie Hypothesis." *American Sociological Review* 57(5): 586–96.

Moody, James. 2001. "Race, School Integration, and Friendship Segregation in America." *The American Journal of Sociology* 107(3): 679–716.

Morgan, Stephen, and Aage Sorsensen. 1999. "Parental Networks, Social Closure, and Mathematics Learning: A Test of Coleman's Social Capital Explanation of School Effects." *American Sociological Review* 64(5): 661–91.

Mouw, Ted. 2002. "Are Black Workers Missing the Connection? The Effect of Spatial Distance and Employee Referrals on Interfirm Racial Segregation." *Demography* 39(3): 507–28.

———. 2003. "Social Capital and Finding a Job: Do Contacts Matter?" *American Sociological Review* 68(6): 868–98.

———. 2006. "Estimating the Causal Effects of Social Capital: A Review of Recent Research." *Annual Review of Sociology* 32: 79–102.

Oliver, Melvin L. 1988. "The Black Urban Community as Network: Toward a Social Network Perspective." *The Sociological Quarterly* 29(4): 623–45.

Oliver, Pamela, Gary Sandefur, Jessica Jakubowski, and James E. Yocom. 2005. "The Effect of Black Male Imprisonment on Black Child Poverty." Paper presented at the meetings of the American Sociological Association, Philadelphia, Pa., August 13, 2005.

Pager, Devah. 2003. "The Mark of a Criminal Record." *The American Journal of Sociology* 108(5): 937–75.

Park, Kyeyoung. 1997. *The Korean American Dream: Immigrants and Small Business in New York City*. Ithaca, N.Y.: Cornell University Press.

Pattillo, Mary. 1999. *Black Picket Fences: Privilege and Peril Among the Black Middle Class*. Chicago, Ill.: The University of Chicago Press.

Paxton, Pamela. 1999. "Is Social Capital Declining in the United States? A Multiple Indicator Assessment." *The American Journal of Sociology* 105(1): 88–127.

Petit, Becky, and Bruce Western. 2004. "Mass Imprisonment and the Life Course: Race and Class Inequality in U.S. Incarceration." *American Sociological Review* 69(2): 151–69.

Popkin, Susan. 2000. *The Hidden War: Crime and the Tragedy of Public Housing in Chicago*. New Brunswick, N.J.: Rutgers University Press.

Portes, Alejandro. 1998. "Social Capital: Its Origins and Applications in Modern Sociology." *Annual Review of Sociology* 24: 1–24.

Portes, Alejandro, and Robert Bach. 1985. *Latin Journey*. Berkeley, Calif.: University of California Press.

Portes, Alejandro, and Ruben Rumbaut. 1996. *Immigrant America: A Portrait*. Berkeley, Calif.: University of California Press.

———. 2001. *Legacies: The Story of the Immigrant Second Generation*. Berkeley, Calif.: University of California Press.

Portes, Alejandro, and Min Zhou. 1993. "The New Second Generation: Segmented Assimilation and its Variants." *Annals of the American Academy of Political and Social Science* 530: 74–96.

Putnam, Robert. 1995. "Bowling Alone: America's Declining Social Capital." *Journal of Democracy* 6(1): 65–78.

Quillian, Lincoln, and Mary Campbell. 2003. "Beyond Black and White: The Present and Future of Multiracial Friendship Segregation." *American Sociological Review* 68(4): 540–66.

Redd, Rozlyn. 2004. "Is There Support for Oppositional Culture in Minority Peer Groups? Evidence from the Adolescent Health Survey Friendship Data." Master's thesis, Department of Sociology, University of Wisconsin-Madison.

Reingold, David. 1999. "Social Networks and the Employment Problems of the Urban Poor." *Urban Studies* 36(11): 1907–32.

Royster, Deidre. 2003. *Race and the Invisible Hand: How White Networks Exclude Black Men from Blue-Collar Jobs*. Berkeley, Calif.: University of California Press.

Rumberger, Russell, and Gregory Palardy. 2005. "Does Segregation (Still) Matter? The Impact of Student Composition on Academic Achievement in High School." *Teachers College Record* 107(9): 1999–2045.

Sacerdote, Bruce. 2001. "Peer Effects with Random Assignment: Results from College Roommates." *Quarterly Journal of Economics* 116(2): 681–704.

Sampson, Robert J., Jeffrey D. Morenoff, and Felton Earls. 1999. "Beyond Social Capital: Spatial Dynamics of Collective Efficacy for Children." *American Sociological Review* 64(5): 633–60.

———. 2005. "Social Anatomy of Racial and Ethnic Disparities in Violence." *American Journal of Public Health* 95(2): 224–32.

Sampson, Robert J., Jeffrey D. Morenoff, and Stephen Raudenbush. 2005. "Social Anatomy of Racial and Ethnic Disparities in Violence." *American Journal of Public Health* 95(2): 224–32.

Sampson, Robert J., Stephen Raudenbush, and Felton Earls. 1997. "Neighborhoods and Violent Crime: A Multilevel Study of Collective Efficacy." *Science* 277(5328): 918–24.

Sanders, Jimy M., and Victor Nee. 1987. "Limits of Ethnic Solidarity in the Enclave Economy." *American Sociological Review* 52(6): 745–73.

Sewell, William, and Robert Hauser. 1975. *Education, Occupation, and Earnings: Achievement in the Early Career*. New York: Academic Press.

Small, Mario. 2004. *Villa Victoria: The Transformation of Social Capital in a Boston Barrio*. Chicago, Ill.: University of Chicago Press.

Smith, Sandra. 2003. "Exploring the Efficacy of African-Americans Job Referral Networks: A Study of the Obligations of Exchange around Job Information and Influence." *Ethnic and Racial Studies* 26(6): 1029–45.

———. 2005. "'Don't Put My Name on It': Social Capital Activation and Job Finding Assistance Among the Black Urban Poor." *The American Journal of Sociology* 111(1): 1–57.

Stanton-Salazar, Ricardo, and Stanford Dornbusch. 1995. "Social Capital and the Reproduction of Inequality: Information Networks among Mexican-Origin High-School Students." *Sociology of Education* 68(2): 116–35.

Teachman, Jay, Kathleen Paasch, and Karen Carver. 1996. "Social Capital and Dropping out of School Early." *Journal of Marriage and the Family* 58(3): 773–83.

Venkatesh, Sudhir. 1997. The Social Organization of Street Gang Activity in an Urban Ghetto. *The American Journal of Sociology* 103(1): 82–111.

Waldinger, Rodger. 1996. *Still the Promised City? African-Americans and New Immigrants in Postindustrial New York*. Cambridge, Mass.: Harvard University Press.

———. 2003. *How the Other Half Works: Immigration and the Social Organization of Labor*. Berkeley, Calif.: University of California Press.

Waters, Mary. 1999. *Black Identities: West Indian Immigrant Dreams and American Realities*. Cambridge, Mass.: Harvard University Press.

White, Michael. 1987. *American Neighborhoods and Residential Differentiation*. New York: Russell Sage Foundation.

Wilson, Franklin. 2003. "Ethnic Niching and Metropolitan Labor Markets." *Social Science Research* 32(3): 429–66.

Wilson, Kenneth, and Allan Martin. 1982. "Ethnic Enclaves: A Comparison of the Cuban and Black Economies in Miami." *American Journal of Sociology* 78(May): 135–60.

Wilson, Kenneth L., and Alejandro Portes. 1980. "Immigrant Enclaves: An Analysis of the Labor Market Experiences of Cubans in Miami." *The American Journal of Sociology* 86(2): 295–319.

Wilson, William Julius. 1987. *The Truly Disadvantaged: The Inner-City, The Underclass, and Public Policy*. Chicago, Ill.: University of Chicago Press.

Zimmerman, David. 2003. "Peer Effects in Academic Outcomes: Results from a Natural Experiment." *Review of Economics and Statistics* 85(1): 9–23.

Zhou, Min, and Carl Bankston. 1998. *Growing Up American: The Adaptation of Vietnamese Adolescents in the United States*. New York: Russell Sage Foundation.

Zhou, Min, and John Logan. 1989. "Returns on Human Capital in Ethnic Enclaves: New York City's Chinatown." *The American Sociological Review* 54(5): 809–20.

Part III

Policy, Race, and Poverty:
Intentions and Consequences

Chapter 8

Race, Place, and Poverty Revisited

Michael A. Stoll

Not long ago, the lens viewing urban America displayed chocolate cities and vanilla suburbs. Popular funk bands of the 1970s, such as Parliament with their megahit "Chocolate Cities," helped mold this understanding through musical lyrics that described American urban areas becoming darker and poorer while suburbs were emerging as white and rich (Avila 2004). U.S. cities were not, of course, always understood in these terms. The great black migrations from the South to the North in the early and mid-1900s, coupled with de jure and de facto discrimination that limited economic and residential opportunities, had tremendous effects on the socioeconomic and racial profiles of cities. This, in conjunction with the rapid suburbanization of mostly middle-income whites in the postwar period, left central cities with growing concentrations of poverty, especially minority poverty, and sealed the connection between race, place and poverty. Central cities were increasingly seen as black and poor, and suburbs were white and the main regions of population, employment, and economic growth.

But a number of factors, including suburban sprawl and massive demographic changes, limited the strong association of cities with poverty and suburbs with white wealth. Sprawl continues to characterize much of metropolitan growth, and immigration, mostly from Latin America and Asia, now drives demographic change in the United States (Portes and Rumbaut 2001). For example, even in the recent decade, the Latino population increased a phenomenal 57.9 percent, from 22.4 million in 1990 to 35.3 million in 2000. In 2000, it represented about 13 percent of the population, up from about 6 percent in 1980, and much of this growth has been driven by immigration. Likewise, the Asian American population continues to grow at an impressive rate, making up about 1 percent of the U.S. population in 1980, but 4 percent in 2000 (Ong and Leung 2003). As a result of these changes, metropolitan America is likely to be more racially and ethnically diverse now than in the past. These changes, among others, have likely altered the colors of poverty across central cities and suburbs and raised questions about the role of place in influencing racial and ethnic differences in poverty.

This chapter revisits several areas of the race, place, and poverty debate: the geography of race, place, and poverty; whether and how they have changed over recent decades; and how patterns and characteristics of place influence observed racial and ethnic differences in poverty. In earlier analyses of these questions, the notion of place was synonymous with the central city-suburban dichotomy for a variety of reasons, including the difficulty of obtaining quality data on place, and especially because of the perceived strong association between place, race and poverty. That is, as American cities declined in the late 1960s, central cities were increasingly characterized by density, minority poverty, crime, and urban problems generally, and newly growing suburban areas were characterized as pockets of new wealth, opportunity, and the absence of poverty and its associated problems. Thus, it was easy to conclude that cities were a source of, and reinforced, poverty, especially minority poverty, and that suburbs were centers of, and influenced, opportunity, especially for whites.

The analysis here confirms the increasingly well-known idea that the central city–suburb dichotomy can be misleading, because of the increasing migration of poor and minority people to the suburbs, the economic decline of many inner-ring suburbs (Holzer and Stoll 2007), and the revitalization of parts of many central cites (Katz 2006). Thus, this categorization of places is of limited value in understanding the role of place in poverty in general, and racial differences in poverty in particular. The growing diversity of places within central cites, suburbs, and rural areas begs for a more local understanding of how place shapes and reinforces poverty and its racial ordering.

However, even when we adopt a more fine-grained approach to categorizing places, we nevertheless see substantial segregation by race, ethnicity, and socioeconomic class. Research has suggested many possible explanations for these patterns. They include micro factors such as neighborhood effects, schools, and networks, and macro factors such as housing market discrimination. Other chapters in this volume focus on the effect of social capital, networks, neighborhoods, and discrimination on racial differences in poverty. This chapter explores the impact of additional factors such as racial segregation and metropolitan decentralization, as well as less often discussed factors such as the geography of low-income housing. We begin by defining place and by reviewing theories about how place might be related to racial and ethnic differences in poverty.

DEFINING PLACE AND ASSESSING ITS CONSEQUENCES

The meaning of place varies a great deal across disciplines and other dimensions. Although a detailed treatment of this discussion is beyond the scope of this chapter, it is important to highlight these different meanings to understand the role place can play in affecting poverty-related economic and social outcomes. To economists and to a large extent many urban planners and geographers, place is the locus of economic activity and amenities that give value to areas. Places are more valuable economically and socially when there is greater density of economic activity (businesses, jobs), and valuable amenities and public goods (good schools and neighbors, parks, low crime, museums) (O'Sullivan 2002). For individuals, attachment to places with these valuable assets is expected to reduce one's risk of poverty because of the positive relationship between locational assets and economic and social mobility. By contrast, living far from these amenities is thought to increase one's risk of being poor. For example, distant jobs are hard to access because of commuting costs and the low probability of being connected to distant job networks.

Sociologist, anthropologists, and some geographers are to some extent concerned with the physical aspects of place, but they mostly concentrate on the social relationships and community identities of sites. The sociological approach and the economic approach are not mutually exclusive, but sociologists are more focused on the spatial ordering of the quality of social ties, the relationships and emotional bonds formed among and between people in a particular spatial context, and the way these relationships enhance or constrain social and economic opportunity and poverty (Jacobs 1961; Gans 1962; Anderson 1976). Thus, residence in longer-term socially stable neighborhoods, or in areas with strong community ties or strong pro-social institutions, is likely to provide better quality of information, better connections to economic and social activities, and stronger role models. Attachment to these networks and communities, themselves influenced by their spatial context, are in turn likely to significantly influence poverty outcomes. For example, residence in places with high turnover, with few working adults, and with weak social institutions, is likely to increase one's risk of poverty by limiting access to resources that can promote social and economic advancement.

Of course, the different meanings of place are strongly related. Places near good jobs, strong economic activities, or amenities are also likely to have well connected residents with good incomes who develop or maintain strong pro-social neighborhood institutions. Thus, the difference in meanings reflects a difference in the mechanisms by and through which individuals access the resources and information required to reduce exposure to poverty risk.

In the past, defining places on the basis of these conceptions has been difficult both because of a lack of theoretical clarity about boundaries, and because of low-quality data. As a consequence, researchers have used broad conceptions of place such as ghettos, barrios, central cities, and suburbs as indicators of the quality of places (Jargowsky 1997; Stoll, Holzer, and Ihlanfeldt 2000). But they do so at the cost of losing sense of the heterogeneity of the economic and social quality within areas. More recently, researchers have examined the nature of place at much lower levels of geography, such as census tracts and zip codes, or by constructing gravity measures, which use better quality data and more powerful computing capacities (Johnson 2006; Ioannides and Loury 2004; Mouw 2000; Raphael 1997; Crane 1991).[1] Yet debate about the boundaries of places and neighborhoods continues, over the specific indicators used to measure the quality of places, and over the mapping of these measures and boundaries onto residents' sense of their own communities (Sampson, Morenoff, and Gannon-Rowley 2002).

More important, there is also debate about whether and how the nature of place, even defined in broad geographic terms, affects poverty outcomes. Since William Julius Wilson's (1987) landmark study of the urban underclass in the late 1980s, there has been a resurgence of scholarship on the effects of place and neighborhood on social and economic outcomes. Although some debate about how we define place and neighborhoods geographically remains, there is greater certainty about the extent of considerable social inequality among neighborhoods with respect to socioeconomic and racial segregation, especially the concentration of disadvantage and geographic isolation of African Americans. We are also more certain that social problems are geographically correlated with social inequality, with poor neighborhoods showing higher levels of crime, school dropout, social and physical disorder, and single-parent households, among other factors. Finally, this ecological concentration of disadvantage has increased considerably during the recent decades, and concentration of wealth has increased as well (Sampson, Morenoff, and Gannon-Rowley 2002; Jencks and Mayer 1990; Quillian and Redd, chapter 7, this volume). What is still in question is the extent to which this concentration of disadvantage limits the social and economic life chances of individuals from these neighborhoods.

On this question, different conclusions have been drawn, depending on what outcomes are studied, by which methods, and for which group. Of course, the major concern in all of these studies is the problem of selection bias, or unobserved heterogeneity. That is, it is difficult to tease out whether individual outcomes are caused by these place-based factors, or by selection (sorting) of individuals with specific characteristics into specific neighborhoods. Do potential suburban characteristics such as more jobs and better quality social networks help reduce poverty exposure, or is it that more advantaged individuals are unlikely to experience poverty and more likely to move to suburbs? On balance, earlier research and research using nonexperimental methods to directly address the selection issues found that neighborhoods play a role in influencing the life chances of individuals (Sampson, Morenoff, and Gannon-Rowley 2002; Brooks-Gunn et al. 1993; Elliott et al. 1996; Crane 1991).

All else equal, neighborhood disadvantage, as measured by such factors as the percent of the neighborhood that is affluent, impoverished, on welfare, or comprised of female-headed households or managers-professionals is negatively correlated with adolescent development outcomes such as dropping out of school, attending college, and achievement test scores (Kling, Ludwig, and Katz 2005; Ioannides and Loury 2004; Sampson, Morenoff, and Gannon-Rowley 2002; Brooks-Gunn et al. 1993; Elliott et al. 1996; Crane 1991). The strength of these correlations is, to some degree, related to the precise measure of neighborhood quality that researchers use (Duncan 1994). Moreover, as noted, estimates of neighborhood effects are commonly overstated if residential choice is not taken into account, as parent's neighborhood of choice is frequently strongly correlated with their expectations of how their children should do in school (Plotnick and Hoffman 1999). The literature indicates that for adults, welfare receipt and exits, men's economic status, and the quality of individuals' social ties are related to the quality of the neighborhood in which individuals live, independent of individuals' personal and family background characteristics (Sampson, Morenoff, and Gannon-Rowley 2002; Vartanian 1997; Osterman 1991; Tigges, Browne, and Green 1998). Finally, some research strongly suggests racial unevenness in these effects. These findings suggest that the characteristics of black neighborhoods are more likely to influence black poverty than for other racial and ethnic groups, thus potentially contributing to racial differences in poverty (Crane 1991).

However, new neighborhood research using experimental methods that directly address the concerns of selection bias has found more mixed results. These studies use what is considered the gold standard in this research: random assignment. Most use data from the Moving to Opportunity (MTO) program to examine the impact of neighborhood quality on adult and adolescent social, economic, or educational outcomes. The research suggests that living in low-poverty neighborhoods has some noticeable impacts on adolescents in the realm of crime, education, and self-esteem, especially for girls, but little effect on adult economic outcomes such as employment or income (Kling, Ludwig, and Katz 2005; Ludwig, Hirschfield, and Duncan 2001; Katz, Kling, and Liebman 2001).

However, research should continue in this area to confirm these results because the validity and generalization of MTO results for adults can be called into question for at least two reasons. The first is that the characteristics of the sample that participated in the program are not generalizable to the poverty population. Most participants were long-term public housing residents who had very little labor market attachment and very limited job skills. It is therefore not surprising that the children of these participants had more favorable economic or social outcomes from moving to low poverty areas than the adults. Skill deficits, the lack of social support, or the absence of programs would likely act to limit the extent to which such adult residents could take advantage of potentially increased economic opportunities in these areas.

Second, the experimental group moved to areas not far from their original residential locations. Furthermore, only half of the experimental group ever moved, leaving the other half in their original places of residence. Thus, most did not fundamentally change the nature of place in their moves, electing to live in or near areas close to home that likely did not have appreciably different economic or social characteristics of place. These problems cast some doubt on the MTO findings, thus leaving one unable to completely rule out the idea that place influences social and economic opportunities.

RACE, PLACE, AND POVERTY TRENDS

Ultimately, our desire is to know more about whether place influences observed racial differences in poverty. Thus, it is important to know more about whether

TABLE 8.1 / U.S. Poverty by Metropolitan Area Type, 2000

	Poverty Rate	Total Population	Poverty Population	Percentage of Poverty Population
Total	14.8	281,421,906	41,650,442	100.0
Nonmetropolitan	18.0	49,963,594	8,993,446	21.6
Metropolitan	14.0	231,458,312	32,404,164	78.4
Central city	22.2	80,105,639	17,744,864	42.6
Suburb	9.7	151,352,672	14,747,230	35.7

Source: Author's compilation.

racial differences in poverty exist across place and whether they have changed over time. To do this, we analyze U.S. Census data from 1960 to 2000 to examine racial differences in poverty across place, looking more precisely at poverty rates within and across places, how the poor are distributed across central cities and suburbs, and the racial and ethnic distribution of the poor within central cities and suburbs. This investigation looks at these questions at the national level to understand general patterns. We also use the old model of looking at place through the lens of central cities, suburbs, and rural areas because of ease of data presentation and to discover whether and how the old model of place fits the place, race, and poverty debate.

First, we look at the distribution of overall poverty across these measures of place in 2000.[2] Table 8.1 shows that on average, poverty rates are slightly higher in rural than metropolitan areas in the United States. Of course, large concentrations of rural poverty are found in Appalachia (for rural whites), the Mississippi Delta (for rural blacks) and the Texas Borderland (for rural Latinos) regions. Although research on rural poverty has lagged behind that of urban poverty in recent years, it shows that this rural effect remains despite explicit controls for a wide variety of factors including demographic characteristics and local economic context (Weber et al. 2005). Whether this rural effect is causal, and what mechanisms drive this rural effect on poverty, however, remain open questions.

But rural poverty rates are lower than those in central city areas of metropolitan areas, and, as table 8.1 indicates, a majority of the poor are located in metropolitan areas. Thus, though rural poverty rates are higher than those in metropolitan areas, rural areas contribute less to the poverty problem in the United States. Moreover, the population of poor people continues to shift from rural toward metropolitan areas as the population in the United States continues to urbanize. Indeed, from 1960 to 2000, the number of poor people in rural areas in the United States declined significantly, from nearly 16 million to 9 million. On the other hand, the number of poor people in metropolitan areas over this period grew from about 17 million to about 32 million, with a slight majority of these still living in central cities in 2000.[3] For these and other reasons, much of the recent U.S. poverty research has tended to focus on metropolitan areas.

As noted throughout this volume, poverty rates are disproportionately higher

TABLE 8.2   /   U.S. Poverty Rates by Race and Metropolitan Area Type, 1960 to 2000

	White	Black	Latino	Asian	Total
Rural					
1960	26.6	79.1	62.4	36.7	33.1
1980	14.9	41.2	29.4	19.1	21.3
2000	15.6	42.3	31.6	23.7	20.1
Central city					
1960	12.1	42.4	43.0	14.4	19.9
1980	9.5	30.4	27.9	16.5	16.9
2000	9.7	27.3	24.6	17.6	18.1
Suburbs					
1960	10.9	44.2	30.7	12.7	13.9
1980	6.8	22.8	19.5	9.1	8.9
2000	4.8	13.4	14.4	7.9	6.7

Source: Author's compilation.

among minorities for a variety of reasons. As other authors in the volume point out, limited access to educational opportunities and inherited wealth, racial discrimination in housing and labor markets, and a disconnect from networks that generate economic rewards are major factors that account for some of the higher poverty rates of minority groups. Does place also contribute to these differences?

Table 8.2 presents 1960 to 2000 U.S. Census data on poverty rates among racial and ethnic groups in rural areas, central cities, and suburbs across the U.S. The table reveals a few key patterns. First, in all areas and for all years, poverty rates for blacks, Latinos, and Asians are higher than those of whites. It also reveals that poverty rates for all groups in all years are higher in rural areas than suburban areas. These findings are consistent with the idea that place, even measured in this geographically gross manner, may influence poverty (or opportunity) given that in the United States, minority groups are more likely to live in rural and central city areas in the United States. Still, as we note, racial differences in poverty are not eliminated in any of these places, meaning that place cannot account for all of the racial differences in poverty.

Second, table 8.2 also shows that for each racial and ethnic group, poverty rates have fallen, in absolute terms or by percentage, most dramatically in rural areas, and have fallen the least in central city areas over this period. The persistence of poverty in the central city again reinforces the notion that place might matter in influencing such poverty. Of course, the general decline in poverty for all groups, but especially for blacks and other minorities over the 1960s and 1970s, is likely accounted for by a variety of factors including the emergence of Great Society programs, increasing civil rights for blacks and other minorities, a strong economy, and affirmative action (Jaynes and Williams 1989).

In metropolitan areas, these trends imply growing poverty rate gaps between central cities and suburbs for all racial and ethnic groups. These trends are consistent with growing suburbanization of the nonpoor or middle income during this

TABLE 8.3 / Racial Differences in U.S. Poverty Rates within Metropolitan Area Type, 1960 to 2000

	Black-White	Latino-White	Asian-White
Rural			
1960	52.5	35.8	10.1
1980	26.3	14.5	4.2
2000	28.7	18.0	10.1
Central City			
1960	30.3	30.9	2.3
1980	21.0	18.4	7.1
2000	17.6	14.9	7.9
Suburbs			
1960	33.3	19.8	1.8
1980	16.0	12.8	2.3
2000	8.6	9.6	3.1

Source: Author's compilation.

period and with two important observations in the literature. First, the steep rise in the poverty rate gap for blacks between central cities and suburbs from the 1960s through the 1980s is consistent with Wilson's (1987) observation of the movement of the black middle class out of central cities to the suburbs, though the suburbs that blacks have been moving to are typically adjacent to central cities (Galster 1991). It is important to note that from 1960 to 1990, the black suburbanization rate rose only about 9 percentage points, from about 23 percent to 32 percent, and the white suburbanization rate rose by about 20 percentage points .[4]

Second, these trends are consistent with the literature on economic segregation. This literature documents the growing degree of economic segregation between the poor and nonpoor. This indicator rose during the 1970s and 1980s, and then leveled off during the 1990s. Although structural economic transformations and related factors likely explain some of this pattern, the full explanation is not yet known (Swanstrom et al. 2004; Madden 2003; Jargowsky 1996).

Finally, table 8.2 reveals that although poverty has fallen across areas and for all groups more generally over this period, the recent patterns in rural areas for Latinos and Asians deviate from these trends. This evidence is consistent with recent immigration research that has identified newly emerging patterns of Latino immigration (Martin, Fix, and Taylor 2006; Singer 2004; Kandel and Cromartie 2004). Latino immigration is increasingly shifting to rural areas (and nontraditional metropolitan areas) for a variety of reasons including demand for agricultural and industrial workers. Whether this is true of Asian immigration and what the mechanisms might be are largely unknown.

Table 8.3 presents 1960 to 2000 racial differences in poverty across central city, suburban, and rural areas. As noted, place cannot account for all of the racial differences in poverty because these differences are not entirely eliminated in any of these places. Yet, racial differences in poverty vary considerably across these ar-

FIGURE 8.1 / Central Cities Within Metropolitan Areas by Race-Ethnicity

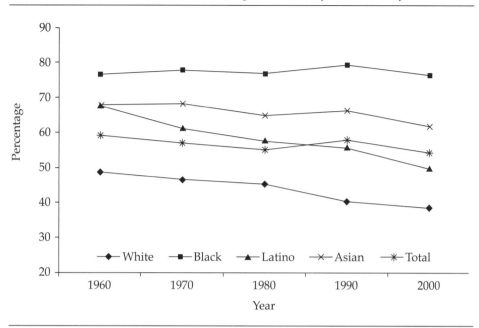

Source: Author's compilation.

eas, suggesting a role for place. The table reveals two important findings. First, racial differences in poverty rates are larger in rural and central city areas than in suburbs, and this is especially true in 2000. Second, racial differences in poverty rates have generally narrowed over time in all areas, but much more quickly in rural and especially suburban areas than in central city areas. This is especially true for black-white differences. For example, the racial poverty gap between blacks and whites was about 30 percentage points in both the central cities and suburbs in the 1960s. By 2000, this racial gap in poverty had declined to about 10 percentage points in the suburbs, but was at 17 percentage points in central cities.

The relative stability of central city poverty rates, especially for blacks, combined with increasing suburbanization, raises questions about the extent to which the poor are concentrated. Figure 8.1 documents the percentage of the metropolitan area poor who live in central cities 1960 to 2000.[5] The figure shows that within metropolitan areas, the percentage of the poor living in central cites declined over this period for most racial and ethnic groups.[6] These declines were especially pronounced for the Latino poor, and somewhat less so for the white poor. By contrast, the percentage of the black poor living in central cities has remained virtually unchanged. These trends are consistent with evidence on the spatial concentration of black and Latino poverty, which has been shown to have increased over the 1980s, but declined over the 1990s (Jargowsky 2003), and on blacks' greater risk of exposure to and inability to migrate out of poor neighborhoods

(Quillian 2003). Although scholars have noted these trends, there is not yet a consensus on why they persist (Frey 2001).

Concerns over the spatial concentration of the poor are clearly warranted. As noted earlier, research on the urban underclass and neighborhood effects demonstrates quite clearly that spatial concentration exacerbates the negative effects of poverty. Less obvious is that the concentration of poor people in central cities has fiscal and tax consequences. Given the large population of poor people in urban areas, cities often have difficulty raising sufficient revenues to meet the expenditure needs of serving a large poor population. The result is a vicious, negative cycle (Orfield 2002). Race itself may further confound the ability of cities or metropolitan areas to solve these fiscal problems if poverty concentration is viewed as a minority rather than a regional problem.

Given these trends, an important question is what the colors of poverty look like in the cities and suburbs and how they have changed over time. Figure 8.2 charts the change in the racial and ethnic composition of the poor in central cities and suburbs over the 1960 to 2000 period. In central cities, the data clearly show the declining shares of the white poor over this period, replaced by a growing presence of the Latino and Asian poor, at least up until 1990. What is more striking is that the poor population in central cities has become even more black over this period, not less so, despite the increasing presence of the immigrant poor in urban America. In particular, about 29 percent of the poor in central cities were black in 1970. By 2000, this percentage had swelled to about 50 percent, despite the fact that the black poverty rate had remained virtually unchanged (see table 8.2), and that their share of the metropolitan area population had also changed very little.[7] The reasons for these changes are not well understood, but could include more rapid suburbanization of other poor populations, such as Asians and Latinos (figure 8.1). Indeed, the share of the central city poor who are Latino declined over the 1990s, which again suggests more rapid suburbanization of this group compared to that of poor blacks.

Where we do find growing diversity of the poor is in the suburbs. Figure 8.2 shows the growing presence of the Asian, Latino, and black poor in suburban areas between 1960 and 2000. In 1960, about 20 percent of the suburban poor were minority, and by 2000 this share had increased to nearly 50 percent. Note again the steady decline in the representation of whites among the poor during this period.[8] The changes observed in suburbs for both the poor and nonpoor are consistent with evidence that suburban areas have experienced great increases in diversity fueled by growth in minority populations, especially those of Asian and Latino ancestry (Frey 2001; Logan 2002).

This brief overview of the basic relationship between race, place and poverty in the United States highlights some important trends. Consistent with the old model of poverty, place, and race, the results reveal that poverty remains concentrated among minority groups, especially among blacks and Latinos, and remains higher in the central cities and rural areas than suburbs. In metropolitan areas, the majority of the poor still live in central cities. This is especially true for blacks, but less so for Latinos and Asians. If these trends persist, most of the Latino poor will

FIGURE 8.2 / Racial and Ethnic Composition of the Poor in Cities and Suburbs

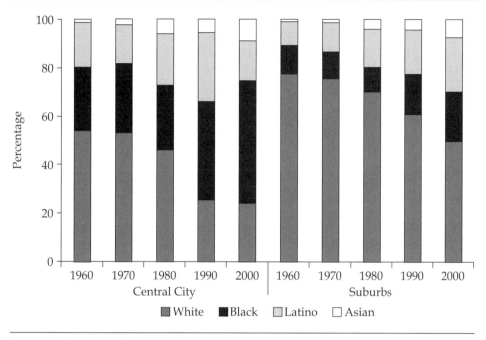

Source: Author's compilation.

live in suburbs in the next decade, even though their presence in rural areas appears to be growing as well. Whites are the racial or ethnic group whose poverty is largely suburbanized. This was true in 1960, and grew more pronounced between 1960 and 2000.

Results also show that despite growing racial and ethnic diversity in the United States, central cities have become much more black since the 1960s, especially among the poor. These patterns require further investigation, but they suggest that the growth of the Latino and Asian populations in the United States is having its greatest impact on poverty populations in suburban areas. Latinos and Asians are suburbanizing at a much faster rate than blacks, and given that whites had already largely left central cities in the 1950s and 1960s, such immigration is leading to slightly more diverse, yet blacker, central cities, and to much greater diversity in suburbs.

Thus, at the national level, the trends observed here indicate that the old model of place, race and poverty—poor chocolate cities and wealthy vanilla suburbs—persists to some degree despite strong demographic changes. Chocolate cities are becoming more chocolate even as they have grown somewhat more diverse, especially among the poor, and vanilla suburbs are becoming ethnically and racially Neapolitan suburbs with poor people increasingly moving there.[9]

Even at this gross level of geography, these trends suggest the role of place in influencing poverty and in accounting for part of the racial differences in poverty. But given the large racial differences in poverty that remain even within suburban, rural, and especially central city areas, what is required is a better understanding of place within these areas. That is, what are the characteristics of places or neighborhoods within these areas that are correlated with poverty or that help account for racial differences in poverty? What are the factors that limit the extent to which the poor, especially the minority (and black) poor, can move to or access areas with greater social and economic opportunity? For example, do the characteristics of certain suburban areas influence poverty among Latinos and Asians and account for part of the growth of the Latino and Asian poor in these areas, or are these areas relatively more accessible (less housing discrimination, or more effective networks or information) for these groups but not for blacks? This is a task for future research.

In the meantime, we want to know some of the key forces that influence and maintain the observed connection between race, place, and poverty. These factors include those that have been documented in the literature, such as racial segregation and decentralization or sprawl. In combination, they have led to significant spatial mismatch between residential and job locations, especially for minority groups in racially segregated cities, thus contributing to their poverty.

But other factors are likely at play as well. The economics and geography of low-income housing may also play an important role in centralizing poverty and limiting the access to economic opportunities in suburban areas. The natural process of filtering in housing markets, as well as where low-income housing is located and why, may also play a role. Suburban efforts that limit the supply of low-income housing surely have played a key role in where low-income housing is located. Finally, given the growing presence of immigrants, especially in suburban areas, questions may be raised about whether there is competition between immigrant and native groups, especially blacks, over access to low-income housing. These factors will be examined in more detail.

RACIAL RESIDENTIAL SEGREGATION

One of the permanent features of urban America is the extent to which racial groups, in particular blacks and whites, are residentially segregated. The physical isolation of blacks and other minority groups has been a major concern because of the social and economic costs of such segregation. Many racially segregated neighborhoods are disadvantaged and suffer disproportionately from problems such as high concentrations of poverty, joblessness, hopelessness, and the political indifference of elites (Massey and Denton 1993). It has frequently been asserted that segregated neighborhoods impose enormous costs on minority residents, such as the unavailability of good schools, worse health outcomes, negative role models, a lack of economic opportunities, and social isolation (Massey and Denton 1993; Wilson 1987). However, there is very little research that shows a direct causal relationship between racial segregation and racial disparities in poverty.

Given open questions about the consequences of racial residential segregation, and growing minority suburbanization, it is important to consider trends in segregation indices. Residential segregation is typically measured using the dissimilarity index, which captures the degree to which two groups are evenly spread across census tracts in a given metropolitan area. The dissimilarity index ranges from 0 to 100, indicating the percentage of one group that would have to move to achieve an even residential pattern in which every tract replicates the group composition in the metropolitan area. For demographers, an index value of 60 or more is considered an extreme level of segregation, values of 40 to 50 are considered moderate, and values of 30 or less are considered low.

Recent research documents a few key trends with respect to segregation in the United States. In general, black-white segregation in metropolitan areas has declined over the recent decades. For example, in 1980, the black-white index of dissimilarity was 73.8 and dropped nearly 9 percentage points to reach 65.0 in 2000 (Iceland, Weinberg, and Steinmetz 2002; Logan 2003). The decline in black segregation over the 1990s seems to have been linked to demographic changes in metropolitan areas. The biggest declines in black segregation occurred in metropolitan areas that were growing quickly, and in places where the percentage of blacks in the population was rising rapidly (Glaeser and Vigdor 2001).

This suggests two possibilities. Black movers within metropolitan areas may be moving to increasingly nonblack neighborhoods: black suburbanization rates have been increasing, which could create lower overall black-white levels of segregation given that segregation is lower there than in cities (Frey 2001). Blacks could also be migrating to metropolitan areas where black segregation is lower than the average: in particular, to the South, where black-white segregation levels are much lower there than in the North or Midwest. Recent evidence shows that the southern share of the black population increased over the 1990s from 53 to 55 percent, and the share of blacks living in the Northeast and Midwest, and to a lesser extent in the West, declined. More direct evidence shows that over the 1990s, the propensity to move to the South was greater for blacks than for whites or other minority groups (Stoll 2004).

The segregation literature and the evidence presented above raises two important puzzles. The first is that the percentage of the black poor living in central cities has remained virtually constant over the past few decades, while black-white segregation levels have declined modestly. At least within metropolitan areas, this suggests that much of the decline in segregation is driven by movements of the black nonpoor. It remains unclear whether segregation levels between the black and white poor have changed over time.

Second, where segregation levels are slightly lower in suburbs than central cities, black-white segregation levels in the suburbs have remained virtually constant over time. Using the dissimilarity index, such segregation dropped only slightly from 59.9 to 56.6 over the 1990s (Frey 2001). This suggests that blacks are moving to largely black suburban areas, which may be only slightly less segregated than neighborhoods in central cities. This idea is consistent with research that indicates that much of black suburbanization is occurring in inner-ring suburbs (usually in close geographic proximity to central city areas), which may not differ dramatically in economic and social conditions from those in the central cities (Galster 1991). Hence, it is an open question as to whether blacks experienced greater economic opportunities as a result of the increased residential mobility over the past decades, though the emergence of some middle class black suburban areas tempers these concerns (Cashin 2004).

The data on the quality of neighborhoods in which blacks and whites live presents a similar dilemma. Black suburbanization does not seem to have translated into moving into better neighborhoods. In 1990, the median neighborhood (census tract) income for a typical black household was $27,808 compared with $45,486 for whites, or a gap of $17,679. By 2000, that gap had increased to $18,112 in constant dollars. Even at households with incomes above $60,000, similar patterns were observed (Logan 2002). The neighborhood gap is smaller between Latinos and whites, but also grew wider over the 1990s, both overall and for Latinos with incomes over $60,000 (Logan 2002).

Still, despite these declines, segregation levels between blacks and whites remain in the extreme segregation range. Moreover, segregation of blacks changed very little in the largest metropolitan areas, where segregation historically has been the highest, and in metropolitan areas where the black population is the largest (Glaeser and Vigdor 2002). The latter trends offer cause for concern because these areas house a disproportionate share of the nation's population in general, and of the black population in particular.

The high degree of racial segregation is influenced by a number of key factors. Among these, suburban housing discrimination plays a key role. This kind of discrimination can take many forms, one of which is discrimination against blacks and other minorities in attaining home mortgages (Pager, chapter 2, this volume). Indeed, there have been numerous studies that document that blacks, and to a lesser extent Latinos, are less likely than whites to be approved for home mortgages even after racial differences in income, debt, credit worthiness, residential location, and other relevant individual-level characteristics are taken into account (Yinger 1997). Housing discrimination can also take the form of discrimination by real estate agents and landlords. Research shows that blacks, and to a lesser extent Latinos, experience discrimination by suburban landlords, whereas real estate agents tend to steer blacks away from neighborhoods that are disproportionately white (Ondrich, Stricker, and Yinger 1999; Ondrich, Ross, and Yinger 2001; Goering and Wienk 1996; Massey and Denton 1993).

Differential racial preferences for integrated neighborhoods also help maintain segregation levels (Charles 2005). By contrast, the evidence indicates that blacks' racial preferences to live near those of their own race play a smaller role in perpetuating segregation (Ihlanfeldt and Scafidi 2002; Massey and Denton 1993). Latino and Asian preferences for coethnic neighborhoods are less well understood. Housing segregation by income seems to play an even smaller role as the black middle class is just as likely to be segregated from whites as the black poor (Massey and Fischer 1999). Less is known about how such segregation affects Latino-white and Asian-white segregation. In general, what is missing is this debate is an empirical accounting of all the relevant factors that explain the high levels of racial segregation in urban America.

The lack of these explanations is evident in the puzzling segregation trends between Latinos and Asians and whites. Over the past two decades, the Latino-white and Asian-white indices of segregation have changed very little. In fact, from 1980 to 2000 the Latino-white segregation index remained virtually unchanged, from 50.7 to 51.5, still remaining in the moderate segregation category. Similarly, the Asian-white index changed only from 41.2 to 42.1 over the same period, also remaining in the moderate category (Logan 2003). Interestingly, the segregation indices have remained unchanged despite the massive growth in the Asian and Latino populations and rapid suburbanization of both the poor and nonpoor in these groups.

Why have these indices remained so steady despite demographic and locational changes? One possibility is that racial preferences by white suburbanites vary with the race or ethnicity of newcomers into the suburbs. Insight into this question may help to explain why Latinos and Asians, especially the poor, have been able to suburbanize much faster than blacks over the past decade. Some research at the metropolitan level has shown that whites' tolerance for residential integration is conditioned by the race of their potential neighbors, with Asians topping the hierarchy, Latinos in the middle, and blacks on the bottom (Charles 2005).

Another possibility is that the neighborhoods in which Latinos and Asians are increasingly living are becoming more concentrated with their respective group members, in both the cities and suburbs. In particular, there is some evidence that in suburban areas, Latino and Asians are increasingly living in neighborhoods with much higher coethnic proportions than was in earlier decades (Frey 2001). These trends raise questions about the types of Latino-Asian-immigrant neighborhoods that are developing in suburban areas: whether they are emerging in inner-ring suburban areas or in newly developing suburban fringes, and whether the poor are isolated in these neighborhoods or are economically integrated with their nonpoor coethnics.

Immigration, however, may have reduced housing segregation among racial and ethnic minority groups. In 2000, the black-white segregation index was 65, the black-Latino index was 51, and the black-Asian level was 55. Moreover, over the 1990s, racial segregation between blacks and other groups declined modestly, and the decline was more dramatic between blacks and Hispanics and blacks and Asians than between blacks and whites. The index of dissimilarity between blacks and whites declined by 3.8 percentage points from 1990 to 2000. The equivalent declines between blacks and Hispanics was 6.1 percentage points, and 5.6 percentage points between blacks and Asians (Stoll 2004).

Interestingly, these declines in segregation among minorities occurred despite their different rates of suburbanization and despite growing Latino and Asian suburban ethnic enclaves. These trends raise questions about the locations of integrated neighborhoods *within* metropolitan areas, and about whether segregation has been changing faster in highly immigrant gateway areas, in large metropolitan regions, or in small metropolitan areas (Farley and Frey 1994). They also raise questions of the socioeconomic mix in these neighborhoods, in particular whether growing integration is generating competition and conflict over local resources.

Although there is an established literature in labor economics on whether and how immigrants impact native workers in the labor market, little research has attempted to investigate how and whether immigrants impact natives, especially blacks, in the housing market. In a competitive model of housing markets where racial preferences of decision makers favor Latinos and Asians over blacks, we may find immigrants competing blacks out of, or displacing them from, certain housing markets. The growth of immigration and its concentration in certain regions and metropolitan areas implies that a large influx of immigrants may also result in substantial increases in housing prices and rents, thus negatively impacting natives' housing choices and consumption.

The thin research in this area suggests that large-scale immigration does affect housing prices in the short run, but not over the longer period, because housing markets seem to adjust quite well to increased demand from immigrants (Greulich, Quigley, and Raphael 2004; Saiz 2003; Susin 2001). It does not, however, examine how these relationships may differ by the race of natives. Immigrant destination points are in many ways nonrandom, following well-established patterns (Singer 2004). Many are located in central cities potentially near black neighborhoods. Combined with racial preferences of housing market decision makers, such as landlords or real estate agents, negative effects of immigration on blacks' housing consumption could well exist but would be masked by these more general aggregate analyses of natives. What is needed is a better understanding of the processes, mechanisms, and reasons for such racial and ethnic change at the neighborhood level between immigrants and natives, especially native blacks, and how these may influence Latinos and Asians' greater suburbanization compared to blacks.

DECENTRALIZATION AND SPRAWL

Another central feature of urban America that influences the race, poverty, and place connection is decentralization, sometimes referred to as sprawl. Urban sprawl, understood as low-density, geographically spreading patterns of development, has been a dominant characteristic of metropolitan growth patterns. Although some debate how to measure sprawl (Lopez and Hynes 2003; Wolman et al. 2002), others debate whether sprawl does in fact characterize development. The growing consensus is that it does (Lopez and Hynes 2003; Glaeser and Kahn 2001). Some basic facts illustrate this point. Between 1950 and 1990, U.S. metropolitan areas grew from 208,000 square miles housing 84 million people, to 585,000 square miles housing 193 million people. Thus, the area in which people live increased by 181 percent, and population increased by 128 percent. Put differently, population density declined from 407 to 330 persons per square mile over this time. In addition, the share of the population in suburbia, which is much more characteristic of sprawl development patterns than central cities, grew from 55.1 percent to 62.2 between 1970 and 2000 (U.S. Department of Housing and Urban Development 2000). This trend accelerated during the 1990s when the suburban population grew by 17.7 percent, compared with just 8.0 percent for central cities (U.S. Census Bureau 2001).

More important, many have examined the causes and consequences of sprawl. Sprawl can be influenced by the physical characteristics of regions, the role of government policy, and preferences and discrimination (Burchfield et al. 2005; Rusk 1993). In particular, many point to white flight, or the structural process of postwar suburbanization fueled in part by white fear, as accelerating sprawl: whites moved to suburbs to separate themselves from what they feared would be concentrations of racialized poverty, and in the process created those concentrations (Squires 2002; Jackson 1985).

The growing empirical literature on the consequences of sprawl has tried to identify its effects, positive or negative, on health problems, pollution, concentrated poverty, and commute times (Bullard, Johnson, and Torres 2000; Heinlich and Andersen 2001; Cieslewicz 2002; Jargowsky 2002; Glaeser and Kahn 2004). For the purposes of this book, however, an important consequence of sprawl is its potential influence on poverty and racial disparities in poverty. One way that decentralization has been connected to the geographic and racial patterns of poverty is through the spatial mismatch hypothesis. John Kain (1968) noted that during the latter half of the twentieth century, the spatial location of employment opportunities within metropolitan areas changed to increase their physical distance from predominantly black residential areas. Urban economists argued that innovations in transportation, such as the development of highways and cargo trucks in the mid-twentieth century, and the availability of cheaper land prices in the suburban fringe caused firms, and therefore employment, to move toward metropolitan area suburbs and exurbs. However, during this same period, the factors that maintain high levels of residential segregation led blacks to remain concentrated in older, central city neighborhoods.

Many argue that this spatial mismatch is partly responsible for the stubbornly inferior labor market outcomes and persistent poverty that African Americans experience. Recent research has been able to quantify spatial mismatch at the national level by adapting the dissimilarity index to compare the spatial distribution of people and jobs (Raphael and Stoll 2002; Martin 2001, 2004). Like the dissimilarity index for racial segregation, the people-total jobs dissimilarity index ranges from 0 to 100, with higher values indicating a greater geographic mismatch between people and jobs. The research finds clear racial-ethnic differences in the degree of mismatch between people and jobs (both in total jobs and low-skill jobs). In 2000, consistent with racial segregation patterns, blacks and jobs were the most spatially mismatched with a dissimilarity index of 53.3. The comparable figures for whites, Latinos, and Asians were 28, 46, and 44, respectively. However, this reflects a decline in spatial mismatch over the 1990s for blacks and Latinos: for blacks, the mismatch index declined by 3.2 points and for Latinos, by 2.5 points. Declines for whites and Asians were trivial (Raphael and Stoll 2002).

Although minority men and women likely face the same spatial mismatch conditions, their impact on the ability to gain employment may differ. Women tend to concentrate their search efforts in a more local area than men because of domestic responsibilities and the joint location problem of work and child care (McLafferty and Preston 1997). But residential locations near central city employment centers may advantage women over men, because women are largely overrepresented in the industrial and occupational employment opportunities available in cities, as in retail trade (Cooke 1997). However, competition for jobs is most severe in these areas because job search efforts are greater in central cities, in turn limiting such employment opportunities for women (Stoll 2000).

One potential explanation for blacks' greater mismatch from jobs is racial segregation. Because geographic job location patterns closely follow the geographic patterns of whites (Bostic and Martin 2003), racial segregation from whites should be a major factor in blacks' greater mismatch. Recent research documents that blacks' mismatch from jobs is strongly related to their segregation from whites. Indeed, nearly 50 percent of blacks' mismatch is accounted for by black-white segregation. Because Latinos are less segregated from whites, such segregation explains much less of their mismatch from jobs (Raphael and Stoll 2002).

Increasing black residential mobility over the 1990s seems to have led to the modestly reduced black segregation from whites (and others), which in turn seems to have led to modest reductions in blacks' segregation from economic opportunities. The declines in blacks' segregation from jobs that occurred during the 1990s were driven entirely by the residential mobility of blacks within metropolitan areas, rather than movements across metropolitan areas. This occurred despite the fact that blacks' migration to the South, where black-white segregation levels are lower, accelerated during the 1990s. In fact, changes in the geographic location of jobs during the 1990s actually militate toward higher levels of black isolation from employment. Had black residential mobility out of mostly disadvantaged black communities not occurred to the extent that it did over the 1990s, blacks' geographic isolation from jobs would have gotten significantly worse during the economic boom (Raphael and Stoll 2002).

What we don't know is whether the residential mobility of the black nonpoor or poor drove this decline. The metropolitan patterns of poverty location for blacks described, where the share of the black poor has remained much more centralized than that of the black nonpoor over time, suggests that the nonpoor drove this decline. This factor needs to be better understood because the poor are much more likely to be harmed by mismatch than the nonpoor, partly because the jobs that are decentralizing fastest are those that require fewer skills (Glaeser and Kahn 2001). Jobs with higher skill requirements tend to be concentrated in central cities, because idea-intensive industries benefit from the positive externalities of knowledge transfers in dense urban areas, and because such industries can operate in vertical towers. These factors are partly the result of central city development patterns caused by scarce land availability and high real estate prices. On the other hand, industries with disproportionately lower skill requirements, such as manufacturing, are more likely to decentralize because their need for horizontal space is more consistent with a suburban location where land is plentiful and cheap (Glaeser and Kahn 2001; Mills 2000). These spatial-skill patterns of opportunity are likely to harm the poor, especially the black poor, because of their location in central cities.

A key empirical question is therefore the relationship between sprawl and the spatial location of concentrated poverty, racial segregation, or mismatch. Some have argued that sprawl could have beneficial effects—specifically, reduce segregation or physical isolation from jobs by increasing housing affordability. Some research has identified such an association. This growth produces housing rapidly relative to demand, lowering housing prices, and thus potentially raising housing consumption, especially that of blacks (Kahn 2001).

In theory, the increases in black residential mobility and the moderate decreases in racial segregation observed over the 1990s suggest that sprawl could have reduced black-white segregation and spatial mismatch. Consistent with this idea, Matthew Kahn (2001) found that all else equal, housing consumption among blacks is higher in sprawling than in nonsprawling metropolitan areas. Because single family homes are disproportionately more available and black homeownership rates are in fact higher in the suburbs, it is likely that the housing changes did in fact lead to greater racial integration and convenient access to jobs.

Other recent research, however, has found evidence counter to this hypothesis. This research demonstrates that at least cross-sectionally, black mismatch levels and black-white segregation levels are much higher in metropolitan areas with high levels of sprawl (Stoll 2005). Moreover, the analysis reveals that variation in the degree of job sprawl explains about a quarter of the variation in the blacks-jobs mismatch index. The results are more striking for blacks than others (Stoll 2005). These results have implications for the findings in Kahn (2001). They suggest that if sprawl is associated with housing affordability that prompts black residential mobility, black residential moves are likely occurring in predominantly black inner suburban neighborhoods. These suburban neighborhoods are adjacent to central cities, leaving black proximity to whites and jobs unchanged, consistent with past research (Galster 1991). If this is true, sprawl is unlikely to lower segregation or mismatch.

Identifying the effect of urban sprawl on segregation and mismatch will likely be difficult, however. The mismatch hypothesis depends largely on the assumption that the forces contributing to sprawl are unrelated to race, segregation, or mismatch. But it is likely that sprawl is indeed influenced by the same considerations. For example, if employers locate to suburban areas to escape black workers because they view them as undesirable (Wilson 1996), or if whites move to suburbs partly to avoid blacks because they view them as bringing down property values or increasing crime, sprawl would be spurred by racial considerations. If this is the case, then racial segregation patterns or mismatch conditions may partly influence the degree of decentralization or sprawl, making inferences about sprawl's effect on these outcomes more difficult. Work by Roberto Fernandez (1994) tempers these assumptions by showing that firm relocations from central city to suburbs are independent of racial considerations. However, the firm sample size in the study was small, making generalizations of findings to all relocating firms more problematic.

The connection of sprawl, racial segregation, and poverty is compounded by factors related to transportation. As jobs, especially low-skill jobs, continue to decentralize to outer suburban fringes, and as racial segregation continues to ensure that racial minorities are more centralized, the increasing distances between jobs and home create problems for employment and concentrated poverty. Given the difficulties of reverse commutes in many metropolitan areas and the fact that traveling long distances takes a high monetary and time toll on commuters, spatial mismatch may literally remove many jobs for which black and other minority workers would otherwise be suited.

Automobile access and the greater flexibility of travel it affords can help improve employment opportunities. But minorities, especially blacks and Latinos, are significantly less likely than whites to have access to cars. This is true regardless of whether car access is measured as car ownership, car access, or cars per adult household member. For example, in the 1990s, about 76 percent of whites owned cars, and the equivalent percentage for blacks and Latinos was about 50 percent. Moreover, these racial differences were greater for the less educated. Car ownership rates for whites, blacks, and Latinos without a high school degree were 65.1, 34.2, and 43.1, respectively (Raphael and Stoll 2001).

Many factors help explain these racial differences in car ownership, including differences in income and earnings, differences in insurance premiums, and discrimination in the car loan market. Indeed, in black and other poor minority neighborhoods, redlining by insurance companies and higher theft and traffic accidents make auto insurance premiums much higher than elsewhere (Ong and Stoll 2007; Ong and Sung 2003). Blacks also tend to be charged significantly higher interest rates for private car loans than similar creditworthy whites and therefore pay significantly more interest over the course of the loan (Cohen 2003).

Given that minorities have less car access, they commute to work more often by public transit. For example, about 15 percent of blacks used public transportation in 2000, compared to only 3 percent of whites (Stoll 2004). Some have argued that that the poor, especially blacks, live in cities precisely because public transit is reasonably available there (Glaeser, Kahn, and Rappaport 1999). But even if this is true, in most metropolitan areas, traveling to work by public transit increases travel burdens in a number of ways and therefore diminishes labor market opportunities. Commuting times by public transit are considerably longer than private travel, so individuals using public transit will be less likely to search for or maintain a distant job. In boom economies like that of the 1990s, this may be less of a problem as central city employment opportunities become relatively more available. During recessions, however, central city employment is usually hit hardest and distant suburban employment becomes more important.

Reverse commutes from central cities to suburbs, where there is greater employment opportunity, are difficult because of the notably fewer services and service routes, particularly for rail. This is partly because such transit systems were designed to move suburban workers to downtown locations, not the reverse

(Wachs and Taylor 1998). Also, relative to other workers, blacks and other minorities are increasingly working nonstandard work schedules, such as the graveyard shift, when public transit is even less available (Beers 2000). Finally, and increasingly as a result of sprawl development patterns, suburban firms are more physically distant from public transit stops than central city firms are, making many suburban employment opportunities even more inaccessible. Indeed, in the mid-1990s, nearly half of all jobs in suburban areas were inaccessible by public transportation (defined over a quarter of a mile away from the nearest transit stop); the comparable figure for jobs in the central city was about 20 percent (Stoll, Holzer, and Ihlanfeldt 2000). Whether firms deliberately locate away from transit stops to avoid racial minorities or others perceived as poor workers remains an open question.

The central question that emerges from this discussion is that if the poor live in cities because public transportation is more easily accessible, then why are the Latino poor, who are just as carless as blacks, increasingly suburbanizing? One explanation is that the carless Latino poor are much more likely to use alternative forms of transit to get to work. One form is camionetas, or small vans, that are used to travel inter-regionally (and even transnationally). These are usually privately owned, but community-based, and targeted at poor Latino communities: they offer accessible, sometimes low priced transportation to areas that may not be well served by fixed-route transit. Such travel is mostly informal because few regulations control its commercial activity, and advertising for this transportation mode is primarily word of mouth or through posters (Valenzuela 2002). Camionetas thus may offer the Latino poor flexibility in transit routes that would allow them to live in suburban areas where public transportation is sparse.

THE GEOGRAPHY OF LOW-INCOME HOUSING

For a variety of reasons, sprawling metropolitan areas are especially likely to create new communities of single-family houses. These houses are built for middle class markets and thus limit the extent to which the poor can move to suburban areas. Thus, the geography of low-income housing is also likely to reinforce the connection between race, place, and poverty, but little research has addressed these associations. To the extent that low-income housing availability is disproportionately located in central city areas, it would be difficult to achieve greater integration of minorities, especially blacks with whites, and of the poor with the nonpoor, even if race-specific barriers to housing mobility were eliminated. But there is little if any research documenting trends in the geography of low-income housing supply, though it seems reasonable to assume that such housing is disproportionately located in central cities.

Both theory and evidence, however, exist to support this possibility. These include theories of housing filtering, the location and effect of development regulations, and government site location for low-income housing assistance. Theories of housing filtering develop a model of urban housing markets where durable dwelling units filter though a quality hierarchy. In this model, the supply of housing of a given quality (or whether it is low-income) is determined by several factors, including the age of the housing, where older housing stocks are more likely to filter to low-income housing (O'Flaherty 1995). To the extent that housing stock is older in central cities than suburbs, as recent census data show, low-income housing is likely to be disproportionately concentrated in central cities.

Development regulations are also likely to shape the geography of low-income housing. Many development regulations affect central cities and suburbs alike, such as requirements for environmental impact studies or toxic cleanup requirements. These may even be especially relevant for development of vacant or abandoned lots, disproportionately located in central cities. But some regulations, such as zoning requirements against multifamily housing and development impact fees, are much more likely to be triggered in suburbs. Many suburban municipalities zone against multifamily housing where newly developed low-income housing is likely to be realized (McDonald and McMillen 2004). In 2000, a much larger percentage of rental housing than of all housing units in metropolitan areas was located in central cities (54 percent to 29 percent).[10]

Development impact fees are assessed on new developments involving undeveloped land, which is typically found on suburban fringes. These fees are assessed to cover infrastructure costs, such as laying water pipes or roads needed for development. However, most agree that such fees contribute to housing price inflation that is capitalized into housing prices and disproportionately paid by consumers of that housing (Evans-Cowley and Lawhon 2003). Obviously, such dynamics will limit the extent to which developers can, or are willing to, pencil in low-income housing projects on undeveloped land, limiting such development in the suburbs (Evans-Cowley, Forgey, and Rutheford 2005).

There is some consensus in the literature that certain development regulations act to decrease low-income housing availability. The critical question in this area is the forces driving these development policies. Of course, the laws of development finance will ensure that infrastructure and other costs are captured during, and capitalized into, development projects for them to be profitable. The implementation of many such regulations, be they for economic, environmental or social reasons, is reasonable. But white suburbanite fears of the poor and minorities could drive these regulations as well. As the infamous Mt. Laurel case shows, racial preferences can influence the erection of zoning regulations, in an effort to limit the development of low-income multifamily housing and thus minority access to suburbs. What is missing, however, is good empirical research that examines the casual link and the magnitude of the relationship between racial preferences and development regulations, and how these influence where the poor live in metropolitan areas.

Finally, the site location of government low-income housing assistance could also influence the geography of such housing. In the past, most large public housing projects were located in predominantly minority neighborhoods, reinforcing the race, place, and poverty connection in urban America. But with a more recent emphasis on scattered-site housing projects and reliance on vouchers and housing choice of the poor, the geography of federal housing assistance may have changed.

The scant research in this area offers a few clues. The most important federal program offering housing assistance is the Low-Income Housing Tax Credit (LIHTC). Recent research on the site location of these tax credits indicates that in metropolitan areas, about 60 percent of such sites are in central city areas. However, housing projects in suburban areas are larger, perhaps because of greater and cheaper land availability. This percentage has changed very little since 1995. LIHTC units are more likely than rental units nationally to be located in poor neighborhoods and in neighborhoods with a large proportion of minorities and female-headed households. In particular, nearly 30 percent of LIHTC units in the central city are located in high-poverty areas, compared to just over 20 percent of rental units overall (Abt Associates 2004). These data suggest that site locations of government low-income housing projects follow the geography of the poor, which in turn reinforces the overall geography of low-income housing and reinforces the race, place, and poverty connection.

The same forces that limit pure private development of low-income housing in suburbs may also limit government subsidized low-income housing. But even if these were to change, locating low-income housing in suburban areas would not come without some cost. The poor, disproportionately reliant on such housing to fill their housing needs, also frequently require access to additional services such as welfare, mental health, and employment services. But these services are themselves disproportionately concentrated in central city areas where poor populations are concentrated. Indeed, on average, poor populations in urban centers have greater spatial access to social services than poor populations living in suburban areas (Allard 2004). Thus, increasingly moving the location of low-income housing assistance to suburbs will, at least in the short run, not match well to the location of social service providers. This pattern has important implications given that greater proximity to these services is associated with greater use of them (Allard, Tolman, and Rosen 2003). More research is needed on whether the use of these services has important and beneficial social or economic effects on the poor.

CONCLUSION

The empirical trends documented here show results fairly consistent with the race, ethnicity, poverty, and suburbanization debates in the literature. Poverty remains concentrated among minority groups, especially among blacks and Latinos, and remains higher in the central cities than suburbs. The majority of the poor in metropolitan areas still live in central cities, especially for blacks, but this pattern is increasingly less true for poor Latinos and Asians.

However, a few less obvious patterns emerge as well. In particular, central cities have become more black since the 1960s, especially among the poor, at least in part because of greater suburbanization of Latinos, Asians, and whites over the past two decades. The phenomenal growth and rapid suburbanization of Latinos and Asians is leading to profound changes in the diversity of populations and poverty in suburban areas. Thus, at the very general level the chocolate cities–vanilla suburbs, poor-rich model of urban America is still relatively applicable today, but is increasingly being replaced with a picture of chocolatier central cities and Neapolitan suburbs (especially for the poor), with growing diversity in the geographic location of the poor, except for the black poor.

These changes have deep implications and raise a number of as yet unanswered questions. Why have the black poor remained centralized over this period despite growing decentralization of the poor more generally? What are the consequences (above and beyond what we already know about the effects of minority concentrated poverty) of these increasingly isolated pockets of deep black poverty in urban America? In addition, the growing diversity of poverty and ethnicity in suburban America begs questions about the types of Latino-Asian-immigrant neighborhoods and black neighborhoods that are developing in suburban areas, whether they are emerging in inner-ring suburban areas or in newly developing suburban fringes, and whether the poor are isolated in these neighborhoods or are economically integrated with their respective coethnic nonpoor.

Over the past two decades, we have learned a great deal about what poverty looks like in central city ghettos, and to a lesser extent barrios, and the effects of this poverty and the mechanisms through which these effects manifest themselves. But we know very little about what poverty looks like in these growing suburban ethnic enclaves, how long such poverty endures, whether the effects of poverty concentration are similar to what we observe for cities, or whether the mechanisms that reinforce such poverty are the same as in cities. These questions become all the more important in light of the fact that though white suburban areas have become much more diverse along these dimensions, racial and ethnic segregation there has virtually remained at the same level over the past decade. The reasons and factors that reinforce suburban racial segregation are important areas of inquiry as well.

But racial segregation among and between racial and ethnic minorities has declined even as such segregation from whites has remained steady, especially in suburban areas and between Latinos and Asians and whites. These trends create questions about where growing minority integrated neighborhoods are within metropolitan areas, and in which metropolitan areas (highly immigrant gateway areas, large or small metropolitan areas) and regions these changes are occurring the fastest. They also beg the question of what the socioeconomic mix of these neighborhoods is, and whether the growing integration of minorities is generating conflict or cooperation for local resources. All of these questions beg for research that digs deeper than the central city–suburban dichotomy to look deeper within central cities and suburbs for the sources of the heterogeneity of place.

To the extent that place plays a role in influencing poverty, and the evidence gathered and analyzed here suggests that it does, the big question going forward is the need to identify the place-based factors likely to continue to influence racial differences in poverty. Suburban sprawl continues at a rapid pace, but the accompanying suburban job growth is located in high-income, largely newer suburban areas where whites increasingly live. Thus, even though blacks and especially Latinos and Asians are suburbanizing rapidly, most minority groups are unlikely to enjoy the job benefits of sprawl because they are locating to lower income, possibly older suburban areas where job growth is relatively weak. These trends also portend relatively stable segregation levels over the next decade. Moreover, such segregation is likely to be reinforced because the geography of low-income housing is unlikely to be significantly altered in the near future, and because of growing competition for suburban housing in the suburbs between and among minority and immigrant groups.

All of this suggests that racial differences in poverty could persist or become exacerbated if low-income suburbs do not become generators of economic opportunities. The same is likely true if economic development does not occur in many central city neighborhoods. The black poor have been slow to suburbanize for reasons that are not fully understood. Gentrification has taken place over the last decade in many central city neighborhoods, but the jury is out on whether the potential benefits of these changes has accrued to poor blacks in central cities. To the extent that it has not, their social and economic isolation will increase and the influence of place in contributing to racial differences in poverty will endure.

The author thanks Amy Friedrich for invaluable research assistance.

NOTES

1. Gravity decay measures weight physical access to economic or social phenomenon, such as access to jobs, to one's own residential location. For example, gravity measures weight jobs closer to one's residential location more heavily than jobs farther away, on the assumption that commuting costs are greater for distant jobs, making them much less accessible.
2. The data presented in this section is based on author's calculations using the Integrated Public Use Micro Samples (IPUMS) for the relevant years.
3. Based on author's calculations using the IPUMS data for relevant years.
4. Based on author's calculations using the IPUMS data for relevant years.
5. This figure is restricted to metropolitan areas for ease of presentation, and because the inclusion of rural areas did not significantly change the basic results.
6. Though not shown, these same basic trends are found for the nonpoor. Both groups were suburbanizing, but the rate of change was much slower for the poor.
7. Calculations from the U.S. Census IPUMS indicate that blacks made up about 10 percent of the U.S. metropolitan population in 1960 and about 14 percent in 2000.
8. Though not shown here, results for urban and suburban nonpoor populations are qualitatively similar to the patterns shown for the poor.
9. Of course, there are a number of nuances in these trends that are likely masked by fo-

cusing at the national level. Metropolitan area size is an obvious dimension by which these patterns are likely to vary: immigrant gateways have historically been larger metropolitan areas, though this is becoming less true over time (Singer 2004). Similarly, regional variations are likely to matter too. Immigration has been regionally concentrated (though this is less true now as a result of recent growth in immigrant populations in such traditionally nonimmigrant areas as the South, Midwest and smaller towns (Suro and Singer 2003) with the coastal regions and southern border states experiencing disproportionate share of such immigration (Singer 2004). In immigrant heavy regions, changes in the connection between race, place and poverty may be very different.

10. Author's calculations based on 2003 data from the American Housing Survey.

REFERENCES

Abt Associates. 2004. *Updating the Low Income Housing Tax Credit (LIHTC) Database: Project Placed in Service Through 2002.* Cambridge, Mass.: U.S. Department of Housing and Urban Development, Office of Economic Affairs.

Allard, Scott. 2004. *Access to Social Services: The Changing Urban Geography of Poverty and Service Provision.* Washington, D.C.: The Brookings Institution, Center on Urban and Metropolitan Policy.

Allard, Scott W., Richard Tolman, and Daniel Rosen. 2003. "Proximity to Service Providers and Service Utilization among Welfare Recipients: The Interaction of Place and Race." *Journal of Policy Analysis and Management* 22(4): 599–613.

Anderson, Elijah. 1976. *A Place on the Corner.* Chicago, Ill.: University of Chicago Press.

Avila, Eric. 2004. *Popular Culture in the Age of White Flight: Fear and Fantasy in Suburban Los Angeles.* Berkeley, Calif.: University of California.

Beers, Thomas M. 2000. "Flexible Schedules and Shift Work: Replacing the '9-to-5' Workday?" *Monthly Labor Review* 123(6): 33–40.

Bostic, Raphael W., and Richard W. Martin. 2003. "Black Home-Owners as a Gentrifying Force? Neighbourhood Dynamics in the Context of Minority Home-Ownership." *Urban Studies* 40(12): 2427–49.

Brooks-Gunn, Jeanne, Greg J. Duncan, Pamela Kato Klebanov, and Naomi Sealand. 1993. "Do Neighborhoods Influence Child and Adolescent Development?" *American Journal of Sociology* 99(2): 353–95.

Bullard, Robert, Glenn Johnson, and A. Torres. 2000. *Sprawl City: Race, Politics and Planning in Atlanta.* Washington, D.C.: Island Press.

Burchfield, Marcy, Henry G. Overman, Diego Puga, and Matthew A. Turner. 2005. "Causes of Urban Sprawl: A Portrait from Space." *Quarterly Journal of Economics* 112(2): 587–633.

Cashin, Sheryll. 2004. *The Failures of Integration: How Race and Class are Undermining the American Dream.* New York: PublicAffairs.

Charles, Camille Zubrinsky. 2005. "Can we Live Together? Racial Preferences and Neighborhood Outcomes." In *The Geography of Opportunity*, edited by Xavier de Souza Briggs. Washington, D.C.: The Brookings Institution Press.

Cieslewicz, David J. 2002. "The Environmental Impacts of Sprawl." In *Urban Sprawl:*

Causes, Consequences, and Policy Responses, edited by Gregory D. Squires. Washington, D.C.: Urban Institute.

Cohen, Mark A. 2003. "Report on the Racial Impact of GMACs Finance Charge Markup Policy," Expert Testimony/Report on the Matter of Addie T. Coleman et al. vs. General Motors Acceptance Corporation (GMAC). Accessed at http://www.consumerlaw.org/initiatives/cocounseling/content/GMAC/CohenReport.pdf.

Cooke, Thomas. 1997. "Geographic Access to Job Opportunities and Labor Force Participation among Women and African-Americans in the Greater Boston Metropolitan Area." *Urban Geography* 18(3): 213–27.

Crane, Jonathan. 1991, "The Epidemic Theory of Ghettos and Neighborhood Effects on Dropping Out and Teenage Childbearing," *American Journal of Sociology*, 96(5): 1226–59.

Duncan, Greg J. 1994. "Families and Neighbors as Sources of Disadvantage in the Schooling Decisions of White and Black Adolescents." *American Journal of Education* 103(1): 20–53.

Elliott, Delbert S., William Julius Wilson, David Huizinga, Robert J. Sampson, Amanda Elliott, and Bruce Rankin. 1996. "The Effects of Neighborhood Disadvantage on Adolescent Development." *Journal of Research in Crime and Delinquency* 33(4): 389–426.

Evans-Cowley, Jennifer S., Fred A. Forgey, and Ronald C. Rutherford.2005. "The Effect of Development Impact Fees on Land Values." *Growth and Change* 36(1): 100–112.

Evans-Cowley, Jennifer S., and Larry L. Lawhon. 2003. "The Effects of Impact Fees on the Price of Housing and Land: A Literature Review." *Journal of Planning Literature* 17(3): 351–59.

Farley, Reynolds, and William H. Frey. 1994. "Changes in the Segregation of Whites from Blacks During the 1980s: Small Steps Toward a More Integrated Society." *American Sociological Review* 59(1): 23–45.

Fernandez, Roberto M. 1994. "Race, Space and Job Accessibility: Evidence from a Plant Retooling." *Economic Geography* 70(4): 390–416.

Frey, William H. 2001. *Melting Pot Suburbs: A Census 2000 Study of Suburban Diversity*. Census 2000 Series. Washington, D.C.: The Brookings Institution, Center on Urban and Metropolitan Policy.

Galster, George G. 1991. "Black Suburbanization: Has it Changed the Relative Location of the Races?" *Urban Affairs Quarterly* 26(4): 621–62.

Gans, Herbert J. 1962. *Urban Villagers: Group and Class in the Life of Italian American*. New York: Free Press of Glencoe.

Glaeser, Edward L., and Matthew E. Kahn. 2001. "Decentralized Employment and the Transformation of the American City." *Brookings-Wharton Papers on Urban Affairs* 2(1): 1–64.

———. 2004. "Sprawl and Urban Growth." In *Handbook of Urban and Regional Economics*, vol. 4, edited by Vernon Henderson and Jacque Thisse. Oxford: Oxford University Press.

Glaeser, Edward L., Matthew Kahn, and J. Rappaport. 1999. "Why do the Poor Live in Cities?" Department of Economics Working Paper. Cambridge, Mass.: Harvard University.

Glaeser, Edward L., and Jacob Vigdor. 2001. *Racial Segregation in the 2000 Census: Promising News*. Census 2000 Series. Washington, D.C.: The Brookings Institution, Center on Urban and Metropolitan Policy.

Goering, John, and Ron Wienk, editors. 1996. *Mortgage Lending, Racial Discrimination, and Federal Policy*. Washington, D.C.: Urban Institute Press.

Greulich, Erica, John M. Quigley, and Steven Raphael. 2004. "The Anatomy of Rent Burdens: Immigration , Growth, and Rental Housing." *Brookings-Wharton Papers on Urban Affairs* 5: 149–87.

Heinlich, Ralph E., and William D. Andersen. 2001. "Development at the Urban Fringe and Beyond: Impacts on Agriculture and Rural Land." ERS Agriculture Economics Report No. 803. Washington: U.S. Department of Agriculture.

Holzer, Harry J., and Michael A. Stoll. 2007. *Where Workers Go, Do Jobs Follow*? Metro Economy Series. Washington, D.C.: The Brookings Institution, Metropolitan Policy Program.

Iceland, John, Daniel H. Weinberg, and Erika Steinmetz. 2002. *Racial and Ethnic Residential Segregation in the United States: 1980-2000*. Series CENSR-3. Washington: U.S. Census Bureau.

Ihlanfeldt, Keith R., and Ben Scafidi. 2002. "Black Self-Segregation as a Cause of Housing Segregation: Evidence from the Multi-City Study of Urban Inequality. *Journal of Urban Economics* 51(2): 366–90.

Ioannides, Y. M., and Linda D. Loury. 2004. "Job Information Networks, Neighborhood Effects, and Inequality." *Journal of Economics Literature* 42(4): 1056–93.

Jackson, Kenneth. 1985. *Crabgrass Frontier: The Suburbanization of the United States*. New York: Oxford University Press.

Jacobs, Jane. 1961. *Death and Life of American Great Cities*. New York: Random House.

Jargowsky, Paul A. 1996. "Take the Money and Run: Economic Segregation in U.S. Metropolitan Areas." *American Sociological Review* 61(6): 984–98.

———. 1997. *Poverty and Place: Ghettos, Barrios, and the American City*. New York: Russell Sage Foundation.

———. 2002. "Sprawl, Concentration of Poverty, and Urban Inequality." In *Urban Sprawl: Causes, Consequences, and Policy Responses*, edited by Gregory D. Squires. Washington, D.C.: Urban Institute Press.

———. 2003. *Stunning Progress, Hidden Problems: The Dramatic Decline of Concentrated Poverty in the 1990s*. The Living Cities Census Series. Washington, D.C.: The Brookings Institution, Center on Urban and Metropolitan Policy.

Jaynes, Gerald D., and Robin W. Williams. 1989. *A Common Destiny: Blacks and American Society*. Washington, D.C.: National Academy Press.

Jencks, Christopher, and Susan Mayer. 1990. "The Social Consequences of Growing Up in a Poor Neighborhood." In *Poverty in the United States*, edited by Gregory D. Squires. Washington, D.C.: National Academies Press.

Johnson, Rucker C. 2006. "Landing a Job in Urban Space: The Extent and Effects of Spatial Mismatch." *Regional Science and Urban Economics* 36(3): 331–72.

Kahn, Matthew E. 2001. "Does Sprawl Reduce the Black/White Housing Consumption Gap?" *Housing Policy Debate* 12(1): 77–86.

Kain, John F. 1968. "Housing Segregation, Negro Employment and Metropolitan Decentralization." *The Quarterly Journal of Economics* 82(2): 175–97.

Kandel, William, and John Cromartie. 2004. *New Patterns of Hispanic Settlement in Rural America*. Washington: U.S. Department of Agriculture, Economic Research Service.

Katz, Bruce. 2006. "The Potential of American Cities." Speech given at the Brookings Institution conference, Reinventing Older Communities: People, Places, Markets. Washington, D.C., April 5, 2006.

Katz, Lawrence, Jeff Kling, and J. B. Liebman. 2001. "Moving to Opportunity in Boston: Early Results of a Randomized Mobility Experiment." *Quarterly Journal of Economics* 116(2): 607–54.

Kling, Jeffrey R., Jens Ludwig, and Larry F. Katz. 2005. "Neighborhood Effects on Crime for Female and Male Youth: Evidence from a Randomized Housing Voucher Experiment." *Quarterly Journal of Economics* 120(1): 87–130.

Logan, John. 2002. *Separate and Unequal: The Neighborhood Gap for Blacks and Hispanics in Metropolitan America*. Albany, N.Y.: University of New York, Lewis Mumford Center.

———. 2003. "Ethnic Diversity Grows, Neighborhood Integration Lags." In *Redefining Urban & Suburban America: Evidence from Census 2000*, edited by Bruce Katz and Robert E. Lang. Washington, D.C.: The Brookings Institution Press.

Lopez, Russ, and H. Patricia Hynes. 2003. "Sprawl in the 1990s: Measurement, Distribution, and Trends." *Urban Affairs Review* 38(3): 325–55.

Ludwig, Jens, Paul Hirschfield, and Greg J. Duncan. 2001. "Urban Poverty and Juvenile Crime: Evidence from a Randomized Housing-Mobility Experiment." *Quarterly Journal of Economics* 116(2): 665–79.

Madden, Janice F. 2003. "The Changing Spatial Concentration of Income and Poverty among Suburbs of Large U.S. Metropolitan Areas." *Urban Studies* 40(3): 481–503.

Martin, Phillip, Michael Fix, and J. Edward Taylor. 2006. *The New Rural Poverty: Agriculture and Immigration in California*. Washington, D.C.: Urban Institute Press.

Martin, Richard W. 2001. "The Adjustments of Black Households to Metropolitan Shifts: How Persistent is Spatial Mismatch?" *Journal of Urban Economics* 50(1): 52–76.

———. 2004. "Spatial Mismatch and the Structure of American Metropolitan Areas, 1970–2000." *Journal of Regional Science* 44(3): 467–88.

Massey, Douglas S., and Nancy A. Denton. 1993. *American Apartheid: Segregation and the Making of the Underclass*. Cambridge, Mass.: Harvard University Press.

Massey, Douglas S., and Mary J. Fischer. 1999. "Does Rising Income Bring Integration? New Results for Blacks, Hispanics, and Asians in 1990." *Social Science Research* 28(3): 316–26.

McDonald, John F., and Daniel P. McMillen. 2004. "Determinants of Suburban Development Controls: A Fischel Expedition." *Urban Studies* 41(2): 341–61.

McLafferty, Sara, and Valerie Preston. 1997. "Gender, Race, and the Determinants of Commuting: New York in 1990." *Urban Geography* 18(3): 192–202.

Mills, Edwin. 2000. "A Thematic History of Urban Economic Research." *Brookings-Wharton Papers on Urban Affairs* 1: 1–52.

Mouw, Ted. 2000. "Job Relocation and the Racial Gap in Unemployment in Detroit and Chicago, 1980 to 1990. *American Sociological Review* 65(5): 730–53.

O'Flaherty, Brenden. 1995. "An Economic Theory of Homelessness and Housing." *Journal of Housing Economics* 4(1): 13–49.

Ondrich, Jan, Stephen L. Ross, and John Yinger. 2001. "Geography of Housing Discrimination." *Journal of Housing Research* 2(2): 217–38.

Ondrich, Jan, Alex Stricker, and John Yinger. 1999. "Do Landlords Discriminate? The Incidence and Causes of Racial Discrimination in Rental Housing Markets." *Journal of Housing Economics* 8(3): 185–20.

Ong, Paul, and Loh-Sze Leung. 2003. "Demographics: Diversified Growth." In *The New Face of Asian Pacific America*, edited by Eric Lai and Dennis Arguelles. Berkeley, Calif.: Asian Week.

Ong, Paul and Michael A. Stoll. 2007, "Redlining or Risk? A Spatial Analysis of Auto Insurance Rates in Los Angeles." *Journal of Policy Analysis and Management* 26(4): 811–30.

Ong, Paul, and Hyun-Gun Sung. 2003. "Exploratory Study of Spatial Variation in Car Insurance Premium, Traffic Volume and Vehicle Accidents." *UCTC* Working Paper No. 654. Berkeley: University of California Transportation Center.

Orfield, Myron. 2002. *American Metropolitics: The New Suburban Reality*. Washington, D.C.: The Brookings Institution Press.

Osterman, Paul. 1991. "Welfare Participation in a Full Employment Economy: The Impact of Neighborhood." *Social Problems* 38(4): 475–91.

O'Sullivan, Arthur. 2002. *Urban Economics*. New York: McGraw-Hill/Irvin.

Plotnick, Robert D., and Saul D. Hoffman. 1999. "The Effect of Neighborhood Characteristics on Young Adult Outcomes: Alternative Estimates." *Social Science Quarterly* 80(1): 1–18.

Portes, Alejandro, and Rubén Rumbaut. 2001. *Legacies: The Story of the Immigrant Second Generation*. Berkeley, Calif.: University of California Press and Russell Sage Foundation.

Quillian, Lincoln. 2003. "How Long Are Exposures to Poor Neighborhoods? The Long-Term Dynamics of Entry and Exit from Poor Neighborhoods." *Population Research and Policy Review* 22(3): 221–49.

Raphael, Steven. 1997. "The Spatial Mismatch Hypothesis and Black Youth Joblessness: Evidence from the San Francisco Bay Area." *Journal of Urban Economics* 43(1): 79–111.

Raphael, Steven, and Michael A. Stoll. 2001. "Can Boosting Minority Car Ownership Rates Narrow Inter-Racial Employment Gaps?" *Brookings-Wharton Papers on Urban Affairs* 2: 99–137.

———. 2002. *Modest Progress: The Narrowing Spatial Mismatch between Blacks and Jobs in the 1990s*. Washington, D.C.: The Brookings Institution, Center on Urban and Metropolitan Policy.

Rusk, David. 1993. *Cities Without Suburbs*. Baltimore, Md.: Johns Hopkins University Press.

Saiz, Albert. 2003. "Room in the Kitchen for the Melting Pot: Immigration and Rental Prices." *Review of Economics and Statistics* 85(3): 502–22.

Sampson, Robert J., Jeffrey D. Morenoff, and Thomas Gannon-Rowley. 2002. "Assessing Neighborhood Effects: Social Processes and New Directions for Research." *Annual Review of Sociology* 28: 443–78.

Singer, Audrey. 2004. *The Rise of New Immigrant Gateways*. Washington, D.C.: The Brookings Institution, Center on Urban and Metropolitan Policy.

Squires, Gregory D. 2002. "Urban Sprawl and the Uneven Development of Metropolitan America." In *Urban Sprawl: Causes, Consequences, and Policy Responses*, edited by Gregory D. Squires. Washington, D.C.: Urban Institute Press.

Stoll, Michael A. 2000. "Search, Discrimination, and the Travel to Work in Los Angeles." In *Prismatic Metropolis: Race, Segregation and Dimensions of Inequality in Los Angeles*, edited by Lawrence D. Bobo, Melvin L. Oliver, James H. Johnson, Jr., and Abel Valenzuela, Jr. New York: Russell Sage Foundation.

———. 2004. *African Americans and the Color Line*. New York: Russell Sage Foundation and Population Reference Bureau.

———. 2005. *Job Sprawl and the Mismatch Between Blacks and Jobs*. Washington, D.C.: The Brookings Institution, Center on Urban and Metropolitan Policy.

Stoll, Michael A., Harry J. Holzer, and Keith R. Ihlanfeldt. 2000. "Within Cities and Suburbs: Racial Residential Concentration and the Distribution of Employment Opportunities Across Sub-Metropolitan Areas." *Journal of Policy Analysis and Management* 19(2): 207–31.

Suro, Roberto, and Audrey Singer. 2003. "Changing Patterns of Latino Growth in Metropolitan America." In *Redefining Urban & Suburban America: Evidence from Census 2000*, edited by Bruce Katz and Robert E. Lang. Washington, D.C.: .Brookings Institution Press.

Susin, Scott. 2001. "The Impact of the Mariel Boatlift on the Miami Housing Market." Washington: U.S. Bureau of the Census.

Swanstrom, Todd, Colleen Casey, Robert Flack, and Peter Dreier. 2004. *Pulling Apart: Economic Segregation Among Suburbs and Central Cities in Major Metropolitan Areas*. Washington, D.C.: The Brookings Institution, Center on Urban and Metropolitan Policy.

Tigges, Leann M., Irene Browne, and Gary P. Green. 1998. "Social Isolation of the Urban Poor: Race, Class, and Neighborhood Effects on Social Resources." *The Sociological Quarterly* 39(1): 53–77.

U.S. Census Bureau. 2001. "Population Estimates of Metropolitan Areas, Metropolitan Areas Inside central cities, Metropolitan Areas Outside central Cities, and Nonmetropolitan Areas by State for July 1, 1999 and April 1, 1990 Population Estimates Base." MA-99-6. Washington: Government Printing Office. Accessed at http://www.census.gov/population/estimates/metro-city/ma99-06.txt.

U.S. Department of Housing and Urban Development. 2000. *The State of the Cities 2000*. Washington: Government Printing Office.

Valenzuela, Abel. 2002. "Planes, Trains, or *Camionetas* (little buses)? A Baseline Study of an Informal Travel Mode." *UCTC* Working Paper 04-2244. Berkeley, Calif.: University of California Transportation Center.

Vartanian, Thomas P. 1997. "Neighborhood Effects on AFDC Exits: Examining the Social Isolation, Relative Deprivation, and Epidemic Theories." *Social Service Review* 71(4): 548–73.

Wachs, Martin, and Brian D. Taylor. 1998. "Can Transportation Strategies Help Meet the Welfare Challenge?" *Journal of the American Planning Association* 64(Winter): 15–20.

Weber, Brue, Leif Jensen, Kathleen Miller, Jane Mosley, and Monica Fisher. 2005. "A Critical Review of Rural Poverty Literature: Is There Truly a Rural Effect." Institute for Research on Poverty Discussion Paper No. 1309-05. Madison, Wisc.: University of Wisconsin.

Wilson, William J. 1987. *The Truly Disadvantaged: The Inner City, the Underclass, and Public Policy*. Chicago, Ill.: University of Chicago Press.

———. 1996. *When Work Disappears: The World of the New Urban Poor*. New York: Vintage Press.

Wolman, Hal, George Galster, Royce Hanson, Michael Ratcliffe, Kimberly Furdell. 2002. "Measuring Sprawl: Problems and Solutions." Paper presented at the Association of Collegiate School of Planning. Baltimore, Md., November 23, 2002.

Yinger, John. 1997. "Cash in Your Face: The Cost of Racial and Ethnic Discrimination in Housing." *Journal of Urban Economics* 42(3): 339–65.

Place, Race, and Access to the Safety Net

Scott W. Allard

T his volume and other research show the clear connections between place, racial segregation, and concentrated poverty in urban and rural communities. Living in impoverished neighborhoods isolated from job opportunities, good schools, and quality housing is associated with negative education, employment, and health outcomes, particularly for racial minorities. To reduce segregation and the isolation of poor populations from opportunity, government housing and redevelopment programs often seek to expand affordable housing options, increase the mobility of poor families to better neighborhoods, and generate job growth within high-poverty communities.

Typically overlooked, however, is the relationship between place, race, and the agencies that administer programs intended to alleviate poverty among nondisabled working-age populations. We assume that the delivery of other antipoverty or safety net programs is targeted, like housing and community development policies, at high-poverty neighborhoods or communities. This is due in part to the poverty literature's focus on public cash assistance programs such as food stamps, Temporary Assistance for Needy Families (TANF) welfare cash assistance, and the Earned Income Tax Credit (EITC) that are perceived to be available regardless of where one lives. Because cash assistance can be delivered directly to recipients through the mail or electronic benefits transfer (EBT) cards, we expect that type of assistance to be well matched to neighborhoods where needs are greatest.

If we broaden our view of antipoverty assistance to include social service programs that seek to promote work activity and greater personal well being among working-age adults through job training, adult education, child care, emergency material assistance, and substance abuse or mental health treatment, these assumptions do not necessarily hold. These types of social services have become central components of safety net assistance for low-income families over the past four decades. But where each year welfare cash assistance, food stamps, and the EITC receive about $80 billion in funding, we likely allocate at least $150 billion in public and private funding to social service programs broadly defined. Unlike cash assistance programs, many social services cannot be delivered directly to an individual at home. Instead, clients typically visit a service agency, quite possibly several times. As a result, social service programs are fundamentally local and vary more widely by place than we tend to realize. Poor persons who do not live nearby relevant providers may either not know about available services or find it difficult to access programs because of the commutes between home, child care, work, and providers' offices. For the poor living far from social service programs, inadequate access to providers is tantamount to receiving no aid.

We should be particularly concerned about whether different race groups in urban and rural areas have spatial access to social service programs. In part this is because racial minorities are more likely to live in impoverished neighborhoods isolated from other types of opportunity and have faced historical discrimination in accessing safety net programs. Evidence that areas with large proportions of racial minorities have little access to services would indicate that programs intended to reduce poverty may in fact reinforce racial disparities in access to economic opportunity. Moreover, recent trends in immigration and shifts in the geography of poverty suggest that poor minorities, particularly Hispanic and Asian populations, are not settling primarily in central city areas as they may have done in the past (see Stoll, chapter 8, this volume). As a result, we should consider whether there are race group differences in access to service agencies across both urban and rural communities.

Yet few studies of race, poverty, and social policy examine the spatial context of social service provision in our communities today. To address this gap in the literature, I review how place matters to safety net programs and compare spatial variation in access to social services in urban and rural communities by neighborhood racial composition. Specifically, I use information about the location of social service providers contained in the Multi-City Survey of Social Service Providers (MSSSP) and the Rural Survey of Social Service Providers (RSSSP) to examine the spatial distribution of service providers in several different communities with large concentrations of poor minorities (Allard 2006a, 2006b). I find evidence of less access to social service providers across predominately poor and minority neighborhoods than across less poor or predominately white ones. Such findings should both inform future research exploring race, place, and poverty, and generate policy implications for a safety net that emphasizes social service programs at least as much as cash assistance.

PLACE, POVERTY, AND GOVERNMENT POLICY

Concentrated, racially segregated urban poverty is one of the most recognizable products of housing discrimination and housing policy in America (Wilson 1987; Massey and Denton 1993). In 1990, roughly 17 percent of all blacks lived in high-poverty areas—census tracts where the poverty rate exceeded 40 percent—and blacks comprised about 50 percent of high-poverty tracts (Jargowsky 1997). By 2000, 27 percent of blacks in central city areas lived below the poverty level, and blacks continued to make up the vast majority of the urban poor (Stoll, chapter 8, this volume). Hispanics are less likely to live in neighborhoods that are highly segregated by race (Massey and Denton 1993; Frey and Farley 1996; Briggs 2005). But almost 50 percent of the nation's Hispanics live in a handful of major metropolitan areas (Frey 2006), and the poverty rate among central city Hispanics was nearly 25 percent in 2000, almost as high as among central city blacks (Stoll, chapter 8, this volume).

Many scholars link persistent race and class segregation to spatial mismatches in the labor market, where job opportunities are in suburban and outer-urban areas so far from low-skill job-seekers in the central city that it is difficult for them to find or keep jobs (Kain 1992; Raphael and Stoll 2002; Stoll, chapter 8, this volume). Distance between jobs and job seekers affects employment outcomes by making commutes to work difficult for central city residents without access to reliable automobile transportation (Coulton, Leete, and Bania 1999; Holzer and Ihlanfeldt 1996; Holzer and Stoll 2001). Distance also is thought to be inversely related to the information job-seekers have about potential job opportunities (Holzer, Ihlanfeldt, and Sjoquist 1994; Rogers 1997; Stoll 1999). Several studies have found low levels of access to labor market opportunities to be related to weaker work outcomes among low-skill workers (Allard and Danziger 2003; Holzer and Stoll 2001; Ong and Blumenberg 1998).

Public policy also has contributed to these patterns. To address deficits in the supply of affordable housing options, federal housing policy in the postwar era subsidized public housing developments for low-income households. Many large-scale public housing developments built during the middle part of the twentieth century concentrated and isolated poor families, often minorities, into deteriorating buildings in unsafe neighborhoods far from labor market opportunities (von Hoffman 1996; Newman and Schnare 1997). In addition, the Federal Housing Administration (FHA) and Home Owners Loan Corporation (HOLC), two prominent New Deal programs established to expand homeownership in the wake of the Great Depression, targeted government loan programs and mortgage insurance to homogeneous white neighborhoods. This valuable assistance was less available to residents of racially or ethnically mixed neighborhoods, exacerbating race and class segregation. These agencies also effectively sanctioned similar discriminatory practices in private lending markets (Jackson 1985; Massey and Denton 1993).

Many of these unfair practices were targeted by civil rights advocates. Federal antidiscrimination and fair housing laws emerged in the postwar era to prevent realtors, private lenders, local governments, and neighborhood associations from overtly opposing racial integration of neighborhoods through discriminatory market practices, mortgage covenants, and intimidation (Sugrue 1996; Hirsch 1983). Enforcement of court decisions and fair housing laws prohibiting discriminatory real estate practices, however, have been criticized as being inconsistent, lackluster, or ineffective in reducing segregation (Jargowsky 1997; Massey and Denton 1993). Instead, two other types of policy responses to race and class segregation predominate: place-based and mobility-based antipoverty programs.

Place-based programs seek to strengthen high-poverty communities, creating job opportunities, improving local housing or schools, or cultivating institutions that may address the results of segregation and concentrated poverty. Model Cities, which emerged early from Lyndon Johnson's Great Society efforts to address urban joblessness and poverty, provided supplemental federal grants to cities to support efforts to revitalize depressed neighborhoods. Unfortunately, participant cities found the process unwieldy, poorly funded, complex, and riddled with delay, which led to modest progress at best and further deteriorating conditions at worst. A more recent example, enterprise zones (EZs) provide tax incentives to private firms if they maintain or expand operations within an impoverished urban or rural area designated by federal or state government. In general, however, these have not been successful at generating greater economic opportunity for the targeted neighborhoods (Greenbaum and Engberg 1998; Peters and Fisher 2002). The most promising contemporary place-based policy is Hope VI housing developments, which replace existing public housing with low-density, mixed-income housing developments designed to attract a range of residents and revitalize impoverished urban neighborhoods (Popkin et al. 2004).

Mobility-based programs, by contrast, facilitate movement away from areas of concentrated poverty, thereby increasing access to opportunity and reducing racial segregation. These have been somewhat successful. Housing vouchers or rent certificates, often provided through the Housing Choice Voucher or Section 8 program, allow recipients to seek housing in a community of their choice. By 2000, about 4 million persons in 1.8 million households received these subsidies, and the average recipient lived in a neighborhood with a 20 percent poverty rate. Compare this to the 2.4 million persons assisted through 1.3 million public housing units, who on average lived in a neighborhood with a poverty rate of 29 percent (U.S. Department of Housing and Urban Development 2000). Sandra Newman and Ann Schnare (1997) found that roughly 5 percent of voucher recipients lived in neighborhoods where the poverty rate exceeds 40 percent, compared to 37 percent of public housing residents. The court-ordered Gautreaux Assisted Housing Program in Chicago used rent subsidies to move more than 7,000 low-income families from high-poverty communities to better neighborhoods, often in the suburbs, between 1976 and 1998. Studies evaluating the impact of Gautreaux found evidence that families who participated in the program on average remain in neighborhoods with lower poverty rates, higher proportions of college graduates, and higher family income (DeLuca and Rosenbaum 2003; Keels et al. 2005). More recently, an experimental housing voucher program called Moving to Opportunity (MTO), which sought to improve the economic outcomes and well being of poor families by helping them move to lower poverty neighborhoods, did not achieve results comparable to the Gautreaux program. Although MTO encouraged families to relocate, many moved to neighborhoods near their initial residence and many others moved back to their original neighborhood over time.

In addition, voucher recipients moving to lower poverty neighborhoods did not experience better work outcomes than those who did not move, though they did experience some physical and mental health gains (Kling, Liebman, and Katz 2006).

Evidence that place- and mobility-based policies have not had significant impact on concentrated and racially segregated urban poverty may mean that antipoverty programs need not have a place-based focus or be viewed as relevant to place. Yet as I discuss shortly, place matters for social programs targeted at individuals, particularly given relatively recent changes in how the safety net delivers assistance to poor persons.

CONNECTING THE GROWTH IN SOCIAL SERVICE PROGRAMS TO PLACE AND POVERTY

Most often when policy makers and researchers talk about antipoverty or safety net assistance, the focus is on particularly salient government programs such as TANF welfare cash assistance, food stamps, and Medicaid. Frequently overlooked are social service programs that seek to promote work activity and greater personal well being through employment services, adult education, child care, child welfare, housing assistance, transportation assistance, emergency or temporary assistance with material needs, or substance abuse and mental health treatment. Social service programs now make up a large share of public and private safety net expenditures. Surprising as this transformation in the safety net may seem, even the most knowledgeable policy expert or community leader may not be aware that the manner in which society and communities help low-income populations has changed so much in recent decades.

There is no single cause to this shift in the composition of safety net assistance. In part it is due to welfare reform and robust economic growth in the 1990s, which led welfare caseloads to fall from a historical high of 14 million in 1993 to fewer than 5 million in 2005. The nearly 70 percent decline led to a simultaneous decline in cash assistance expenditures (in 2006 dollars) from about $32 billion in 1993 to approximately $12 billion in 2004. Thus, welfare cash assistance today is a much smaller component of the safety net than it was even ten years ago. In addition, recurring monthly welfare checks are no longer the primary mode of welfare assistance. Instead, TANF programs in 2004 spent about $17.5 billion on social services promoting work activity, temporary or one-time cash assistance, and transfers to other service programs (U.S. Congress 1998, 2004; U.S. Department of Health and Human Services 2006, 2007a, 2007b).

By comparison, funding for means-tested social service programs for persons living near or below the poverty line have steadily expanded since 1970. Such programs began to grow after the war on poverty through the different public titles of the Social Security Act (SSA), and now receive funding through a wide range of public sources (Smith and Lipsky 1993). The federal Social Services Block Grant (SSBG) program, which originated as Title XX of the SSA, provides billions of dollars to local agencies for services that promote economic self-sufficiency, well being, and child welfare. Other federal programs include the Community Services Block Grant (CSBG) and the Community Development Block Grant (CDBG), which provide grants to local agencies that provide employment and support services to impoverished communities, and the Child Care and Development Block Grant (CCDBG), which seeks to improve the affordability and availability of child care assistance to low-income families. Beyond federal programs and expenditures, there are thousands of state, county, and locally funded social service programs that address the employment, health, and well being needs of low-income populations.[1]

The Congressional Research Service (CRS) estimated that means-tested spending on a variety of social services, including job training, housing, adult education, and energy assistance, increased from $47 billion to $110 billion (in 2006 dollars) between 1975 and 2002 (Burke 2003). This is a lower-bound estimate, however, because it excludes a wide array of employment, counseling, substance abuse treatment, mental health treatment, child care, and temporary assistance programs funded by federal, state, and local governments. To put the scope of social service provision into perspective, cash assistance programs such as food stamps, TANF welfare cash assistance, and the Earned Income Tax Credit provide about $80 billion in total aid to working poor families each year (U.S. Congress 1998, 2004; U.S. Department of Health and Human Services 2007b). Medicaid, among the largest of the public safety net programs, spent about $70 billion on coverage to roughly 30 million nonelderly, nondisabled families in 2003 (Holahan and Ghosh 2005, Zedlewski et al. 2006).

Offering a sense of recent trends in safety net expenditures, figure 9.1 compares CRS data on federal, state, and local expenditures for a limited number of social service programs—specifically job training, child care programs, and SSBG—to data from other sources tracking welfare cash assistance and EITC expenditures from 1975 to 2002. These are the best annual data available, but represent just a fraction of public social service expenditures today. As shown, federal, state, and local government spent $18.5 billion (in 2006 dollars) on this very narrow set of social services in 1975, roughly half that spent on welfare cash assistance ($31.5 billion). Public expenditures almost doubled in real dollars between 1975 and 2002, reaching approximately $34 billion. In contrast, federal and state welfare cash assistance expenditures declined by two-thirds during the same period, and have hovered near $11 or $12 billion for the last several years. The EITC has expanded to become the largest means-tested program providing cash assistance to low-income households in America.[2]

Not only do these data underestimate pubic expenditures for social service programs, but they also do not account for the important contributions of private nonprofit organizations. Government agencies in many communities depend heavily on nonprofit agencies to deliver publicly funded social service programs to the poor at the street level. As Steven Smith noted, "nonprofit social service agencies have a more central role in society's response to social problems than ever before" (2002, 150). Increases in public expenditures for social service pro-

FIGURE 9.1 / Federal, State, and Local Cash Assistance, Social Services, and Earned Income Tax Credit Expenditures

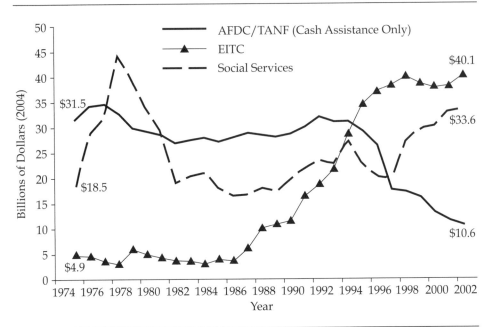

Source: Burke (2003); U.S. Congress (1998, 2004); U.S. Department of Health and Human Services (2007b).

grams over the past four decades has led to an increase in both the number of nonprofit service agencies and the total revenues of the nonprofit service sector. Lester Salamon (2002) found that the total number of nonprofit human service organizations filing as tax exempt with the Internal Revenue Service (IRS) increased by 115 percent between 1977 and 1997. Including only nonprofits registering with the IRS that are most likely to provide services to low-income working-age adults, I estimate that the number of nonprofit human service and job training service providers increased by about 65 percent between 1990 and 2003. Annual expenditures by this set of providers totaled roughly $80 billion in 2003 (in 2006 dollars). Like estimates of the public social service sector, these figures underestimate the size of the nonprofit social service sector because they exclude nonprofit mental health and substance abuse service providers, health-related services, youth development programs, housing and shelter providers, and civil rights or legal aid programs, as well as religious congregations and small nonprofits not required to file with the IRS.[3]

Generating accurate estimates of total public and private social service expenditures is challenging because of the difficulty in collecting accurate and detailed information from the thousands of governmental and nongovernmental agencies that deliver services. Such challenges are compounded by the limitations of IRS data on tax-exempt organizations. Contracts and fee-for-service arrangements between government and nonprofit agencies also may lead to double-counting of program expenditures or revenues. With these caveats and concerns in mind, I estimate that governmental and nonprofit agencies combined spend at least $150 billion for social services targeted at disadvantaged populations each year, and probably much more. Contrary to popular impressions about antipoverty assistance, therefore, the American safety net spends about fifteen times as much on social services for poor people as it does on welfare cash assistance and likely several times as much as it does on the EITC.

Place can affect the delivery of cash assistance programs. Income maintenance programs such as welfare cash assistance and food stamps have rules that vary by state and can vary within counties of a given state (Soss and Schram, chapter 11, this volume; Schram et al. 2007). But these cash assistance programs typically do not vary in benefit level or eligibility within a particular city or community. Benefits from these programs also are often mailed or electronically transferred to clients, regardless of their place of residence within a community.

I argue, however, that place is more central to administering and delivering human or social service programs than cash assistance programs. One can receive a welfare check in the mail or have a food stamp allocation placed on an EBT card, but job training services or domestic violence counseling cannot be typically delivered to one's home. Applying the spatial mismatch hypothesis to social service delivery, therefore, we should expect greater proximity to service providers to increase the likelihood that a person in need receives help. To participate in a social service program, a poor person often must make repeated visits to an agency. As with job or education opportunities, we assume that individuals are more likely to have information about agencies operating in their immediate community or neighborhood. For their part, caseworkers also are more likely to refer clients to programs and agencies located near their homes. Individuals seeking help may trust agencies from the immediate community more than those located farther away. Proximity also matters because many low-income adults fit visits to service agencies within daily commutes to work and child care that are already complicated by inadequate access to reliable automobile or efficient public transportation. Mismatches or inadequate access to social service programs can be viewed as tantamount to being denied aid.

Spatial variation in access to social service programs is a product of the location decisions of providers. A number of factors may shape where agencies locate and whether they will be readily accessible to persons living in high-poverty neighborhoods. Of primary importance, it can be difficult for agencies to find affordable and adequate office space near or within high-poverty areas. Location choices may be driven by the need to access revenues from government sources, charitable foundations, or private giving. Because social service programs are not entitlements, such as Medicaid or food stamps, state and local governments choose how to fund services and these choices create variation in public support for programs. At times, agencies can run into difficulty finding suitable locations when confronted with not in my backyard (NIMBY) sentiment, in which neighborhoods resist the presence of social service agencies. Nonprofit service organizations may be attracted to neighborhoods with strong community-based institutions and high levels of civic engagement or social capital. Organizational commitments to serving particular populations or neighborhoods and staff preferences to work in certain neighborhoods also shape location decisions. Moreover, we should keep in mind that location incentives will vary across service sectors. For example, job-training programs might locate closer to employers than to program clients because proximity to employers may be critical to building the relationships necessary to place clients and to replicating for clients the process of going to work. In the end, service providers must locate with the interests and needs of multiple stakeholders, constituencies, and obligations in mind. Proximity to clients is only one of many considerations.

The few studies that have explored social service accessibility in poor communities find evidence of mismatches. Kirsten Grønbjerg and Laurie Paarlberg (2001) found that counties in Indiana with higher poverty rates had fewer nonprofit organizations per capita than counties with lower poverty rates. Controlling for potential demand for assistance when considering access to nonprofit service providers in Phoenix, Laura Peck (2008) concluded that nonprofits were less accessible to high-poverty areas near the central city than to low-poverty areas away from the central city. Examining the location of nonprofit service providers in southern California, Pascale Joassart-Marcelli and Jennifer Wolch (2003) presented evidence that nonprofit organizations in poorer municipalities had lower expenditures and face greater demand for assistance than nonprofits in more affluent communities. Similarly, a survey of nonprofit agencies in Los Angeles County revealed that high-poverty neighborhoods in South and East Los Angeles were underserved compared to other impoverished areas of the county (Mosley et al. 2003).

Linking place to the delivery of social services is particularly relevant to discussions of race and poverty. The safety net has a historical legacy of treating racial and ethnic minorities differently than other population groups. Well into the middle part of the twentieth century, states and communities denied poor blacks access to a range of safety net programs (Lieberman 1998; Schram, Soss, and Fording 2003; Soss et al. 2001). To the extent that access to social services likewise varies by race and place, there may be disparities in access between poor minority populations and both whites and those living outside of central cities. A safety net mismatched from those in need cannot alleviate the social problems created by persistent poverty and residential segregation of racial and ethnic minorities.

Although much of the work exploring nonprofit service provision and service accessibility considers only urban settings, we should expect access to services to matter in rural places as well. Providers in one town or county seat may be willing to serve populations outside those municipal limits, but most rural towns are a considerable distance apart. These distances often make accessible only those programs or providers in the immediate town or community. Moreover, the dispersal of population and low densities of potential clients outside of main town areas may prevent service providers from locating outside county seats or population centers, even if unmet needs are recognized in more isolated portions of a rural community. In rural places, therefore, having access to a reliable automobile or living in a population center may be even more critical determinants of service access than in urban places.

Shifts in the racial and ethnic geography of poverty over the past decade also affect social service accessibility. Alan Berube and Elizabeth Kneebone (2006) found that though poverty rates in larger cities remained twice as high as in suburbs in 2005 (18.8 versus 9.4 percent), the number of poor people grew much faster in suburbs than in central cities between 1999 and 2005. Although poor minorities remain concentrated in central cities, the proportion of poor blacks living in high-poverty neighborhoods declined from 30 percent in 1990 to 19 percent in 2000 (Briggs 2005; Jargowsky 2003). Hispanic and other immigrant populations are also moving to new metropolitan areas and regions (Singer 2004). William Frey (2006) found Hispanic population growth since 1990 to be particularly high in metropolitan areas of the Southeast—such as Charlotte, North Carolina, and Atlanta, Georgia—and the West—such as Riverside, California. Service agencies, often less mobile than poor populations, may find it challenging to adequately respond to these shifts in the geography of poverty. Many providers own their buildings or are locked into long-term leases and thus cannot easily pick up and leave one neighborhood to move to another. These agencies may find it difficult to maintain funding or client caseloads amidst the decentralization of poverty. Yet low-income families moving away from central city neighborhoods still struggle with barriers to employment or with finding good paying jobs. And, few destination communities commit significant public or private resources to address the needs of the working poor. The result is a growing mismatch between those seeking help and those capable of providing it.

DATA AND METHODS

To assess the accessibility of social service providers to poor minorities in urban communities, I analyze data from two surveys: the Multi-City Survey of Social Service Providers and the Rural Survey of Social Service Providers (Allard 2006a, 2006b). The MSSSP conducted telephone survey interviews with executives and managers from 1,487 social service providers in three metropolitan areas— Chicago, Los Angeles, Washington, D.C. The RSSSP interviewed administrators from 724 agencies in southeastern Kentucky, south-central Georgia, southeastern New Mexico, and the mountainous forested Oregon-California border counties. Each survey collected detailed information about service delivery, clients, funding, and geographic location from governmental and nongovernmental agencies operating in one of several service areas—adult education, job training, outpatient mental health, outpatient substance abuse, emergency assistance. With response rates that exceed 60 percent in each site, these surveys contain the most unique, comprehensive, and geographically sensitive data about social service provision currently available.[4]

The standard measure of concentrated poverty—the percentage of poor in a census tract—needs to be adapted for social service provision. An accurate understanding of service accessibility should take into account the range of providers within a reasonable commuting distance, not just those located in a particular census tract or neighborhood. Measures of service access also should control for both the supply of assistance available and demand for that assistance. A provider that serves 100 clients in a neighborhood where 200 persons are in need is more accessible than a provider serving 100 in a neighborhood where 1,000 are in need. All things being equal, it is assumed that services are more readily accessible if a person seeking help is nearby an agency that offers relevant services, has resources available, and is not overwhelmed by demand for assistance from the surrounding community.

To provide insight into the accessibility of service providers to concentrations of need in the three MSSSP sites, I calculate a service accessibility score that reflects a residential census tract's access to social service opportunities within three miles relative to the average tract in Chicago, Los Angeles, and Washington, D.C. These scores weight for supply of services by summing the number of clients served within three miles of a given residential tract and for potential demand by accounting for the number of poor persons within three miles.[5] One can use service accessibility scores to compare types of census tracts or neighborhoods. For example, Neighborhood A with an access score of 1.10 is within three miles of 10 percent more service opportunities than the metropolitan mean tract (score of 1.00). If Neighborhood B has an access score of 0.90, it can be said to be near 10 percent fewer service opportunities than the metropolitan mean tract. It can also be said that Neighborhood A has access to 22 percent more service opportunities than Neighborhood B (1.10 ÷ 0.90 = 1.22). If providers and programs are more likely to locate near or within impoverished neighborhoods, then service accessibility scores should be at or above 1 in high-poverty neighborhoods. Scores do not speak to how all public and nonprofit resources are allocated across a community or whether the supply of services is adequate to meet the need. Also, access scores do not account for whether programs are high or low quality, or for the length of time in which a client typically participates in a program.

Three access scores are presented in table 9.1: one measuring accessibility to employment services (for example, job training, job placement, adult education), one measuring access to basic needs assistance (such as emergency cash or food assistance), and one measuring access to services promoting broader personal well being (such as outpatient mental health or substance abuse treatment).

ACCESS TO SOCIAL SERVICES ACROSS RACE GROUPS IN URBAN AMERICA

The differences that emerge when comparing service access in tracts with large percentages of blacks or Hispanics to tracts with few minorities are startling. The top panel of table 9.1 contains access scores for census tracts according to race composition. Looking at access to employment-related services in column 1, residents of predominately black census tracts—more than 75 percent black—have access to 38 percent fewer employment-related service opportunities than the average tract (column 1, access score of 0.62). Predominately Hispanic tracts are proximate to 20 percent fewer employment service providers than the average tract (access score of 0.80). Predominately white neighborhoods have access far above the mean levels in their communities—approximately 21 percent more employment service opportunities than the metropolitan mean tract (access score of 1.21).

Contrasting black and Hispanic tracts to mostly white tracts yields large race differences in access to employment-related services. Predominately black tracts have half as much access to employment services as predominately white tracts (0.62 versus 1.21, respectively). Similarly, predominately Hispanic tracts have access to 50 percent fewer employment service opportunities than their predominately white counterparts (0.80 versus 1.21, respectively).

Differences in service accessibility across race group composition in a tract persist when examining other types of services. Basic needs assistance—typically emergency cash, clothing, utility, and food assistance provided to the most disadvantaged populations—is much more accessible in neighborhoods with smaller shares of racial minorities and higher shares of whites (see column 2). For instance, predominately black tracts have access to roughly 40 percent fewer basic needs assistance opportunities than the average tract (0.63 versus 1.00) and access to half as many providers as predominately white tracts (0.63 versus 1.28). Smaller gaps in access to basic needs assistance exist between predominately Hispanic and white neighborhoods. Further, column 3 shows even larger race differences in access to mental health or substance abuse programs that promote personal well being.

The bottom panel of table 9.1 examines service accessibility across majority black, Hispanic, and white tracts with different levels of poverty. Even when controlling for the poverty rate, predominately black and Hispanic tracts have far less access to social service agencies than predominately white areas. For instance, in tracts where the poverty rate ranges from 21 percent to 40 percent, majority black and Hispanic areas have access to 32 percent and 22 percent fewer employment service opportunities than the metropolitan mean tract (scores of 0.68 and 0.78 respectively). Majority white tracts in these same types of high poverty tracts have slightly higher levels of access to employment services than majority minority tracts (score of 0.87). Majority white tracts in low poverty areas have access to social services that far exceeds that in the average tracts or high poverty majority minority tracts.

Because table 9.1 aggregates across the three MSSSP study sites, the access scores reported mask some of the extremely low levels of service access in many high poverty and racially segregated areas. Thus, figures 9.2 and 9.3 map access to employment-related services in the central city areas of Chicago and Los Angeles respectively. Darker areas reflect places with greater access, lighter areas those with less access. Because access to employment service agencies is comparable to

TABLE 9.1 / Access to Social Services by Race in Chicago, Los Angeles, and Washington, D.C.

Type of Census Tract	Employment-Related Services (1)	Basic Needs Services (2)	Services Addressing Personal Well Being (3)
Percentage of tract population black			
0 to 25	1.11[abc]	1.09[ab]	1.11[abc]
26 to 50	0.82[a]	0.93[c]	0.82[a]
51 to 75	0.63[b]	0.81[a]	0.67[b]
More than 75	0.62[c]	0.63[bc]	0.60[c]
Percentage of tract population Hispanic			
0 to 25	1.08[ab]	1.10[abc]	1.12[ab]
26 to 50	0.98	0.89[a]	1.06[c]
51 to 75	0.82[a]	0.80[b]	0.79[a]
More than 75	0.80[b]	0.85[c]	0.56[bc]
Percentage of tract population white			
0 to 25	0.68[abc]	0.68[abc]	0.62[ab]
26 to 50	1.11[ad]	0.87[ade]	0.71[cd]
51 to 75	1.01[be]	1.07[bdf]	1.10[ace]
More than 75	1.21[cde]	1.28[cef]	1.43[bde]
Poverty rate 0 to 20 percent	1.09[ab]	1.05[ab]	1.10[ab]
Poverty rate 21 to 40 percent	0.81[a]	0.88[a]	0.76[a]
Poverty rate more than 40 percent	0.74[b]	0.85[b]	0.78[b]
Majority black census tracts with . . .			
Poverty rate 0 to 20 percent	0.52[a]	0.63[ab]	0.59[a]
Poverty rate 21 to 40 percent	0.68[b]	0.68[c]	0.62[b]
Poverty rate more than 40 percent	0.81	0.81	0.68[c]
Majority Hispanic census tracts with . . .			
Poverty rate 0 to 20 percent	0.98	0.85	0.57[d]
Poverty rate 21 to 40 percent	0.78[c]	0.85[d]	0.69
Poverty rate more than 40 percent	0.59	0.82	0.76
Majority white census tracts with . . .			
Poverty rate 0 to 20 percent	1.14[abc]	1.18[acd]	1.30[abcd]
Poverty rate 21 to 40 percent	0.87	1.17[b]	0.99
Poverty rate more than 40 percent	0.97	1.15	1.44

Source: Allard (2006a).
Note: Numbers reported are mean service accessibility scores reflecting access to all social service providers and controlling for potential demand in the surrounding area.
[a, b, c, d, e, f] Notations identify sets of paired cells where the mean difference in service access between the two cells is significant at the .10 level or below.
N = 4,275.

FIGURE 9.2 / Access to Employment-Related Services in Chicago

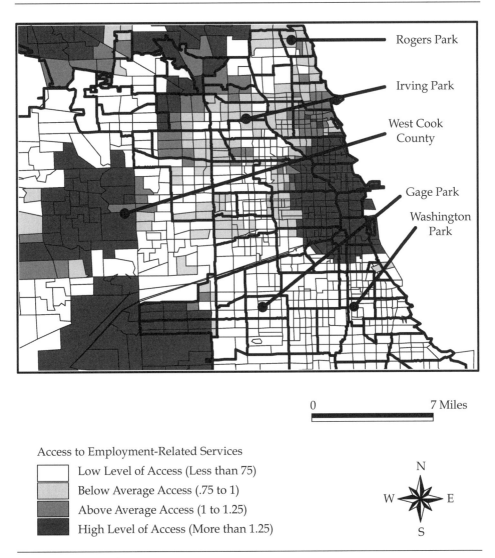

Access to Employment-Related Services

- ☐ Low Level of Access (Less than 75)
- ▨ Below Average Access (.75 to 1)
- ▥ Above Average Access (1 to 1.25)
- ■ High Level of Access (More than 1.25)

Source: Allard (2006a).

other types of services, figures 9.2 and 9.3 can approximate the spatial distribution of safety net assistance of all types in urban communities.

Consistent with explanations for mismatches in social service provision, figures 9.2 and 9.3 show that employment service providers tend to be located outside the core central city. With the exception of the downtown Loop area of Chicago along the eastern edge of the city, the central cities of Chicago and Los Angeles have

FIGURE 9.3 / Access to Employment-Related Services in Los Angeles

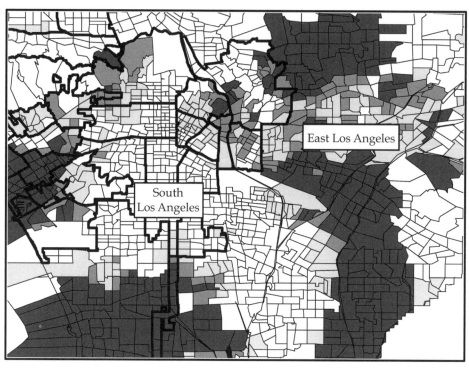

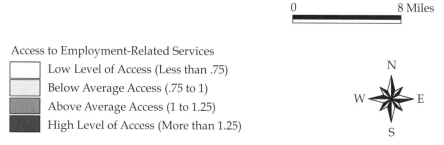

Access to Employment-Related Services
- ☐ Low Level of Access (Less than .75)
- ☐ Below Average Access (.75 to 1)
- ☐ Above Average Access (1 to 1.25)
- ■ High Level of Access (More than 1.25)

Source: Allard (2006a).

very low levels of access to service providers. Access is much greater in the communities outside of Chicago in the western portion of Cook County and in the communities south and east of Los Angeles.

Predominately black neighborhoods like Washington Park on the south side of Chicago or in South Los Angeles have particularly low levels of access. Although these areas are labeled as having little access, the actual access scores are far below the metropolitan mean. For example, the historically black neighborhoods of

Crenshaw, Watts, and Compton in South Los Angeles have access scores of 0.25 to 0.4, 60 to 75 percent fewer providers than the average neighborhood. The same is true for the black neighborhoods south of the Loop in Chicago, with 75 percent fewer services than the mean tract.

Although Hispanics appear to have better access than blacks, variation across Hispanic neighborhoods is wide. In Chicago, neighborhoods to the northwest of Loop, such as Irving Park, and to the southwest, such as Gage Park, are home to large concentrations of Hispanics. Access to social services, in this case employment services, is much higher in the Irving Park area and in the mixed-race Rogers Park neighborhood than in the southwest corner of the city. Communities in the northwest approach, and in some instances exceed, metropolitan mean levels of service accessibility; neighborhoods in the southwest have access to even fewer service providers than predominately black neighborhoods south of downtown. Several miles from service-rich neighborhoods to the west, predominately Hispanic communities such as Gage Park typically post service access scores of 0.25 or lower. Likewise, Southeast Los Angeles and East Los Angeles are predominately Hispanic communities straddling the Los Angeles city limits. Although they are somewhat proximate to each other, Hispanics in Southeast Los Angeles have access to about one-fifth to one-quarter as many employment services as their counterparts in East Los Angeles.

The MSSSP documents that primarily poor black tracts have far less access to social service programs than poor white or Hispanic tracts. Though poor whites have the highest levels of access to social service agencies, many poor Hispanics living in mixed-race communities have greater access to service providers than poor blacks. Despite living in less segregated neighborhoods than blacks, however, many predominately Hispanic communities also have extremely low levels of access.

SERVICE PROVISION IN RURAL AMERICA

Poverty is a rural as well as an urban problem—rural rates approach those in central cities. Roughly 18 percent of rural Americans live below the poverty line, compared to 22 percent of central city residents and almost 10 percent of suburban residents. The rural poor account for nearly 25 percent of the total poor population. Poverty rates remain quite high among racial minorities living in rural areas and are much higher than those for rural whites. For instance, 42 percent of rural blacks and almost 32 percent of rural Hispanics lived below the poverty line in 2000, compared to less than 16 percent of rural whites (Stoll, chapter 8, this volume).

Do we see race group disparities in access to the safety net in high poverty rural areas similar to those observed in urban areas? Service agencies operating in rural areas often have fewer resources, operate across a much wider geographic area, and confront declining economic opportunity, making it easy to assume that mismatches in service access will be similar across rural and urban places. Yet service accessibility has a different meaning in rural areas and measures of accessibility are more difficult to calculate. The most suitable space for social service agencies is in or near town centers. Remote rural areas have few poor people numerically, making it difficult for providers to support operations even if they were to relocate there. Given that rural populations travel farther to get to work, or even to go shopping, the commuting distance expected of the rural poor are also different—even though access to automobiles is no different than among the urban poor. Access scores calculated at three-mile radii have less meaning in rural than in urban areas. Although they are not representative of rural white, black, or Hispanic poverty nationally, here I briefly examine the spatial distribution of service opportunities in the New Mexico and Georgia sites of the RSSSP.[6]

In southeast New Mexico, predominately cattle and oil country, 20 percent of the region's population are poor, and the population of the region is primarily of white and Hispanic. When speaking with service providers throughout this region, it is common for program managers to identify where poor Hispanics live. Although low density, these rural barrios have the same features as segregated urban ghettos: poor quality housing, low quality public infrastructure, few commercial stores or shops, high crime rates, low literacy rates, and low levels of educational achievement. Even in a region that is not particularly affluent, these racially segregated rural barrios can be a world away from the chain stores and nicer homes in other areas of the community.

With a regional economy based in the service industry, manufacturing, agriculture, and timber, south-central Georgia has a poverty rate of about 20 percent across the eight-county region. This area of Georgia is more sparsely populated than the southeast New Mexico site and about 25 percent of the population is black. Poor blacks are primarily concentrated in Ben Hill County and in the cities of Douglas and Waycross.

Figures 9.4 and 9.5 map social service agencies weighted by average monthly caseload in southeastern New Mexico and south-central Georgia. Immediately apparent is the clustering of service agencies around town centers, with street locations on the primary commercial street or near the county government centers.[7] Providers tend to locate near population centers for several reasons. Agencies have difficulty maintaining enough clients for operation and even more difficulty finding qualified staff if offices are not centrally located. Also, to a greater extent than their urban counterparts, rural social service agencies struggle to find office space.

Most low-income persons in need of assistance, particularly poor minorities, however, do not live along these main thoroughfares. In many smaller cities and towns in these areas of Georgia and New Mexico, the typical social service agency is more than three miles away from neighborhoods with large percentages of blacks or Hispanics. Lack of access to service providers can be a formidable problem, given that 80 percent of providers in rural New Mexico and Georgia report inadequate transportation resources as a frequent or occasional barrier to service use. Often without access to reliable automobile transportation and with few or no public transportation resources, poor people in these segregated communities may have to walk up to five miles one way in some places to reach an agency.

FIGURE 9.4 / Access to Social Service Providers in Southeast New Mexico

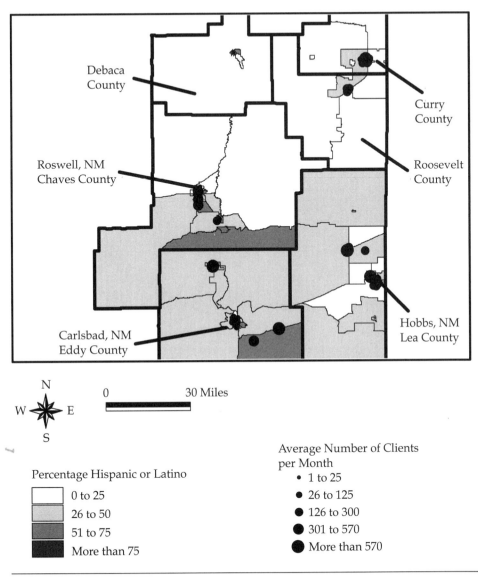

Debaca
County

Curry
County

Roswell, NM
Chaves County

Roosevelt
County

Carlsbad, NM
Eddy County

Hobbs, NM
Lea County

N
W ⬥ E
S

0   30 Miles

Percentage Hispanic or Latino

☐ 0 to 25
▨ 26 to 50
▨ 51 to 75
■ More than 75

Average Number of Clients
per Month
• 1 to 25
● 26 to 125
● 126 to 300
● 301 to 570
● More than 570

Source: Allard (2006b).

A snapshot of service provision in one New Mexico community highlights the challenges. A large county agency had just relocated to new office space in a more affluent neighborhood, on the opposite end of town from its previous location near one of the poorest barrios in its part of the state. Suitable space was hard to find in other parts of town and the new location provided more accommodating

FIGURE 9.5 / Access to Social Service Providers in South-Central Georgia

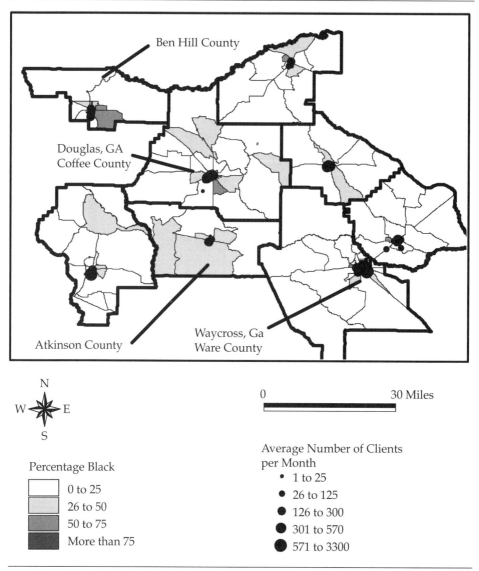

Source: Allard (2006b).

offices. Echoing comments that providers often made in each rural region, an administrator from a nonprofit community agency in the barrio that formerly housed the county agency explained it this way:

> A lot of people don't have a vehicle, for example, to come down [to receive assistance]. The fact that we have our offices in the barrio, for me that is a very positive

thing. However the [county agency] used to be located closer, and has now moved to another part of town. It's a problem for people because they have to walk a long ways. Most of the people on human services are from this area and they have to walk up there now. We don't have any public transportation.

At the same time that this county agency left, demand for assistance from nonprofits remaining in the barrio had risen due to increased housing and energy costs in the community. Highlighting the challenges that families who could not make it to the county agency might face in seeking help from local nonprofits, the administrator noted that agencies in that barrio were not able to accommodate additional demand. Resources for emergency or food assistance were depleted early each month. Later he remarked that his office would try to coordinate volunteers or staff with cars to help clients get to the county agency.

The maps in figures 9.4 and 9.5 also show that the remote communities outside of main population centers and away from clusters of service providers often have large percentages of racial minorities. Moreover, the poverty rates in these areas exceed 20 percent and are higher than remote areas with few minorities. The poor blacks and Hispanics in these rural areas, however, may need the most help and have access to the fewest labor market opportunities. For poor persons living even on the edge of a rural town or city limit, there may be no public transportation and walking into town is prohibitively time consuming. Even for those with access to automobiles, commutes to service providers may be anywhere from fifteen minutes to more than a half hour. Further complicating the dilemma, three-quarters of all service providers in the RSSSP indicated that inadequate access to child care was an occasional or frequent problem for clients making appointments and completing programs. In many of these communities, there may be no certified or licensed child care providers nearby to watch children while parents keep appointments.

With few transportation resources to offer poor clients, rural service agencies often rely on client resourcefulness to deliver services. Recognizing that many of his clients did not have access to a car or public transportation, but still managed to travel from outside the town limits to his office, one program administrator said, "They just get here. I don't know how they do it. But they do it." Another program manager operating in a rural New Mexico barrio repeated a conversation he frequently had with clients who did not have a car: "Don't worry [program manager], I'll get there somehow, I'll get there. . . I'll find a way, I'll walk, I'll ride my bike, I'll take the bus."

On the other hand, the great distances that many must travel may be too difficult even when clients are motivated. It is challenging to keep appointments when transportation depends on a combination of ingenuity, luck, and the reliability of others. The same program manager who discussed how clients promise to get to his office by any means noted, "Maybe 75 percent of the time they do make it. The other 25 percent, they lose out."

Navigating the geography of the safety net and social service providers is an everyday challenge. For low-income individuals in both urban and rural areas who cannot easily access social services, losing out when trying visit a social service agency can translate into being sanctioned by a welfare-to-work office, falling behind in an already-demanding adult education course, missing the one day a month that a church hands out emergency food boxes, or failing to get needed health treatment. In the end, the price of living in a segregated and isolated community is not just the difficulty of accessing economic opportunities. It is also the challenge of accessing the safety net resources that are supposed to set people on better economic trajectories.

CONCLUSION

The expansion of social service programs in the last forty years has transformed the way communities and the safety net help low-income populations. In contrast to popular impressions, expenditures for social service programs that address barriers to employment and obstacles to personal well being are at least as large as total expenditures for more commonly identified cash assistance programs. Delivered by thousands of local governmental and nonprofit agencies, social service programs have become a primary vehicle for antipoverty assistance in America today.

This shift in the safety net and antipoverty assistance has a number of implications for scholarship on race, place, and poverty, as well as for practice and policy. Of primary importance is ensuring that the poor have adequate access to social service programs and providers. Unlike other forms of person-based assistance, service provision varies by place and services are not entitlements. Not all neighborhoods are home to the same bundle of service agencies.

As shown here, living in a neighborhood highly segregated by race diminishes one's access to the social service agencies that are an increasingly important part of the contemporary safety net. I document that a poor person living in a predominately black or Hispanic neighborhood will have access to roughly half as many social services as a poor person living in a predominately white neighborhood. For many poor minorities in highly segregated communities, disparities in access to social services are even larger.

Racial disparities in access to support services combine with existing mismatches and discrimination in the labor market to create more formidable obstacles to finding and keeping a job. Inadequate access to job training and adult education programs reinforce the poor quality of public schools in many low-income areas to further increase the barriers to self-sufficiency and economic advancement. Despite the prevalence of mental health and substance abuse problems in poor rural and urban areas, most poor communities and poor minorities have access to few program resources to address such problems. Poverty, inequality, and joblessness therefore persist in highly segregated and high-poverty communities. Policy tools and safety net programs developed to alleviate social problems are not readily accessible to the populations most in need, a mismatch that reinforces the structural and individual-level barriers that poor persons, particularly poor minorities, face.

Why are there these disparities and inequalities in access to social services across tracts with different racial make-ups? First, just like residents of high poverty segregated communities seeking quality affordable housing, service agencies may struggle to find suitable office space. Second, many service providers may choose to locate away from concentrated poverty to reduce the isolation of clients and to help clients avoid potential negative influences of those neighborhoods, at least temporarily. For example, employment service agencies may choose to locate near employers, which are located increasingly farther away from low-income central city areas. Racial discrimination also may play a role. Whether out of personal preferences or concerns about losing other tenants, it is possible that some landlords and commercial property owners are hesitant to rent to agencies that primarily serve racial minorities.

Mismatches also exist because the supply of services in high poverty neighborhoods falls short of demand for assistance. If these access scores are accurate, it appears we commit inadequate public and private resources to social service programs in relation to the levels of demand for help. Moreover, government service programs and contracts often do not require organizations to locate in specific areas or communities. To the extent that nonprofit service organizations or contractors are not proximate to concentrations of low-income minorities, public program dollars may not be as equitably targeted by race as we might think. As is the case in understanding patterns of residential segregation, it is likely that government policies contribute to some of the race group disparities observed here.

The changing geography of poverty in America also has implications for the safety net. In an era when geographic mobility among poor and nonpoor households has steadily increased, government funding for a wide range of social service and antipoverty programs remains siloed within municipal or county jurisdictions. Assistance is often limited to those who live within those boundaries, despite the fact that poor persons are living, working, and commuting across many jurisdictions in a given day. In effect, the safety net remains predicated on the limited mobility of the poor and the concentration of poverty within municipal boundaries. As greater numbers of the poor move away from high-poverty neighborhoods and the central city, it will not take long before the demand for social assistance in lower poverty and suburban areas exceeds the ability of those communities to provide. Working poor families moving to lower poverty areas will still need assistance finding work, keeping jobs, making it through temporary loss of work, and advancing into better jobs. Suburban communities currently provide assistance that is reasonably well matched to need, but there are few public or private resources for additional programming.

Even the movement of a small percentage of poor persons from central cities to suburban areas will lower service accessibility in suburban communities substantially. Moreover, agencies that remain in central cities may find it difficult to stay in operation given the changes in their surrounding communities. In an ironic twist, therefore, poor minorities remaining in high-poverty central city neighbor-hoods may have access to even fewer service opportunities in the wake of the de-centralization of poverty. Unless communities begin to address the connections between the safety net and the geography of poverty, it is likely that safety net programs will become less able to address the future needs of low-income popu-lations, regardless of where they live.

In addition, rural areas may face additional challenges to connecting the poor to the safety net. More than one-third of service agencies in rural New Mexico and Georgia report that inadequate access to transportation resources and lack of af-fordable child are frequent obstacles to service receipt, which will compound the challenges that distance to agencies poses. In addition, the nonprofit sectors in many high-poverty rural communities are not as well developed as those in the three urban communities of the MSSSP. Rural service providers have fewer re-sources than their urban counterparts overall, but the communities in the RSSSP depend much more heavily on government service providers than those in the MSSSP do. Poorly resourced rural nonprofit service sectors should translate into fewer programs and fewer partners for government programs looking to contract out services or seek grants. It is not surprising, therefore, that many rural commu-nities in the RSSSP do not provide critical employment, mental health, or sub-stance abuse services necessary to help poor persons trying to become more self-sufficient.

Even with all these concerns, social service programs in urban and rural areas receive only modest attention from poverty researchers. A host of important re-search questions relating to the challenges communities and agencies face when delivering social service programs go unanswered. Program effectiveness and ef-ficiency likely suffer because we devote so little attention to implementing social service programs. In addition, scholars might think about better ways to capture the opportunity structures that more accurately capture the environment in which low-income households live, work, raise their children, and attach to community organizations. This chapter generates initial insight into issues of service accessi-bility, but future research might go further and develop more precise measures of access, including those that take program quality into account. To see how access matters to individual-level outcomes, we need to examine the needs of working poor families and the factors shaping the use of services that address those needs. Finally, to permit meaningful comparisons across communities, we could pursue data collection efforts that are geographically representative of several rural re-gions or metropolitan areas and would allow us to assess the spatial dimensions of the social service sector.

As future research continues to explore patterns of service accessibility and use, policy makers and community leaders might consider a number of policy options to reduce mismatches and improve access to providers. Improved access to the safety net will hinge on building information technology systems that better link persons in need with community resources and service providers. More attention could be paid to the space and facility needs of service organizations. Efforts to provide agencies with a mix of technical assistance for facilities planning, data resources to aid facilities decision making, and access to financial resources that can help acquire or expand facilities may be particularly useful in closing mismatches. Initiatives to strengthen the service delivery capacity of faith-based and community-based nonprofits may be critical in increasing the availability of assistance to racially segregated communities because these organizations may be most likely to operate and be trusted in neighborhoods with large proportions of racial minorities. Another step would be to cultivate greater fundraising capacity to diversify nonprofit funding portfolios and increase their long-term stability. Beyond private giving, we would also do well to maintain our public financial commitments to social service programs. Cuts in public expenditures will increase the vulnerability of local nonprofits, the lynchpins of the contemporary American safety net. A retrenchment of social welfare programs, therefore, jeopardizes the very foundations of the safety net more profoundly than is commonly realized.

The disparities and inequalities in access to the social service components of the safety net would be unthinkable in most other contemporary social welfare programs. Although states vary eligibility and administration in many antipoverty programs, few implement programs that treat residents of the same community so differently from each other. Imagine the controversy if poor black or Hispanic families in one city received 75 percent less in food stamp assistance or a 75 percent lower Medicaid reimbursement rate than a comparable poor white family in the same city, only because the white family lived in a different neighborhood. The negative impact of such disparities on the health of poor black and Hispanic families would be striking. Yet such disparities exist in other critical service areas. Policy makers, advocates, community leaders, and scholars need to pay more attention to mismatches in safety net assistance to ensure that people seeking help get there, rather than lose out.

This project was supported by research grants from the Brookings Institution, Brown University, Department of Housing and Urban Development (HUD), University of Kentucky Center for Poverty Research, the RUPRI Rural Poverty Research Center, and the West Coast Poverty Center at the University of Washington, as well as support from the Institute for Policy Research at Northwestern University. The author would like to thank Eduardo Moncada, the RUPRI Community Information Resource Center, and Scott Bell at the Spatial Structures in the Social Sciences Initiative at Brown University for assistance with data preparation.

NOTES

1. Social services received initial support from Title IV-A of the Social Security Act (SSA) in the late 1960s. Eventually these funds were transferred to Title XX and then consolidated into the SSBG in 1981. Later, programs such as the Comprehensive Employment

and Training Act (CETA), Job Training Partnership Act (JTPA), and Workforce Investment Act (WIA) would fund tens of billions of dollars in employment services to low-income youth and adults. The CSBG, CDBG, and the Substance Abuse and Mental Health Services Administration (SAMHSA) have administered billions of dollars in grants and contracts to social service agencies. Medicaid also has provided states and communities with several billion dollars in fees and reimbursements for substance abuse and mental health programs in recent years.

2. CRS estimates of social service spending cited here exclude government expenditures on means-tested medical benefits, food benefits, and cash assistance.

3. Data on nonprofit employment and human service organizations come from the National Center for Charitable Statistics at the Urban Institute. These estimates include only organizations with National Taxonomy of Exempt Entities codes likely corresponding to provision of direct services. I exclude mental health and substance abuse service providers, housing and shelter, and civil rights or legal aid programs because it is difficult to discern which agencies within these categories are most likely to provide direct services to working age adults on-site or in an out-patient capacity.

4. Respondents were drawn from databases of governmental and nongovernmental service agencies constructed for each city or rural region from community directories, social service directories, county agency referral lists, phonebooks, and internet searches. Agencies were included in the study if they advertised programs for nondisabled working age low-income adults. MSSSP interviews in metropolitan Washington, D.C., included agencies located in the District of Columbia, as well as Prince George's County and Montgomery County in Maryland to the northeast and communities in northern Virginia—Alexandria, Arlington, Loudoun County, Fairfax County, and Prince William County.

5. Ideally, I would have data that links individual-level service utilization to information about service provision in the community surrounding that individual. Such data is not readily available. Few data sets contain precise information about social service utilization or contain enough observations in a given community to permit spatial analysis. Based on previously calculated job accessibility scores (see Allard and Danziger 2003), I compute city-specific service accessibility scores with data from the MSSSP as follows. First, I determine which nonprofit and government agencies currently are operating programs on site available to nondisabled working poor adults. Next, I total the number of clients served by all agencies or a particular type of agency located within three miles of each residential census tract (using tract centroid-to-centroid distances). To account for potential demand for services, I sum the number of individuals with income below the poverty line within three miles of each residential tract, and then divide the number of clients served by the total number of persons in poverty. Thus I calculate a set of demand-, distance-, and organization-weighted service accessibility scores as follows: $A_i = \Sigma(CS_i) \div \Sigma(P_i)$, where A_i is the initial access score for tract i. CS_i reflects the number of providers offering a particular service (S) to low-income adults within three miles of tract i, multiplied by the number of clients served in each agency in a typical month (C). To account for potential demand, I divide by the total number of persons living below the poverty line (P_i) within three miles of

tract *i*. To be able to compare tracts to each other, I divide this tract-specific access score by the average of that access score for the metropolitan area.

6. Among the four rural sites in the RSSSP, only the Georgia and New Mexico sites had meaningful numbers of poor minorities. The south-central Georgia site is made up of eight rural counties: Atkinson, Bacon, Ben Hill, Berrien, Coffee, Jeff Davis, Pierce, and Ware. The site in southeast New Mexico is a six-county region: Chaves, Curry, DeBaca, Eddy, Lea, and Roosevelt.

7. Although not shown here, service agencies locate similarly in the Kentucky and Oregon-California sites.

REFERENCES

Allard, Scott W. 2006a. Multi-City Survey of Social Service Providers (MSSSP). Providence, R.I.: Brown University.

———. 2006b. Rural Survey of Social Service Providers (RSSSP). Providence, R.I.: Brown University.

Allard, Scott W., and Sheldon Danziger. 2003. "Proximity and Opportunity: How Residence and Race Affect the Employment of Welfare Recipients." *Housing Policy Debate* 13(4): 675–700.

Berube, Alan, and Elizabeth Kneebone. 2006. "Two Steps Back: City and Suburban Poverty Trends, 1999–2005." *Living Cities Census* Series. Washington, D.C.: The Brookings Institution, Center on Urban and Metropolitan Policy.

Briggs, Xavier de Souza. 2005. "More Pluribus, Less Unum? The Changing Geography of Race and Opportunity." In *The Geography of Opportunity*, edited by Xavier de Souza Briggs. Washington, D.C.: The Brookings Institution Press.

Burke, Vee. 2003. *Cash and Noncash Benefits for Persons with Limited Income: Eligibility Rules, Recipient and Expenditure Data, FY2000–FY2002*. Report RL32233. Washington: Congressional Research Service.

Coulton, Claudia, Laura Leete, and Neil Bania. 1999. "Housing, Transportation, and Access to Suburban Jobs by Welfare Recipients in the Cleveland Area." In *The Home Front*, edited by Sandra J. Newman. Washington, D.C.: Urban Institute Press.

DeLuca, Stefanie, and James E. Rosenbaum. 2003. "If Low-Income Blacks Are Given a Chance To Live in White Neighborhoods, Will They Stay? Examining Mobility Patterns in a Quasi-Experimental Program with Administrative Data." *Housing Policy Debate* 14(3): 305–45.

Frey, William H. 2006. "Diversity Spreads Out: Metropolitan Shifts in Hispanic, Asian, and Black Populations Since 2000." Living Cities Census Series. Washington, D.C.: The Brookings Institution, Center on Urban and Metropolitan Policy.

Frey, William H., and Reynolds Farley. 1996. "Latino, Asian, and Black Segregation in U.S. Metropolitan Areas: Are Multi-Ethnic Metros Different?" *Demography* 33(1): 35–50.

Greenbaum, Robert T., and John B. Engberg. 1998. "The Impact of State Urban Enterprise Zones on Business Outcomes." U.S Census Bureau Center for Economic Studies Working Paper CES-WP-98-20. Washington: Government Printing Office.

Grønbjerg, Kirsten A., and Laurie Paarlberg. 2001. "Community Variations in the Size and Scope of the Nonprofit Sector: Theory and Preliminary Findings." *Nonprofit and Voluntary Sector Quarterly* 30(4): 684–706.

Hirsch, Arnold R. 1983. *Making the Second Ghetto*. Cambridge: Cambridge University Press.

Holahan, John, and Arunabh Ghosh. 2005. "Understanding the Recent Growth in Medicaid Spending, 2000–2003." *Health Affairs: The Policy Journal of the Health Sphere*. Web Exclusive. Accessed at http://content.healthaffairs.org/cgi/reprint/hlthaff.w5.52v1.

Holzer, Harry J., and Keith R. Ihlanfeldt. 1996. "Spatial Factors and the Employment of Blacks at the Firm Level." *New England Economic Review* May/June: 65–82.

Holzer, Harry J., Keith R. Ihlanfeldt, and David L. Sjoquist. 1994. "Work Search and Travel Among White and Black Youth." *Journal of Urban Economics*. 35(3): 320–45.

Holzer, Harry J., and Michael A. Stoll. 2001. "Meeting the Demand: Hiring Patterns of Welfare Recipients in Four Metropolitan Areas." Survey Series. Washington, D.C.: The Brookings Institution, Center on Urban and Metropolitan Policy.

Jackson, Kenneth T. 1985. *Crabgrass Frontier*. Oxford: Oxford University Press.

Jargowsky, Paul A. 1997. *Poverty and Place*. New York: Russell Sage Foundation.

———. 2003. "Stunning Progress, Hidden Problems: The Dramatic Decline of Concentrated Poverty in the 1990s." Living Cities Census Series. Washington, D.C.: The Brookings Institution, Center on Urban and Metropolitan Policy.

Joassart-Marcelli, Pascale, and Jennifer R. Wolch. 2003. "The Intrametropolitan Geography of Poverty and the Nonprofit Sector in Southern California." *Nonprofit and Voluntary Sector Quarterly* 32(1): 70–96.

Kain, John F. 1992. "The Spatial Mismatch Hypothesis: Three Decades Later." *Housing Policy Debate* 3(2): 371–460.

Keels, Micere, Greg J. Duncan, Stefanie DeLuca, Ruby Mendenhall, and James Rosenbaum. 2005. "Fifteen Years Later: Can Residential Mobility Programs Provide a Long-term Escape from Neighborhood Segregation, Crime, and Poverty?" *Demography* 42(1): 51–73.

Kling, Jeffrey R., Jeffrey B. Liebman, and Lawrence F. Katz. 2006. "Experimental Analysis of Neighborhood Effects." *Econometrica* 75(1): 83–119.

Lieberman, Robert C. 1998. *Shifting the Color Line: Race and the American Welfare State*. Cambridge, Mass.: Harvard University Press.

Massey, Douglas S., and Nancy A. Denton. 1993. *American Apartheid*. Cambridge, Mass.: Harvard University Press.

Mosley, Jennifer E., Hagai Katz, Yeheskel Hasenfeld, and Helmut A. Anheier. 2003. "The Challenge of Meeting Social Needs in Los Angeles: Nonprofit Human Service Organizations in a Diverse Community." Los Angeles, Calif.: University of California, School of Public Policy and Social Research, Center for Civil Society. Accessed at http://www.spa.ucla.edu/ccs/docs/challenge.pdf.

Newman, Sandra J., and Ann B. Schnare. 1997. "'. . . And a Suitable Living Environment': The Failure of Housing Programs to Deliver on Neighborhood Quality." *Housing Policy Debate* 8(4): 703–41.

Ong, Paul, and Evelyn Blumenberg. 1998. "Job Accessibility and Welfare Usage: Evidence from Los Angeles." *Journal of Policy Analysis and Management*. 17(4): 639–57.

Peck, Laura R. 2008. "Do Anti-Poverty Nonprofits Locate Where People Need Them? Evidence from a Spatial Analysis of Phoenix." *Nonprofit and Voluntary Sector Quarterly* 37(1): 138–51.

Peters, Alan H., and Peter S. Fisher. 2002. *State Enterprise Programs: Have They Worked?* Kalamazoo, Mich.: W. E. Upjohn Institute for Employment Research.

Popkin, Susan J., Bruce Katz, Mary K. Cunningham, Karen D. Brown, Jeremy Gustafson, and Margery A. Turner. 2004. "A Decade of Hope VI: Research Findings and Policy Challenges." Washington, D.C.: The Urban Institute. Accesed at http://www.urban.org/UploadedPDF/411002_HOPEVI.pdf.

Raphael, Steven, and Michael A. Stoll. 2002. "Modest Progress: The Narrowing Spatial Mismatch between Blacks and Jobs in the 1990s." Living Cities Census Series. Washington, D.C.: The Brookings Institution, Center on Urban and Metropolitan Policy.

Rogers, Cynthia L. 1997. "Job Search and Unemployment Duration: Implications for the Spatial Mismatch Hypothesis." *Journal of Urban Economics* 42(1): 108–32.

Salamon, Lester M. 2002. "The Resilient Sector: The State of Nonprofit America." In *The State of Nonprofit America*, edited by Lester M. Salamon. Washington, D.C.: The Brookings Institution Press.

Schram, Sanford F., Joe Soss, and Richard C. Fording, editors. 2003. *Race and the Politics of Welfare Reform*. Ann Arbor, Mich.: University of Michigan Press.

Schram, Sanford F., Joe Soss, Richard C. Fording, and Linda Houser. 2007. "Deciding to Discipline: A Multi-Method Study of Race, Choice, and Punishment at the Frontlines of Welfare Reform." *National Poverty Center* Working Paper Series #07-33. Ann Arbor, Mich.: University of Michigan Press.

Singer, Audrey. 2004. "The Rise of New Immigrant Gateways." Living Cities Census Series. Washington, D.C.: The Brookings Institution, Center on Urban and Metropolitan Policy.

Smith, Steven Rathgeb. 2002. "Social Services." In *The State of Nonprofit America*, edited by Lester M. Salamon. Washington, D.C.: Brookings Institution Press.

Smith, Steven Rathgeb, and Michael Lipsky. 1993. *Nonprofits for Hire*. Cambridge, Mass.: Harvard University Press.

Soss, Joe, Sanford F. Schram, Tom Vartanian, and Erin O'Brien. 2001. "Setting the Terms of Relief: Explaining State Policy Choices in the Devolution Revolution." *American Journal of Political Science* 45(2): 378–95.

Stoll, Michael A. 1999. "Spatial Job Search, Spatial Mismatch, and the Employment and Wages of Racial and Ethnic Groups in Los Angeles." *Journal of Urban Economics* 46(1): 129–55.

Sugrue, Thomas J. 1996. *The Origins of the Urban Crisis*. Princeton, N.J.: Princeton University Press.

U.S. Congress. House. Committee on Ways and Means. 1998. *1998 Green Book*. Washington, D.C.: Government Printing Office.

———. 2004. *2004 Green Book*. Washington, D.C.: Government Printing Office.

U.S. Department of Health and Human Services. Administration for Children and Families. 2006. "Average Monthly Families and Recipients for Calendar Years 1936–2001." Washington, D.C.: Government Printing Office. Accessed October 2006 at http://www.acf.hhs.gov/news/stats/3697.htm.

———. 2007a. "Characteristics and Financial Circumstances of TANF Recipients Fiscal

Year 2005." Washington: Government Printing Office. Accessed at http://www.acf
.hhs.gov//programs/ofa/character/FY2005/indexfy05.htm.

————. 2007b. "TANF Financial Data." Washington: Government Printing Office. Accessed
at http://www.acf.hhs.gov/programs/ofs/data/index.html.

U.S. Department of Housing and Urban Development. 2000. "Picture of Subsidized Housing in 2000." Washington: Government Printing Office. Accessed at http://www
.huduser.org/picture2000/index.html.

Von Hoffman, Alexander. 1996. "High Ambitions: The Past and Future of American Low-
Income Housing Policy." *Housing Policy Debate* 7(3): 423–46.

Wilson, William Julius. 1987. *The Truly Disadvantaged: The Inner City, the Underclass, and Public Policy*. Chicago, Ill.: University of Chicago Press.

Zedlewski, Sheila, Gina Adams, Lisa Dubay, and Genevieve Kenney. 2006. "Is There a System Supporting Low-Income Working Families?" *Low-Income Working Families* Series, no.
4. Washington, D.C.: The Urban Institute. Accessed at http://www.urban.org/upload-
edPDF/311282_lowincome_families.pdf.

Chapter 10

Punishment, Crime, and Poverty

Darren Wheelock and Christopher Uggen

The association between crime, punishment, and poverty has long been the subject of sociological and criminological investigation. Recent work has shifted attention to the role of criminal punishment in explaining contemporary trends in inequality (Clear 2007; Clear, Rose, and Ryder 2001; Pager 2003; Petersilia 2003; Pettit and Western 2004; Western 2006; Western and Pettit 2000). Despite the strides in this area, research linking racial disparities in criminal sanctions to different domains of inequality remains incomplete and largely segmented. For example, although studies have examined the impact of felon disenfranchisement on the democratic process (Uggen, Manza, and Thompson 2006), its impact on the voting patterns of racial and ethnic minorities has received less fanfare (for a notable exception, see Demeo and Ochoa 2003).

In this chapter we describe and explain how the role of formal and informal consequences of criminal sanctions may perpetuate racial and ethnic inequality. We contend that felony convictions and incarceration entrench individuals more deeply in disadvantage, with effects that ripple outward to affect larger communities. We offer a brief overview of the emerging literature that examines the consequences of criminal sanctions. Building on that work, we argue that criminal punishment forms a system of disadvantage that sustains and exacerbates racial and ethnic inequalities.

Our systems of disadvantage framework rests on the premise that individuals with felony convictions face a host of restrictions on their socioeconomic, political, and family life that should be viewed as interconnected rather than separate consequences of their felon status. These barriers conjoin for individuals and groups, contributing to both cumulative disadvantage for individuals and concentrated disadvantage for communities. As discussed throughout this volume, the persistence of poverty and inequality is largely due to its diffuse nature. In developing our thesis, we begin by asking whether and how criminal sanctions embed disadvantaged individuals more securely in poverty.

To be sure, communities may benefit when the criminal justice system removes violent and disruptive offenders. Public safety represents a delicate balance between demands for strict crime control and the just and equitable treatment of those accused of crime. Since the mid-1970s, the United States has embarked on a historically unprecedented program of racialized mass incarceration, with profound and far-reaching effects for communities of color (Bobo and Thompson 2006). Many observers now argue that the rate and severity of punishment levied on African Americans, in particular, far exceeds that needed to preserve public safety (Clear 2007; Uggen, Manza, and Thompson 2006; Western 2006).

Those at greatest risk of contact with the criminal justice system and criminal victimization—young black men—are clearly the most vulnerable to their deleterious consequences. Young African American men with low levels of education are far more likely than any other social group to be incarcerated (Western 2006), and to become victims of homicide or robbery (U.S. Department of Justice 2005; U.S. Department of Justice, Federal Bureau of Investigation 2004). The growing numbers of young black men with felony convictions and histories of imprisonment has led to an ever-increasing criminal class: a group excluded from the social institutions that may alleviate economic hardship and diminish further criminal involvement (Uggen, Manza, and Thompson 2006).

In examining how punishment may sustain racial and ethnic inequality, we focus specifically on the formal and informal consequences of felony conviction. Despite hopes and expectations that released prisoners and other felons will reintegrate into their communities, state and federal laws prohibit convicted felons from fully participating in social institutions that would facilitate this process. These formal laws and administrative regulations, collectively known as collateral consequences, exclude felons and ex-felons from social institutions such as the labor market, higher education, the political process, and public assistance. Informal consequences are equally salient in this regard, yet operate through complex social processes involving stigma and discrimination. Informal consequences suppress employability and occupational attainment (Western 2002; Western, Kling, and Weiman 2001), disrupt family ties (Uggen, Wakefield, and Western 2005; Edin, Nelson, and Paranal 2004; Hagan and Dinovitzer 1999) and impose debilitating stigmas (Pager 2003). Together, formal and informal consequences act to translate criminal punishment into a system of disadvantage. Just as rates of criminal punishment vary dramatically across racial and ethnic groups, so too do collateral consequences that ripple outward to affect the families and communities of those who are punished.

With hundreds of thousands of individuals exiting the penal system each year and even more receiving felony convictions, millions of individuals now face the difficult challenge of reentering society despite having low skills and meager

FIGURE 10.1 / Correctional Populations in the United States

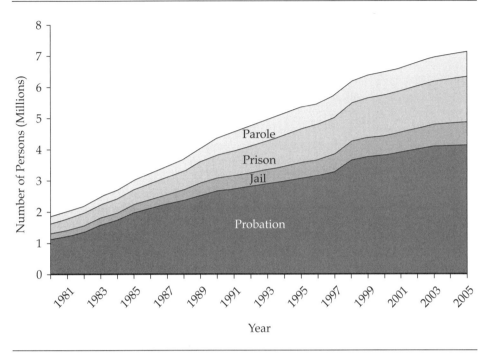

Source: Authors' compilation.

prospects for improving their economic situation. Children and caregivers must adjust to the removal of parents and the reduced household income from their diminished employment prospects when released (Wakefield 2007). Furthermore, the spatial concentration of released prisoners, and the probationers and parolees who remain under correctional supervision in their communities, engenders similar processes at the neighborhood level. Disadvantaged neighborhoods face the difficult task of reintegrating large numbers of released prisoners while dealing with the socially divisive impact of offending and victimization (Clear 2007).

RACE, POVERTY, AND PUNISHMENT

As many social scientists have noted, rates of criminal punishment in the United States have soared in the past thirty years. As shown in figure 10.1, all categories of correctional populations—prisoners, parolees, probationers, and jail inmates—have undergone dramatic increases. In 2005, some 7.1 million people were under some form of correctional supervision, relative to 1.8 million in 1980. Incarceration represents the most severe form of supervision and American prisons and jails now house more than 2.2 million inmates, an overall incarceration rate of 750 per 100,000 in the population (U.S. Department of Justice 2007). By comparison, the imprisoned population in 1974 was approximately 210,000 (U.S. Department of Justice 2003a). The number of probationers and parolees has grown rapidly as well. In 1980, there were only 1.1 million probationers and 220,000 parolees, compared to about 4.2 million probationers and 784,000 parolees in 2005. In short, more people are incarcerated and more nonincarcerated felons are serving sentences than at any other time in American history.

The increased use of imprisonment as a form of punishment marks what some scholars have termed the new penology (Feeley and Simon 1992). This era is characterized by a shifting punitive ideology of management over rehabilitation and increasing numbers of police, criminal defendants, and criminal justice expenditures. Perhaps its most distinctive feature, however, has been the increasing representation of African American men in prisons.

Racial and Ethnic Disparities in Criminal Punishment

The African American incarceration rate has increased so dramatically that the topic has generated voluminous research (Beckett and Sasson 2000; Blumstein 1982, 1993, 1998; Bobo and Thompson 2006; Chiricos and Crawford 1995; Steffensmeier, Ulmer, and Kramer 1998; Lusane 1991; Mauer 1999; Miller 1992; Myers 1993; Pettit and Western 2004; Sampson and Lauritsen 1997; Spohn and Holleran 2000; Tonry 1995; Western 2006). Figure 10.2 compares the racial and ethnic distribution of prisoners with the racial and ethnic distribution of males aged twenty-five to thirty-four in the general population. The prisoners are approximately 47 percent African American, 33 percent white, and 17 percent Hispanic, whereas the general population is approximately 13 percent African American, 69 percent white, and 13 percent Hispanic.

Young African American men are at the greatest risk of incarceration. In 2006, the incarceration rate for African American men was 4,789 per 100,000; that is, about 5 percent of all African American male adult residents were incarcerated in that year. The corresponding rate for white men is 736 inmates per 100,000, or about 0.7 percent of all white male adult residents. Based on these estimates, the rate of incarceration for African American men is more than six times greater than for white men. If current trends of incarceration continue, a Justice Department study calculates that the percentage of males born in 2001 who will go to prison during their lifetimes is 32 percent for African Americans, 17 percent for Hispanics, and 5 percent for whites (Bonczar 2003; see also Western 2006). These patterns are especially pronounced in some urban areas. Katherine Beckett and Theodore Sasson (2000) report that more than half of all African American men between the ages of eighteen and thirty-five are currently under criminal justice supervision in Baltimore and Washington, D.C.

FIGURE 10.2. / Race and Ethnicity of U.S. Prisoners Versus U.S. Males Age Twenty-Five to Thirty-Four

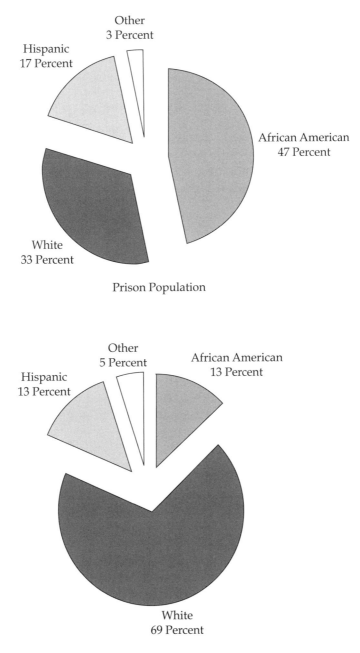

Source: Authors' compilation.

FIGURE 10.3 / Estimates of Incarcerated, Poor U.S. Residents Age Eighteen and Older

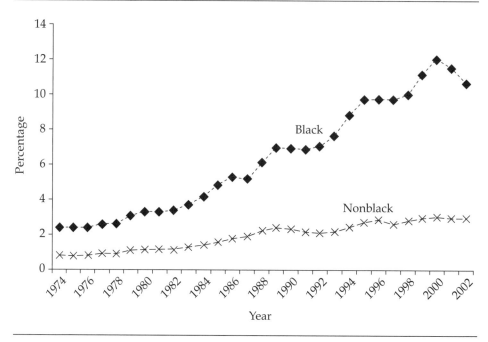

Source: Authors' compilation.

As Becky Pettit and Bruce Western (2004) pointed out, more African American men were imprisoned in 2003 than were attending college or serving in the military that year. Incarceration has become so commonplace among young black males that they liken it to a common life course event: "recent birth cohorts of black men are more likely to have prison records (22.4 percent) than military records (17.4 percent) or bachelor's degrees (12.5 percent)" (2004, 164). Figure 10.3 illustrates this pattern by plotting changes over time in the percentage of all poor African Americans and poor non–African Americans who are imprisoned. This graph shows a dramatic increase in incarceration rates for poor blacks, rising from slightly more than 2 percent in 1974 to more than 10 percent in 2002. The corresponding percentage for nonblacks is far lower, rising from nearly 1 percent in 1974 to close to 3 percent in 2002.

These trends are wholly consistent with Pettit and Western's (2004) argument that incarceration increases have particularly affected the less educated, the less skilled, and the poor. They estimated that 60 percent of African American men born in the late 1960s with no more than a high school education have a prison record by their mid-thirties. Considering these findings, it would be difficult to overstate the importance of social class, race, and gender as risk factors for incarceration. Although incarceration has also risen for men of other races and for women, the increases for these groups have been more modest and the initial base incarceration rates had been much lower. Not surprisingly, class disparities in imprisonment mirror those for racial and ethnic differences.

National incarceration data for racial groups other than whites and African Americans are sparse, making it difficult to detect national changes in the ethnic distribution of the incarcerated population. Nevertheless, the available information suggests that there are large ethnic disparities in incarceration, with Hispanic rates approximately 1.8 times those of non-Hispanic whites (Mauer and King 2007). Some sources of official criminal justice statistics provide estimates for Hispanics and combine all other racial and ethnic categories into Other. Unfortunately, this makes broad cross-race national comparisons impossible, though it does allow for comparisons between select ethnicities and races. It is also possible to observe trends in certain states for racial groups other than African Americans and whites.

There appear to be substantial ethnic disparities in incarceration between non-Hispanics and Hispanics, though the differences are smaller in magnitude than the differences between whites and African Americans. The Sentencing Project finds Hispanic overrepresentation in thirty-two of forty-one states for which data were available (Mauer and King 2007). A recent report from the Mexican American Legal Defense Fund (Demeo and Ochoa 2003) similarly concludes that Latinos were overrepresented among the convicted felon population in nine of ten states examined. This study found that adult Latinos are disproportionately represented in the convicted felon population in Texas, California, Florida, Nebraska, Nevada, New York, North Carolina, Arizona, and Washington.[1] Excluding those whose race was not reported in the most recent census of state and federal correctional facilities, approximately 46 percent of all prison inmates were African American, 36 percent white, 16 percent Hispanic, 1 percent American Indian or Alaska Native, and 1 percent Asian or Pacific Islander (U.S. Department of Justice 2003b). Additional research is needed, however, to determine whether the formal and informal consequences of punishment disadvantage other groups to the extent that they disadvantage African Americans.

Criminal Punishment and Social Class

Variation in criminal punishment, of course, is also linked to economic deprivation. It is virtually impossible to discuss the prevalence of racial and ethnic minorities in the criminal justice system without discussing crucial group differences in socioeconomic backgrounds. The U.S. Department of Justice regularly conducts a large, nationally representative survey of state prison inmates and occasional surveys of probationers and parolees. As shown in table 10.1, men and racial minorities are vastly overrepresented in these populations relative to the general population. For the most recent survey years, 94 percent of all prison inmates, 90 percent of parolees, and 79 percent of probationers were males. African Americans make up almost 50 percent of the prison and parole populations and

TABLE 10.1   /   Characteristics of Prison Inmates, Parolees, and Felony Probationers

	Prison Inmates			Parole	Felony Probation	Men Twenty-Five to Thirty-Five
	1974	1986	1997	1999	1995	1997
Education						
Years of education	9.9	10.9	10.7			
Percentage with high school diploma or GED	21.1	31.9	30.6	49.2	54.4	87.3
Employment						
Percentage full-time employed	61.6	57.3	56.0			77.0
Percentage part-time or occasionally employed	7.3	11.6	12.5			12.1
Percentage looking for work	12.5	18.0	13.7			3.9
Percentage not employed and not looking for work	18.5	13.0	17.8		7.0	
Sex (percent male)	96.7	95.6	93.7	90.1	79.1	100
Current age	29.6	30.6	34.8	34.0	31.9	29.7
	(10.0)	(9.0)	(10.0)			
Age at admission to prison	26.5	27.6	32.5			
	(9.3)	(8.7)	(10.4)			
Race						
Percentage black, non-Hispanic	49	45	47	47.3	31	12.8
Percentage white, non-Hispanic	39	40	33	35.4	55	68.9
Percentage Hispanic	10	13	17	16.1	11	13.2
Percentage other	2	3	3	1.2	3	5.0
Family status						
Percentage never married	47.9	53.7	55.9		50.8	40.4
Percentage married	23.7	20.3	17.7		26.8	53.0
Percentage with children	60.2	60.4	56.0			
Number of children	1.7	2.3	2.5			
	(2.0)	(1.7)	(1.9)			
Conviction offense						
Percentage violent	52.5	64.2	46.4	24.4	19.5	
Percentage property	33.3	22.9	14.0	30.8	36.6	
Percentage drug	10.4	8.8	26.9	35.3	30.7	
Percentage public order	1.9	3.3	8.9	9.0	12.1	
Percentage other	2.0	0.9	3.7	0.5	1.0	

Source: Adapted from Manza and Uggen (2006).
Note: Standard deviations for continuous variables in parentheses.

almost 30 percent of the felony probation population, as compared with 12 percent of the general population and 13 percent of the population aged twenty-five to thirty-four.

As the rate and absolute number of incarcerated persons have grown since the early 1970s, the composition of prisoners by offense type has also undergone important changes. Drug offenses, which had accounted for about 10 percent of the prison population in the 1970s, have increased sharply to more than 26 percent. Property offenders have declined from 33 to 14 percent, and the percentage of those incarcerated for violent offenses has declined from 53 to 46 percent. The relationship between offense type, socioeconomic status, and race-ethnicity is difficult to unpack. Minorities, particularly those in poverty, tend to be overrepresented as offenders in violent crime convictions, which receive the most severe penal sanctions (Hagan and Peterson 1995). Yet the increasing proportion of nonviolent offenders in the prison population suggests that differential offending patterns can no longer account for the persistent racial and ethnic disparities in penal sanctions for minority groups. Now more than ever, the poor and disadvantaged are disproportionately funneled into the penal system for both violent and nonviolent offenses (Western 2006).

Other trends in the data indicate that the average age of prison entry has risen steadily since the 1970s, with prisoners now averaging over thirty years of age at the time of admission. Despite their advancing age, however, prisoners remain socioeconomically disadvantaged relative to the general population. They have very low levels of education, fewer than 30 percent having received a high school diploma when interviewed in prison. Employment levels at the time of arrest have declined gradually since 1974, with a slim majority (56 percent) holding a full-time job before their most recent arrest in the 1997 survey. By comparison, more than 75 percent of males of comparable age in the general population held full-time jobs and 87 percent had attained a high school degree.

Based on these inmate surveys and self-reported income information, we calculated the percentage of prisoners falling below inflation-adjusted federal poverty guidelines at the time of their most recent arrest. We must caution that the inmate surveys do not include an independent verification of prisoners' self-reported income information and that these data are therefore subject to potential validity and reliability problems. Nevertheless, they are useful for showing trends in the percentage of inmates who report very low incomes. As figure 10.4 shows, the share of inmates that report being impoverished fluctuated between 40 and 60 percent in the past thirty years. Nevertheless, the total number of inmates in poverty has increased dramatically with the prison population, as shown in the dotted line of the figure. In 1974, fewer than 100,000 prisoners had been in poverty before their most recent arrest. In 2004, by contrast, that figure exceeded 600,000. The data thus suggest that prisoners have always been poor but that imprisonment is now, relative to thirty years ago, much more prevalent among those in poverty.

FIGURE 10.4 / Poverty Status of State Prison Inmates

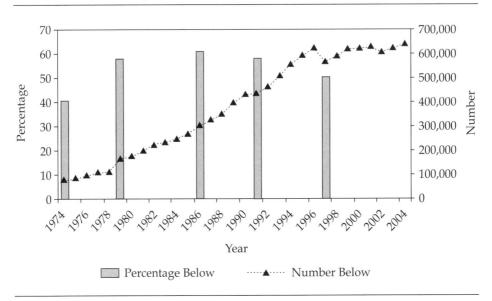

Source: Authors' compilation.

ACCOUNTING FOR DISPARITIES IN CRIMINAL PUNISHMENT

Scholars of social control, punishment, and criminal justice policy have attributed increases in the prevalence of imprisonment to numerous factors. State-level variation appears to coincide with homicide rates (Oliver and Yocum 2004). David Greenberg and Valerie West (2001) find that state-level incarceration growth between 1971 and 1991 is partly a function of violent crime rates. During the period of greatest prison growth, the mid-1970s to the late 1990s, however, crime rates were mostly stable (Blumstein 1998), suggesting a tenuous correlation between crime and punishment in the past thirty years. Rather, research has indicated that criminal justice policy during this era has become more sensitive to political factors than in the past (Stucky, Heimer, and Lang 2005; Jacobs and Carmichael 2001; Greenberg and West 2001; Beckett and Sasson 2000; Savelsberg 1994). The crux of this argument is that crime control is a highly charged political issue on which many candidates base their election campaigns. Such candidates may gain votes by calling for increased sentences (especially for drug offenders), repeal of parole programs, and mandatory minimum sentences (see, for instance, Mendelberg's 2001 account of George H.W. Bush's 1988 presidential campaign). Not only have get-tough arguments been immune from political criticism, but few economic limits have been imposed on punitiveness or public expenditures on punishment.

As previously mentioned, Malcolm Feeley and Jonathan Simon (1992) described these increases as part of the new penology, which includes the emergence of new discourses in punishment and new criminal justice objectives. These rationales emphasize management of threatening and dangerous groups rather than rehabilitation of individual offenders. Feeley and Simon further asserted that conceptions of dangerousness are, in large part, tied to a group's economic marginality:

> The underclass is understood as a permanently marginal population, without literacy, without skills, and without hope—a self-perpetuating and pathological segment of society that is not integratable into the larger whole, even as a reserve labor pool. Conceived this way, the underclass is also a dangerous class, not only for what any particular member may or may not do, but more generally for collective potential misbehavior. It is treated as a high-risk group that must be managed for the protection of the rest of society. (467)

Nevertheless, it would be careless to reduce all racial differences in criminal punishment to recent shifts in the structure of crime control efforts. Such a position disregards compelling evidence concerning group differences in criminal offending.

There have been numerous attempts to explain racial and ethnic disparities in the criminal justice system. Research frequently attributes some portion of recent disparities to changes in the prosecution and punishment of drug-related and other nonviolent offenses and the host of sentencing laws enacted during the early 1980s (Beckett and Sasson 2000; Blumstein 1998; Mauer 1999; Tonry 1995). Policies such as mandatory minimum sentences, three strikes laws, and sentencing guidelines have clearly increased the use of imprisonment in addressing crime in the United States. These legislative changes alone, however, cannot account for long-standing disparities that existed prior to such laws. At the risk of oversimplifying a large body of literature, we discuss two broad explanations for persistent disparities in punishment: differential rates of offending across these groups and differential treatment of racial and ethnic minority groups.

The basic idea behind the differential offending position is that social inequality or other factors lead a disproportionate share of racial and ethnic minorities to engage in violent and criminal behavior, which, in turn, explains much of the racial and ethnic disparities in imprisonment. Researchers have focused on various mechanisms through which deprivation leads to greater crime and violence, such as street credibility (Anderson 1990), residential segregation (Massey 1995), social isolation (Sampson and Wilson 1995), and social disorganization (Morenoff and Sampson 1997). The differential offending position is largely supported by official homicide statistics. These data clearly reveal higher rates of homicide victimization and offending among African American males relative to any other social group (LaFree 1995; U.S. Department of Justice 2004). During the early 1990s, homicide was the leading cause of death among young black men, at least 80 percent of whom were killed by other young African American men (Hagan and Peterson 1995). One oft-cited, albeit dated, study (Blumstein 1982) estimated that at least 80 percent of the racial differences in incarceration were due to differences in arrest rates (which were taken in the study as a proxy for offending differences).

Although Alfred Blumstein (1993) and others later reduced these early estimates, researchers continue to provide empirical evidence that differential offending plays a role in criminal punishment disparities (DeLisi and Regoli 1999; DiIulio 1994; Sampson and Lauritsen 1997).

In contrast, differential treatment explanations emphasize the role of discrimination in contributing to racial and ethnic gaps in punishment. A long line of research shows that African American and Hispanic criminal defendants are treated more harshly than their white counterparts by the police (Chambliss 1994), by judges (Hagan and Peterson 1995; Steffensmeier, Ulmer, and Kramer 1998; Spohn and Holleran 2000) and by parole and release boards (Myers 1993). One promising line of research explores the possible role of racial threat in penal policy. Originally conceived in intergroup conflict literature, the racial threat concept borrows heavily from Herbert Blumer (1958) and Hubert Blalock's (1967) work concerning discrimination and prejudice. Supporting notions of intergroup conflict, studies have found that net of crime rates, the percentage of African American residents is a significant predictor of crime control activities such as policing (Earl, Soule and McCarthy 2003; Jackson 1989; Jackson and Carroll 1981), incarceration (Greenberg and West 2001; Jacobs and Carmichael 2001; Myers 1990; Stucky, Heimer, and Lang 2005), and the death penalty (Paternoster 1991). Researchers have interpreted these findings as evidence that racial threat fuels punitive penal practices and in some cases, predicts the intensity of racial disparities in punishment as well.

Although a few sociologists and criminologists dogmatically adhere to either the differential offending or the differential treatment position, most today acknowledge that both factors help explain racial and ethnic gaps in criminal punishment (for a concise summary of this integrated perspective, see Hagan and Peterson 1995). To be sure, both factors interact in complex ways across time, place, and subgroup characteristics. While the explicit racial and ethnic discrimination in the criminal justice system of previous eras has largely been eliminated, many argue that it has been replaced with more subtle forms of discrimination. Although more difficult to detect, modern forms of laissez-faire racism (Bobo and Smith 1998) can also prove harmful to racial and ethnic minorities (Sampson and Lauritsen 1997). It is also plausible that discrimination plays an indirect role in offending patterns. Furthermore, African American men with criminal records are doubly stigmatized in the labor market (Pager 2003), and employment status is closely tied to recidivism patterns (Sampson and Laub 1990; Uggen 2000). Hence, labor market discrimination could plausibly account for some portion of the race gap in criminal offending.

Theory regarding social class differentials in criminal punishment also splits along the differential offending and differential treatment perspectives noted above. Since the advent of self-reported crime surveys in the late 1950s, criminologists have found relatively meager associations between socioeconomic status and self-reported crime, in contrast to arrest and incarceration data that show substantial differences (Braithwaite 1981; Elliot and Ageton 1980; Tittle, Villemez, and Smith 1978; Wright et al. 1999; Uggen 2001). Even now little consensus has been reached on whether economically disadvantaged individuals indeed commit more crime than other groups, or the extent to which this pattern could account for their overrepresentation in correctional populations. It is plausible that a large share of the class disparities in punishment stem from systematic biases that penalize the poor more harshly than the wealthy, rather than from disproportionate offending patterns. Theoretical approaches that integrate both perspectives perhaps best capture the origins of class differences in punishment. Nevertheless, it is an undeniable empirical fact that the lion's share of the prison population comes from extremely disadvantaged social circumstances.

IMPACT OF FELON STATUS ON FUTURE LIFE CHANCES

The expansion of criminal punishment is essential to our claim that current penal policies have maintained or exacerbated racial and ethnic inequalities. But punishment does not stop at the prison gates. As correctional populations have risen, so have the ranks of the formerly incarcerated, who continue to face the barriers that accompany their original conviction. In recent years, more than 600,000 prisoners have been released annually (Petersilia 2003) and more than 2 million probationers also leave supervision (U.S. Department of Justice 2004). Apart from the flow out of the system, the number of new convictions is also rising. In 2002, there were more than 1 million state felony convictions (U.S. Department of Justice 2003b). Forty-four percent of those convicted were African American, 54 percent were white, and the remaining 2 percent other racial groups. Approximately 81 percent of these convictions were for nonviolent offenses and about 31 percent resulted in probation rather than prison sentences.

Based on analysis of demographic life tables, Christopher Uggen, Jeff Manza, and Melissa Thompson (2006) estimated the 2004 population of former felons at 11.7 million, after accounting for recidivism and mortality. This estimate represents about 5.4 percent of the adult population, 9.2 percent of the adult male population, and 23 percent of the African American adult male population. After combining the number of current felons and former felons, the estimated total population is approximately 16 million (Uggen, Manza, and Thompson 2006). This is approximately 7 percent of the adult population and 33 percent of the adult African American male population. The criminal class includes millions of individuals with felon status who are now off-paper as they rebuild their work and family lives. Most important for our purposes, these individuals and their communities remain subject to the long-term consequences of felony convictions.

After release, prisoners re-entering their communities often face discrimination, low levels of human and social capital, and legal restrictions that affect their ability to earn a living and obtain basic necessities such as housing. There is little doubt that these barriers adversely affect future occupational attainment, labor force participation, and economic security. It is only recently, however, that researchers have begun to estimate the magnitude of punishment effects on the well being of individuals (Western 2006) and communities (Clear 2007). Current research has also begun to disentangle the impact of criminal sanctions from self-selection into crime in other arenas of social life, such as the family, educational attainment, and civic engagement.

FORMAL CONSEQUENCES OF CRIMINAL SANCTIONS

The millions who have been convicted of felonies have lost numerous rights and privileges due to provisions known as civil disabilities or collateral consequences. Researchers have begun to explore the origins of such limitations (Behrens, Uggen, and Manza 2003; Keyssar 2000), their implications for citizenship and democracy (Uggen and Manza 2002), their legal status (Behrens 2004; Damaska 1968; Love 2003; Snyder 1988), and their importance for social policy (Mauer 2002; Rubinstein and Mukamal 2002; Travis 2002). Overlooked, in our view, are the role of collateral sanctions in perpetuating and often exacerbating racial inequalities. These provisions disproportionately affect the socioeconomic and community standing of disadvantaged groups. They reduce employment prospects, erode civic participation, bar receipt of federal funding for higher education, and remove parental rights, with consequences falling particularly heavily upon the many poor and working class members of racial and ethnic minority groups.

We approach these issues with a conceptual framework presented in other work (Wheelock 2005) that packages collateral consequences as classes of restrictions. We view them as an interconnected system of disadvantage that amplifies disparities across diverse markers of economic and social well being. Although we initially conceived the systems of disadvantage framework to apply to legal restrictions, it could also be applied to the informal consequences associated with criminal convictions. Both formal and informal consequences of criminal punishment interact to block numerous avenues for upward social mobility. In this way, criminal punishment is one of the many social mechanisms that make movement out of poverty so difficult, in keeping with the cumulative disadvantage concept discussed elsewhere in this volume (see chapter 1). This approach allows us to discuss and describe the diffuse yet important role of punishment in broader patterns of stratification. Turning our attention to formal consequences, we distinguish three broad groups of restrictions: occupational, public aid, and civic. We briefly discuss each and provide an example of how such a restriction either maintains or worsens inequality for racial minorities and the poor.

First, work and occupational restrictions have perhaps the most direct impact on inequality in the labor market. This group of laws excludes individuals with felon status from holding specific types of employment either through outright bans or by disqualifying them from eligibility for occupational licensure (Dietrich 2002; May 1995). Some of these restrictions are clearly justified as public safety measures (for example, barring those who have committed crimes against children from driving school buses), but the list of restricted occupations spans diverse fields and activities. In New York, ineligible occupations include barbershop owner, boxer/wrestler, commercial feed distributor, and emergency medical technician (Samuels and Mukamal 2003). Table 10.2 provides a list of occupations restricted by statute in Florida, which includes acupuncturist, chiropractor, speech-language pathologist, and cosmetologist. It seems unlikely that all former felons could pose such a danger in these occupations that they should be categorically locked out as a group.

We do not suggest that every occupational restriction has significant implications for racial and ethnic inequality. In some cases, convicted felons may lack the human capital to seek such occupations in the first place. For example, it is unlikely that large proportions of individuals with felon status are pursuing positions as speech-language pathologists. Nevertheless, New York and Florida (both with very large released-felon populations) also prohibit individuals with felon status from less-skilled positions such as taxi driver, junk dealer, farm laborer, and even telephone seller (Samuels and Mukamal 2003). Furthermore, in light of the sheer numbers of felons and the broad scope of these restrictions it would seem plausible that lifetime occupational bans not only diminish offender reintegration and reentry, but also exacerbate racial and ethnic inequality in the labor market.

In addition, the federal government bars people with felon status from government positions. Census data indicate that African Americans are more heavily concentrated than whites in government sector employment (U.S. Census Bureau 2003), so felon restrictions on government work, again, exert a disproportionate impact on racial and ethnic minorities. In sum, there are significant direct impacts of occupational restrictions on stratification outcomes. To the extent that those with felon status are relegated to marginal work with little opportunity for advancement, there are long-term effects on socioeconomic status over the life course.

Public aid restrictions disqualify felons from government assistance because of their criminal records. This class of disqualifications includes eligibility for federal college loans and grants, welfare assistance, public housing, and military benefits. The consequences of these bans are most keenly felt in the critical months immediately following release from correctional supervision, when the likelihood of recidivism is at its apex (Uggen 2000). Few researchers have systematically examined the impact of these restrictions, but we can offer a preliminary look based on the impact of the 1998 Higher Education Act Reauthorization (20 U.S.C. 1091(r)). This federal legislation disqualified individuals with drug offenses (including nonfelony drug convictions) from receiving federal aid for higher education. Individuals with three possession convictions or two distribution convictions receive lifetime bans on receipt of federal education monies. We hypothesize that this single piece of legislation likely accounts for a nontrivial portion of the racial gap in educational attainment. Although no empirical study to date has estimated the magnitude of the impact, we can bring some preliminary data to bear on the question.

TABLE 10.2 / Occupations Affected by Employment Restrictions in Florida (ACLU)

Statute	Occupation	Statute	Occupation
F.S. 457.101	acupuncture	F.S. 481.201	interior design
F.S. 458.301	medical practice	F.S. 481.311	landscape architecture
F.S. 458.301	medical faculty	F.S. 482.001	pest control
F.S. 459.001	osteopaths	F.S. 483.101	clinical laboratories
F.S. 460.401	chiropractors	F.S. 483.30	multiphasic health testing centers
F.S. 483.825	clinical lab personnel	F.S. 483.825	clinical laboratory personnel
F.S. 461.001	podiatrist	F.S. 483.825	medical physicists
F.S. 462.01	naturopathy	F.S. 484.001	dispensing of optical devices
F.S. 463.001	optometry	F.S. 484.0401	hearing aid specialist
F.S. 464.001	nursing	F.S. 486.001	physical therapy practice
F.S. 465.001	pharmacy	F.S. 489.101	contracting
F.S. 466.001	dentistry, hygiene, and dental labs	F.S. 489.501	electrical and alarm system contracting
F.S. 467.001	midwifery	F.S. 489.551	septic tank contracting
F.S. 468.1105	speech-language pathologist, audiologist	F.S.490.009	psychological services and clinical
F.S. 468.1635	nursing home administration	F.S. 491.006	counseling and psychotherapy services
F.S. 468.201	occupational therapy	F.S. 492.105	professional geology
F.S. 468.3001	radiologic technology	F.S. 493.6105	private investigative, private security and repossessive services
F.S. 468.35	respiratory therapy	F.S. 112.001	public officers and employees
F.S. 468.381	auctioneers	F.S. 112.531	law enforcement and correctional officers
F.S. 468.401	talent agencies	F.S. 112.80	firefighters
F.S. 468.433	community associ- ation management	F.S. 494.0031	mortgage brokers
		F.S. 494.0061	mortgage lenders
F.S. 468.451	athletes' agents	F.S. 469.009	asbestos abatement
F.S. 468.501	dietetics and nutrition practice	F.S. 469.409	professional fundraising consultant
F.S. 468.520	employee leasing agency	F.S. 496.410	professional solicitors
F.S. 468.601	building code admin- istrators	F.S. 497.433	funeral and cemetery services
F.S. 468.70	athletic trainers	F.S. 501.605	telephone sellers
F.S.468.80	orthotics, prosthetics, pedorthics	F.S. 516.05	consumer finance
F.S. 469.001	asbestos abatement	F.S. 517.12	securities transactions
F.S. 470.001	funeral directing	F.S. 320.27	motor vehicle dealers
F.S. 470.001	embalming	F.S. 648.27	bail bond agents and runners
F.S. 470.001	direct disposition	F.S. 310.071	(boat) pilots

TABLE 10.2 / *Continued*

Statute	Occupation	Statute	Occupation
F.S. 471.001	engineering	F.S. 484.056	dispensing of optical devices and hearing aids
F.S. 472.001	land surveying and mapping	F.S. 476.024	barbering
F.S. 473.301	public accountancy	F.S. 477.012	cosmetology
F.S. 474.201	veterinary medical practice	F.S. 478.41	electrolysis
F.S. 475.001	real estate broker, salespersons, schools and appraisers	F.S. 480.031	massage practice
		F.S. 481.201	architecture

Source: Authors' compilation.

According to research by the National Center of Education Statistics, black-white racial gaps in high school completion and dropout have decreased in recent years, though racial gaps in college attendance and completion have either remained stagnant or worsened slightly (U.S. Department of Education 2001). College attendance rates for African Americans between the mid-1970s and the late 1990s remained 83 to 85 percent of white rates. The racial gap in college completion, however, has actually increased during this period, rising from 13 percent to 17 percent (U.S. Department of Education 2001). The 1998 Reauthorization has likely contributed to this widening gap.

A report by the U.S. Government Accountability Office (GOA) (2005) finds that more than 142,000 federal education aid applicants were ineligible due to a drug conviction for the 2001 to 2002, 2002 to 2003, and 2003 to 2004 academic school years alone. The report also found that approximately 100,000 applicants who would otherwise have received funding were denied on the basis of drug convictions, totaling at least $341,000,000 dollars in lost higher education assistance. Although we cannot determine how many of these individuals are minorities, it seems plausible that this practice disproportionately affects African Americans. Blacks are more likely than other groups to be convicted of drug felonies and more likely to rely on federal assistance to help fund college tuition and expenses (U.S. Department of Education 2001).[2]

In many states, those convicted of drug felonies also sacrifice their eligibility to receive public assistance (Allard 2002). Such disqualifications exact a heavy toll on felons in poverty and their families. Approximately two-thirds of female state prison inmates are mothers of minor children and 64 percent reported living with their children before incarceration (U.S. Department of Justice 2000b). Again, public assistance disqualifications exacerbate racial inequalities, because African American women face an incarceration rate over six times that of white women (U.S. Department of Justice 2000a). Although far more information is needed to assess the magnitude and significance of these effects, it is clear that public aid restrictions worsen racial and ethnic stratification.

Finally, civic restrictions such as felon disenfranchisement, jury exclusion, and disqualification for public office prevent individuals with felon status from fully participating as citizens. Felon disenfranchisement research indicates that excluding individuals with felon status has influenced recent senatorial and presidential elections (Uggen and Manza 2002). In addition, this body of work has drawn attention to the implications of restoring the right to vote for the successful reintegration of former felons (Uggen and Manza 2004). The impact of civic restrictions on racial and ethnic inequality, however, is likely indirect. It seems plausible that felon voting bans maintain inequality by quelling the political voices of the economically disadvantaged and socially marginalized. To some extent, restrictions on jury service and office-holding may also diminish the pool of otherwise eligible citizens and further dilute the political power of groups overrepresented in correctional populations. Community-level research on felon-jury restrictions provides an intriguing example of how collateral consequences exacerbate racial inequalities in the administration of justice.

Based on U.S. Census and Georgia Department of Corrections[3] (GDOC) data, Wheelock (2006) examined the community-level impact of rules that exclude felons from jury service on the racial composition of jury pools. Because almost 30 percent of all adult African American men in Georgia are felons, Darren Wheelock (2006) finds that jury exclusion rules dramatically shift the demographic composition of eligible jury pools. On average, 31 percent of African American men are excluded from juror service across Georgia counties due to a felony conviction, though the rate is as high as 70 percent in one county, Whitfield. As figure 10.5 shows, in sixteen counties, more than half of all African American men are excluded from jury service due to a felony conviction, including Atlanta's Fulton County.

These estimates might seem unreasonably high but they are consistent with recent research by Becky Pettit and Bruce Western (2004), which identifies incarceration as an increasingly common life event for many young African American men, especially those with low levels of educational attainment and bleak employment prospects.

This study demonstrates the profound community-level effects of legal restrictions on the composition of jury pools. Felon jury exclusion removes large portions of African American men from the pool of eligible jurors, calling into question the fairness of jury selection. The implication is that because black men are overrepresented as criminal defendants, they are also more likely to be excluded from participating in the administration of justice, which may ultimately contribute to their overrepresentation as criminal defendants. Pertinent to our broader thesis is that individuals with felon status are not only excluded from jury service, but from myriad other rights and responsibilities afforded to individuals without a felony conviction. Thus, one-third of adult African American men in Georgia are also unable to hold numerous occupations, receive many forms of public assistance, or engage in other activities afforded adult citizens.

FIGURE 10.5 / Adult Black Males Excluded from Juror Service in Georgia, by County

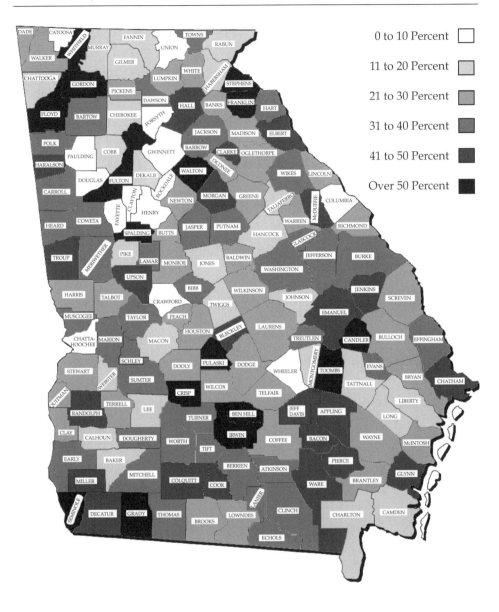

Source: Wheelock (2006).

FIGURE 10.6 / Criminal Deportations

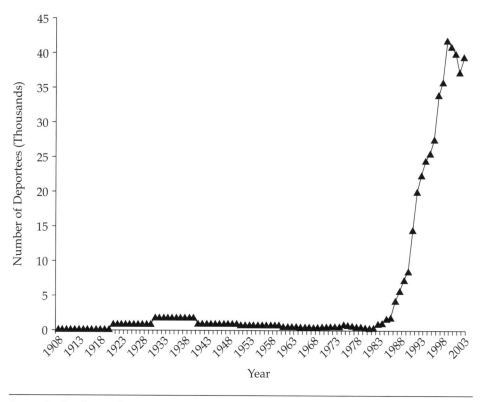

Source: Authors' compilation.

For noncitizens, the most serious civic consequence of a felony conviction is the possibility of deportation (Kanstroom 2000, 2005). Regrettably, many immigrants who agree to a guilty plea (typically in exchange for a reduced period of confinement) are never informed that they may face deportation as a consequence of their plea agreement (Ferster and Aroca 2005). In 2003, the U.S. Bureau of Immigration and Customs reported that of 11,317 immigrants held in federal and state detention centers, 10,763 had been convicted of criminal offenses and 1,725 had pending criminal cases (U.S. Department of Justice 2003a). The long-term trend in deportation reveals sharp increases in recent years. Figure 10.6 is based on decennial deportation data from 1908 to 1960 and annual information from 1960 to 2003 in U.S. criminal deportations (Immigration and Naturalization Statistical Yearbook, 1908-2003). Until the mid-1980s, there were fewer than 5,000 criminal deportations per year. By 1990, however, there were more than 8,500 such deportations, and by 2000, more than 40,000. Although many immigrants do not have the rights and privileges of American citizens, these deportations clearly affect the socioeconomic standing of the families left behind.

As the number of felons rises, collateral sanctions are likely to play an ever-larger role in racial and ethnic stratification, operating as an interconnected system of disadvantage. Given the high rates of felony conviction in minority communities and the expansiveness of collateral consequences for released felons, we expect these effects to ripple outward to affect nonfelons in these communities as well. When a significant proportion of a group is locked out of the political process, barred from jury service, and ineligible for public assistance and educational aid, the economic and political power of that group is correspondingly diminished. To date, however, research linking stratification and collateral sanctions is in its infancy, as even the most rudimentary descriptive statistics and summary counts are often unavailable. We now discuss a more mature line of research regarding the informal consequences of criminal sanctions.

INFORMAL CONSEQUENCES OF CRIMINAL SANCTIONS

In recent years, new research has begun to specify the informal effects of incarceration and felon status. One line of strong empirical research has estimated the effects of incarceration on future economic well being (Western 2002, 2006; Western and Pettit 2000) and life course outcomes (Pettit and Western 2004). These studies indicate that stints in prison significantly depress future employability and earnings. Other research suggests that imprisonment leads to family instability (Hagan and Coleman 2001; Lopoo and Western 2005). Despite low rates of marriage (18 percent in 1997), most inmates are parents (Wakefield 2007). Long periods of confinement away from family often erode whatever ties might have been intact before imprisonment. Devah Pager's experimental audit study convincingly demonstrates how a criminal record reduces employment prospects, particularly for African American men (2003). She finds that men with criminal records are significantly less likely to be called back when they submit job applications, with African American males effectively screened out of even entry-level employment. Such evidence highlights the important intersection of race and criminal convictions. The combined discriminatory impact of race and felon status thus locks many released felons out of the labor market altogether.

A body of related work examines the impact of criminal punishment with a different lens, focusing more intently on the experiences and understandings of young African American men, particularly those in disadvantaged inner-city housing projects. Alford Young (2004) provided insights into the strategies that those with criminal records employ to regain balance and control of their lives while embedded in disadvantaged communities. Of course, some communities house more than their share of the felon, ex-felon, and gang-involved populations. Work by Sudhir Venkatesh (2000) and Mary Pattillo (1998) sheds light on techniques that such communities employ to promote stability and security. As noted, we are only beginning to understand how the release of hundreds of thousands of former prisoners each year impacts socioeconomic well being at the individual and community level. To be sure, the judicious use of criminal punishment is vital to maintaining public safety. Nevertheless, Todd Clear (2007) and a rising chorus of scholars are beginning to show how extreme levels of concentrated incarceration has undermined the safety and security of the most disadvantaged neighborhoods.

Of course, it is difficult to disentangle imprisonment effects from the selection processes that lead to differential rates of incarceration. It could be the case that many convicted felons would remain disadvantaged even in the absence of their felony conviction. If this is true, then the impact of criminal punishment on racial and ethnic inequality would be negligible. A recent group of studies endeavor to address the selection conundrum. Studies have used experimental methods (Pager 2003; Uggen 2000), panel data models (Kling 2006; Western 2006), and propensity score matching (Massoglia 2005) to address selectivity effects. For example, Massoglia (2005) used propensity score matching to estimate sizable incarceration effects on mental and physical health at midlife, net of selection into incarceration. In other words, he found that individuals who have been incarcerated tend to have more mental and physical health problems later in life than their counterparts who have not been incarcerated. Such findings are consistent with our argument that criminal punishment maintains racial and ethnic inequality above and beyond the selectivity processes that lead individuals into disadvantaged circumstances.

Removal from the labor force, disrupted ties to families and communities, and social stigma all work to place released prisoners at the very rear of the labor queue and at the highest risk of poverty. Many return to their communities with few marketable skills, minimal education, splintered personal relationships with family members (Petersilia 2003), and few of the weak ties that nonfelons use to obtain employment (Granovetter 1983). Stable employment, so critical to successful reintegration (Sampson and Laub 1990; Uggen 2000), also remains elusive for individuals with a felony criminal record (Petersilia 2003). Former prisoners earn significantly less than those who were never incarcerated, though the absolute duration of imprisonment does not appear to exact additional wage penalties (Kling 2006). According to Western (2002), incarceration can reduce wages by 10 to 20 percent and reduce wage growth by 30 percent. In sum, criminal punishment not only decreases the probability of obtaining employment but it reduces future earnings. Prison and jail inmates lag the farthest behind their contemporaries in the general population, and probationers and parolees are somewhat better off socioeconomically. All, however, face challenges in rebuilding their lives after they have served their sentences. The implications of these informal consequences for racial and ethnic inequality are clear. They interact with formal criminal and collateral sanctions to restrict or shut down the standard avenues for socioeconomic success.

FIGURE 10.7 / Serious Violent Victimization by Race

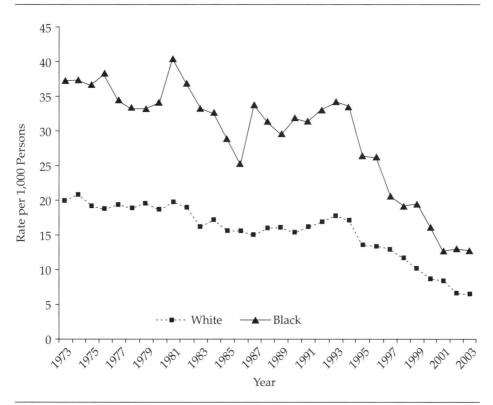

Source: Authors' compilation.

CRIMINAL VICTIMIZATION, RACE, AND SOCIAL CLASS

Although we have argued that punishment may sustain or worsen racial inequalities, it would be irresponsible to advance such arguments without also articulating the need to address the serious crime problems confronting disadvantaged communities. Crime victims as well as offenders are also more likely to be drawn from the ranks of racial minorities and the poor. Data from the National Crime Victimization Survey, for example, show widely varying rates of victimization across race and ethnicity. African Americans and, to a lesser extent, Hispanics, report being victimized at higher rates than whites and non-Hispanics, particularly for violent offenses. As shown in figure 10.7, African Americans report significantly higher rates of serious violent victimization (homicide, rape, robbery, and aggravated assault) than do whites (U.S. Department of Justice 2005).

Nevertheless, due to a declining rate of criminal violence, African American

FIGURE 10.8 / Violent and Property Victimization by Income, 2003

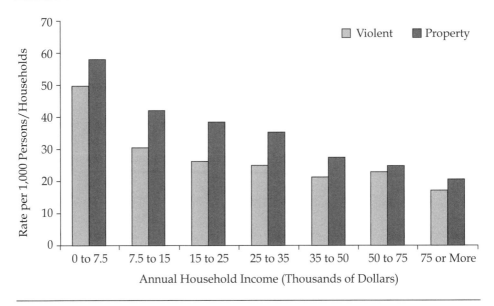

Source: Authors' compilation.

victimization rates for 2001 to 2003 are well below white rates from the 1970s to the early 1990s. Hispanics were victims of overall violence at about the same rate as non-Hispanics: Hispanic persons age twelve and older made up 13 percent of the population and experienced about 14 percent of all violent crime.

Criminal victimization is also stratified by socioeconomic status. Figure 10.8 shows rates of violent and property victimization by income categories. For both types of crime, the greatest victimization occurs among households earning less than $7,500 per year. The personal victimization rate of 49.9 per 1,000 households in the lowest income group is double that of households earning $25,000 to $35,000 per year and almost triple that of households earning greater than $75,000 per year.

Similar to criminal punishment, however, criminal victimization also has collateral effects. Ross Macmillan (2000, 2001) finds evidence that violent victimization, especially during adolescence, exerts long-term effects on psychological distress, future involvement in crime, and even educational and occupational attainment. In an analysis of National Youth Survey data, for example, victimization is associated with a $1 per hour wage reduction, net of gender, age, race, family structure, urban residence, family socioeconomic status, delinquency, and delinquent peers (Macmillan 2000). This effect appears to be driven, in large part, by diminished educational attainment and occupational status among crime victims. Any calls for scaling back criminal punishment must therefore be made with the public safety of disadvantaged communities in clear sight. We would argue that some

sanctions, such as voting restrictions for crimes committed decades earlier or restrictions on public assistance for those most in need, may be pared back without
in any way compromising crime control efforts.

CONCLUSION

We have described the relationship between criminal punishment and racial and
socioeconomic stratification. In doing so, we hope to have shown how criminal
punishment might act as a system of disadvantage that maintains and exacerbates
existing inequalities. We close on a programmatic note, calling for further research
on the impact of collateral sanctions on the communities and family members of
those convicted of crime. As punishment has risen in the past three decades, an
ever-larger proportion of minorities and those in poverty have become felons,
and hence subject to both the formal and informal consequences of felony convictions. As the data and literature reviewed make clear, the impact of crime and
punishment lingers long after these felons are released from supervision, either
removing or impeding their opportunities.

What policy interventions might be undertaken to reduce the impact of criminal sanctions on racial, ethnic, and socioeconomic inequality? We view the harsh
consequences of low-level and nonviolent convictions to be especially problematic. Permanently disenfranchising a young man who serves a year in prison for a
drug crime, for example, will diminish not only his political power but that of his
community as well. Sentencing reform in targeted areas, such as addressing the
disparity in penalties for possessing crack versus powder cocaine, will likely reduce racial disparities in criminal punishment (Beckett et al. 2005). More generally, reducing the scope and duration of criminal punishment for nonviolent offenses would reduce the size of the criminal class and the social deficits that
accompany criminal sanctions. With regard to collateral consequences, we suggest a thoughtful reassessment of the sanctions that sap the social, economic, and
political strength of the poor and disenfranchised. What public safety purpose is
served by the lifetime voting ban for former felons in Alabama? Or the lifetime restriction on obtaining a Florida cosmetologist's license? In such instances, pru-
dently extending basic rights—to work, to vote, and to participate in social life—
may reduce the deleterious impact of crime and punishment on inequality.

Increasing interest in the informal consequences of criminal punishment has
yielded an important line of research that informs much of this chapter. There is
far less attention paid to the impact of formal consequences, however, despite
their important role in maintaining racial and ethnic inequality. Future studies
must begin by cataloguing the restrictions and describing the number and social
distribution of those affected by jurisdiction. Even the most rudimentary information, such as the extent of employment restrictions by state, is often unavailable.
Future research and policy efforts would also be well served by examining the impact of legal restrictions across domains of disadvantage (civic, service and aid,
and employment). State-level analyses are well suited to testing hypotheses con-

cerning the impact of collateral sanctions, since there is great regional variation in these laws. For example, a future study might address the degree to which state occupational licensure restrictions account for racial inequality in employment and earnings. Until such gaps are filled, researchers are left speculating about the total effect of criminal punishment, even as it has become a modal life experience for recent cohorts of less-educated African American men.

We thank all the reviewers who helped us improve this chapter especially Alford Young, Ted Mouw, Kia Heise, Jeff Morenoff, David Harris, and Ann Chih Lin. We are also indebted to Kim Gardner, Heather McLaughlin, and Pamela Parnell for research assistance.

NOTES

1. The authors found that Virginia is the only state they examined that did not have an overrepresentation of Hispanics in the convicted felon population.
2. The National Center of Education Statistics found that people of color have the highest proportional need of specific state loans and grants, such as the Pell Grant, in order to attain education beyond high school (Riccobono 2000). In 1998 and 1999, approximately 3.8 million students were receiving Pell Grants. For both public and private four-year institutions, a greater percentage of minority undergraduates received Pell Grant funding than white students. In most cases, the percentage of minority undergraduates that received a Pell Grant was two to three times greater than for white undergraduates.
3. The GDOC data are a count of individuals that have either served a prison sentence or were sentenced to probation for a felony conviction since 1971 in Georgia, including all individuals under sentence that year.

REFERENCES

Allard, Patricia. 2002. *Life Sentences: Denying Welfare Benefits to Women Convicted of Drug Offenses*. Washington, D.C.: The Sentencing Project.

Anderson, Elijah. 1990. *Streetwise: Race, Class, and Change in an Urban Community*. Chicago, Ill.: University of Chicago Press.

Beckett, Katherine, Kris Nyrop, Lori Pfingst, and Melissa Bowen. 2005. "Drug Use, Drug Possession Arrests, and the Question of Race: Lessons from Seattle." *Social Problems* 52(3): 419–41.

Beckett, Katherine, and Theodore Sasson. 2000. *The Politics of Injustice: Crime and Justice in America*. Thousand Oaks, Calif.: Pine Forge Press.

Behrens, Angela. 2004. "Voting—Not Quite a Fundamental Right? A Look at Legal and Legislative Challenges to Felon Disfranchisement Laws." *Minnesota Law Review* 89(1): 231–75.

Behrens, Angela, Christopher Uggen, and Jeff Manza. 2003. "Ballot Manipulation and the 'Menace of Negro Domination:' Racial Threat and Felon Disenfranchisement in the United States, 1850–2002." *American Journal of Sociology* 109(3): 559–605.

Blalock, Hubert M. 1967. *Toward a Theory of Minority-Group Relations.* New York: John Wiley & Sons.

Blumer, Herbert. 1958. "Race Prejudice as a Sense of Group Position." *The Pacific Sociological Review* 1(1): 3–7.

Blumstein, Alfred. 1982. "On the Racial Disproportionality of United States' Prison Population." *The Journal of Criminal Law and Criminology* 73(3): 1259–81.

———. 1993. "Racial Disproportionality of United States' Prison Populations Revisited." *University of Colorado Law Review* 64(3): 743–60.

———. 1998. "U.S. Criminal Justice Conundrum: Rising Prison Populations and Stable Crime Rates." *Crime & Delinquency* 44(1): 127–35.

Bobo, Lawrence D., and Ryan A. Smith. 1998. "From Jim Crow Racism to Laissez-Faire Racism: The Transformation of Racial Attitudes." In *Beyond Pluralism: The Conception of Groups and Group Identities in America,* edited by Wendy F. Katkin, Ned Landsman, and Andrea Tyree. Chicago, Ill.: University of Illinois Press.

Bobo, Lawrence D., and Victor Thompson. 2006. "Unfair by Design: The War on Drugs, Race, and the Legitimacy of the Criminal Justice System." *Social Research: An International Quarterly of Social Sciences* 73(2): 445–72.

Bonczar, Thomas P. 2003. *Prevalence of Imprisonment in the U.S. Population, 1974–2001.* Bureau of Justice Statistics Special Report. Washington: Government Printing Office.

Braithwaite, John. 1981. "The Myth of Social Class and Criminality Reconsidered." *American Sociological Review* 46(1): 36–57.

Chambliss, William. 1994. "Policing the Ghetto Underclass: The Politics of Law and Law Enforcement." *Social Problems* 41(2): 177–94.

Chiricos, Theodore, and Charles Crawford. 1995. "Race and Imprisonment: A Contextual Assessment of the Evidence." In *Ethnicity, Race, and Crime: Perspectives Across Time and Place,* edited by Darnell Hawkins. Albany, N.Y.: State University of New York Press.

Clear, Todd. 2007. *Imprisoning Communities: How Mass Incarceration Makes Disadvantaged Neighborhoods Worse.* New York: Oxford University Press.

Clear, Todd, Dina Rose, and Judith Ryder. 2001. "Incarceration and the Community: The Problem of Removing and Returning Offenders." *Crime & Delinquency* 47(3): 335–51.

Damaska, Mirjan A. 1968. "Adverse Legal Consequences of Conviction and Their Removal: A Comparative Study." *The Journal of Criminal Law, Criminology, and Police Science* 59(3): 347–52.

DeLisi, Matt, and Bob Regoli. 1999. "Race, Conventional Crime and Criminal Justice: The Declining Importance of Skin Color." *Journal of Criminal Justice* 27(5): 549–57.

Demeo, Marisa J., and Steven A. Ochoa. 2003. *Diminished Voting Power in the Latino Community: The Impact of Felon Disenfranchisement Laws in Ten Targeted States.* Los Angeles, Calif.: MALDEF.

Dietrich, Sharon M. 2002. "Criminal Records and Employment: Ex-Offenders Thwarted Attempts to Earn a Living for Their Families." In *Every Door Closed: Barriers Facing Parents with Criminal Records*. Washington, D.C.: Center for Law and Social Policy.

DiIulio, John, Jr. 1994. "The Question of Black Crime." *The Public Interest* 117(Fall): 3–32.

Earl, Jennifer, Sarah A. Soule, and John D. McCarthy. 2003. "Protest Under Fire? Explaining the Policing of Protest." *American Sociological Review* 68(4): 581–606.

Edin, Kathryn, Timothy J. Nelson, and Rechelle Paranal. 2004. "Fatherhood and Incarceration as Potential Turning Points in the Criminal Careers of Unskilled Men." In *Imprisoning America: The Social Effects of Mass Incarceration*, edited by Mary Pattillo, David Weiman, and Bruce Western. New York: Russell Sage Foundation.

Elliot, Delbert, and Susan Ageton. 1980. "Reconciling Race and Class Differences in Self-Reported and Official Estimates of Delinquency." *American Sociological Review* 45(1): 95–110.

Feeley, Malcolm, and Jonathan Simon. 1992. "The New Penology: Notes on the Emerging Strategy of Corrections and Its Implications." *Criminology* 30(4): 449–74.

Ferster, Lucian E., and Santiago Aroca. 2005. "Lawyering at the Margins: Collateral Civil Penalties at the Entry and Completion of the Criminal Sentence." In *Civil Penalties, Social Consequences*, edited by Christopher Mele and Teresa Miller. New York: Routledge.

Granovetter, Mark S. 1983. "The Strength of Weak Ties: A Network Theory Revisited." *Sociological Theory* 1: 203–33.

Greenberg, David, and Valerie West. 2001. "State Prison Populations and their Growth, 1971–1991." *Criminology* 39(3): 615–53.

Hagan, John, and Juliegh Petty Coleman. 2001. "Returning Captives of the American War on Drugs: Issues of Community and Family Reentry." *Crime & Delinquency* 47(3): 352–67.

Hagan, John, and Ronit Dinovitzer. 1999. "Children of the Prison Generation: Collateral Consequences of Imprisonment for Children and Communities." *Crime and Justice* 26: 121–62.

Hagan, John, and Ruth Peterson. 1995. "Criminal Inequality in America." In *Crime and Inequality*, edited by John Hagan and Ruth Peterson. Stanford, Calif.: Stanford University Press.

Jackson, Pamela. 1989. *Minority Group Threat, Crime, and Policing: Social Context and Social Control*. New York: Praeger Press.

Jackson, Pamela Irving, and Leo Carroll. 1981. "Race and the War on Crime: The Sociopolitical Determinants of Municipal Police Expenditures in 90 Non-southern U.S. Cities." *American Sociological Review* 46(3): 290–305.

Jacobs, David, and Jason Carmichael. 2001. "The Politics of Punishment across Time and Space. A Pooled Time-Series Analysis of Imprisonment Rates." *Social Forces* 80(1): 61–91.

Kanstroom, Daniel. 2000. "Deportation, Social Control, and Punishment: Some Thoughts about Why Hard Laws Make Bad Cases." *Harvard Law Review* 113(8): 1890–935.

———. 2005. "Immigration Law as Social Control: How Many People Without Rights Does it Take to Make You Feel Secure." In *Civil Penalties, Social Consequences*, edited by Christopher Mele and Teresa Miller. New York: Routledge.

Keyssar, Alexander. 2000. *The Right to Vote*. New York: Basic Books.

Kling, Jeffery. 2006. "Incarceration Length, Employment and Earnings." *American Economic Review* 96(3): 863–76.

LaFree, Gary. 1995. "Race and Crime Trends in the United States, 1946–1990." In *Ethnicity, Race, and Crime: Perspectives Across Time and Place,* edited by Darnell Hawkins. Albany: State University of New York Press.

Lopoo, Leonard M., and Bruce Western. 2005. "Incarceration and the Formation and Stability of Marital Unions." *Journal of Marriage the Family* 67(3): 721–34.

Love, Margaret Colgate. 2003. "Starting Over with a Clean Slate: In Praise of a Forgotten Section of the Model Penal Code." *Fordham Urban Law Journal* 30(5): 1705–41.

Lusane, Clarence. 1991. *Pipe Dream Blues: Racism and the War on Drugs.* Boston, Mass.: South End Press.

Macmillan, Ross. 2000. "Adolescent Victimization and Income Deficits in Early Adulthood: Rethinking the Costs of Criminal Violence from a Life Course Perspective." *Criminology* 31(2): 553–87.

———. 2001. "Violence and the Life Course: Assessing the Consequences of Violent Victimization for Personal and Social Development." Annual Review of Sociology 27: 1–22.

Massey, Douglas. 1995. "Getting Away with Murder: Segregation and Violent Crime in Urban America." *University of Pennsylvania Law Review* 143(5): 1203–32.

Massoglia, Michael. 2005. Health Consequences of Crime and Punishment. *Ph.D. dissertation, Department of Sociology, University of Minnesota.*

Mauer, Marc. 1999. *Race to Incarcerate.* New York: The Sentencing Project.

———. 2002. "Mass Imprisonment and the Disappearing Vote." In *Invisible Punishment: The Collateral Consequences of Mass Imprisonment,* edited by Marc Mauer and Meda Chesney-Lind. New York: The New Press.

Mauer, Marc and Ryan King. 2007. *Uneven Justice: State Rates of Incarceration by Race and Ethnicity.* Washington, D.C.: The Sentencing Project.

May, Bruce E. 1995. "The Character Component of Occupational Licensing Laws: A Continuing Barrier to the Ex-Felon's Employment Opportunities." *North Dakota Law Review* 71(1): 187–210.

Mendelberg, Tali. 2001. *The Race Card: Campaign Strategy, Implicit Messages, and the Norm of Equality.* Princeton, N.J.: Princeton University Press.

Miller, Jerome G. 1992. *Search and Destroy: African-American Males in the Criminal Justice System.* Cambridge: Cambridge University Press.

Morenoff, Jeffery and Robert Sampson. 1997. "Violent Crime and the Spatial Dynamics of Neighborhood Transition: Chicago." *Social Forces* 76(1): 31–64.

Myers, Martha A. 1990. "Black Threat and Incarceration in Postbellum Georgia." *Social Forces* 69(2): 373–93.

Myers, Samuel, Jr. 1993. "Racial Disparities in Sentencing: Can Sentencing Reforms Reduce Discrimination in Punishment?" *University of Colorado Law Review* 64(3): 781–808.

Oliver, Pamela E., and James E. Yocum. 2004. "Explaining State Black Imprisonment Rates 1983–1999." Paper presented at the annual meetings of the American Sociological Association. San Francisco, Calif., August 14, 2004.

Pager, Devah. 2003. "The Mark of a Criminal Record." *American Journal of Sociology* 108(5): 937–75.

Paternoster, Raymond. 1991. *Capital Punishment in America.* New York: Lexington Books.

Pattillo, Mary E. 1998. "Sweet Mothers and Gangbangers: Managing Crime in a Black Middle Class Neighborhood." *Social Forces* 76(3): 747–74.

Petersilia, Joan. 2003. *When Prisoners Come Home Parole and Prisoner Reentry*. London: Oxford University Press.

Pettit, Becky, and Bruce Western. 2004. "Mass Imprisonment and the Life Course: Race and Class Inequality in U.S. Incarceration." *American Sociological Review* 69(2): 151–69.

Riccobono, John A. 2000. *1999–2000 National Postsecondary Student Aid Study*. Washington D.C.: National Center for Education Statistics.

Rubinstein, Gwen, and Debbie Mukamal. 2002. "Welfare and Housing—Denial of Benefits to Drug Offenders." In *Invisible Punishment: The Collateral Consequences of Mass Imprisonment*, edited by Marc Mauer and Meda Chesney-Lind. New York: The New Press.

Sampson, Robert J., and John H. Laub. 1990. "Crime and Deviance over the Life Course: The Salience of Adult Social Bonds." American Sociological Review 55(5): 609–27.

Sampson, Robert J., and Janet L. Lauritsen. 1997. "Racial and Ethnic Disparities in Crime and Criminal Justice in the United States." In *Ethnicity, Crime, and Immigration: Comparative and Cross-National Perspectives*, edited by Michael Tonry. Vol. 21, *Crime and Justice*. Chicago, Ill.: University of Chicago Press.

Sampson, Robert, and William Julius Wilson. 1995. "Race, Crime, Urban Inequality." In *Crime and Inequality*, edited by John Hagan and Ruth Peterson. Stanford, Calif.: Stanford University Press.

Samuels, Paul, and Debbie Mukamal. 2003. *After Prison: Roadblocks to Reentry*. New York: Legal Action Center.

Savelsberg, Joachim J. 1994. "Knowledge, Domination, and Criminal Punishment." *American Journal of Sociology* 99(4): 911–43.

Snyder, B. Steven. 1988. "Let My People Run: The Right of Voters and Candidates Under State Laws Barring Felons from Holding Elective Office." *Journal of Law and Politics* 4(3): 543–77.

Spohn, Cassia, and David Holleran. 2000. "The Imprisonment Penalty Paid By Young, Unemployed Black and Hispanic Male Offenders." *Criminology* 38(1): 281–306.

Steffensmeier, Darrell, Jeffery Ulmer, and John Kramer. 1998. "The Interaction of Race, Gender, and Age in Criminal Sentencing: The Punishment Cost of Being Young, Black and Male." *Criminology* 36(4): 763–97.

Stucky, Thomas D., Karen Heimer, and Joseph B. Lang. 2005. "Partisan Politics, Electoral Competition and Imprisonment: An Analysis of States Over Time." *Criminology* 43(1): 211–458

Tittle, Charles, Wayne Villemez, and Douglas Smith. 1978. "The Myth of Social Class and Criminality: An Empirical Assessment of the Empirical Evidence." *American Sociological Review* 43(5): 643–56.

Tonry, Michael. 1995. *Malign Neglect: Race, Crime and Punishment in America*. New York: Oxford University Press.

Travis, Jeremy. 2002. "Invisible Punishment: An Instrument of Social Exclusion." In *Invisible Punishment: The Collateral Consequences of Mass Imprisonment*, edited by Marc Mauer. New York: The New Press.

Uggen, Christopher. 2000. "Work as a Turning Point in the Life Course of Criminals: A Duration Model of Age, Employment and Recidivism." *American Sociological Review* 65(4): 529–46.

———. 2001. "Crime and Class." In *International Encyclopedia of the Social and Behavioral Sciences*, edited by Neil J. Smelser and Paul B. Baltes. New York: Elsevier.

Uggen, Christopher, and Jeff Manza. 2002. "Democratic Contraction? Political Consequences of Felon Disenfranchisement in the United States." *American Sociological Review* 67(6): 777–803.

———. 2004. "Voting and Subsequent Crime and Arrest: Evidence from a Community Sample." *Columbia Human Rights Law Review* 36: 193–215.

Uggen, Christopher, Jeff Manza, and Melissa Thompson. 2006. "Citizenship, Democracy, and the Civic Reintegration of Criminal Offenders." *The Annals of the American Academy of Political and Social Science* 605(1): 281–310.

Uggen, Christopher, Sara Wakefield, and Bruce Western. 2005. "Work and Family Perspectives on Reentry." In *Prisoner Reentry and Crime in America*, edited by Jeremy Travis and Christy Visher. New York: Cambridge University Press.

U.S. Census Bureau. 2003. *Statistical Abstract of the United States*. Washington: Government Printing Office.

U.S. Department of Education. 2001. *Educational Achievement and Black-White Inequality*. Washington: Government Printing Office.

U.S. Department of Justice. 2000a. *Women Offenders Revised*. Washington: Government Printing Office.

———. 2000b. *Incarcerated Parents and Their Children*. Washington: Government Printing Office.

———. 2003a. *State Court Sentencing of Convicted Felons, 2000 Statistical Tables*. Washington: Government Printing Office.

———. 2003b. *Census of State and Federal Correctional Facilities, 2000*. Washington: Government Printing Office.

———. 2004. *Sourcebook of Criminal Justice Statistics*. Washington: Government Printing Office.

———. 2005. *Criminal Victimization in the United States, 2003 Statistical Tables*. Washington: Government Printing Office.

———. 2007. *Prison and Jail Inmates at Midyear 2006*. Washington: Government Printing Office.

U.S. Department of Justice, Federal Bureau of Investigation. 2004. *Crime in the United States*. Washington: Government Printing Office.

U.S. Government Accountability Office. 2005. *Drug Offenders: Various Factors May Limit the Impacts of Federal Laws that Provide for Denial of Selected Benefits*. Report to Congressional Requesters. Washington: Government Printing Office.

U.S. Immigration and Naturalization Service. 1908–2003. *Statistical Yearbook of the Immigration and Naturalization Service*. Washington: U.S. Government Printing Office.

Venkatesh, Sudhir Alladi. 2000. *American Project: The Rise and Fall of a Modern Ghetto*. Cambridge, Mass: Harvard University Press.

Wakefield, Sara E. 2007. "The Consequences of Incarceration for Parents and Children." Ph.D. dissertation, University of Minnesota.

Western, Bruce. 2002. "The Impact of Incarceration on Wage Mobility and Inequality." *American Sociological Review* 67(4): 526–46.

———. 2006. *Punishment and Inequality in America*. New York: Russell Sage Foundation.

Western, Bruce, Jeffery Kling, and David Weiman. 2001. "The Labor Market Consequences of Incarceration." *Crime & Delinquency* 47(3): 410–38.

Western, Bruce, and Becky Pettit. 2000. "Incarceration and Racial Inequality in Men's Employment." *Industrial and Labor Relations Review* 54(1): 3–16.

Wheelock, Darren. 2005. "Collateral Consequences and Racial Inequality: Felon Status Exclusions as a System of Disadvantage." *Journal of Contemporary Criminal Justice* 21(Special Issue: Collateral Consequences of Criminal Sanctions): 82–90.

———. 2006. "A Jury of 'Peers:' Felon Jury Exclusion, Racial Threat, and Racial Inequality in United States Criminal Courts." Ph.D. dissertation, University of Minnesota.

Wright, Bradley R. Entner, Avshalom Caspi, Terrie E. Moffitt, Richard Miech, and Phil Silva. 1999. "Reconsidering the Relationship Between SES and Delinquency: Causation but Not Correlation." *Criminology* 37(1): 175–94.

Young, Alford. 2004. *The Minds of Marginalized Black Men: Making Sense of Mobility, Opportunity, and Future Life Chances*. Princeton, N.J.: Princeton University Press.

Chapter 11

Coloring the Terms of Membership

Joe Soss and Sanford F. Schram

Most studies of racial and ethnic inequalities focus on how discrete, measurable things get allocated across groups. "Who benefits," researchers ask as they examine the allocation of goods, "and why do some get more than others?" Such questions rightly lie at the heart of our collective effort to understand how inequalities persist and change. Yet they are not the whole of it. Disparities exist, not only in who gets more or less, but also in how social groups are positioned in relation to one another and major societal institutions (Tilly 1998).

In this chapter, we explore racial and ethnic disparities associated with recent changes in U.S. policies toward low-income populations. We focus primarily on welfare policy and, secondarily, on criminal justice. Likewise, our analysis centers on African Americans, though we consider the positioning of other groups intermittently. Our chapter is not a study of distributive disparities; it does not focus on who gets more or less and why. Rather, it is a study of civic disparities: it asks how recent policy changes position different groups vis-à-vis major institutions of the state, market, and civil society. Civic and distributive disparities are, of course, related. We focus on the terms of a group's societal inclusion partly because they are significant in their own right and because we assume that outcomes of the "who gets what, when, how" variety depend, at least partly, on how groups are positioned in relation to societal institutions.

In this respect, our analysis builds on a long intellectual tradition of conceptualizing civic and distributive disparities as two sides of a single transaction. This is the tradition of Jane Addams (1902), who viewed poverty as a combination of economic deprivation and social marginality, and who linked both to processes of assimilation in which denigrated "others" were told to act "more like us." It is also the tradition of scholars who have argued that poverty and inequality cannot be decoupled from the social question of solidarity (Heclo 1995), conceptions of social citizenship (Marshall 1949/1964), and processes of civic incorporation into societal institutions (Lieberman 2005). This tradition invites us to rethink the theme of this volume, racial and ethnic disparities, in terms of societal membership. Specifically, we ask: in the United States today, how do welfare and criminal justice policies organize governance and establish terms of membership in distinctive ways for different racial and ethnic groups?

Gosta Esping-Andersen (1990, 23) once observed that "the welfare state is. . . in its own right, a system of stratification." Its policies can classify and locate social groups in ways that disrupt or consolidate preexisting patterns of disparity. In what follows, we suggest that contemporary U.S. policies intersect with race in ways that promote uneven patterns of civic incorporation. To be sure, race is less decisive for civic incorporation today than it was in Jane Addams's time. Nevertheless, race continues to influence the kinds of societal institutions that individuals encounter and the kinds of institutional positions they occupy (King and Smith 2005; Brown et al. 2003). This interplay of race and policy has profound implications for the future of citizenship and democracy in the United States, and it deserves a central place in the study of how goods, risks, and opportunities are distributed across social groups in America.

In addition to raising enduring questions of membership, the theme of this chapter is also a timely one. In recent years, arguments over societal inclusion have risen to the forefront of welfare state politics. Across Europe, debates over civic inclusion have gathered momentum as governments have struggled to cope with immigration, economic integration, changing domestic populations, and the shifting relationship between economic disadvantage and social marginality (Blank 2003). The language of social exclusion now routinely frames European discussions of unemployment and welfare (Silver 1994). Labor activation policies are cast as ways to bring marginal groups into the societal mainstream, primarily by assimilating the long-term unemployed into the consistently working labor force (Handler 2004).

In the United States, the politics of welfare reform has followed its own politics of inclusion grounded in the new paternalism (Mead 1997, 2–3), a directive and supervisory approach to the poor that emphasizes the need to enforce civic obligations and present an appropriate "operational definition of citizenship" (Mead 1986, 7). Because the poor have failed to work and form families in the manner expected by "the societal mainstream," paternalists argue, effective civic incorporation requires new disciplinary policies that "tell the poor what to do" (Mead 1998). It is only by meeting the threshold requirements of full and equal membership—the civic minimum (White 2003)—that the poor can be incorporated as first-class citizens who deserve the rights, benefits, and privileges associated with that status.

When federal lawmakers passed the Personal Responsibility and Work Opportunity Reconciliation Act of 1996 (PRWORA), they sought to restate the rights and obligations of societal membership. PRWORA explicitly stated that citizens are not entitled to public aid and that work and marriage should be promoted as the "foundation of a successful society" (PL 96-104). It imposed new eligibility restrictions along civic lines, placing bars on minors (who lack the full civic standing of adults) and on noncitizen immigrants (Fix and Zimmerman 2002). The new Temporary Assistance for Needy Families (TANF) program imposed time limits and work requirements as conditions of aid and encouraged states to experiment with ways to assimilate the poor into a life of work and family (Winston 2002). Today, the TANF program is less about income support than about integrating the poor into mainstream institutions and behaviors. Work and marriage, valued by many in their own right, are treated in the program as stepping stones to full, self-sufficient membership in mainstream society (Edin and Kefalas 2005).

In what follows, we analyze the TANF program as just such a project of incorporation. On its face, the TANF program is a race-neutral policy that holds all recipients (with limited exceptions) to the same behavioral standards. It is an effort to integrate poor people—regardless of race or ethnicity—into a social order where women, including single mothers, increasingly engage in paid employment (Orloff 2001). In some respects, this is indeed the program's effect. In practice, however, welfare reform also operates in ways that generate civic disparities related to race, ethnicity, and immigrant status. As Joel Handler (2004) explained in his recent book on what he calls the paradox of inclusion, policies that aim to incorporate the poor into mainstream institutions may do so in ways that actually reinforce their status as second-class citizens. We suggest that the TANF program operates in this fashion and that its paradoxes are rooted in the complex landscape of race, ethnicity, and immigration in the contemporary United States.

We begin by tracing the historical relationship between U.S. welfare provision and questions of citizenship and race.

A HISTORY OF THE PRESENT: WELFARE POLICY AND CIVIC INCORPORATION

Welfare policy in the United States has always been entwined with the politics of race and ethnicity, class and gender, immigration, and citizenship. It has been debated and used as a tool of civic incorporation, and its implementation has both reflected and redefined prevailing terms of inclusion in mainstream society. Throughout this history, the civic consequences of welfare policy have depended greatly on the division of policy authority across—and the structure of relations between—national, state, and local governments (Lieberman 1998; Mettler 1998).

Mothers' Pensions were first enacted by states during the Progressive era, partly to reduce the number of children being placed in orphanages because their impoverished mothers could not care for them (Crenson 1998). Many of the reformers who championed these pensions did so explicitly in the name of republican motherhood, a woman's special civic duty and right to care for the next generation of citizens (Skocpol 1992; Gordon 1994). Republican motherhood, for these reformers, reflected the race-specific meaning of American citizenship that prevailed at the time (Smith 1997). White mothers were understood as the primary targets of assistance, and Mothers' Pensions were cast as a way to fight back the "race death" threatened by the growing numbers of immigrant families that reformers considered nonwhite (Berg 2002). Even so, Mothers' Pension advocates were typically the racial liberals of their time, emphasizing that race death could be avoided through civic incorporation. As Linda Gordon explained:

> Conservatives tended to view non-WASPs as irremediably inferior. Liberals tended to regard them as inferior in culture but potentially responsive to a socialization that could bring them "up" to "American" standards. . . . Mothers' aid supporters frequently spoke of building citizenship as one of the goals of the program, and they meant raising not only children but also mothers to that level. The supervision [of recipients] embedded in the mothers' pension plans aimed at raising recipients to "American" standards. (1994, 47)

Mothers' Pensions served as the policy vehicle for significant efforts to Americanize Polish, Irish, German, and Italian immigrant families, who made up a disproportionate number of recipients. Mothers' aid was more typically withheld from black and Latina women, either because their poverty was ignored or because they were considered undeserving. "Groups today regarded as minorities received only a tiny proportion of mothers' aid. . . . In Los Angeles, Mexicans were excluded from the mothers-aid on the grounds that their inferior background made it too likely that they would abuse it. Sometimes minorities were excluded from programs; at other times programs were not established in locations with large minority populations" (Gordon 1994, 48). Thus, Mothers' Pensions reflected a strange mixture of nationalism, maternalist politics, and racially disparate goals related to civic incorporation. These state programs became the foundation for more ambitious federal action in 1935.

The federally funded Aid to Families with Dependent Children (AFDC) program that ended in 1996 began as the Aid to Dependent Children (ADC) program, a minor element of the Social Security Act of 1935. The 1935 law produced a two-tiered system of welfare provision, with social insurance programs run at the national level and means-tested public assistance programs administered at the state and local levels. The two tiers divided along class, race, and gender lines. Social insurance disproportionately benefited the families of white male workers, actively excluding occupations heavily populated by women and minorities, such as domestic and agricultural workers (Lieberman 1998; Katznelson 2006). As a result, public aid programs controlled at the state and local levels became the primary source of aid for poor female-headed families who were more likely to include racial minority groups (Gordon 1994).

The subsidiary status of the ADC program reflected a particular combination of civic understandings and material interests. As Hugh Heclo explained, the 1935 law institutionalized a historically specific "settlement" to the social question: it gave civic priority to "the male breadwinner and the family dependent on his earnings;" it emphasized "security against income loss not economic equality;" and it identified "the nation-state as the appropriate arena" of social welfare for citizens in full standing (1995, 667–68). Exclusion from the national system of so-cial insurance meant being incorporated into the civic order on decidedly inferior terms (Mettler 1998). For African Americans, this exclusion had its basis in the racial caste system of the Old South. In the 1930s, southern congressmen and agri-cultural interests worked to ensure that public aid would not disturb the southern sharecropping system that relied on poor black families to work the fields (Lieber-man 1998). They sought and won federal aid programs that gave the states sub-stantial control over eligibility, benefit levels, and program rules.

In the decades that followed, southern relief workers offered black families only limited access to public aid, calibrated to the planting and harvesting sea-sons. As black women entered the rolls, some southern states shored up these practices by purging recipients for violations of "suitable home" rules and by in-stituting "employable mothers" rules "in areas where seasonal employment was almost exclusively performed by nonwhite families" (Bell 1965, 46; Piven and Cloward 1993, 134). Throughout the country, such practices in the ADC program contrasted with the broader move toward a rights-based system of national in-come support. But because poor black women were concentrated in the southern political economy, they dealt with the state through ADC programs that were markedly stricter and more focused on labor enforcement. Thus, the New Deal in-corporated poor black mothers into the welfare-state regime through an inferior channel that was segregated from national insurance, designed to support ex-ploitative labor relations, and governed differently than the ADC policies affect-ing most white mothers.

This program, later renamed AFDC, expanded dramatically in the 1960s, and again the politics of civic incorporation played a key role. AFDC expansion coin-cided with the tumultuous period in which racial minorities finally achieved meaningful citizenship in the United States (Quadagno 1994). Indeed, the timing was no coincidence. Changes in welfare access were part of a broad reconstruc-tion of the civic order that reflected the politics of race. The Voting Rights Act of 1965 joined the Civil Rights Act of 1964 and the Economic Opportunity Act of 1964 to form a new system of political, civil, and social rights for racial minorities. Expansions of public aid were spurred in part by black migration out of the South, a confrontational civil rights movement, and race-based changes in the electoral circumstances of the Democratic Party (Piven and Cloward 1974, 1977). State-level welfare expansion tracked closely with black insurgency and electoral power (Fording 1997). And, ultimately, the war on poverty was fought through a host of local conflicts that gravitated toward issues of Black Power, white privi-lege, and competing visions of how race would operate in the new civic order (Quadagno 1994).

This confluence of events turned a policy that had long been racialized in prac-tice into a policy that was also racialized in media coverage and in the public mind (Kellstedt 2003). As Martin Gilens (2003) showed, it was at this historical moment that "the poor became black"—not just nonwhite, but specifically black—in media coverage of poverty and welfare and in the perceptions of many Americans. In the years that followed, the Democratic Party became closely asso-

FIGURE 11.1 / Perceptions of Poverty and Welfare Policy as Important National Problems

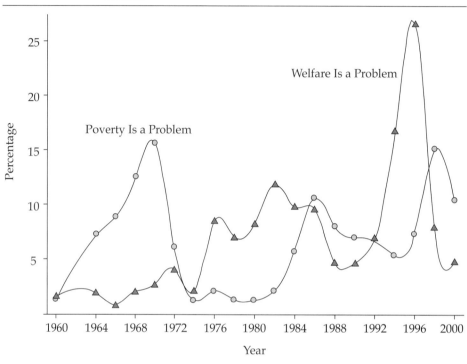

Source: American National Election Studies time series, 1960 to 2000.
Note: Lines indicate the percentage of respondents in each year naming poverty or welfare in response to the open-ended question, "What do you think are the most important problems facing this country?"

ciated with welfare for the black poor (Edsall with Edsall 1991), and attitudes toward blacks became a key predictor of white Americans' welfare policy preferences, partisan loyalties, and voting behaviors (Carmines and Stimson 1989; Kinder and Sanders 1996; Gilens 1999).

This racial context played an important role in the political run-up to welfare reform in 1996. Figure 11.1 shows the percentage of Americans who cited poverty and welfare when asked to name the most important national problems, 1960 to 2000. Few Americans focused on welfare as an important national problem before 1992 or after 1996. Concern about this policy spiked between 1992 and 1996, without a corresponding rise in concern about poverty. Kent Weaver (2000) outlined the crucial political role that this aroused public played in constraining liberal opponents of conservative reforms, raising the question of who was aroused.

Based on an analysis of panel data running from 1992 to 1996, Joe Soss (n.d.) found a striking pattern. The aroused segment of the public did not have distinctive demographic characteristics, political values, or partisan attachments. Rather, the Americans activated by the antiwelfare campaign came disproportionately from the subset of individuals who viewed blacks as lazier than whites. The perception of welfare as a major societal problem became more widespread and more closely tied to stereotypes of black laziness between 1992 and 1996. The mobilization and racialization of mass opinion rose and fell in tandem. Both were weak in 1992, shot up between 1992 and 1996, and dissipated after the passage of welfare reform.

Thus, despite the fact that reform advocates avoided explicit racial language, disparaging images of poor black women mattered greatly for the making of PRWORA (Hancock 2004). The campaign for reform emphasized deviance from civic norms regarding work, sex, and marriage. Reformers called for a more paternalist approach that would require and encourage more mainstream behavior (Weaver 2000). Although the issue of race was rarely explicit, such us-compared-to-them arguments tended to carry a racial subtext because so many Americans identified welfare recipients with poor black women. When asked whom they thought of when they heard about someone on welfare in 1995, more than twice as many Americans named black women as any other group.[1] The significance of this fact is suggested by survey data on stereotyping. In 2000, 30 percent of Americans said they thought most blacks were lazy, 18 percent thought Hispanics were, and 7 percent though whites were (Fox 2004). In 2002, 42 percent of surveyed Americans said they thought most black women were sexually irresponsible, 29 percent thought Hispanic women were, and 18 percent thought white women.[2]

Nevertheless, it would be a mistake to view the racial politics of welfare reform solely in black-white terms. Although stereotypes of Hispanics have a less robust relationship to public welfare attitudes, there is evidence that they were a significant influence on white welfare attitudes in the 1990s (Fox 2004). Moreover, concerns about immigration helped fuel the campaign for reform. Ultimately, immigrants—usually but not always presumed to be Hispanic—were singled out for some of the toughest policy changes passed in 1996.

Between 1980 and 2000, the number of foreign-born people in the United States more than doubled, rising from an estimated 14.1 million to 31.1 million (Tumlin and Zimmerman 2003). This growth was accompanied by rising concerns about how to assimilate immigrants from Latin America and Southeast Asia and by anxieties that U.S. welfare benefits might serve as a magnet for poor people from these parts of the world (Borjas and Hilton 1996). When welfare reform came in 1996, it drew a bright line between citizens and noncitizens. PRWORA barred future legal immigrants arriving after the law's passage from receiving Medicaid, Food Stamps, Supplemental Security Income, and TANF benefits, lifting this ban only after citizenship was gained. The law allowed states to choose whether to offer federally funded Medicaid and TANF benefits to "pre-enactment" noncitizen immigrants; it offered Food Stamps only if these immigrants were over age sixty-five, under eighteen, or became disabled. The Congressional Budget Office (1996, 27) estimated that almost half of the $54 billion savings initially attributed to the welfare reform bill could be traced directly to restrictions on immigrant use of welfare.

In this manner, PRWORA carried forward a long tradition in U.S. welfare politics. It reflected the enduring complexity of civic understandings rooted in behavioral expectations, nativity, class, gender, race, and ethnicity. It also expressed the age-old hope that welfare policy could be used to incorporate poor and racially identified Others into the societal mainstream.

POVERTY POLICY AS A POLITICAL PROCESS

However much race may have contributed to the politics of welfare reform, PRWORA itself contained no race-specific provisions. Blacks, Hispanics, and Native Americans were not singled out for distinctive treatment. State programs were not made subject to racial standards of evaluation. PRWORA denied aid to many immigrants, but this action was based on citizenship rather than the race or ethnicity of the immigrant. PRWORA limited forms of aid that went disproportionately to nonwhites, and it put conditions on aid that nonwhite clients might have more difficulty meeting (Schram 2005). But the work requirements, family caps, and other restrictions were race-neutral in the law: they applied to types of behavior, not people. In short, if federal legislation was all that mattered, our analysis of civic disparities in the TANF program would be a short story focused on the temporary bans on immigrants prior to naturalization.

That is why it would be a grievous mistake for students of racial disparities to equate welfare reform with the federal law known as PRWORA. Welfare reform is best viewed as an ongoing political process. To understand how it generates or ameliorates civic inequities, one must follow its path down through a cascade of institutional choice points. The TANF program is a complex system of incentive and oversight mechanisms that traverses levels of governance. Its operation depends on the opportunities and incentives that federal lawmakers create for states, states create for local governing boards, governing boards create for service providers, service providers create for frontline workers, and frontline workers create for TANF participants.

In a system defined by policy devolution, outsourcing to private providers, and frontline discretion, clients who live in different locales can encounter radically different versions of the TANF program. Decentralized discretion can facilitate tailored policy solutions and dynamic local experimentation. No small benefits, to be sure. But as our brief historical review should make clear, decentralized discretion can also underwrite large differences in the treatment accorded to social groups. As Robert Lieberman noted, "the distinction between national and local control and the extent of decentralized bureaucratic discretion have been crucial in determining how social policy treats African Americans" (1998, 228–29).

PRWORA created strong incentives for state lawmakers to develop their TANF programs in restrictive directions. Block grants meant that states could save money by paring back services and benefits; they would have to foot the bill if they chose to be more generous. Federal rules also limited some state choices solely to restrictive options. Thus, states could shorten but not lengthen the sixty-month lifetime limit that federal lawmakers placed on TANF participation (unless they were willing to bear the full costs of the longer limit), and they could shorten but not lengthen the twenty-four-months before work requirements kicked in. Performance bonuses and penalties were designed so that states would have clear incentives to emphasize caseload reduction and work promotion. As the TANF rolls fell sharply in the late 1990s, the states reaped caseload reduction credits that eased the pressures of some federal rules. They also enjoyed surplus block-grant funds that allowed for greater investment in transitional supports. These credits and surpluses were short-lived, however, and the vast majority of states "used their new authority to limit access to social provision and, most especially, to shift the balance in welfare policy design from rights to obligations" (Mettler 2000, 26).

Given this context, it is striking that policy choices made after 1996 mainly served to reduce civic disparities related to immigrant status. Federal lawmakers told the states to choose whether noncitizens who arrived before the enactment of PRWORA would be eligible for federally funded programs such as TANF and Medicaid. All but Alabama opted to make this group eligible (Fix and Zimmerman 1999). Moreover, in response to the federal decision to bar postenactment noncitizen immigrants from receiving Food Stamps, Supplemental Security Income (SSI), TANF, and Medicaid, many states acted to provide at least a partial state-funded substitute (Zimmerman and Tumlin 1999).[3] Officials from states with large immigrant populations also urged the federal government to soften PRWORA's immigrant bans. Substantial forms of access to Food Stamps, Medicaid, and SSI were reinstated through federal laws passed in 1997, 1998, and 2002.[4]

Today, immigrants—who are disproportionately from racial minorities—occupy a position in the welfare state that remains inferior to that of full citizens. They confront more categorical bars to eligibility and are subject to more strenuous income-deeming rules that can render them ineligible for aid. Moreover, states that provide immigrants with greater access to TANF benefits also tend to reduce benefits more than other states (Hero and Preuhs 2007). Thus, immigrants occupy a distinctively inferior position in the TANF program, but it is one that arises from the original provisions of PRWORA in 1996; later policy choices primarily functioned to soften the immigration-based civic disparities created by the federal law.

When we turn from immigrant status to race and ethnicity per se, we find the reverse pattern. PRWORA made no overt distinctions along racial lines, but as states elaborated their TANF programs, their policy choices followed a racialized pattern. A number of studies have demonstrated the political nature of state policy choices under welfare reform, linking them to policy-maker ideology, levels of party competition, and class biases in voter participation (for example, Avery and Peffley 2005; Fellows and Rowe 2004; Soss et al. 2001). Across these studies, racial composition has emerged as one of the most consistent predictors of restrictive policies. Under TANF, states with more blacks and Hispanics in their welfare caseload have been more likely to impose strict lifetime limits on aid, family caps on benefits for women who have children while receiving aid, and tougher sanctions for noncompliance with program rules (Soss et al. 2001). The correlation between racial composition and restrictive state welfare rules extends back to policy choices made under the AFDC waiver system (Fording 2003) and out to policy choices regarding TANF eligibility rules and the degree of flexibility in state welfare-to-work requirements (Fellows and Rowe 2004).

The same racialized pattern appears for state choices to devolve TANF policy authority down to the local level. Local control of welfare policy is a key mechanism for civic disparities. It facilitates the application of different rules to different social groups (Lieberman 1998) in ways that can be calibrated to the needs of local employers and other elites (Piven and Cloward 1993). Thus, it is important to note that, under the TANF program, most states now allow important aspects of implementation to vary somewhat across local providers. Some states, however, have devolved more substantial control over policy and contracting down to counties or regional governing bodies (Nathan and Gais 1999; Gainsborough 2003). In recent research with Richard Fording, we find that such "second-order" devolution has been significantly more likely in states where African Americans are more prevalent in the population and more unevenly distributed across local jurisdictions (Soss, Fording, and Schram 2008). This pattern of local devolution is significantly less related to the presence of Hispanic populations.

To illustrate, figure 11.2 shows the predicted effects of a rising black presence on the welfare rolls for a hypothetical state with average values on all other variables included in the authors' regression models.[5] As the black percentage of the rolls rises across its observed range, so too do the odds that a state will devolve TANF authority to the local level, adopt a full-family sanction, impose strict time limits on TANF participation, and place a family cap on aid for children born to participants. Indeed, the magnitude of these effects is quite striking, with predicted probabilities for all four policy choices ending above .90. We find similar results for the presence of Hispanics in two areas—time limits and family caps.

Such patterns tell us little about policy makers' motivations. They could arise because lawmakers have acted on racialized images of welfare recipients. Or they could arise from aspects of institutional racism that have little to do with individuals' attitudes and beliefs. Or they could arise, not because of contemporary racial politics, but because of the different ways race has shaped political development in different states. One could list many possibilities. The key issue, for us, is not the presence or absence of racist motivation. It is the potential for state policy choices to generate disparities in the ways that social groups are positioned vis-à-vis the state.

Because the presence of African Americans has such a strong influence on state TANF policy choices, we find that black TANF recipients are consistently (and significantly) more likely than their white counterparts to participate under the four restrictive policy elements shown in figure 11.2 (Soss, Fording, and Schram 2008). That is, they are more likely to be participating in a state where no additional aid is provided for a child conceived by a TANF participant, lifetime limits on aid are set shorter than the federal requirement, noncompliance

FIGURE 11.2 / Effect of Black Caseload Percentage on Welfare Policy Choices in
Hypothetical Average State

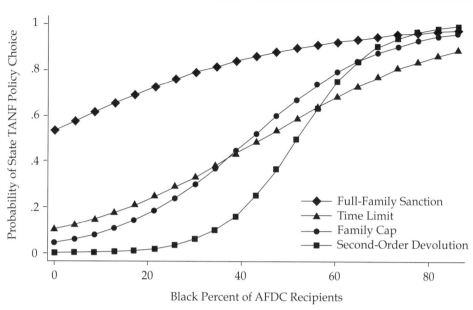

Source: Authors' compilation based on Soss et al. (2001); Fording, Schram, and Soss (2005).
Note: All variables, other than the black percentage of AFDC caseloads in 1996, were set to their
means for purposes of calculating average effects. For second-order devolution, state-level control variables include government ideology, AFDC participation rate, unmarried birth rate, unemployment rate, party competition, population per square mile, per capita tax revenues, increases in incarceration between 1990 and 1996, policy innovation score, class bias in voter
turnout, and Hispanic percent of AFDC participants in 1996. For the other three policies, state-
level controls include government ideology, AFDC participation rate, unmarried birth rate, unemployment rate, party competition, increases in incarceration between 1990 and 1996, policy
innovation score, lower-class voter turnout, and Hispanic percent of AFDC participants in 1996.

can generate a full-family sanction, and TANF policy is controlled primarily at
the local level.

Indeed, if we treat these four policies as constituent elements of the overall
TANF regime designed by each state, we find a remarkable pattern of black-white
racial disparity. The horizontal axis of figure 11.3 indicates how many of the four
TANF policies (shown in figure 11.2) that a given state applies: seven have none;
fourteen have one; fifteen have two; seven have three; and four have all four program elements. The bars on the left side of figure 11.3 show the average percentage black and white for clients in states with each regime type. White families average 69 percent of the caseload in states that have neither devolved TANF control
nor adopted any of the three restrictive rules, and black families average only 13
percent. As one moves to the right, toward the most stringent and devolved

FIGURE 11.3 / Cumulative Exposure to TANF Program Features by Race of Family, 2001

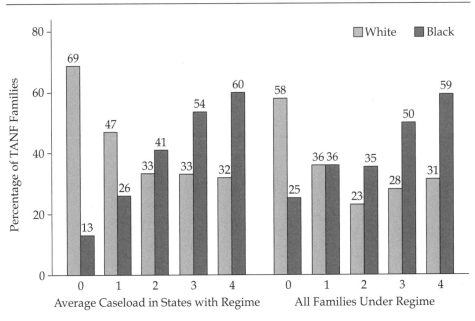

Source: Authors' compilation from Soss, Fording, and Schram (2008).
Note: Calculations are based on TANF caseload data from the U.S. Department of Health and Human Services for October 2000 to September 2001; state TANF policies are also for 2001 and are drawn from the Urban Institute Welfare Rules Database and Gainsborough (2003). Policy regimes are defined by the presence of 0-4 of the program elements shown in figure 3. All relationships shown here are statistically significant.

regimes, the white percentage falls as the black percentage rises. In regimes that combine the most restrictive rules with local program authority, whites average only 32 percent of the caseload and blacks 60 percent.

The right side of figure 11.3 extends the analysis to national patterns, addressing the question of what percent of all American families participating under each type of TANF regime type are white and what percent are black? Once again, the results are dramatic. Of all families participating under the most lenient regime type (0 of 4 rules), 58 percent are white and only 25 percent are black. This 33 point gap evaporates immediately as one looks to the right. Black families become more prevalent in a stair-step pattern, with the black-over-white gap rising from 0 points to 12, then 22, and finally 28. Of all TANF families participating under the most stringent and localized regime type, blacks make up 59 percent and whites only 31 percent. Here, we see a key dynamic related to racial inequality in the contemporary United States: large disparities emerge, not in the visible form of a single decision, but instead from the less visible accumulation of smaller differences.

Indeed, these differences continue to multiply as the operation of TANF policy moves down from the state to the local level. Under local program administration, racial equity in American welfare provision has often been sacrificed to the exigencies of local labor markets and political pressures (Gooden 2003). Contemporary evidence suggests this pattern is not entirely a thing of the past. A recent study of Missouri's TANF program, for example, found that black recipients were more likely to be sanctioned than whites in every county in the state (Keiser, Meuser, and Choi 2004). Moreover, as the black percentage of county residents rose, sanctioning rates rose as well—right up to a tipping point where counties with very large numbers of black residents (presumably capable of attaining greater political control) produced dramatically lower sanctioning rates.[6]

Our study of sanctions in the Florida TANF program, conducted with Richard Fording, offers further evidence of how race and place intersect in local welfare implementation. For white TANF clients, we found that the likelihood of being sanctioned has no significant relationship to whether the individual is participating in a liberal versus a conservative county. By contrast, for blacks and Hispanics, sanction rates are substantially higher in politically conservative locales than in politically liberal locales, even after controlling for other observable differences at the individual and community levels (Fording, Soss, and Schram 2007). Thus, under contemporary welfare devolution, it appears that local political contexts continue to matter greatly for the extent of racial and ethnic disparities.

Before moving on, one last point must also be made about disparities within the TANF program. Our discussion in this section has assumed that people participating under the same TANF rules are, in fact, similarly situated. This assumption is unwarranted, and it serves to understate the disparate positioning of social groups in the TANF program.

A race-neutral program that demands work first from everyone, and then evaluates and sanctions clients based on work-related outcomes, will predictably convert a group's labor-market disadvantages into program disadvantages. For example, as Georgia Pabst noted in the *Milwaukee Journal Sentinel*, policies that demand work first and offer little time or assistance for English acquisition have distinctive implications for immigrants ("Refuge is Not Quite Sanctuary: Bureaucracy, Language Barriers Leave Many Hmong in Frustration," August 1, 2005). Thus, although welfare reform ultimately did little to change the immigrant proportion of the welfare caseload,[7] Karen Tumlin and Wendy Zimmerman (2003) reported that this observation papers over critical differences: "immigrants are getting on welfare at lower rates than citizens" but they are "having a harder time getting off TANF because they face significant barriers to employment, are less likely to work while on TANF, and are often the last ones "called up' for the remaining employment services available under TANF" (2003, 7). Similarly, Sanford Schram (2005) reviewed evidence that racial differences in access to education, job openings, and social capital make it harder for nonwhite clients to meet work requirements and to leave welfare for paid work or marriage to a working spouse. Partly for these reasons, whites have left TANF faster than nonwhites, and nonwhites have been more likely to exhaust their allowable program time, get sanctioned off welfare, and cycle back to welfare after leaving for work (Schram 2005).

Thus, racial and ethnic groups differ in what they bring to the TANF program, and these background differences serve as a multiplier for the policy-design disparities they encounter within the program. Thus, the logic of racial disparity unfolds slowly, as various disadvantages accumulate and life disadvantages enhance the effects of inferior institutional positioning.

PATERNALISM, DISPARITY, WELFARE, AND CRIMINAL JUSTICE

The civic consequences of a public policy flow not only from how various groups are positioned within it, but also from how it positions its targets in relation to the broader citizenry and state. We suggest that recent changes in welfare and criminal justice policies have combined to create a distinctively marginal position in American civic life.

As the twentieth century drew to a close, two rising forces in U.S. politics—neoliberal (free market) conservatism and paternalist (social order) conservatism—reshaped public policy for low-income citizens. On one side, governance of the poor was redesigned to emphasize privatization, competition, and devolution—a reinvention of government along neoliberal lines. On the other, policies for the poor began to place a greater emphasis on direction, supervision, and punishment—a set of developments that Lawrence Mead (1997) praises as the new paternalism and that Charles Murray (1999) laments as a form of custodial democracy. Together, these changes have forged a distinctive logic of poverty governance that is more muscular in its normative enforcement and more dispersed in its organizational forms. Loic Wacquant (2005) refers to this new regime as the neoliberal paternalist state.

Traditional theories of social control treat welfare and criminal justice policies as related tools for regulating the poor (Fording 2001), and it is striking how the changes in these policy areas have paralleled each other. The long run-up to federal welfare reform coincided with a restructuring of criminal sentencing practices and a dramatic increase in incarceration (Garland 2001; Mauer and Chesney-Lind 2002). Figure 11.4 illustrates the stunning transformation that occurred in the 1990s. In just a decade's time, the number of Americans receiving cash welfare dropped by more than 50 percent, and the number incarcerated rose by more than 50 percent.[8]

Recent developments in welfare and criminal justice are connected not only in time and the arguments of social control theorists; they are also joined by the politics of race. As figure 11.5 illustrates, the accumulation of race-based disadvantage shown earlier for state TANF regimes extends to state approaches to criminal justice. African Americans are disproportionately subject to state policy regimes that combine locally managed welfare paternalism with a stronger emphasis on carceral control. The horizontal axis of figure 11.5 replicates the measure of TANF

FIGURE 11.4. / Proportional Change in Rates of Incarceration and AFDC/TANF Receipt

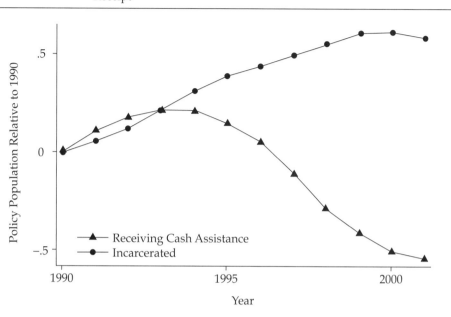

Source: Authors' compilation.
Note: TANF caseload data are from the Administration for Children and Families, U.S. Department of Health and Human Services, accessed at http://www.acf.dhhs.gov/news/stats/3697.htm. Incarceration data are from the U.S. Bureau of Justice Statistics, accessed at http://www.ojp.usdoj.gov/bjs/glance/incrt.htm.

regime stringency used earlier in figure 11.3. The bars correspond to the left-vertical axis, indicating the average black percent of population for states with each TANF regime type.[9] The dots plotted in this figure show how the average level of state corrections spending (as a percentage of total direct expenditures) changes as TANF regimes become more stringent and localized. Such spending appears to track closely with both the black percentage of state population and TANF regime types. This apparent relationship is confirmed by the curved line in the figure—a simple quadratic slope generated by regressing corrections spending on TANF regime stringency and its square. The relationship between average state corrections spending and TANF regime stringency is very strong: the R-squared for the quadratic slope is .83.

Taken together, the results in this figure suggest a strong state-level pattern of racialized social control. Looking across the American states, one finds a tightly configured relationship consisting of rising black population rates, more stringent and locally controlled TANF regimes, and higher levels of investment in incarceration.

This combination, we argue, is crucial for understanding the persistence of dis-

FIGURE 11.5 / Black TANF Caseload and State Corrections Spending by TANF Regime Type

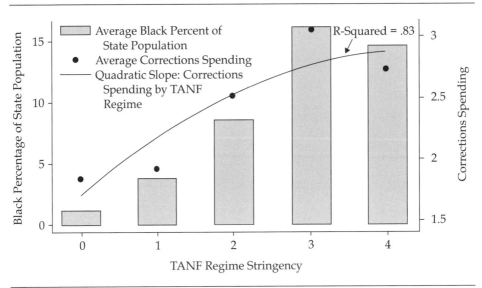

Source: Authors' compilation.
Note: TANF regime stringency are based on 2001 state TANF policies as measured by the Urban Institute and Gainsborough (2003); corrections spending data are from *Sourcebook of Criminal Justice Statistics 1999.*

advantage for poor people of color in the contemporary United States. The consequences of rising incarceration are, of course, covered in greater detail elsewhere in this volume (see Wheelock and Uggen, chapter 10, this volume). We address them briefly here to clarify how rising incarceration intersects with welfare reform to create a distinctive civic position for low-income racial minorities in the United States.

Rising incarceration has, of course, affected poor communities most intensely (Reiman 2004). Its greatest effects, however, have been concentrated in poor minority communities. Today, Latinos are almost twice as likely as whites to be incarcerated; blacks are about eight times as likely (Pettit and Western 2004). By their early thirties, around 14 percent of white men lacking a high school diploma can expect to have spent time in prison; the rate for black men in this educational group is 59 percent (Pettit and Western 2004). These numbers are staggering, but to grasp their import for poor blacks and Hispanics, one must consider how their effects ripple through social networks, family trees, neighborhoods, and community organizations. The transformation of criminal justice policy in the United States is a palpable presence in the lives of large numbers of poor blacks and Hispanics. For white and most Americans, these policy changes are little more than news dispatches from a distant front.

A parallel story can be told for welfare retrenchment. Social welfare supports have been dwindling for all Americans (Hacker 2006), but direct contact with welfare state paternalism remains a more restricted experience. National social insurance programs and private employee benefits remain the civic norm. Most Americans have no experience with social policies that seek out drug usage and penalize felony records, that condition aid on behavioral obligations related to work and family, that require a discretionary relationship with a caseworker, or that use the overt threat of sanctions to enforce a mandatory schedule of weekly appointments. These sorts of program rules define the experience of government for only a small segment of the citizenry—a group of people who are poor and disproportionately black and Hispanic.

For these Americans, prisons and welfare agencies are critical sites of citizenship, as are courts and other components of government related to crime and welfare. These are the places where the rights and obligations of citizenship get negotiated, asserted, and imposed. They are the sites where public policies get translated—by police and prison guards and welfare case managers—from abstract legislative words into real decisions that affect real lives. Hence, they are places where the capacity to speak, to influence decisions, and to make use of procedural protections count in unusually direct and consequential ways. They are also places where citizens learn basic lessons about their relationship to the state and develop consequential beliefs about whether it is wise or effective to try to influence government (Soss 2000).

Thus, it matters quite a bit for American civic life that the operating principles of these institutions have changed profoundly under neoliberal paternalism. Over the past few decades, we have witnessed the rise of the supermax prison and broader moves toward restricted-activity warehousing, a growing tendency to transfer prisoners to distant states and remote rural areas, the pruning of rehabilitation and leave programs, and the passage of the Prison Litigation Reform Act of 1996, which raised the statutory standards for a prisoner pursuing a case in court. These and other changes have increased the isolation and vulnerability of people sentenced to prison, further multiplying the accumulating institutional disadvantages for racial minorities we have already documented in this chapter (Feeley and Swearingen 2004; Rhodes 2004; Garland 2001; Wacquant 2001). Today, as Mary Fainsod Katzenstein (2005) noted, prisoners occupy a gray area of civic status; they possess, at best, a limited form of rights without citizenship.

Welfare provision has been the site of parallel changes. Policy devolution and work-first have been accompanied by the loss of substantive entitlement and by significant limitations on due process rights, grounds for grievances, and access to fair hearing procedures (Mink 2002). This dramatic loss of standing for clients has been paired with expanded authority for caseworkers through new capacities to sanction and new forms of discretion over the kinds of information and resources provided to clients. In short, if we examine the relationship between state and citizen as it now plays out inside U.S. welfare agencies and prisons, we find that an increasingly custodial form of governance has emerged. Because poor blacks and Latinos are disproportionately the objects of this governance, neoliberal paternalism implies a significant change in the quality of citizenship these groups experience relative to others in society.

The distinctive terms of this civic membership become even more apparent if one considers how welfare and criminal justice systems now contribute to the disproportionate targeting of poor blacks and Hispanics for ongoing government surveillance. As poverty governance has moved in a more custodial direction, it has strengthened its reach beyond the brick-and-mortar boundaries of welfare agencies and prisons. Today, more than 80 percent of people leaving prison are placed on parole, and the number of those sent back to prison for parole violations is seven times higher than it was twenty years ago (Travis 2005, 40).[10] As David Garland (2001, 178) explains, this postprison supervision entails a civic status inferior to what most Americans experience and what most ex-convicts used to experience.

Offenders released into the community are subject to much tighter control than previously, and frequently find themselves returned to custody for failure to comply with the conditions that continue to restrict their freedom. For many of the parolees and ex-convicts, the community into which they are released is actually a closely monitored terrain, a supervised space, lacking much of the liberty that one associates with normal life.

Thus, incarceration begets civic marginality not just because of the prison experience and its social and economic consequences (see Pager and Wheeler and Uggen, chapters 2 and 10, this volume), but also because ex-prisoners are "subjected to ever longer and broader post-detention forms of social control and symbolic branding that durably set them apart from the rest of the population" (Wacquant 2001, 112). Release into a poor minority neighborhood now usually signifies a shift rather than a break in the governance relationship established by criminal conviction and incarceration: "With fully 54 percent of offenders failing to complete their term of parole in 1997 (compared to 27 percent in 1984), and parole violators making up a third of all persons admitted in state penitentiaries every year (two-thirds in California), parole has become an appendage of the prison which operates mainly to extend the social and symbolic incapacities of incarceration beyond its walls" (Wacquant 2001, 113).

On the welfare side, we find a less substantial but parallel erosion of the line between program insiders and leavers. As official TANF caseloads have declined and transitional work support programs have grown, there has been an increase in the number of ex-TANF recipients who have an ongoing administrative relationship with the state.[11] This expansion of transition services has already stimulated calls to extend the reach of paternalist supervision to program leavers. Lawrence Mead, for example, has argued that administrative enforcement serves clients well in the TANF program and, hence, the state should not abandon them after they leave the program for paid employment. He has called for a more expansive "post-exit paternalism" that conditions the provision of wage supplements and support services, including the Earned Income Tax Credit (EITC) program, on behavioral obligations enforced through administrative oversight.[12] These forms of supervision would augment the new forms of monitoring and work enforcement Mead argued should be applied to low-income men who become involved with welfare-related child support enforcement or re-enter communities after a stay in prison (2006).

It is too early to know what these emerging developments will produce. But if a more broadly applied welfare paternalism combines with the greatly expanded postprison supervision now in place, it will have major implications for the civic status of poor minorities. In many low-income black and Hispanic neighborhoods, we face a real prospect of having large segments of the community placed under direct, ongoing state supervision related to postprison re-entry, welfare-to-work transition, child support enforcement, and ongoing needs for income support. To the extent that this supervision actually moves poor minorities into the societal mainstream—toward greater social and economic opportunities—one must do some complicated balancing to assess its net effects on civic disparities. To date, however, welfare leavers have remained overwhelmingly poor,[13] as have ex-prisoners (Pettit and Western 2004). For poor racial minorities, and especially blacks, neoliberal paternalism has manifestly created a more distinctive civic status and a distinctively vulnerable position vis-à-vis the state. Its positive contributions toward civic incorporation remain decidedly more difficult to ascertain.

ADVANCED MARGINALIZATION, RACE, AND CLASS

The policy dynamics we have discussed have the potential to isolate low-income racial minorities, not just from white Americans but also from middle class racial minorities, including many new immigrant groups as well as middle class blacks and Latinos. Indeed, some of the policy effects we have discussed are more likely to be experienced by a poor white person than by a more affluent minority individual. Thus, to understand how changes in welfare and criminal justice policy are reshaping citizenship in the United States, one must pay close attention to the intersection of social locations and identities.

Intersectionality refers to the idea that plural social categories create more than just identity alternatives (for example, experiencing social identity in one context as a woman and in another as a Jew) and more than just additive effects (as when the consequences of being a woman augment the separate consequences of being a Jew). Intersectionality suggests that social categories also intersect in a multiplicative way to produce specific social identities and social locations (such as that of a Jewish woman). Dimensions of identity become meaningful in combination. Thus, to be a poor black woman in the United States is to occupy an identity that can be distinguished from being poor and white, from being black and middle class, and from being white or middle class.

Because it foregrounds subgroup differences, attention to intersectionality complicates generalizations about racial and ethnic disparities. It does so, not only by demanding caveats (such as, the preceding effects apply to subgroup A more than subgroup B) but, more fundamentally, by challenging us to ask how civic disparities for different segments of a particular racial or ethnic group take on different forms and fit together. Consider, for example, gender differences among African Americans. Today, roughly 90 percent of adult TANF recipients are women, and about 90 percent of adult prisoners are men. Thus, in poor black communities, women are the primary recipients of welfare-paternalism's rehabilitative agenda, and their male counterparts cycle through a prison system that has, in most respects, abandoned rehabilitation as a policy goal. Poor black women are channeled into marriage promotion efforts as a way to promote self-sufficiency and civic incorporation. Poor black men in their communities are swept away to distant prisons, returning years later as less attractive marital partners (Western 2006). In short, the trade-offs and interplays that occur between mass incarceration and welfare reform in the United States transpire across a gender-based divide (Haney 2004). The effects that these policies have on racial disparities hinge, to a significant degree, on the ways they fit into and reshape gender relations in communities defined by race and class.

But it is not just gender that intersects with the construction of racial disparities; class position is equally important. In this final section, we explore the intersection of race and class, asking how the rise of neoliberal and paternalist-custodial policies is changing the civic position of low-income blacks vis-à-vis the black middle class.

The rise of neoliberal paternalism has coincided with remarkable social and economic advancement for many African Americans. Today, income inequalities are greater among African Americans than among white Americans (Hochschild 1995, 48). In political science, the question most often asked about this class polarization is whether it has undermined black solidarity or the cohesiveness of black political interests and behaviors. The answer from survey researchers has been a resounding "no." Numerous studies suggest that feelings of linked fate continue to be widespread among African Americans and that middle class blacks remain committed to a race-based conception of their political interests (Dawson 1994; Tate 1993).

These studies offer important insights into individual-level opinion, but they do so in a way that pays remarkably little attention to "politics among black people" (Reed 2004, 127). In asking whether class polarization now trumps racial solidarity, these studies rarely stop to ask how class-based privileges and organizations may shape the terms of racial cohesion and the articulation of black interests. Critics, such as Adolph Reed, have argued that "the generic politics of racial advancement [has become] skewed to programmatic agendas that confer concrete benefits disproportionately on those [in the] petit bourgeois strata. . . . [It is] a singular class vision projected as the organic and transparent sensibility of [blacks] as a whole." (2004, 133-4). Going further, and echoing a broader historical literature on "racial respectability" (Wolcott 2001; White 2001), Cathy Cohen (1999) suggested that the partial incorporation of more elite members of a subordinate group may generate pressures to reform, regulate, or suppress the problems of more marginal group members under a political logic she calls "advanced marginalization."

As many African Americans struggle to maintain some decent standard of living under a pattern of advanced marginalization, others have secured unprecedented access to dominant institutions and find themselves solidly integrated at multiple levels into the state apparatus. Those marginal group members who are close to the edges of dominant power, where access and involvement in decision making actually seem possible, confront incentives to promote and prioritize those issues and members thought to enhance the public image of the group, controlling and making invisible those issues and members perceived to threaten the status of the community (Cohen 1999, 27).

Here again, we confront the importance of cumulative disadvantage as intersecting dimensions of marginality compound in the lives of the lowest-status group members. This dynamic has far-reaching implications for the civic disparities generated by neoliberal paternalism. At a minimum, recent policy changes widen the social gap between poor and middle class blacks. Welfare offices and prisons may serve as key sites of interaction with the state for poor African Americans, but they are rarely experienced by middle- and upper-income blacks. As incarceration rates for high school-educated black men have soared in recent decades, the risk of imprisonment for college-educated black men has actually declined (Pettit and Western 2004, 161). Thus, as the state's new approach to poverty governance places poor blacks in an increasingly distinctive and isolated civic position, it simultaneously increases the potential for divergence between the political interests of poor blacks and the political agendas articulated by middle class black political organizations (see Strolovitch 2006).[14]

Indeed, it is not just effects on poor black communities that may widen this gap. The same policies that have exposed low-income African Americans to increasing surveillance and punishment have, in many cases, generated good civil service jobs for middle class blacks. To be sure, black professionals work in many fields that have nothing do with these policies. But today, middle class African Americans are disproportionately likely to work in criminal justice, social work, and social welfare professions that focus on managing the problems of poor black communities (Cohen 1999). Roger Waldinger highlighted one potential consequence of this fact in arguing that "while the black middle class largely works in government, the black poor are its dependents. . . . Public sector concentration thus pits the interests of the city's black middle class against the interests of its black poor" (1996, 252). Emphasizing this possibility, Cathy Cohen argued that advanced marginalization "not only allows for limited mobility on the part of some marginal group members, but also transfers much of the direct management of other, less privileged marginal group members to individuals who share the same group identity" (1999, 27).

The concentration of middle class blacks in policing and social work jobs means that poor and affluent blacks often occupy opposing roles in social control relationships. It would oversimplify these relationships to assume that they necessarily pit the interests of one against the other. Middle class people from disadvantaged groups may function as bureaucratic representatives working on behalf of the group rather than as gatekeepers policing their own (Selden 1997; Keiser, Meuser, and Choi 2004). Yet as Celeste Watkins (2003) demonstrated, the politics of racial respectability can be a powerful force in welfare agencies, leading black case managers to embrace the state's paternalism as a means to discipline their own. Concentration in such managerial positions means that middle class blacks often work in jobs where they confront, time and again, the most distressing behaviors and choices to be found in poor black neighborhoods. Beyond this minimum, middle class blacks may embrace the state's supervision of poor blacks in the name of racial uplift and in the interest of preserving group respectability.[15]

All of this suggests that the new approach to poverty governance may promote civic disparities between poor and middle class blacks—differences in the ways they are positioned in relation to the state and to each other. A November 2004 column written by Marcellus Andrews in *The Black Commentator* portrayed these strains in strong terms, highlighting the complexity of racial solidarity under stress. Pointing to the "fraying of a historic bond between the black middle class and the black poor," Andrews argued: "Bill Cosby's complaint about poor black people, unfair as it is, is nonetheless the view of many middle class black people who see poverty as a trap made worse by self-destructive behavior. . . . It is perfectly possible for middle class blacks to be angry at conservative white people and poor black people at the same time" (2004).

These arguments suggest a uniquely intense form of social exclusion for poor blacks—not only in relation to whites but also in relation to middle class blacks. Yet the key point, for our purposes, is that this distinctive isolation is largely a construction of public policy—especially the divergent fortunes of policies affecting different segments of the African American population (Lieberman 2005). These policy dynamics operate in a broader societal context where many shared conditions continue to connect the lives of poor and middle class blacks. Indeed, alternative policies that work to dampen the class-based civic divide among African Americans might find fertile soil for a politics of civic solidarity.

For example, the arrival of significant numbers of blacks in the American middle class has occurred just as economic and policy changes have made middle class status less stable than it used to be (Hacker 2006). In fact, the risk of falling from the middle class is generally greater for blacks than for whites because, though they are middle class by virtue of their annual incomes, they rarely hold significant assets (Shapiro 2004). Most people in the black middle class have little to fall back on in the event of an unanticipated illness or an especially costly decision. Moreover, they are likely to have poor friends and family whose needs can easily turn into drains on their limited resources. Middle class whites, by contrast, accumulate and consolidate advantage by virtue of having extended social networks that present them with fewer crises and demands for resources.

Indeed, one should not overestimate the existing social distance between poor and middle class African Americans. As Mary Pattillo-McCoy (1999) described it in *Black Picket Fences*, the kin networks of middle class blacks are rarely devoid of poor relatives in need of assistance. Middle class black neighborhoods are often close to poorer black neighborhoods, with considerable traffic across the neighborhood line. Pattillo-McCoy suggested that middle class blacks may not be so insulated from the problems of poor black neighborhoods after all. For many middle class blacks, the effects of the new poverty governance may be quite a bit more meaningful than a news dispatch from a distant front. These policies are likely to have affected a relative, friend, or acquaintance; they are likely to have affected someone connected to a son or daughter. Such connections to welfare and criminal justice policies are, of course, less direct than the experiences of low-income African Americans. But they offer an important counterpoint to our theme, holding out the potential for cross-class racial solidarity and shared civic experience.

CONCLUSION

In an essay on social citizenship published a decade ago, Hugh Heclo argued that the old settlement of the social question that Americans embraced in the midtwentieth century was being swept away and that a new settlement would need to be forged (1995, 667–70). In this essay, we have explored several implications of the new settlement. A new approach to poverty governance has emerged, with important implications for racial and ethnic disparities in the United States. The state's new orientation toward marginal populations blends neoliberal commitments to devolution, privatization, and market incorporation with paternalist commitments to directive, supervisory, and punitive mechanisms of social control. We say blends because, although market liberalism and statist paternalism may have their tensions as ideologies, together they now constitute a coherent regime of practice for regulating the poor.[16] Our goal here has been to show how specific features of this regime—features embedded in and enacted through public policy—are reshaping civic disparities for African Americans but other racialized groups as well.

   Three propositions lie at the heart of our analysis. First, neoliberal policy devolution operates in practice as a mechanism that creates racial disparities in the context of overtly race-neutral policy. Its cascade of choice points introduces and compounds racial differences. The result is a system in which low-income blacks and Hispanics occupy a distinctive position in relation to the state. They confront a regime of practice that more often operates according to the toughest rules and with the most local discretion. Second, the new poverty governance subjects poor minorities to a system of social control that is more muscular than policies experienced only a few decades ago, and that is far removed from the experiences of most Americans today. Third, the implications of this new approach to poverty governance vary greatly by class, fueling complex dynamics of advanced marginalization within disadvantaged racial and ethnic groups. In an era in which some black people have gained new access to advanced degrees and other credentials that facilitate incorporation, the poorest African Americans are branded with the mark of a criminal record and the stigma of welfare dependence. The civic positions of these two groups are growing more distant from each other, but they are also tied to one another through the emergence of a significant black professional class employed in positions that manage the social problems (and people) found in poor black communities.

The neoliberal policy changes that have contributed to a distinctively isolated civic position for low-income African Americans may eventually have parallel consequences for low-status segments of other groups such as Latinos and Asians. Recent debates about immigration policy underscore this possibility by distinguishing sharply between undocumented immigrants who engage in illegal activity and legal immigrants who play by the rules. Such distinctions occur, not just in the realm of policy argument, but also in immigration policy itself—as, for example, when lawmakers create separate immigration categories for high-skilled and low-skilled workers, who are likely to come from different racial-ethnic groups or from different gender and class positions within a racial-ethnic group.

Over the past few decades, racial politics has played a key role in the rise of neoliberal paternalism. Welfare and criminal justice policy are among the most race-coded government activities in the American polity. This race-coding helped smooth the way for a new approach to poverty governance, and it has shaped the trajectory of this regime over time. Public policies, however, are not just products of politics, racial or otherwise. They are also political forces in their own right with the power to reorganize the civic order. Today, neoliberal paternalism in the United States is reinventing the divided citizenry along racial and ethnic lines. Its operation warrants close scrutiny from all who hope to achieve an inclusive democracy in America.

NOTES

1. NBC News Poll, Roper Center at University of Connecticut, Public Opinion Online, June 8–12, 1995.
2. These figures are based on analysis of the authors' data.
3. Twenty-eight states created at least one state-funded program in these areas, fifteen provided at least two, ten offered at least three, and two offered all four (Zimmerman and Tumlin 1999). As of 2003, nineteen states used state funds to provide TANF-like assistance to legal immigrants who arrived after the passage of PRWORA. These programs offer aid on largely the same terms as these states' TANF programs for citizens (Tumlin and Zimmerman 2003).
4. The Balanced Budget Act of 1997, the Agricultural Research, Extension, and Education Reform Act of 1998, and the Farm Bill of 2002 (see Haider et al 2004, 749).
5. Predicted probabilities second-order devolution are based on the model presented in Soss, Fording, and Schram 2008. All others shown in this figure are based on models presented in Soss et al. 2001.
6. Because of this tipping point, black recipients actually had a slightly lower sanctioning rate for the state as a whole (see Keiser, Meuser, and Choi 2004).
7. Tumlin and Zimmerman reported: "As of 2000, noncitizens accounted for 10 percent of all families reporting TANF receipt, the same share as in 1994. Adding refugees (2 percent) and naturalized immigrants (4 percent) brings the foreign-born share of all TANF families to 16 percent—marginally higher than their 15 percent share in 1994." (2003, 7).

8. The dramatic increase in incarceration, of course, began long before 1990 (Travis 2005, 21–38).

9. The pattern of bars in figure 11.5 offers additional corroboration of the relationship between percent black and "neoliberal paternalism" in the TANF program shown in figure 11.4.

10. In fact, the number of people sent back to prison for parole violations each year is now as high as the total number of prison admissions was in 1980 (Travis 2005, 40).

11. Recent estimates suggest that TANF caseloads would rise by 50 to 100 percent if families that received TANF-funded post-exit services, but not cash assistance, were included in the caseload count (Fernstad and Neuberger 2002).

12. See Mead 2004 and Mead's roundtable comments at the annual conference of the Midwest Political Science Association (2005).

13. Steve Schultze, "W-2's Poor Stay Poor, Audit Finds: Most Still Earn Poverty Wages after Leaving Welfare Program," *The Milwaukee Journal Sentinel*, April 7, 2005, accessed at http://www.jsonline.com/news/state/apr05/316168.asp.

14. Consistent with this analysis, Michael Dawson reported that "affluent African Americans are much less likely to support economic redistribution than those with fewer resources [and] the most affluent African Americans hold views more consistent with those of the conservative white mainstream" (1994, 205, 181–99).

15. Of course, the politics of racial respectability may also bolster the forces we have already identified as encouraging black middle class silence on the problems confronting black welfare recipients and current and former prisoners. As Cathy Cohen noted in her study of AIDS and black politics: "Those groups suffering most from AIDS in African-American communities were constructed as standing outside the indigenous moral and racial codes of the community as defined in part by the black church. Members of these subgroups were perceived as a disgrace to 'the community' and thus not worth the expense of the limited political capital controlled by black elites" (1999, 346).

16. Our formulation here, "regime of practice for regulating the poor," intentionally draws together Michel Foucault (1991) and Frances Piven and Richard Cloward (1993). For related arguments, see Loïc Wacquant (2005).

REFERENCES

Addams, Jane. 1902. *Democracy and Social Ethics*. New York: The Macmillan Company.

Andrews, Marcellus. 2004. "No Exit in Black: Trapped by the Economy and Politics." *The Black Commentator*. Accessed at http://www.newamerica.net/index.cfm?pg=article &DocID=2044

Avery, James M. and Mark Peffley. 2005. "Voter Registration Requirements, Voter Turnout, and Welfare Eligibility Policy: Class Bias Matters." *State Politics & Policy Quarterly* 5(1): 47–67.

Bell, Winifred. 1965. *Aid to Families with Dependent Children*. New York: Columbia University Press.

Berg, Allison. 2002. *Mothering the Race: Women's Narratives on Reproduction, 1890-1930*. Chicago, Ill.: University of Illinois Press.

Blank, Rebecca. 2003. "U.S. Welfare Reform: What's Relevant for Europe?" *CE-Sinfo Economic Studies* 49(1): 26.

Borjas, George and Lynette Hilton. 1996. "Immigration and the Welfare State: Immigrant Participation in Means-Tested Entitlement Programs." *Quarterly Journal of Economics* 111(2): 575–604.

Brown, Michael K., Martin Carnoy, Elliott Currie, Troy Duster, David B. Oppenheimer, Marjorie M. Schultz, and David Wellman. 2003. *Whitewashing Race: The Myth of a Colorblind Society*. Berkeley, Calif.: University of California Press.

Carmines, Edward G. and James A. Stimson. 1989. *Issue Evolution: Race and the Transformation of American Politics*. Princeton, N.J.: Princeton University Press.

Cohen, Cathy J. 1999. *The Boundaries of Blackness: AIDS and the Breakdown of Black Politics*. Chicago, Ill.: University of Chicago Press.

Congressional Budget Office. 1996. *Federal Budgetary Implications of the Personal Responsibility and Work Opportunity Reconciliation Act of 1996*. Washington: Congressional Budget Office.

Crenson, Matthew A. 1998. *Building the Invisible Orphanage: A Prehistory of the American Welfare State*. Cambridge, Mass.: Harvard University Press.

Dawson, Michael. 1994. *Behind the Mule: Race and Class in African American Politics*. Princeton, N.J.: Princeton University Press.

Edin, Kathryn, and Maria Kefalas. 2005. *Promises I Can Keep: Why Poor Women Put Motherhood Before Marriage*. Berkeley, Calif.: University of California Press.

Edsall, Thomas Byrne with Mary D. Edsall 1991. *Chain Reaction: The Impact of Race, Rights, and Taxes on American Politics*. New York: Alfred A. Knopf.

Esping-Andersen, Gosta. 1990. *Three Worlds of Welfare Capitalism*. Cambridge: Polity Press.

Feeley, Malcolm M. and Van Swearingen. 2004. "The Prison Conditions Cases and the Bureaucratization of Incarceration" *Pace Law Review* 24(2): 433–76.

Fellows, Matthew C., and Gretchen Rowe. 2004. "Politics and the New American Welfare States." *American Journal of Political Science* 48(2): 362–73.

Fernstad, Shawn and Zoe Neuberger. 2002. *TANF's "Uncounted" Cases: More than One Million Working Families Receiving TANF-funded Services Not Counted in TANF Caseload*. Washington, D.C.: Urban Institute Press. Accessed at http://www.cbpp.org/4-24-02tanf.htm

Fix, Michael and Wendy Zimmerman. 1999. *All Under One Roof: Mixed-Status Families in an Era of Reform*. Washington, D.C.: Urban Institute Press.

———. 2002. "Assessing Welfare Reform's Immigrant Provisions." In *Welfare Reform: The Next Act*, edited by Andrew Weil and K. Finegold. Washington, D.C.: Urban Institute Press.

Fording, Richard C. 1997. "The Conditional Effect of Violence as a Political Tactic: Mass Insurgency, Welfare Generosity, and Electoral Context in the American States." *American Journal of Political Science* 41(1): 1–29.

———. 2001. "The Political Response to Black Insurgency: A Critical Test of Competing Theories of the State." *American Political Science Review* 95(1): 115–30.

———. 2003. "Laboratories of Democracy or Symbolic Politics: The Racial Origins of Welfare Reform." In *Race and the Politics of Welfare Reform*, edited by S.F. Schram, J. Soss, and R.C. Fording. Ann Arbor, Mich.: University of Michigan Press.

Fording, Richard, Joe Soss and Sanford F. Schram. 2007. "Distributing Discipline: Race, Politics, and Punishment at the Frontlines of Welfare Reform." University of Kentucky Poverty Center Discussion Paper Series 2007-04. Lexington, Ky.: University of Kentucky Center for Poverty Research. Accessed at http://www.ukcpr.org/Publications/DP2007 -04.pdf.

Foucault, Michel. 1991. "Questions of Method." In *The Foucault Effect: Studies in Governmentality with Two Lectures by and an Interview with Michel Foucault*, edited by Graham Burchell, Colin Gordon and P. Miller. Chicago, Ill.: University of Chicago Press.

Fox, Cybelle. 2004. "The Changing Color of Welfare? How Whites' Attitudes Toward latinos Influence Support for Welfare." *American Journal of Sociology* 110(3): 580–625.

Gainsborough, Juliet F. 2003. "To Devolve or Not to Devolve? Welfare Reform in the States." *Policy Studies Journal* 31(4): 603–23.

Garland, David. 2001. *Culture of Control: Crime and Social Order in Contemporary Society*. Chicago, Ill.: University of Chicago Press.

Gilens, Martin. 1999. *Why Americans Hate Welfare: Race, Media, and the Politics of Antipoverty Policy*. Chicago, Ill.: University of Chicago Press.

———. 2003. "How the Poor Became Black: The Racialization of Poverty in the Mass Media." In *Race and the Politics of Welfare Reform*, edited by Sanford F. Schram, Joe Soss, and Richard C. Fording. Ann Arbor, Mich.: University of Michigan Press.

Gooden, Susan. 2003. "Contemporary Approaches to Enduring Challenges: Using Performance Measurement to Promote Racial Equality under TANF." In *Race and the Politics of Welfare Reform*, edited by Sandford F. Schram, Joe Soss, and Richard C. Fording. Ann Arbor, Mich.: University of Michigan Press.

Gordon, Linda. 1994. *Pitied But Not Entitled: Single Mothers and the History of Welfare*. New York: Free Press.

Hacker, Jacob S. 2006. *The Great Risk Shift: The Assault on American Jobs, Families, Health Care, and Retirement—and How You Can Fight Back*. New York: Oxford University Press.

Haider, Steven J., Robert F. Schoeni, Yuhua Bao, and Caroline Danielson. 2004. "Immigrants, Welfare Reform, and the Economy." *Journal of Policy Analysis and Management* 23(4): 745–64.

Hancock, Ange-Marie. 2004. *The Politics of Disgust: The Public Identity of the Welfare Queen*. New York: New York University Press.

Handler, Joel F. 2004. *Social Citizenship and Workfare in the United States and Western Europe: The Paradox of Inclusion*. New York: Cambridge University Press.

Haney, Lynne. 2004. "Introduction: Gender, Welfare, and States of Punishment." *Social Politics* 11(3): 333–62.

Heclo, Hugh. 1995. "The Social Question." In *Poverty, Inequality, and the Future of Social Policy*, edited by K. McFate, R. Lawson, and W.J. Wilson. New York: Russell Sage Foundation.

Hero, Rodney E., and Robert R. Preuhs. 2007. "Immigration and the Evolving American Welfare State: Examining Policies in the U.S. States." *American Journal of Political Science* 5(3): 498–517.

Hochschild, Jennifer. 1995. *Facing Up to the American Dream*. Princeton, N.J.: Princeton University Press.

Katzenstein, Mary Fainsod. 2005. "Rights Without Citizenship: Activist Politics and Prison Reform in the United States." In *Routing the Opposition: Social Movements, Public Policy, and Democracy*, edited by D. S. Meyer, V. Jenness, and H. Ingram. Minneapolis, Minn.: University of Minnesota Press.

Katznelson, Ira. 2006. *When Affirmative Action Was White: An Untold History of Racial Inequality in Twentieth-Century America*. New York: W. W. Norton.

Keiser, Lael R., Peter Meuser, and Seung-Whan Choi. 2004. "Race, Bureaucratic Discretion and the Implementation of Welfare Reform." *American Journal of Political Science* 48(2): 314–27.

Kellstedt, Paul M. 2003. *The Mass Media and the Dynamics of American Racial Attitudes*. New York: Cambridge University Press.

Kinder, Donald, and Lynn Sanders. 1996. *Divided by Color: Racial Politics and Democratic Ideals*. Chicago, Ill.: University of Chicago Press.

King, Desmond S., and Rogers M. Smith. 2005. "Racial Orders in American Political Development." American Political Science Review 99(1): 75–92.

Lieberman, Robert. 1998. *Shifting the Color Line: Race and the American Welfare State*. Cambridge, Mass.: Harvard University Press.

———. 2005 *Shaping Race Policy: The United States in Comparative Perspective*. Princeton, N.J.: Princeton University Press.

Marshall, T.H. 1949/1964. "Citizenship and Social Class." I. *Class, Citizenship, and Social Development: Essays by T.H. Marshall*, Seymour Martin Lipset. Chicago, Ill.: University of Chicago Press.

Mauer, Marc, and Meda Chesney-Lind, editors. 2002. *Invisible Punishment: The Collateral Consequences of Mass Imprisonment*. New York: The New Press.

Mead, Lawrence. 1986. *Beyond Entitlement: The Social Obligations of Citizenship*. New York: Free Press.

———, editor. 1997. *The New Paternalism: Supervisory Approaches to Poverty*. Washington, D.C.: The Brookings Institution Press.

———. 1998. "Telling the Poor What to Do." *The Public Interest* 132(Summer): 97–112.

———. 2004. *Government Matters: Welfare Reform in Wisconsin*. Princeton, N.J.: Princeton University Press.

———. 2005. Roundtable comments at the annual conference of the Midwest Political Science Association, Chicago, Ill., April 8, 2005.

———. 2006. "Toward a Mandatory Work Policy for Men." Unpublished manuscript. Accessed at http://www.nyu.edu/gsas/dept/politics/faculty/mead/Research/Brookings_3rd_draft.pdf

Mettler, Suzanne. 1998. *Dividing Citizens: Gender and Federalism in New Deal Public Policy*. Ithaca, N.Y.: Cornell University Press.

———. 2000. "States' Rights, Women's Obligations: Contemporary Welfare Reform in Historical Perspective." *Women & Politics* 21(1): 1–34.

Mink, Gwendolyn. 2002. "Violating Women: Rights Abuses in the Welfare Police State." In *Lost Ground*, edited by Randy Albelda and Ann Withorn. Cambridge, Mass.: South End Press.

Murray, Charles. 1999. "And Now for the Bad News." *Society* 37(1): 12–15.

Nathan, Richard P., and Thomas L. Gais. 1999. *Implementing the Personal Responsibility Act of 1996: A First Look*. Albany, N.Y.: State University of New York.

Orloff, Ann Shola. 2001. "Ending the Entitlements of Poor Single Mothers." In *Women and Welfare*, edited by N.J. Hirschmann and U. Libert. New Brunswick, N.J.: Rutgers University Press.

Pattillo-McCoy, Mary. 1999. *Black Picket Fences: Peril and Privilege among the Black Middle Class*. Chicago, Ill.: University of Chicago Press.

Pettit, Becky, and Bruce Western. 2004. "Mass Imprisonment and the Life Course: Race and Class Inequality in U.S. Incarceration." *American Sociological Review* 69(2): 151–69.

Piven, Frances Fox, and Richard A. Cloward. 1974. *The Politics of Turmoil*. New York: Vintage Press.

———. 1977. *Poor People's Movements*. New York: Vintage Press.

———. 1993. *Regulating the Poor: The Functions of Public Welfare*. New York: Vintage Books.

Quadagno, Jill. 1994. *The Color of Welfare: How Racism Undermined the War on Poverty*. New York: Oxford University Press.

Reed, Adolph. 2004. "The Study of Black Politics and the Practice of Black Politics: Their Historical Relation and Evolution." In *Problems and Methods in the Study of Politics*, edited by I. Shapiro, R.M. Smith, and T.E. Mamoud. New York: Cambridge University Press.

Reiman, Jeffrey. 2004. *The Rich Get Richer and the Poor Get Prison: Ideology, Class, and Criminal Justice*. Boston, Mass.: Allyn & Bacon.

Rhodes, Lorna A. 2004. *Total Confinement: Madness and Reason in the Maximum Security Prison*. Berkeley, Calif.: University of California Press.

Schram, Sanford F. 2005. "Contextualizing Racial Disparities in American Welfare Reform: Toward a New Poverty Research." *Perspectives on Politics* 3(2): 253–68.

Selden, Sally Coleman. 1997. *The Promise of Representative Bureaucracy: Diversity and Responsiveness in a Government Agency*. Boston, Mass.: M.E. Sharpe.

Shapiro, Thomas 2004. *The Hidden Cost of Being African American: how Wealth Perpetuates Inequality*. New York: Oxford University Press.

Silver, Hilary. 1994. "Social Exclusion and Social Solidarity: Three Paradigms." *International Labour Review* 133(5/6): 531–78.

Skocpol, Theda. 1992. *Protecting Soldiers and Mothers: The Political Origins of Social Policy in the United States*. Cambridge: The Belknap Press of Harvard University Press.

Smith, Rogers. 1997. *Civic Ideals: Conflicting Visions of Citizenship in U.S. History*. New Haven, Conn.: Yale University Press.

Soss, Joe. 2000. *Unwanted Claims: The Politics of Participation in the U.S. Welfare System*. Ann Arbor, Mich.: University of Michigan Press.

———. n.d. "Welfare Reform and the Mobilization of Racial Bias: Mass Arousal in the Policy Process." Unpublished manuscript. On file with author.

Soss, Joe, Richard C. Fording, and Sanford F. Schram. 2008. "The Color of Develolution: Race, Federalism, and the Politics of Social Control." *American Journal of Political Science* 52(3).

Soss, Joe, Sanford F. Schram, Thomas P. Vartanian, and Erin O'Brien. 2001. "Setting the Terms of Relief: Explaining State Policy Choices in the Devolution Revolution." *American Journal of Political Science* 45(2): 378–95.

Strolovitch, Dara Z. 2006. "Do Interest Groups Represent the Disadvantaged? Advocacy at the Intersections of Race, Class, and Gender." *Journal of Politics* 68(4): 894–910.

Tate, Katherine. 1993. *From Protest to Politics: The New Black Voters in American Elections.* Cambridge, Mass.: Harvard University Press.

Tilly, Charles. 1998. *Durable Inequality.* Berkeley: University of California Press.

Travis, Jeremy. 2005. *But They All Come Back: Facing the Challenges of Prisoner Reentry.* Washington, D.C.: Urban Institute Press.

Tumlin, Karen C., and Wendy Zimmermann. 2003. *Immigrants and TANF: A Look at Immigrant Welfare Recipients in Three Citie*s. Occasional Paper 69. Washington, D.C.: Urban Institute Press.

Wacquant, Loïc. 2001. "Deadly Symbiosis: When Ghetto and Prison Meet and Mesh." *Punishment & Society* 3(1): 95–134.

——— 2005. "Social Insecurity, Racial Division, and the Penalization of Poverty in the U.S. and Western Europe, 1975–2005" Paper presented at the Annual Meeting of the American Sociological Association, Philadelphia, Pa., August 14, 2005.

Waldinger, Roger. 1996. *Still the Promised City? African Americans and New Immigrants in Postindustrial New York.* Cambridge, Mass.: Harvard University Press.

Watkins, Celeste. 2003. *The Incomplete Revolution: Constraints on Reform in Welfare Bureaucracies.* Ph.D. dissertation, Harvard University.

Weaver, R. Kent. 2000. Ending Welfare as We Know It. Washington, D.C.: The Brookings Institution Press.

Western, Bruce. 2006. *Punishment and Inequality in America.* New York: Russell Sage Foundation.

White, E. Frances. 2001. *Dark Continent of Our Bodies: Black Feminism and the Politics of Respectability.* Philadelphia, Pa.: Temple University Press.

White, Stuart. 2003. *The Civic Minimum: On the Rights and Obligations of Economic Citizenship.* Oxford: Oxford University Press.

Winston, Pamela. 2002. *Welfare Policymaking in the States: The Devil in Devolution.* Washington, D.C.: Georgetown University Press.

Wolcott, Victoria W. 2001. *Remaking Respectability: African American Women in Interwar Detroit.* Chapel Hill, N.C.: University of North Carolina Press.

Zimmermann, Wendy, and Karen Tumlin. 1999."Patchwork Policies: State Assistance for Immigrants Under Welfare Reform." Washington, D.C.: The Urban Institute.

Index

Boldface numbers refer to figures and tables.

Index

Flat Broke with Children (Hays), 82
Fording, Richard, 302, 305
formal consequences of criminal sanctions, 261, 262, 274–81
Fosse, Nathan, 85
Fox, Cybelle, 61
frames, culture as, 80–81, 90
friendship networks, 174, 175, 184–89, 190, **191,** 191*n*3

Gates, Susan, 40–41
Gautreaux Assisted Housing Program, 235
Geertz, Clifford, 79
gender: and academic achievement inequalities, 119–21; health status, **147,** 148–49; and incarceration, 262, 264, 266, **268,** 271, 278, 281; and individualistic vs. structural explanations for inequality, 56, 57; and intersectionality of identities, 312; low-income black men's differential attitudes, 85–86; and poverty, 54, 295–96; and spatial mismatch, 218; in welfare policy history, 295–96
genetic arguments for minorities' inferiority, 59
geographic factors in disadvantage. *See* place
Gilens, Martin, 297
Gilliam, Franklin, 55
Goffman, Erving, 80
Gordon, Linda, 296
Gornick, Marian, 139
government. *See* legislation
Greenberg, David, 270
Grissmer, David, 122–23
Grønbjerg, Kirsten, 240

Hall, L. Shane, 125
Halpern, David, 172
Handler, Joel, 295
Hannerz, Ulf, 82
Harding, David, 81
Harris, Kathleen, 185
Hart, Betty, 114
Hays, Sharon, 82
Head Start program, 121, 123–24, 127
health: discrimination effects, 24, 28, **36,** 138–39, 148, 163–64; gender factor, **147,** 148–49; and housing discrimination, 34; immigrant

status, 139–40, 146, 148, 149–61, 163–64; policy issues, 140–42, 161–62; and race-ethnicity, 137–40, 141, 142–49, 152–61; and SES, 135–48, 149–57, 160, 161–64
Heckman, James, 38–39
Heclo, Hugh, 296, 315
Hedges, Larry, 122
heritability of intelligence, 59
Herrnstein, Richard J., 59
heterogeneity: among national origin groups, 143, **144,** 181; cultural differences within poor groups, 81, 82–83, 91; in immigrant education outcomes, 149, 152; and place effects, 204
Hispanics: categorization complications, 6; criminal victimization levels, 283, 284; cumulative disadvantage, **112,** 113; discrimination against, 43*n*7, 214, 272, 302, 305; education outcomes, 111, 113, 117, **118,** 119, **120, 121,** 122–23, 126–27, 143; ethnic enclave advantage for, 32–33; friendship networks, 186, **187, 188**; health status, 137, 139, 140, **145, 147,** 148, 149, 152, **153, 155,** 157, **158,** 160; heterogeneity among, 143, **144**; and incarceration, 264, **265,** 267, **268,** 308; individualistic vs. structural explanations for inequality, 56–57; job networks, 177; language issue in school readiness, 112; media underrepresentation among poor, 55; parental education level, 112; place effects, 201, 207, 208, 209, 210–11, 215, 217, 218, 221, 223–24; population share, 5–6; poverty levels, 54, 111, 143, **144, 150**; school readiness, 115, 116, 117; social class level, 111; social service access disparities, 242–43, **244,** 247, 248, 251; stereotyping of, 25; welfare policy disparities for, 61, 296, 299
Holzer, Harry, 39
homophily: definition, 173–74; friendship networks, 185, 186; job networks, 177, 178; and promotion of inequality, 175, 190

Hope VI housing developments, 235
housing: discrimination in, 28, 34–35, **36,** 39, 40–41, 43*n*6–7, 214, 233–35; low-income, 221–23, 234; rental assistance programs, 163, 235; and social services access, 233–36
housing filtering theories, 221–22
Hoxby, Caroline, 185
human capital, 113, 181. *See also* education
Hunt, Matthew, 56–57
Huston, Aletha, 126
Hutchings, Vincent, 26

identity construction, 64–67, 84–86
ideological foundations of inequality. *See* attitudes about inequality
immigrants: abolishment of ethnic quotas in immigration policy, 5–6; advanced marginalization of, 316; advantage of ethnic enclaves, 9–10; black immigrants vs. native blacks, 6, 152, **153, 155**; civic disparities for, 295; deportation of felon, 280–81; educational attainment, 119, **120,** 149, 152; emotional well-being, 152, **153–54,** 157; and health status, 139–40, 146, 148, 149–61, 163–64; language issue, 111–12, 119, **120,** 127; mortality rates of, 137; place effects, 201, 215–16, 241; poverty levels, **150–51**; SES heterogeneity among, 149; social capital of, 181–84, 190, **191**; and welfare reform, 299–300, 301, 305. *See also* Asians; Hispanics
incarceration-imprisonment: cumulative disadvantage consequences, 274, 282, 309; felon status and life chances, 261, 273–82, 285; formal consequences of criminal sanctions, 261, 262, 274–81; increased levels of, 263–64; informal consequences of criminal sanctions, 261, 262, 281–82; and loss of neighborhood efficacy, 181; policy recommendations, 273–74, 285–86; racial-ethnic dispari-